The publisher and the University of California Press Foundation gratefully acknowledge the generous support of the Ahmanson Foundation Endowment Fund in Humanities.

A Sea of Wealth

THE CALIFORNIA WORLD HISTORY LIBRARY

Edited by Edmund Burke III, Kenneth Pomeranz, and Patricia Seed

A Sea of Wealth

THE OMANI EMPIRE AND THE MAKING OF AN OCEANIC MARKETPLACE

Nicholas P. Roberts

UNIVERSITY OF CALIFORNIA PRESS

University of California Press
Oakland, California

Library of Congress Cataloging-in-Publication Data

Names: Roberts, Nicholas P. author
Title: A sea of wealth : the Omani Empire and the making of an oceanic marketplace / Nicholas P. Roberts.
Other titles: California world history library 33.
Description: Oakland, California : University of California Press, [2025] | Series: The California world history library ; 33 | Includes bibliographical references and index.
Identifiers: LCCN 2024058421 (print) | LCCN 2024058422 (ebook) | ISBN 9780520415775 cloth | ISBN 9780520415782 paperback | ISBN 9780520415799 ebook
Subjects: LCSH: Saʿīd bin Sulṭān, Sultan of Zanzibar, 1791–1856 | Oman—Commerce—History | Oman—Globalization | Oman—Foreign relations
Classification: LCC DS247.067 R63 2025 (print) | LCC DS247.067 (ebook) | DDC 303.48/25353—dc23/eng/20250312
LC record available at https://lccn.loc.gov/2024058421
LC ebook record available at https://lccn.loc.gov/2024058422

GPSR Authorized Representative: Easy Access System Europe, Mustamäe tee 50, 10621 Tallinn, Estonia, gpsr.requests@easproject.com

34 33 32 31 30 29 28 27 26 25
10 9 8 7 6 5 4 3 2 1

For my teachers

My sealed orders were to determine the shape of the world. The final report is that all presumptions are in error. The blasted thing is nearly upside down.

JOHN A. MCGLYNN JR., *An Old Man's Rules for Hitchhiking*

CONTENTS

Note on Spelling ix
Acknowledgments xi
Maps xvi

Prelude 1

1 · Writing Omani History 8

2 · The Emergence of Empire 26

3 · Contesting the Gulf 56

4 · Moving to Zanzibar 82

5 · Politics of the Marketplace 115

6 · Enslavement and Human Trafficking 141

7 · The Omani Empire in World History 170

Notes 185
Bibliography 237
Index 261

NOTE ON SPELLING

In this book I have minimized the use of diacritics. Scholars who work with Arabic-language materials often use diacritics to transliterate Arabic words into English. There are two main systems for doing this: the United States Library of Congress system and the *International Journal of Middle East Studies* system. Strictly following either of these systems, the country Oman would appear as ʿUmān and the name Saʿid bin Sultan would appear as Saʿīd bin Ṣulṭān. This appeals to some Arabic-language specialists, a very small number of readers. Generally, I have removed diacritics from this text except for the Arabic *ʿayn*—without it, the name Saʿid would appear Said. Full diacritics are found in footnotes and citations and at some points throughout the text where I refer on occasion to specific words or phrases. When repeatedly referring to the same family group, like the Al-Qawasim, I have dropped the Al- to make the text more concise and accessible in its English-language printing. Unless noted, all translations in this book are my own, as are any errors.

ACKNOWLEDGMENTS

In his memoir *Travels with a Donkey in the Cevennes*, Robert Louis Stevenson remarked that every book is like a letter to an author's friends. Throughout its pages, Stevenson wrote, readers find private messages and assurances of love. They find gratitude dropped for them in every corner. I hope my readers find the same things here, but in this prefatory note I shall be more specific. This book is the culmination of a decade of study; thousands of miles of travel; countless emails, WhatsApp messages, and phone calls; and many hours of laboring and waiting. There is a long list of persons to whom I am grateful. Each influenced this project in different ways. I shall start from the beginning of my graduate training.

At Georgetown University, John Voll shaped how I think of world history and the histories of Islamicate societies. A distinguished scholar, he was also an artist in the classroom. When I was a professor, I often thought of my time in his classes, wishing I could mold a discussion as gracefully as he. He is the embodiment of Norman Maclean's line that all good things come by grace, and grace comes by art, and art does not come easy. Also at Georgetown, David Goldfrank early became a strong advocate and mentor, and I hope I continue to live the rest of my life according to the promises he asked me to keep on graduation day: to never stop asking hard questions, to always allow facts to change my mind, and to never stop being a contrarian voice. I hope the work I am embarking upon now in international law lives up, at least in part, to Professor Goldfrank's belief in me.

It is not an overstatement to say that I was among the most fortunate PhD students in the world at the University of Notre Dame, where the Department of History offered me a significant annual travel fund. Without it, the initial research for this book would have been nearly impossible, even with a generous fellowship and outside funding. I remain deeply grateful for that support, knowing that such resources are increasingly rare in academia. My adviser, Ebrahim Moosa, remained supportive and patient as I changed paths from what I had applied to study and began focusing more on this area of history. He was unafraid to pound on doors to advocate for me. He challenged me to dive deep into details, to pearl over minutiae, and then to dive even deeper. He is a model of how to be an eminent scholar and to fight for global justice. It remains my honor to consider John McGreevy among my most dedicated mentors. Though we study different fields, Provost McGreevy has read multiple versions of this project. He never flinched in his support and guidance. His voice has been in my head as I have written these pages, urging me to consider the perennial question of History: "So what?"

I would not have completed this project without Fahad Bishara. An external member of my dissertation committee, Professor Bishara was a critical teacher during my graduate studies. He has remained one since. He is the epitome of a superior teacher: I am often unsure where my thoughts begin and his end. His expertise was pivotal in completing this project, even in helping me establish connections with archivists overseas. My time in Zanzibar was so delightful in no small part because of a key introduction he made for me. I will never be able to repay him for all the time and space he has devoted to me. Professor Bishara also introduced me to two friends, each of whom has helped shape this book: Joshua Morrison and Ahmed al-Maazmi. I thank Josh and Ahmed for countless messages, innumerable shrewd insights, comments on drafts, and more over the years.

Fahad Bishara also served as my supervisor at the University of Virginia, where I completed a year as the inaugural W. Nathaniel Howell Postdoctoral Research Associate for Arabian Peninsula and Gulf Studies. This fellowship year provided respite from a crushing teaching and service load, and very directly made this book possible. I am grateful to the Howell family for the opportunity, and I hope that this work helps speak to the memory and legacy of the late Ambassador Howell. At the conclusion of my fellowship year, Professor Bishara organized a workshop to discuss this manuscript at UVA with Jeremy Prestholdt, Thomas McDow, and Mandana Limbert. Their insights and encouragement were integral to its further refinement.

As I type this paragraph, I am a law student in the heat of midterms. My law studies cap what will ultimately be a decade of graduate school. Until I met my legal writing teacher, Professor Jennifer Cupar, I was unsure if I could be pushed more than I already had been by extraordinary writing teachers. She ranks among the kindest, most exceptionally talented, dedicated, and influential teachers I have had. There are sure to be some "there ares" throughout this manuscript, and I take full responsibility for any errors—with apologies to Professor Cupar.

At the University of California Press, editor Niels Hooper did for me what the very finest editors can do: he found the most qualified scholars and gracious colleagues to serve as reviewers. Both Dodie McDow and John Willis provided sharp, patient reviews that tremendously enhanced this work. I am grateful to them, and I am grateful to Niels for setting up the privilege of having them review my work. At UCP, I am also thankful for my editorial assistant, Nora Becker, who was always gracious, kind, and efficient. My production project manager, Jon Dierten, was the consummate professional who was also very efficient. One of my world history mentors, Professor Alfred Andrea, once remarked to me: "If it is not written well, it is not History." Indeed, many historians throw fits when others touch their writing, but it was a delight having my work edited by Sharon Langworthy, my superb copy editor.

My former student at Norwich University Ethan Trask created beautiful maps for me. At Norwich, I was lucky to be part of a uniquely warm, collegial, and friendly department. My colleagues there, especially Michael Thunberg and Jeff Casey, never hesitated to lend an ear or offer support. When administrators cut faculty funds for research and conference travel, precluding me from presenting aspects of this work at the Middle East Studies Association annual meeting, my department chair, Steve Sodergren, wrote me a personal check—and insisted that I cash it. That is a model of service to others that I shall not soon forget.

This book is the result of eighteen months of research across four continents, made all the more meaningful by the generosity of those who hosted me. My time in Muscat, Zanzibar, Mumbai, and New Delhi was particularly shaped by the kindness of scholars, archivists, and local communities, whose hospitality and insights enriched this work beyond what I could have gathered from documents alone. The locations of the homes I stayed in during my research reflect the international system this book traces: Bill and Joan in Salem; Christopher and Allison in Washington, DC; Dario in London; Abdullah in Muscat; Petra in Zanzibar; and Thane in Mumbai and Muhammad Ali in New Delhi —among others.

I am especially grateful for the talented, generous archivists and librarians who assisted me in uncountable ways throughout my research. The archivists at the Phillips Library, part of the Peabody Essex Museum in Salem, graciously allowed me to arrive early and depart late, knowing I had to sift through enormous collections in a short time. Lucy Hereford, associate reference librarian at the Phillips Library, helped me procure two images for this book. Archivists at the Library of Congress in Washington, DC taught me a crucial skill for a historian: how to use a microfilm reader, and I am still sorry that I broke the first one I ever touched. The archivists at The British Library in London are quintessential professionals, and I miss seeing them every morning while beginning a rigorous day of reading and writing. The British National Archives is a historian's dream palace, and the staff and archivists there have mastered the art of efficiency, making research there a true delight. In Muscat, Abdulrahman Al-Salimi and Hilal al-Hajri helped me on numerous trips, especially procuring Arabic-language books. I am not sure I have ever been happier than I was sitting in the reading room at the Zanzibar National Archives. I drafted many of the following pages there, listening to the island's life and the archive's voices as the equatorial sun alternated with monsoon rains. I woke every morning excited to arrive in the reading room and embarrass myself trying to speak Swahili with the archivists; they were the most patient of teachers. In India, I wish I could have bought more gulab jamoon for the archivists and staff of the Maharashtra State Archives, who pretended to not see the thousands of photographs I took while they quite literally sweated for me, carrying dusty, heavy records up and down stairs all day long.

No words can express the tenderness I hold for my Arabic tutor, Ustaza Wa'ed, with whom I studied in Amman, Jordan, for six months while reading Omani chronicles and other Arabic-language materials. I still hear her in my head, lovingly scolding me when I would make mistakes: "Rakkiz [focus], ya Nicholas!!" As I write this, above me on my bookshelf is a piece of paper on which she wrote for me one of the greatest lessons of my life, far more important than any lesson she taught me about Arabic grammar:

ضع قليلا من عقلك على قلبك ليستقيم وضع قليلا من قلبك على عقلك ليلين

Basically, put a little of your brain in your heart to keep it true, and put a little of your heart in your brain to keep it soft.

One of the most delightful parts of my study and research for this project was an Omani-Ibadhi summer school hosted on Procida Island off the Amalfi Coast by Professor Ersilia Francesca of University Naples

"L'Orientale" and Professor Angeliki Ziaka of Aristotle University of Thessaloniki. I thank them for insisting that I eat at least two full entrees at every dinner, but also for providing a space for graduate students and junior scholars to meet and form connections that many of us will maintain for the rest of our lives.

Even if they are unnamed here, many of my graduate student and junior scholar colleagues have helped me in more ways than they will ever know, just by being there as we—together—have gone up against a system in academia that is without question demanding unprecedented standards of excellence while also offering the lowest chances of success or livelihood, even when those standards are surpassed. Like many early-career scholars, especially in the humanities, I faced financial pressures during my time at Norwich and during my fellowship year. I was privileged to have the skills to work in the trades on nights and weekends—pouring concrete, patching roofs, building decks, blazing trails—to supplement my income and keep inevitable debt at bay. The reality of balancing intellectual and physical labor reinforced my appreciation for an unpredictable academic landscape. I will always be grateful to the people of rural Vermont, where I lived for three years after earning my PhD, for providing me those opportunities to help make a living. I was told I was one of the lucky ones to obtain a tenure track position in 2021 at the height of COVID. I consider myself lucky for leaving it. I admire those who remain in academia and continue fighting for it, and I hope for a future in which scholars are better supported in their work and in their well-being. In this way, I thank Philip Gooding for being the first person I have seen to give voice in his own book's acknowledgments to the cost of this current culture of academia—especially in the humanities—to mental health. To my fellow junior scholars or graduate students: You are more than enough. Your work is better than superb.

In nearly every archive that kept a register, I consistently found one name of a person who had viewed the same sources before me, handwritten, decades ago: Abdul Sheriff. I end this note by thanking him. Living near Professor Sheriff in Zanzibar, I was privileged to spend hours in his garden with him, discussing Saʿid bin Sultan, the history he helped shape, and how best to tell it. *A Sea of Wealth* builds on his foundational work and in some places offers a different interpretation. I offer those different interpretations with the utmost humility and respect for his scholarship, as well as for every other scholar and teacher who has come before me.

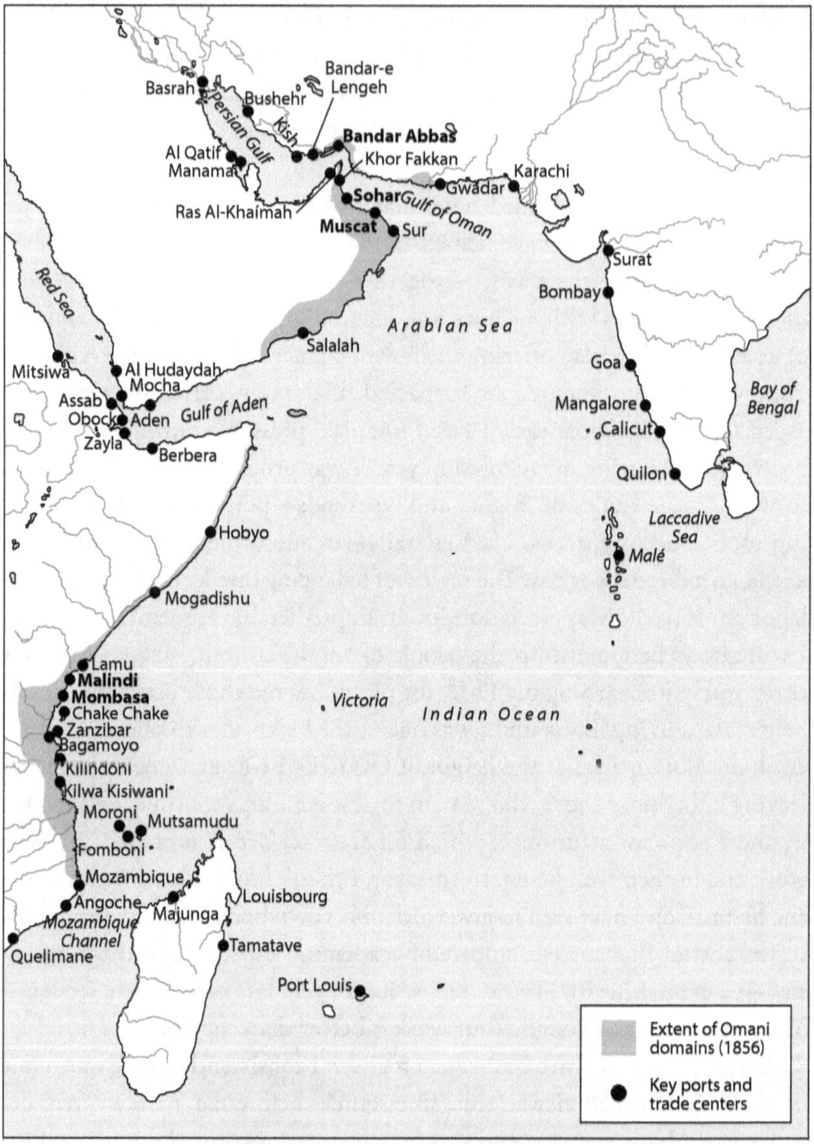

MAP 1. Western Indian Ocean. Designed by Mr. Ethan Trask.

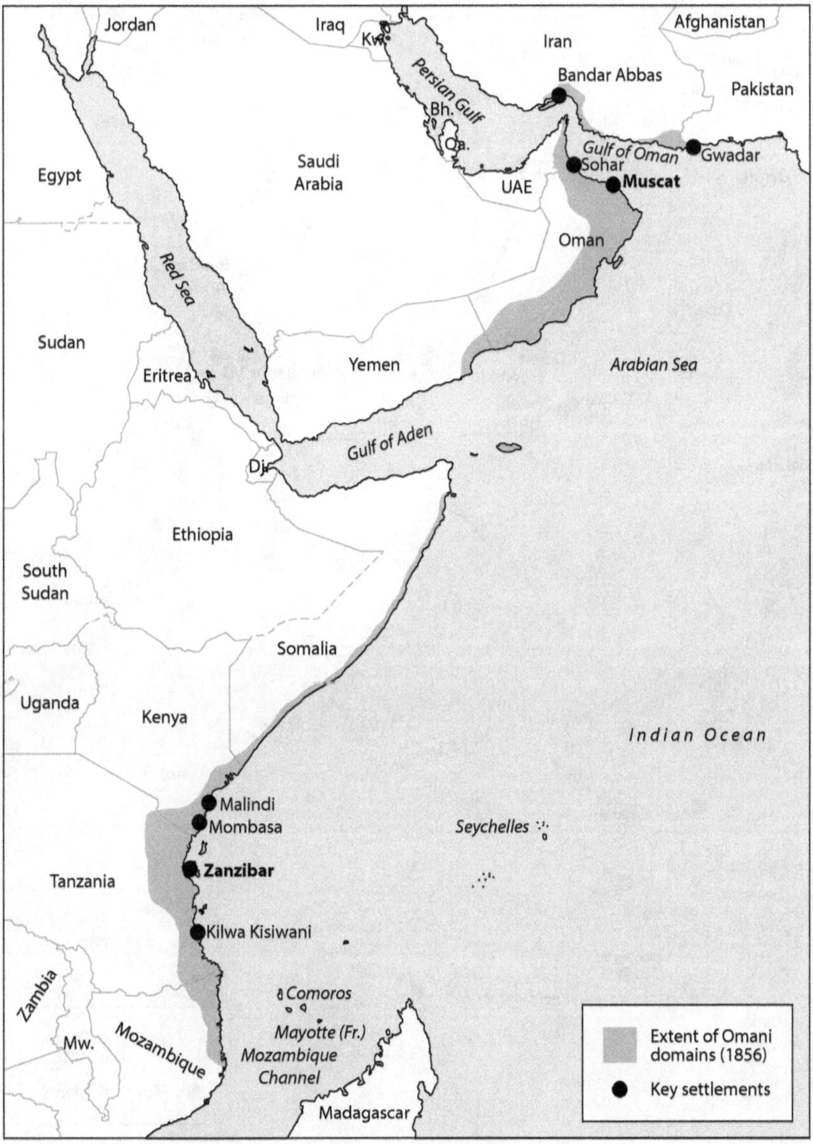

MAP 2. The Omani Empire. Designed by Mr. Ethan Trask.

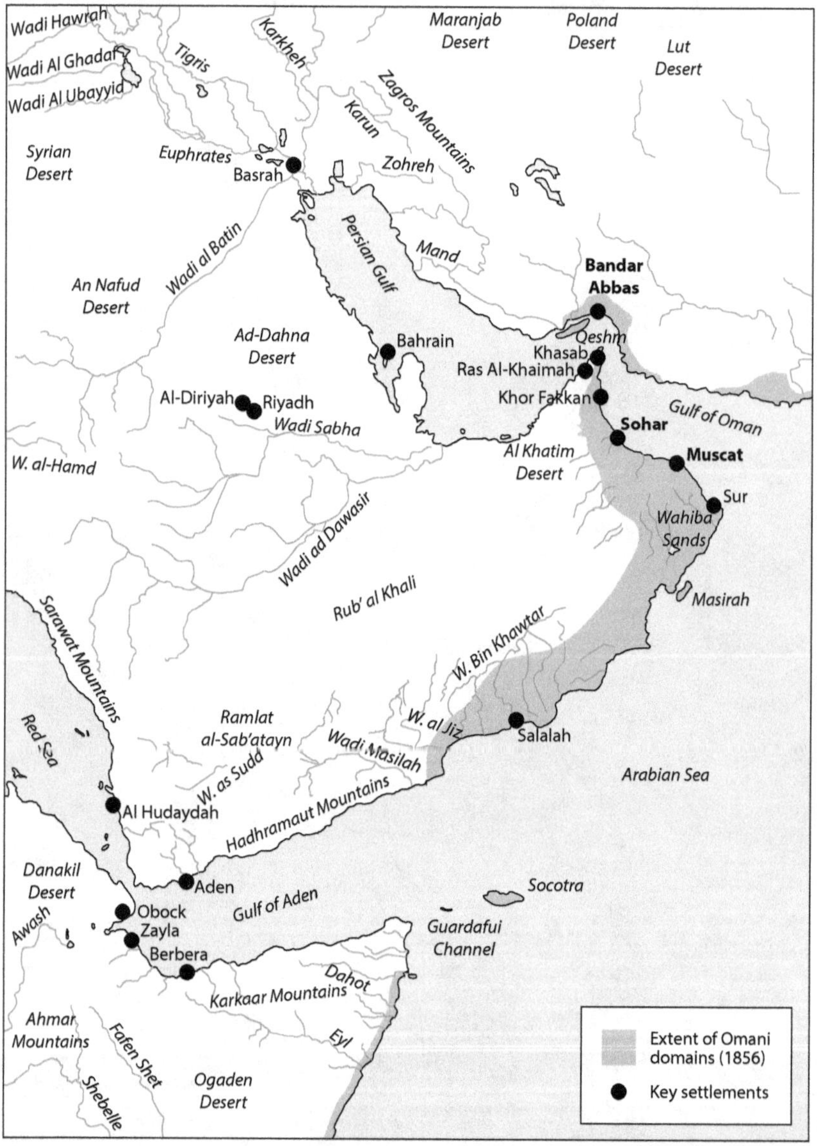

MAP 3. The Arabian Peninsula. Designed by Mr. Ethan Trask.

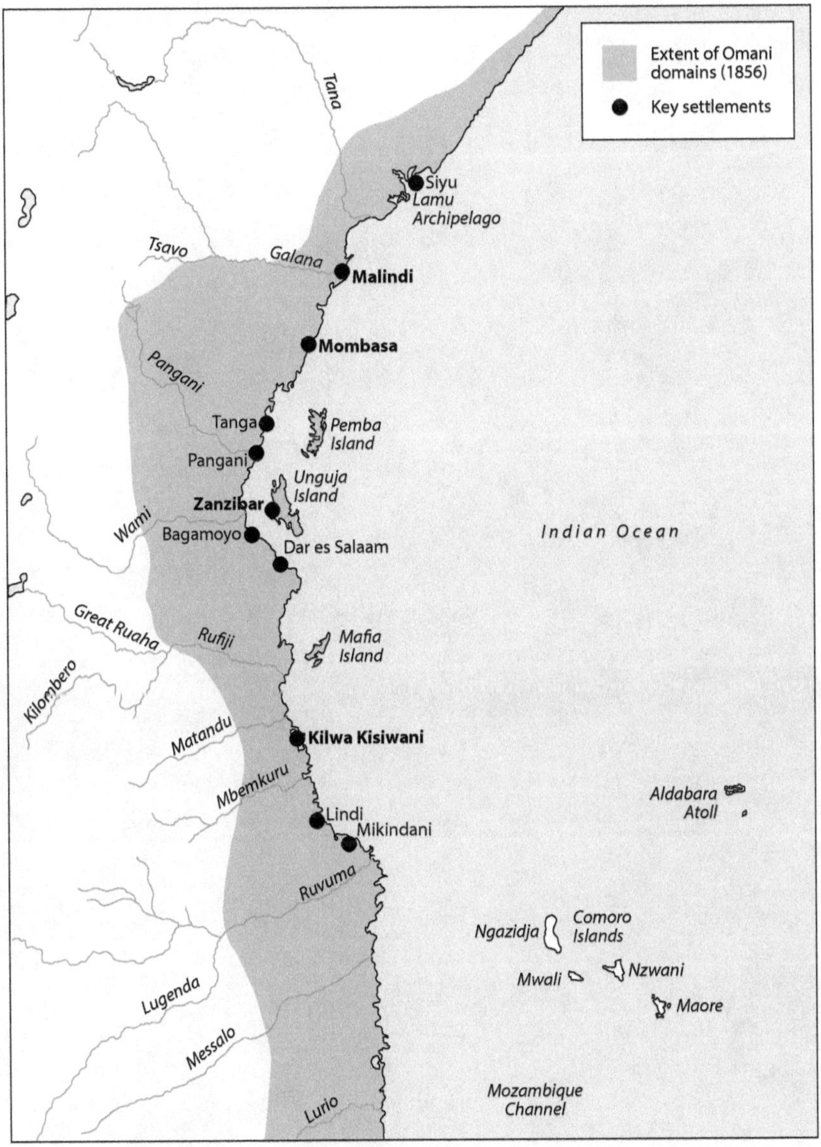

MAP 4. The Swahili Coast. Designed by Mr. Ethan Trask.

Prelude

SA'ID BIN SULTAN was refusing Charles Guillain's overtures. It was August 1840, and the French naval officer was waiting aboard his flagship, *La Dordogne*, anchored in Muscat harbor. Guillain was not supposed to be there. In fact, he was not supposed to be anywhere in the Persian Gulf. He had been ordered to sail for Zanzibar, a small island thousands of miles south of Muscat off Africa's eastern coast. Eight years earlier, Sa'id bin Sultan, leader of the Omani Empire, had made Zanzibar his capital, capping a centuries-long process of Omani expansion through East Africa in pursuit of entwined political and commercial aspirations. Guillain's superiors had sent him there to try to negotiate a commercial treaty with Sa'id. A treaty would bolster French commerce in East Africa, they reasoned, augmenting their own imperial ambitions in the Western Indian Ocean. The French had reasons to be hopeful. For centuries French merchants had traded along East Africa's coast, where they were especially involved in human trafficking. Alongside Arab, East African, and South Asian counterparts, the French trafficked enslaved humans as laborers for their claims in Mauritius and La Réunion, islands east of Madagascar.

Yet when Guillain had anchored in Zanzibar harbor and gone ashore, Sa'id was nowhere to be found. Sa'id had left and sailed for Muscat to gather family members and bring them to Zanzibar. Exasperated, Guillain reboarded his ship and sailed for Muscat. As the winds pulled the *La Dordogne* north, Guillain decided to air his grievances with Sa'id in a formal letter. Guillain's career was at stake, but so was the success of French commerce in Omani domains. The first thing Guillain wrote to Sa'id, therefore, was that he preferred written communication. As he stated to Sa'id, Guillain was frustrated by the difficulty of arranging meetings with him. He

FIGURE 1. Watercolor of Zanzibar harbor and seashore around 1840, showing the US consulate (left), the Customs House (center), and the fort (right), which still stands today. Ships from the Atlantic and Indian Oceans are in the harbor. Artist in Zanzibar, view of Zanzibar, about 1840, gouache and watercolor, image 15½ × 35¼ in. (39.37 × 89.54 cm), museum purchase, 1974, M15708. Courtesy of the Peabody Essex Museum.

was also wary of relying on oral correspondence through messengers, as was Saʿid's preference. Guillain feared that such oral communication without a written record could be "misinterpreted." Like his British counterparts, Guillain was an agent of an imperial apparatus based on paper. He wanted an archive of his diplomacy with Saʿid.

More than his frustration with such ostensible informality, however, Guillain described his offense at Saʿid's decision to ignore French attempts to establish a consulate. The French had already sent someone to be a consul to Saʿid in Zanzibar, just as the Americans and the British had. When that person went to Zanzibar, however, Saʿid had rebuffed him, ignoring his presence. There was no written correspondence to reference, but Guillain claimed that Saʿid had agreed to host a French consul, as he did for Great Britain and the United States. "These are literally your words," he groaned, adding: "They are not in any way changed." He could not understand why Saʿid would feel hostile toward the French. He claimed to Saʿid that they had never done anything "without your consent." Having now followed Saʿid across the ocean, Guillain was committed to meet and, he hoped, finally conclude a written treaty. "When you have finished reading this letter, Your Highness will be pleased to return me a reply," Guillain implored, before reiterating his point: "I hope whatever you may intend to communicate to me will be in writing."[1]

Saʿid responded in writing but did not indicate any willingness to meet. His reply was unusually terse. Saʿid declared that he did not recall ever granting the French permission to send a consul to Zanzibar. His French-Arabic interpreter, with him in Muscat, also did not recall such an agreement. He challenged Guillain, asking him if he had any piece of paper stating otherwise. More important for Saʿid, however, was telling Guillain that his rank was not equal to his tone or his demands. He told Guillain that he would instead communicate directly with the French emperor's ministers in Paris. He ended his response with a lesson for Guillain: "There is a particular way for every object arrived at."[2]

This exchange between Saʿid bin Sultan and Charles Guillain provides a glimpse into the makings of the modern world as it unfolded in ways different from conventional depictions. That moment in 1840 off the coast of Muscat offers a lens into modern world history through the Omani Empire. Saʿid bin Sultan was the leader of the Omani Empire from 1806 until his death in 1856. He remains Oman's longest-serving ruler. As his exchange with Guillain reflected, Saʿid and others in the Omani Empire dealt with Europeans and Americans from positions of parity and sometimes from positions of superiority, at least throughout Saʿid's reign. Saʿid was understood in his lifetime to be an important leader on the world stage. He communicated with American presidents, British royals, the queen of Madagascar, Mohammad Ali of Egypt, and he negotiated with countless powerful social groups throughout East Africa and Arabia. Saʿid's lesson to Guillain that there was a particular way of doing things in his domains encapsulates this book's argument: there was an Omani Empire, and in this empire Arabs, Africans, and Asians actively shaped the conditions of commercial engagement in the Western Indian Ocean, uniting the empire's domains into a single oceanic marketplace in which Europeans and Americans had to accede if they wished to succeed.

Saʿid's movement between East Africa and Arabia was not unusual, either in the first half of the nineteenth century or in the millennia-old longer arc of the Western Indian Ocean's history. Since long before Saʿid's lifetime, countless numbers of Omanis had moved between parts of East Africa and Arabia, settling and resettling with the monsoon winds. Beginning in the seventeenth century, Omani migrations around the Western Indian Ocean took on increasingly imperialist hues, with more concerted acts of Omani state power manifest through violent acts of expansion, expropriation, and enslavement, backed by political machinations.[3] Guillain's struggles to ingratiate himself with Saʿid were also not unusual. They can be read as part of a larger world historical phenomenon of Europeans acquiescing to and accommodating other societies' ways of doing things.[4]

Just as Guillain was frustrated that Saʿid preferred to not write anything down, historians might feel the same. We know remarkably little about Saʿid. Like his predecessors, he did not maintain an official archive. He left behind no logbooks, no diaries, almost no diplomatic correspondence, and almost no records of personal affairs.[5] While limiting, this lack of sources is also an opportunity to think in creative ways about reading sources in combination and against each other, to think through a kind of prosopography: uncovering the dynamics of a historical period by finding overlapping themes and characteristics of a group of people, whose individual biographies might in fact be largely untraceable. Prosopography interprets the history of an individual in reciprocity with the history of larger structures and phenomena, viewing an individual as one of a group of other actors.[6] Compared to later periods, historians have relatively few sources for understanding Omani history in the first half of the nineteenth century and before. In the sources we do have, Saʿid is prominent, but nearly every source that includes Saʿid also brings other actors to center stage. Examining history through Saʿid reveals a polyphonic narrative, in which diverse voices form an interwoven yet distinct whole—each necessary, none dominant.[7]

Rather than writing a history *of* Saʿid, therefore, we can instead write a history *through* him, piecing together a kind of prosopography to uncover sediments of a world in the making, rather than one foretold.[8] And in doing so, the multiple voices of this period can be seen not only as interdependent but also as interactive, reciprocal, and mutually constitutive. Saʿid bin Sultan and the Omani Empire upturn many received narratives about how our shared global present came to be. By 1840 Arabs, East Africans, and South Asians had transformed Zanzibar into a bustling commercial hub, a monied metropolis. Yet for many it remained a place of misery. Zanzibar's station as the capital of the Omani Empire and its place in interoceanic commerce was rooted in the evisceration of entire human communities forced into slavery and human trafficking. In fact, Saʿid bin Sultan was one of the most prolific human traffickers in the Western Indian Ocean. He received a personal tax on every human trafficked through the empire's domains.

In Oman today, Saʿid looms large in national mythology. His family, the Al Bu Saʿid, remain in power. In Zanzibar his grave and former residence bustle with tourists. Omanis and Zanzibaris alike burst into smiles when they hear his name, eager to regale visitors with tales of his legacy as a golden age. There is one primary difference between the ways Omani and non-Omani scholars have written about Saʿid's reign and the Omani

Empire: almost as a rule, Omanis try not to discuss slavery. When it is discussed, it is generally in censored and apologetic ways.[9] The exceptions to this, generally, occur among Omanis of East African descent.[10] Enslavement and human trafficking were the core of the Omani Empire, sustained by deeply ingrained and violent racial, religious, and tribal hierarchies, some of which remain in Omani society today.[11] There is little, if any, mention of this history in Omani secondary literature, secondary school curriculum, museums, media, or general public discourse. Saʿid's decisions and actions as leader of the Omani Empire were part of a broader world historical period that brought great affluence and leisure to many, including many Omanis. His decisions and actions also ravaged the lives of many more.

Historians have debated the language used to discuss slavery.[12] Some argue that *slave* erases the violence of traffickers and objectifies the enslaved, preferring *enslaved person* instead.[13] Others have criticized such terminology, claiming that it alludes to a sense of personhood or autonomy that simply was never there in American or Atlantic history.[14] In the Omani Empire, however, we might suggest the opposite. *Enslaved person* carries more purchase than *slave* because, under Islamic law, slaves had legal personhood; they were not chattel property as in the Atlantic.[15] As shown in chapter 6 of this book, slavery was bound up with every aspect of the Omani Empire, but the enslaved had varying degrees of autonomy and power, whether they were laborers, governors, or mothers of future sultans. Yet any of these words—slavery, enslavement, slave trade, human trafficking—can occlude what was taking place. Led by Omanis but also facilitated by other Arabs, Persians, Central Asians and South Asians, Europeans, Americans, and others, in the Omani Empire this was the efficient, calculated, and systematic evisceration of entire human communities, born from the pursuit of wealth.

Already in his lifetime Saʿid was mythologized. One American diplomat lauded him as the "Haroun al Raschid" of the time, referring to the famous Abbasid caliph whose reign ushered in a flowering of Islamicate civilization.[16] The British and the French often called him "His Highness." Sometimes the British wrote of him in less celebratory terms, but still steeped in Orientalist myths of Arab rulers as patriarchal despots.[17] Today, the Omani nation-state casts Saʿid's reign as the country's "golden age."[18] Beginning in the third grade, teachers have instructed Omani schoolchildren that Saʿid "built a very large Omani Empire (*al-imbaraturiya al-ʿUmaniya*) across Asia, including Oman and the East African coast as far north as Mogadishu and as far south as Mozambique."[19] They have cast Saʿid as a national hero who extended the empire as far inland in East Africa as the Congo. This view echoes a popular nineteenth-century Omani proverb: if someone played a *mizmar* in Zanzibar, people would dance on Africa's Great Lakes.[20]

In reality, Saʿid was neither as powerful nor as wealthy as Haroun al-Rashid. Nor was he simply a patriarch. Saʿid's sovereignty and the influence of the empire on peoples in Africa were never as complete as many Omanis might like to portray. Reading a history of empire through Saʿid, while seeing him as one part of a broader whole, helps us peel apart these layers of historiography and mythology. For as privileged as Saʿid was, he died deeply in debt to his Gujarati customs master. Dualities central to Saʿid's life mirror the Omani Empire's contradictions and themes of modern world history: connections forged by violent disconnections, power built on exploitation, wealth amassed through displacement, and commerce shaped by coercion and monopoly.

Saʿid's life and reign are thus like a keyhole through which we can peer into local, regional, and global history.[21] His life prompts us to question the labels we use for interpreting the world of which he was a part. For instance, his aunt who orchestrated his seizure of power in 1806 was known as Bibi Moza.[22] That he and his family members—native Arabic speakers—referred to Moza by the prefix *Bibi* reflects multilingual currents of the Indian Ocean world. *Bibi* is not originally an Arabic word. It is a traveling word, an Indian Ocean artifact that moved between Persian, Swahili, and South Asian languages into Arabic.[23] Individuals moved between these worlds, too. One of the first things Saʿid did upon seizing power was appoint Durrah bin Jumʿah as Muscat's governor.[24] Durrah was a Baloch, coming from the coastal region of present-day Iran or Pakistan. Baloch mercenaries and guards remained central to the Omani Empire's military forces well into the late nineteenth century.[25]

Like many Omanis today, Saʿid was an Ibadi Muslim – neither Sunni nor Shiʿi. Put most basically, Ibadi Islam emerged among the first generation of Muslims in the context of disagreements over political succession, governance, and leadership after the Prophet Muhammad's death. For centuries before Saʿid, leaders of the Ibadi community in Oman held the title *imam.* Upon reaching consensus, certain male community members bestowed this title upon another person chosen as the leader for perceived character, reputation, piety, and learning. Ibadi notions of governance surrounding the position of imam formed deeply rooted traditions in Oman and filled thousands of pages of Ibadi jurisprudence. By all accounts a pious and educated person, Saʿid would have known these traditions and this history. Yet Saʿid never once referred to himself as *imam*, nor did he ever seek the title. Sometimes American or European observers mistakenly referred to him as such. At other times they referred to him, also in error, as a *sultan*. But Saʿid was also technically not a sultan.[26] In Islamic history, the word sultan comes from the Arabic word for power or sovereignty, and it developed into a particular form of political leadership. In Omani history before Saʿid's death, sultan was a derogatory title, equated with tyranny.[27] The word sultan can also be a person's name, however, as in Saʿid bin Sultan, indicating that Saʿid was the son of a man named Sultan.

Instead of either imam or sultan, Saʿid used the label *sayyid,* a relatively generic honorific used to refer to an esteemed person.[28] We do not know why he chose this title. We do not know why he chose to not pursue the title of imam, as his grandfather had but not his father. He left no sources on these matters. What we do know reveals an empire at its zenith in the early nineteenth century, shaped by Omani, East African, and South Asian actors alike.

This book tells the history of how that empire came to be. It begins with an introductory chapter interweaving the history and historiography that frames the book and discusses more elements and challenges of crafting this history. The second chapter traces the emergence of the Omani Empire in the centuries before Saʿid's reign, showing how Omanis reduced arriving Europeans into subordinate competing factions while augmenting their control over Gulf commerce as they began to increasingly set their sights on East Africa. The third chapter frames and reframes Gulf history in the first three decades of the nineteenth century by tracing Saʿid's uses of violence and negotiations with other powerful regional groups and emerging states, showing how those groups helped delimit the boundaries of the Omani Empire. The fourth chapter maps how, having established himself in the Gulf, Saʿid moved to Zanzibar and put in place certain policies and institutions aimed at catalyzing interoceanic commerce while also exploiting the island's physical geography and remaking its social landscape, establishing the empire's new capital in Zanzibar. The fifth chapter traces negotiations between Saʿid, the British, and the Americans in ratifying commercial treaties, and reveals how local peoples exploited the British-American rivalry for their own financial gains, reducing Atlantic merchants to minority middlemen and forcing them to conduct business according to Indian Ocean institutions. The final chapter breathes historical life into the tens of thousands of unnamed enslaved humans who sustained the Omani Empire and, ultimately, the nineteenth-century world economy.

ONE

Writing Omani History

THE SKETCH WAS DRAWN for Benjamin Fabens, one of the wealthiest merchants in Salem, Massachusetts. We do not know who drew it. It is a loose-leaf drawing in the Fabens Family Papers housed in the Phillips Library, part of the Peabody Essex Museum.[1] The sketch was probably drawn by one of the sailors Fabens contracted as part of his firm's extensive business in the Western Indian Ocean, where the firm sold American cotton, brass wire, sometimes muskets, and other goods to discerning East African, Arab, and South Asian consumers. In turn, the Fabens firm procured dates, cloves, ivory, coffee, and other products, fueling a reciprocal consumerism in Salem and elsewhere in the United States.[2]

The sketch showed the Western Indian Ocean's interconnected waterways, highlighting the major commercial centers: Zanzibar, off the coast of present-day Tanzania; Aden and Mocha in Yemen; Muscat in Oman; and Bombay, today known as Mumbai, in India. It details the different monsoons and the dates of their seasons, with the directions of the winds that carried ships around the ocean. The sketch also noted the best products that could be procured in each port during the different seasons. In Muscat, September was the best season for procuring dates, especially the coveted *fard* variety, the best that the "Near East and Persian Gulf produces."[3] From Muscat, it was about a twenty-day voyage east to Bombay, where all kinds of "produce" flowed in from across the ocean in the Red Sea and Africa. Though the sketch was probably drawn in the 1840s, in showing these connections, it could have been drawn a millennium prior: peoples from East Africa, Arabia, and South Asia had crisscrossed the sea for centuries, exploiting the monsoon winds as an engine for fueling a carousel-like, enduring commercial world.[4]

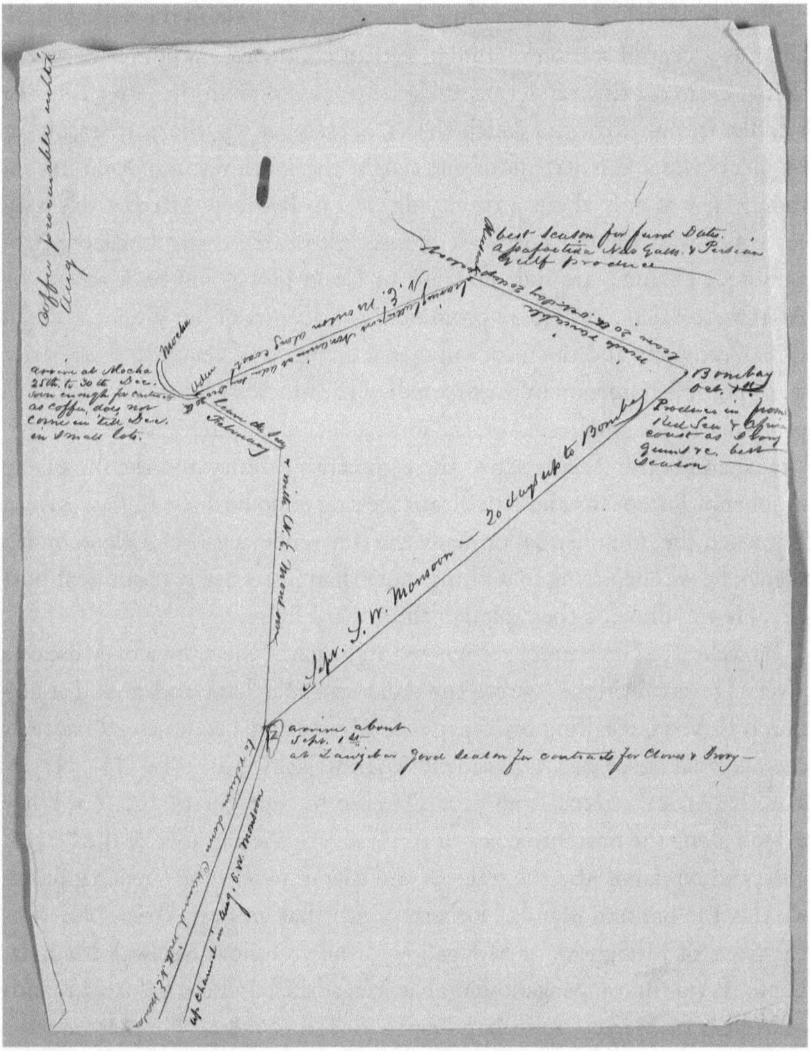

FIGURE 2. Sketch of oceanic trade routes in the Western Indian Ocean, drawn for Benjamin Fabens by an unknown sailor in the 1840s. It shows the interconnected routes between the Arabian Peninsula, East Africa, and South Asia, with a tiny rendering of Zanzibar island. Letter Book, 1844–1848, Fabens Family Papers, MH 94, box 2, folder 10. Courtesy of Phillips Library, Peabody Essex Museum, Rowley, MA.

But the sketch also shows something decisively new to the period: Zanzibar as a central station of Indian Ocean commerce. Whoever drew the sketch created a tiny rendering of Zanzibar island, with the letter Z in the middle. In Zanzibar, the sketch shows, September was the best season for buying cloves and ivory, and if one caught the southwest monsoon in that month, it was only about a twenty-day sail to Bombay. Alternatively, sailors could wait for the northeast monsoon to carry them down the Mozambique channel, around the Cape of Good Hope, and back across the Atlantic to Salem. Zanzibar's prominence as a center of the Western Indian Ocean economy and the most important commercial center in East Africa was a new phenomenon in the first half of the nineteenth century. Its rise to prominence was predicated on the movements of countless Arabs, East Africans, and South Asians across the eighteenth century and the increasing number of Europeans and Americans seeking to do business in East Africa. But when the unnamed sailor made the tiny rendering of the island on his sketch, he was depicting something more than just a newly prominent port city. He was drawing the capital of the Omani Empire.

Travelers to the empire recognized its reach. "The sultan of Muscat is a very powerful prince," wrote the American merchant and diplomat Edmund Roberts, recalling his experience negotiating a commercial treaty as the personal envoy of US president Andrew Jackson in 1832. "His possessions in Africa, stretch from cape Delgado to cape Guardafui. . . . [T]hey extend along the northern coast of Arabia . . . to the entrance of the Persian gulf: and he claims also the seacoast and islands *within* the Persian gulf, including the Bahrein islands." Roberts added that, in East Africa, "he owns the ports of Monghow, or Mongallow, Lyndy, Quiloa (Keelwa), Melinda, Lamo, Patta, Brava, Magadosha (alias Magadshe), and the valuable islands of Mofeea or Mafeea, Zanzibar, Pemba, Socotra . . . &c." He then added a qualification, something that puzzled many Europeans and Americans. "It is true," Roberts observed, "that only a small part of this immense territory is garrisoned by his [Saʿid bin Sultan's] troops, but all is tributary to him."[5]

How could there be a "prince" ruling over such vast domains without troops holding them together? Many historians have grappled with this question, as well as how to label and interpret the makeup of the domains Roberts identified. Every study of Oman and the Western Indian Ocean in this period acknowledges some form of imperial formation and qualifies the empire using a mixture of adjectives. This book asserts that there was an Omani Empire, and this empire reached the apex of its flourishing and its influence in the first half of the nineteenth century, during Saʿid's reign from 1806 to 1856. Emanating from Arabia and the Gulf down the coast of East Africa, the Omani Empire was forged through military power, political machinations and negotiations, and commercial networking to encompass loosely linked individual markets, towns, and cities into a single oceanic-oriented marketplace. By 1832 that marketplace was centered on Zanzibar, where Saʿid moved his court, contained Atlantic merchants, and established his primary Customs House, through which all customs duties and other revenues flowed. The Omani Empire was thus an integral actor in forging a coherent political and commercial entity in the Western Indian Ocean in the first half of the nineteenth century.

The empire reshaped commerce and life from East Africa to Arabia, sometimes through violence, other times through negotiation. Ultimately the empire's rise introduced new financial arrangements allowing for the more effective proliferation of networks of credit and foreign capital, all undergirded by enslavement and human trafficking.[6] The domains Roberts identified were part of a single, multidimensional political and economic formation emanating from a home area and from a single ruler as part of a ruling family. That ruler used increasingly powerful mechanisms of state control, whether force, negotiations, or incentives, to expand and expropriate the earth and lands of other peoples, coercing them to adhere to a set of political and commercial institutions and structures. This was evident to the French diplomat Édouard Loarer, who traveled throughout the Omani Empire during Saʿid's reign and wrote an extensive report on what he observed. Loarer echoed Roberts, also noting Saʿid's sovereignty over these territories. He acknowledged that there were vast distances between different parts of the empire and that some parts might have had more autonomy than others; nonetheless, there were "particular" administrative structures that harnessed these domains into a single entity—"one and the same state"—a state under the "immediate authority" of Saʿid and centered on Zanzibar.[7]

The Omani Empire's history upturns conventional narratives of our modern world. It is one part of how our modern world came to be. In describing a single state, Loarer was observing an entity that held together an oceanic marketplace, a space in which the Atlantic and Indian Oceans were stitched together. Yet the Omani Empire uncovers a different perspective on this process of two oceanic spaces coming to meet. It challenges basic Western imperialist epistemological convictions that continue to inform the writing of history, our conception of what and where the Middle East is and has been, and thinking on our shared global present. Many historians have called for understanding world history from below.[8] Such an approach might be conceived as something more than thinking about the past through the experiences and perspectives of the marginal and the exploited. From the perspective of the discipline of world history, especially treatments of empires in global contexts, the Omani Empire itself is marginalized. In one representative global history of empire, John Darwin referred to Saʿid bin Sultan and his "Omani domain" and acknowledged how peoples in this "Omani domain" turned Europe's markets and merchants to its advantage while forming a "mercantile empire" centered on Zanzibar by the 1840s. But that is less than one paragraph in a one-thousand-page-long book and is only in the context of questioning why the British ostensibly "chose" to "exempt" this mercantile empire from their ban on the slave trade.[9]

A Sea of Wealth turns such narratives on their heads. It reframes the Omani Empire as a pivotal force in nineteenth-century global trade, not a peripheral entity. The empire set the terms of engagement for Europeans and Americans, not the other way around. Amplifying the voices and agencies of the marginal and the exploited might be facilitated by also identifying them as parts of larger categories, like an empire, important to the shaping of modern world history. Peoples comprising this empire—whether elite or marginalized, free or enslaved, man or woman, Arab or South Asian—were part of global processes that shaped the direction and character of connectivity in the Western Indian Ocean and beyond. Omani imperialism foremost involved the consolidation of smaller markets into a larger market connecting East Africa with Arabia and the Gulf and maintained by a central political formation with an Omani leader at its helm.

Omani leaders often dictated trade terms to European and American merchants, integrating them into existing networks. All these trade terms were predicated on the violent expropriation of certain peoples and political negotiations with others, both processes aimed at incorporating local and regional groups into the empire's economic orbit. The Omani Empire held together an oceanic marketplace centered on Muscat and then Zanzibar through military force, forms of political power and negotiations, labor organization rooted in enslavement and human trafficking, and dynamic mechanisms of credit and debt. The sketch in the Fabens collection demonstrated connectivity, perhaps the central theme in Indian Ocean history, but connectivity does not just exist. Connections are forged, and by the time Saʿid bin Sultan made

Zanzibar his capital in 1832, peoples in the Omani Empire had connected markets across East Africa and into Arabia into an imperial space that subordinated Europeans and Americans, at least for a time.

World historian Marshall Hodgson noted how, in 1698, one defining event in the history of the Islamic world between the years 1500 and 1698 was when the "sultanate of Muscat" drove the Portuguese from Zanzibar, which he labeled a "major commercial center" of East Africa.[10] Writing before the defining monographs of Omani history had been published, Hodgson was shrewd in noting the importance of Omani expansion in East Africa. But the Omanis did not drive the Portuguese from Zanzibar, which in 1698 was still a relatively minor part of the East African maritime commercial realm. The Omanis drove the Portuguese from Mombasa. Later, Hodgson referred to the "sultanate of Zanzibar" as among parts of the world that held a "special niche in the world market." Hodgson noted that in 1832 Saʿid bin Sultan, whom he categorized as "lord of Muscat," made Zanzibar his capital to "better control and extend his dominions along the Swahili African coast."[11] As Hodgson's characterizations highlight, the idea of some sort of Omani imperial formation is familiar, especially to specialists of East Africa, Arabia, or the Western Indian Ocean. Less familiar, however, is understanding it as an empire helping drive modern world history in ways other than merely being incorporated into a Western world.[12]

In a defining work of Omani and Indian Ocean history, Abdul Sheriff analyzed a "commercial empire" based in Zanzibar, which the Omanis established as their capital while acting as an "alien power."[13] Omani imperialism in the form of expansion, expropriation, and enslavement is standard to the histories of eighteenth- and nineteenth-century Oman. John Wilkinson concluded that Omanis forged a "major" economic empire that ultimately developed into a "quasi-colonial empire."[14] Responding to both, Reda Bhacker countered that, although Saʿid and his predecessors exerted "some degree of control" over "far-flung dominions," those dominions were never "a homogenous entity constituting an 'empire' or even a 'state' in the modern European sense."[15]

Bhacker's claim reflects an approach to interpreting this history that continues to inform much scholarship, even if in more subtle and implicit ways. Bhacker made explicit the tendency to use Europe as a central reference for interpreting history, including the histories of non-European peoples and their societies. His claim also belies a reductive understanding of European history: European empires were not homogenous entities either.[16] Such a claim reveals a deeply rooted tendency in the discipline of history and the broader academy to use a "hyperreal Europe" as the central reference for evaluating humans and their societies anywhere in the world.[17] Running through these older-style histories of Oman was the idea of an outside world acting upon Oman, as peoples in Omani domains reacted. Wilkinson, for instance, departed from the assumption that Oman was "effectively an island," surrounded by sea on one side and sand on the other.[18]

The history of Oman was thus one of an "outside world" that "forced itself" over time on the island of Oman, which was "fixed within a more or less rigid geographical and economic framework" that operated according to "an antique social and religious structure." According to Wilkinson, this meant no development: no transformation of the land, no urbanization, no evolution of class and political structures, no changing of institutions. Because of this, Wilkinson concluded, Oman was a "sociological *cul de sac*."[19] Sheriff took a more expansive view of Omani history, highlighting its imperial nature and its expansionist dynamics in East Africa. While Sheriff eschewed the idea of an isolationist Oman, he nonetheless concluded that, by the end of the eighteenth century, Europeans had transformed the Omani Empire into a "compradorial state" that was entirely "politically dependent on Britain."[20]

A Sea of Wealth asserts that the Omani Empire was not a compradorial state and that its history more broadly cannot be reduced to a veritable cul de sac.[21] The Omani Empire, like other parts of the world, did not recede in the face of European intrusions.[22] As a part of the Indian Ocean and a part of the Middle East, the Omani Empire can join land and sea into a single formation and help answer the call of many historians to seek new historical lines of inquiry for reimagining these spaces in modern world history.[23] Whether standing in the harbor of Muscat, Mombasa, or Zanzibar, looking out from the Omani Empire toward the seas offers a modern world history that can be different from those already written. This history is one in which Arabs, Africans, and Asians used Europeans and Americans to enrich their own lives and fortify their own ambitions. In this way, Marshall Hodgson remains instructive. Decades ago, Hodgson sought to reorient our understanding of our modern world, showing how the arrival of Europeans in the Indian Ocean was far from the beginning of any sort of European dominance. In fact, he argued, Muslim societies in the Indian Ocean actually *contained* Europeans, "reducing them to one element among others in the multinational trading world of the Southern Seas."[24]

As shown throughout *A Sea of Wealth,* the Omani Empire opens vistas of possibilities for seeing how Indian Ocean peoples—Arabs, Africans, Asians, and others—did just that. They were neither brokers of the West nor mere *compradors* forming a dominated service bourgeoisie.[25] In the Omani Empire, local peoples ferociously preserved their own agencies and subordinated Europeans and Americans as they pursued wealth by controlling markets. Looking into this world through Saʿid prompts us to question European power and, at certain times, to cast it aside entirely. In doing so, this book builds upon and is indebted to a formidable foundation provided foremost by Jeremy Prestholdt, Thomas McDow, and Fahad Bishara.

In his masterful telling, Prestholdt also sought to upturn many received assumptions about the modern world. He placed East African consumers—not mere producers—at the fore of global processes shaping the lived worlds of Europeans and Americans. Prestholdt uncovered reciprocities and interrelations at the core of our present-day global economic system. Peoples in the Western Indian Ocean, especially the Swahili-speaking peoples of East Africa, obsessed over materiality and the pursuit of wealth. That these people pursued wealth, he demonstrated, is not an etic abstraction. It was central to the way they built and conceived of their worlds. Pursuing wealth, not only in material things but also in terms of status and perception, was integral to social life in this time and space. The arrival of European and especially American persons in the Western Indian Ocean did not minimize this but rather gave these local consumers newfound levers of social, political, and commercial power.[26] Prestholdt acknowledged that Omani power in Zanzibar and the consolidation of Omani rule elsewhere in East Africa brought rapid changes to the region with great economic repercussions. Most important, Prestholdt stated, was that Omani control in Zanzibar bound other parts of East Africa within the same Zanzibar-centered "cultural-economic zone."[27]

McDow and Bishara entered the world Prestholdt uncovered, and in doing so they both named the empire. McDow noted that Saʿid ruled over "an empire that connected three sides of the Western Indian Ocean."[28] In this empire and around it, McDow illustrated how Africans, Arabs, and South Asians used credit and kinship to facilitate their mobility and pursue commercial gain throughout the empire, knitting its domains together in denser ways in which coast and interior—in Arabia as in East Africa—were interlinked with the ocean.[29] For Bishara, there was a discernible political economy at the core of the "trans-oceanic empire," and the law was integral to it.[30] Bishara showed how Omani jurists developed legal frameworks allowing people to capitalize on conditions of possibility predicated by imperial expansion by taking on debt and extending credit, also linking the empire's domains ever tighter together. Peoples in the Omani Empire drew upon legal compendiums that did more than delineate rules and guide individual actions. Bishara argued that the law was constitutive of wealth itself and, by extension, of the Western Indian Ocean as a coherent arena. "The challenge," instructed Bishara, "is to find the voices of the thousands of migrants who traversed these imperial realms and remade the boundaries between law, empire, and economic life."[31] *A Sea of Wealth* shows how those imperial realms came to be the Omani Empire, and does so to recenter our understanding of this history not as separate, preformed worlds coming to meet and to overlap but rather as part of one total world historical process.

No two empires are the same, but in many ways the Omani Empire and the craft of writing its history are like another, oceans and continents away, one that many historians have also struggled with. Contrary to conventional interpretations of American history, Pekka Hämäläinen boldly argued that there was a Comanche Empire, one that also expanded, expropriated, and enslaved its way into forcing Europeans to resist, retreat, and struggle. Hämäläinen's conception of the Comanche Empire helps us think about the Omani Empire. As he wrote, the Comanche Empire was powered by violence but was ultimately an economic construction. "At its core," Hämäläinen stated, the Comanche Empire "was an extensive commercial network that allowed Comanches to control nearby border markets and long-distance trade [and] swing surrounding groups into their political orbit."[32] Similarly, *A Sea of Wealth* shows how the Omani Empire leveraged force to build extensive commercial networks allowing Omanis and other imperial elites to control an interregional oceanic marketplace, orbiting around Zanzibar. The Omanis, to borrow from Hämäläinen, were an interregional power with an imperial presence. This imperial presence had borders, though they were fluid. It was held together by a single central authority, and though it was heterogeneous, it was characterized by a deep social hierarchy formed through expropriation and exploitation, most of all for commercial control and gain.

Hämäläinen's work raised the question of whether his category was an etic, or outsider, interpretation.[33] In Islamic and Middle Eastern history there is a grand tradition of empire and imperialism. In fact, the Omani Empire emerged in the age of the famous Islamic gunpowder empires: the Ottomans, the Mughals, and the Safavids.[34] Each of these empires is the subject of enormous scholarship, and scholars have debated what constituted them as empires. These and many other empires have been debated as entities that are more than the basic assumption of empire as a "political unit that is large and expansionist . . . reproducing differentiation and inequality among the people it incorporates."[35] Yet the elements of expansionism, differentiation, inequality, and incorporation are basic building blocks of an empire from which other elements, such as ideology, arts and culture, and more, emanate.

As shown throughout this work, those who traveled through the Omani Empire understood it as a political structure with Zanzibar as its center. All peoples in the empire, as Edmund Roberts explained, were in tribute to Saʿid; certain structures facilitating that tribute would have been visible. Though its borders might have been somewhat fluid, the empire's domains were physically identifiable: whether caravan waystations or port cities, land and sea spaces were part of the Omani Empire if there were customs officials and often mercenary security forces funneling prescribed duties, commodities, and people directly to Zanzibar. The second American consul in Zanzibar, Charles Ward, observed how central the management of customs duties was to the functioning of the empire. "The Custom master has his revenue officers in every town and village and the duties on the coast are regulated by him, and all is included in the Zanzibar district," he observed.[36]

Force held this system together, as well. Though Saʿid did not have a regular army, he was able at times to marshal powerful land forces. His navy, however, was the core of how he projected power. One American sailor described the Omani navy as a "force of no common kind."[37] Edmund Roberts similarly remarked that Saʿid possessed "a more efficient Naval force than all the native Princes combined from the Cape of Good Hope to Japan."[38] And this navy was one way Saʿid ensured peoples throughout the empire understood they were tributary to him, as Roberts's previous quote revealed.

That peoples in the Omani Empire were tributary to Saʿid not only indicates varying degrees of autonomy and subjecthood, but it also belies the existence of a complicated commercial system. Whether it was in the form of actual payments of tribute or customs duties or other taxes, tribute itself was predicated upon sets of commercial networks, which themselves were predicated upon an organized system of labor, a multidimensional system bound up with enslavement and human trafficking.[39] That system of labor moved people, capital, and currency toward Zanzibar beginning in 1785, when Saʿid's predecessors appointed the Shivji family firm to farm customs there. The consolidation of Zanzibar as an imperial center of a vast commercial world became further instantiated in 1832 when Saʿid moved his capital there and again in 1835 when he granted the Shivji firm continuing management of the empire's customs. As demonstrated especially in chapter 6, Saʿid understood his empire in this way, with Zanzibar at the center of a labor system moving people, capital, and currency from India, Arabia, and Africa's interior toward Zanzibar.

The English-language word *empire* holds great currency in European history and thought, with a repertoire of forms and meanings. Certainly the word has purchase in other societies as well.[40] The word has correlates but not cognates in Islamic political philosophy, Middle Eastern history, and Middle Eastern languages. Yet it is not an etic label for Omani history if we conceive of empires as many historians have called for: as constructions comprised of peoples from myriad national, ethnic, or religious backgrounds. The history of the British Empire in the world can be interpreted as different societies coming to look more like Britain in terms of laws, language, and norms, but in many ways, Britain also came to look more like other societies, with Britons drinking coffee, eating curry, peppering their food, wearing silk, or polishing their ivory jewelry.

Jeremy Prestholdt's call for uncovering alternative genealogies of globalization and thus our basic epistemological framework for interpreting the modern world can also be applied to how we think about empires, as mutually determinative, reciprocal culminations of relationships between peoples in multinational spaces. And in this way, the adjective *Omani* becomes especially apt. To be Omani, especially in Saʿid's lifetime, was to bear out in literal ways a reciprocal, mutually determinative oceanic world, embedded in the language they used to understand it.[41] Like Omanis today, when Saʿid's family sat down to a meal of lentils they would have referred to them as *daal*, like people in South Asia, rather than *ʿadas*, like people in Egypt or the Levant. Saʿid's daughter Salameh remembered how, in the royal residence where she grew up in Zanzibar, a "babel" of languages was spoken: Arabic, Swahili, Persian, and Circassian and Abyssinian languages.[42] Accordingly, the Omani Empire was a composite or "conglomerate state," a polity not so unique after all, consisting of several territories held together by a "ruling house," but one in which "each territory—or rather the social elite of each territory—had its distinctive relation to the ruler."[43]

Yet stating the existence of the Omani Empire is not enough. Saʿid and his imperial agents did things: they contained Europeans and Americans while monopolizing trade in favor of Arab, African, and Asian persons; they destroyed human communities and uprooted family units; they enslaved and trafficked countless numbers of humans; they exploited the earth and changed the physical landscape of entire geographic spaces, like Zanzibar. In doing all this, they consolidated connections for the pursuit of wealth. Those connections left a history that can help bridge historiographical divides, especially by questioning geographic labels and fields.[44] Around the middle of the nineteenth century, the British explorer Richard Burton began a book on the history of East and Central Africa by declaring that, contrary to what encyclopedias and the press stated, the island of Zanzibar was not part of the Persian Gulf.[45] That Burton felt the need to correct the period's assumption that Zanzibar and the Persian Gulf were part of the same geographic space reflects how people understood it in this time as a connected, mutually intelligible space. Since long before Saʿid's lifetime, the Arabian Peninsula and the Gulf had been parts of the broader Indian Ocean world, enmeshed throughout history with East Africa, South Asia, and the ocean itself.[46]

In our understandings of world history, Allen Fromherz pointed out that there has long been a "gulf" because the Gulf has tended to be overlooked.[47] Studies on Oman, especially the relatively smaller number that focus on the first half of the nineteenth century and before, have all departed from certain European imperialist frameworks of world history.[48] *A Sea of Wealth* fills this gap and yet does not begin its interpretation by explaining ostensible "roots of British domination."[49] Bishara suggested that imperial history can blur the agencies of local Indian Ocean peoples, but imperial history does so if the empires in question are, almost by default, assumed to be European. Centering the Omani Empire in the Indian Ocean can be part of a world historical reorientation that amplifies non-European power and the agencies of Indian Ocean peoples who co-opted the interests, actions, and strengths of Europeans and Americans well into the nineteenth century, all while folding the relatively new North Atlantic into the enduring Indian Ocean world. Thus peoples in the Omani Empire and elsewhere in the Indian Ocean were not acting in response to the "*arrival* of modern capitalism in the region."[50]

In the Omani Empire, Arabs, Africans, and Asians were *cocreators* of a new world in the making, actively bound up in the creation of modern capitalism from its inception.[51] Peoples in the Omani Empire were not merely responding to ideas and institutions brought to their shores and their doors on the decks of Atlantic ships. They were taking part in the creation of something new. This was a time and a space in which peoples in the Omani

Empire used new transoceanic markets for pursuing wealth not only as an end unto itself, but to remake values, class and racial structures, societal and individual behaviors, and political hierarchies. People in the Omani Empire were not responding to global dynamics in local vernaculars; they were taking part in the shaping of those dynamics from their global genesis.

This book draws on published and archival sources in three languages from more than a dozen archives, libraries, and museums across four continents. I have tried as much as possible to use sources from the period under study. A major challenge in writing this book has been dealing with the number and type of sources from the first half of the nineteenth century and before. Archival sources from the second half of the century and the twentieth century are quantitatively more numerous and qualitatively far better preserved. The quantitative imbalance is especially apparent when it comes to slavery.[52] Many works thus fast-forward through he century to their primary focus on the latter decades. In his study of East African wage labor relative to the caravan system, Steven Rockel acknowledged this, noting the "extremely limited data surviving from before the 1850s."[53]

Other examples are the works of McDow and Bishara and the contracts they used as their primary source bases. There are thousands of these contracts from the latter decades of the nineteenth century and even more from the twentieth century. As McDow stated, however, only a "small number" exist from before the 1860s—about one dozen from the 1840s or before.[54] Pekka Hämäläinen faced a similar problem in his work, and discussed the problems and possibilities in what he called "upstreaming": working backward from "more recent and more complete" sources.[55] I have sought to minimize my reliance on upstreaming. I have also sought to write this history forward, rather than using a starting point like "British domination" and then moving backward to explore its ostensible roots. Using British domination or European hegemony as a starting point is common in histories of Africa and the Middle East.[56] Much history has been written as a quest for the "precursors of supposedly inevitable European success, and the equally inexorable failure of everyone else."[57]

Seen through Saʿid's eyes and those of persons whose lives intersected with his, British domination seemed anything but certain. In using Saʿid as a platform for reimagining this history, I have drawn upon a rich literature on microhistory and global microhistory. Tonio Andrade urged historians to fortify large-scale narratives with the "human dramas that make history come alive."[58] Inspired by Andrade, I have sought to balance the forces of structure and agency or macro and micro by taking them as a duality, each at least in some part constitutive of the other. Like every individual, Saʿid was both empowered and hampered by structures, but he and others also affected the very structures that acted upon them.[59] Fine-grained details, which often manifest from interactions between two individuals, can augment our understanding of large structures, to include world history itself. Seemingly innocuous things like passing remarks, scribbles in a diary, or paintings hung in houses all contain what Carlo Ginzburg called "clues" for enriching our understanding of lived worlds.[60] Every exchange that took place in its domains can be seen as instances of a larger world historical process collapsing distances on a global scale. Each Boston fruitcake spiced with cloves and every American cotton cloth worn in Tanganyika reflected the empire's global dimensions. The Omani Empire was helping to connect the world in the first half of the nineteenth century, and the process by which this unfolded occurred by means of the grand—like international treaties—and the mundane—like retrieving lost ship anchors.

The Omani Empire opens a window for dismissing the notion of an "outside" world and instead taking all peoples as part of one world, against the canvas of world history, in which all peoples in all parts of the world have taken part in its historical unfolding.[61] Many historians have questioned rise-of-the-West style narratives of the world.[62] Amplifying the movements, actions, and ideas of non-European peoples, especially in the Indian Ocean, has nonetheless been cast within a paradigm of counterhegemonic discourses. As historian Sujit Sivasundaram shrewdly demonstrated, in the Indian Ocean world non-European peoples wielded "indigenous agency," exerting themselves across the eighteenth and nineteenth centuries in ways that displace the "pernicious assumption that the soul of the world was crafted in the West and travelled east."[63] In a similar work, Sugata Bose sought to show how certain peoples exerted or maintained their agency *despite* European hegemony, but European hegemony nonetheless remained the accepted analytical point of departure, and the backdrop against which this history is explained.[64] Sivasundaram made this clear: while Indian Ocean peoples took from Europeans as they resituated their own traditions, beliefs, and commitments, they did so while the British "co-opted the dreams of the global South and sent these dreams into reverse gear," folding and overtaking the "aims and agency" of indigenous people.[65] As for the Gulf in this time, it is important because it was the site of major transformations, "as also the narrative of the steady but uneven rise of Britain."[66] Such a framework mirrors the reduction of the Omani Empire to something imperial, but perhaps only a lowercase empire, not like a capitalized European Empire. The discipline of world history, which informs the way we conceive of spaces like the Gulf or Indian Ocean, continues to use epistemological forms and categories of Western modernity.[67] All parts of the world are thus explained as aspects of the rise of the West, as if world history can be drawn as a line graph beginning with Plato and ending with NATO.

THE PURSUIT OF WEALTH

In 1844 the American consul in Zanzibar, Richard Waters, wrote to one of his favored Omani commercial partners, Sadick bin Barack, acknowledging that their goal in working together was to "make all the money we can."[68] Like many in East Africa, Richard Waters and Sadick bin Barick sought wealth. Their commercial partnership crossed oceans, continents, religions, languages, ethnicities, and cultures. Such a partnership would not have been surprising to any person from the Indian Ocean world. It exemplified continuity with centuries of history. From Africa through the Arabian Peninsula to Central Asia, Southeast Asia, and back, in Islamicate societies had for centuries been a complex world of *tijara*, commerce, in which peoples crossed physical, social, and political boundaries in the pursuit of wealth long before Americans and Europeans began arriving in arena after 1500. Seen from the perspective of Islamicate Afro-Asian history, it is thus not surprising that a Muslim person from the Arabian Peninsula moved about the Indian Ocean, particularly to East Africa, as part of a vast commercial world pursuing wealth.[69] Especially in East Africa, societies had developed a "seemingly infinite vocabulary" for wealth and its pursuit.[70] East African political-economic vocabularies reflected sophisticated understandings of markets, especially those rooted in consumer demand.

But Sadick bin Barack was trading with an American, and they were not trading in Mombasa or Kilwa or Mogadishu or Bombay, any of the major ports throughout Western Indian Ocean history. Sadick was trading with an American in Zanzibar. American commerce in East Africa had only begun in the first few decades of the nineteenth century and coincided with Zanzibar reaching its new apex of commercial prominence under Omani imperialism. While two merchants from different linguistic, religious, ethnic, and national backgrounds pursuing wealth in the Indian Ocean was nothing new in terms of world history, that they were in Zanzibar and one of them was American was strikingly new.

Indian Ocean societies had well-developed concepts of commerce, profit, and wealth long before European arrival. These concepts were not mere borrowings from an ostensibly preordained and preformed Western capitalism. As historian Andrew Liu has said, focusing on Afro-Asian connections in the Indian ocean can present a history of capitalism's truly global genesis in ways different from past paradigms, ways that challenge the continued embeddedness of North Atlantic exceptionalism and explore more truly global conceptions of capital accumulation and structures and institutions of exchange.[71] Andrew Liu is one voice among many historians who, across decades, have challenged the notion of the world as Immanuel Wallerstein depicted it: a dominant European core peripheralizing non-European spaces to suit European ends.[72] The Omani Empire's history disrupts Eurocentric narratives and enriches Middle East historiography. It adds another angle for challenging, as historian of Egypt Peter Gran put it, the "Western-centered structure of the discipline of history."[73]

The Omani Empire can thus help add a richer portrait to understanding the Middle East in the modern world. It can be read alongside the histories of other parts of the Middle East in the same period, especially regarding economic transformations, and contribute to our understanding of global processes of accumulation and capitalist practices.[74] Peoples in the Indian Ocean, and in other parts of the Middle East, like the Levant or North Africa, engaged in wealth-building practices resembling certain components of modern capitalism long before European intervention. As Gran boldly asserted, questioning our analytical categories and upturning European epistemologies allows us not only to set aside any notion of European peripheralization of non-European peoples but also to contend with non-European roots of capitalism.[75]

Others have made similar arguments. Kenneth Cuno and Beshara Doumani uncovered in Egypt and in Palestine rich, complex socioeconomic capitalist practices embedded in Egyptian and Palestinian society before any notion of European incorporation. Capitalist practices that Doumani highlighted in Palestine were similar to those taking place in Omani domains, as shown throughout this book, including social differentiation and exploitation; the creation of new urban centers and the integration of those centers with rural or interior places; the exploitation and commoditization of land; and the monetization, emanating from urban centers, of larger expanses of rural or interior economies, all driven by expansive systems of centralized moneylending.[76] Seen from this framework, much of the Middle East in modern world history can be interpreted as one of local peoples maintaining dynamic capitalist strategies for confronting European competitors while shaping their own agencies over their own worlds and futures.[77] The modern history of much of the Middle East, including Oman and its domains throughout East Africa, can be interpreted from the perspective of the period from the first half of the nineteenth century and before to see a different set of historical dynamics, in which any notion of European hegemony was not only far from certain but in many ways far-fetched.

Muslim merchants in the Afro-Asian world, especially those traversing the Indian Ocean, practiced sophisticated forms of commerce, finance, and wealth accumulation. Many historians have written about the European *commenda* contract. Islamicate societies had their own equivalent—not a borrowing—called a *muḍāraba* contract.[78] Muḍāraba basically means profit sharing. The concept and practice of a muḍāraba contract is not found in the Qur'an; the earliest communities of Muslims relied upon it in conducting trade. It is an equity financing instrument, based on profit sharing and profit loss sharing, in which one party supplies capital to another party who sells, trades, or otherwise transacts in that capital for a profit, which is then shared between the parties. One leading Muslim jurist-scholar of the eleventh century expounded upon this type of contract and made clear the impetus behind its development and use: obtaining profit, by means of trading capital.[79] Seeking profits was the domain of commerce, but commerce was not simply just bartering and trading. As the great fourteenth-century intellectual Ibn Khaldun wrote: "Commerce means the attempt to earn a living by expanding your capital (*bi tanmīyat al-māl*) and the extent by which capital is increased is called profit." And the basis of all commerce, Ibn Khaldun added, was labor: "the essential basis of all profit and accumulation of capital."[80]

Already by the tenth century Muslim merchants were at the heart of a world on the move, emanating from Arabia to cross vast continental and oceanic spaces.[81] Their ability to cross these distances was facilitated by a legal-economic lexicon, legible and actionable to any person in this world. This entire legal corpus shaped politics, social understandings, and commercial exchange. Enshrined within this corpus were the clearly understood concepts of wealth (*māl*), profit (*ribh*), financing (*mutamawwal*), and capital accumulation (*tanmīyat al-māl*).[82]

The purpose in stating the preceding is to clarify a set of questions and perspectives that inform this book. That persons in the Indian Ocean and in the Atlantic worlds had their own respective notions of wealth, capital, profit, and their accumulation prompts reflection on how these peoples and their ideas merged into a transoceanic marketplace. The Omani Empire opens a framework for transcending the domination-subordination narrative that continues to underly so much scholarship about these human communities. It provides a useful category for interpreting the makings of our modern world as one of cocreation, in which multiple peoples at simultaneous times around the world participated in a polyphonic, multidimensional process in which it becomes difficult to isolate any one component.

Though they did not ever use the word *capitalism*, the persons under study would have used its vocabulary: markets, supply, demand, market saturation, risk, investments, profit, time, wealth, property, and more. Any historian working on issues of capitalism or issues that speak to our understanding of capitalism risks certain perils, the first being defining the term.[83] At least one leading historian has argued that we should not seek to define it, because doing so reduces its explanatory power by flattening its historical dynamism, complexities, and contradictions—the very things that historians tease out.[84] Others have tried to elaborate theoretical and conceptual tools for defining it.[85] To be clear, in this book I do not presume to offer a definition of capitalism, nor do I consider it a history of capitalism as such. Global capitalism is one part of modern world history, and in reimagining this history in the Western Indian Ocean I am interested more in the contours of the adjective *global* than I am in the mechanics of the noun *capitalism*.

Zanzibar's Customs House embodied an oceanic marketplace, where buyers and sellers converged on the seashore. On many occasions Saʿid used his sovereignty to maintain the central position of the Customs House. Richard Waters once tried to skirt the marketplace's rules and have American cargo be unloaded in front of his residence, rather than be unloaded and passed in front of the Customs House. Saʿid put an immediate stop to that.[86] But it was also a broader system that stitched together caravan waystations and port cities north from Zanzibar, along East Africa's littoral, to Arabia and the Gulf. In the Omani Empire, the commercial practices that formed the marketplace were defined primarily by first carving out control over geographic spaces by military coercion and political machinations; by credit lending from a central customs house farmed out by the empire's ruler; and by the proliferation of slave labor and human trafficking.

TWO

The Emergence of Empire

INTRODUCTION

In April 1847 the American merchant vessel *Cherokee* pulled up anchor in Salem, Massachusetts, and sailed toward the Indian Ocean. Arriving in Zanzibar several months later, the ship's log keeper, twenty-two-year-old Horace Putnam, was taken aback. Gazing from the *Cherokee*'s deck, he wondered if the verdant island before him might have been the Garden of Eden. "No one could picture in his imagination a port more grand or beautiful," he described. "The clime is healthy and at this season of the year is cool. The breezes that blow from the sea by day and from the land by night make it all that one could wish." Beyond the harbor, Putnam rhapsodized about lush forests "so thick that the rays of the sun are not able to penetrate." He went on, musing: "It would be a beautiful place to spend a few hours in retirement, and to hold communion with the God of Nature. It would be like the Elysian fields in fabled times. . . . There is a long, extended beach before the palms which the waves of old oceans wash with their never ceasing tide. White sands and shells of the most beautiful kinds slush beneath its surface, which, added to the rays of this summer, make it look like a sea of liquid fire."[1]

Horace Putnam had indeed sailed into an old ocean. For thousands of years, the Indian Ocean's tides had facilitated the movements of peoples. Since long before Putnam's arrival, the ocean surrounding Zanzibar had been an avenue for collapsing distance in pursuit of fortunes.[2] Putnam, however, was seeing Zanzibar at the height of its flourishing. As Putnam and his crewmates went about their work in Zanzibar harbor, they would have mirrored other sailors and merchants aboard hundreds of other ships—many of them *dhows*, some of them ships of war, and others still commercial vessels like the *Cherokee*.

Putnam's presence in Zanzibar marked a historic shift, in which Indian Ocean peoples stitched relatively new Atlantic markets into their enduring commercial world. By Putnam's arrival, Zanzibar was a monied metropolis founded on oceanic exchange and fueled by slavery. Like many other American merchants, the *Cherokee*'s crew had been encouraged to sail for the Indian Ocean by the US government, but the Americans were late to the race. Europeans had been vying for influence since the sixteenth century, investing in its booming cities and commercial networks as soon as they began building ships capable of sailing there. Coveted riches like ivory, pearls, silk, spices, perfumes, porcelain, coffee, and more began to fuel European consumerism. Already for centuries, many of these same goods and products had flowed through markets in Persia, Damascus, Baghdad, India, China, and throughout Africa. As one sixteenth-century sailor put it, you went to the Indian Ocean to "find what you want, and sometimes more than you are looking for."[3] Finding more than what you are looking for—the pursuit of unprecedented wealth as an unceasing end unto itself—was one component in the unfolding of modern world history. The increasingly connected political and economic threads coursing throughout the Indian Ocean and beyond were already apparent to traders in the sixteenth century. In 1512 one seafarer concluded: "Whoever is lord of Malacca has his hand on the throat of Venice."[4]

The arrival of Europeans strengthened commerce for local peoples.[5] In 1765 one young British merchant wrote to his father, telling him how doing business in the area was a "sure path" to wealth. He added: "A moderate share of attention, and your being not quite an idiot, are ample qualities for the attainment of riches."[6] The exhortation to not be an idiot contains a clue to understanding this history in ways attuned to local perspectives. The arrival of Europeans and, later, Americans, in the Indian Ocean did not bring about a break in its history. Indian Ocean peoples, especially the Omanis, subsumed these new visitors within their political and commercial world as new actors. Newly arriving Europeans and Americans had to carefully navigate a foreign commercial world, adapting to local norms and power structures. Zanzibar's rise as the empire's capital stemmed from centuries of Omani expansion, expropriation, and enslavement. Though Omani by virtue of its ruler and geographic starting point, this empire was comprised of peoples from around the Indian Ocean who used Europeans as fuel for their own commercial and social engines. This process was characterized by elements of both continuity and change in Indian Ocean history. Certain age-old elements of this history did not end with the expansion of empires, whether Omani or European, but rather gained new purchase in sustaining interhemispheric, transoceanic commerce.

THE WORLD OF EMPORIA

The history of Oman is entwined with the sea. Located on the southeast edge of the Arabian Peninsula, Oman abuts the Persian Gulf, the Sea of Oman, the Arabian Sea, and the Indian Ocean. Muscat, its capital today, is nestled in a bay, its shore encircled by mountains. In antiquity the Greek geographer Ptolemy described Muscat's privileged location, referring to it as the "hidden harbor" of the Indian Ocean.[7] More modern writers also highlighted its unique geography. "The location of this place is far different from any that I have yet seen," wrote Horace Putnam in 1847 after he sailed north from Zanzibar. He continued: "Were it not for an island that serves as a landmark outside the harbor, it would be difficult to find."[8] Putnam's apparent difficulty finding Muscat belies its historical significance as part of an interconnected Indian Ocean world—a terraqueous arena connecting Africa with China and all points in between. Since even before Islam's revelation in the seventh century AD, Omanis were so thoroughly enmeshed within this oceanic world that early Arab-Muslim invaders referred to the land of present-day Oman as part of *ardh al-Hind*, "the land of India."[9]

Although the sea has always been important in Oman's history, Oman's geography also provided access to important land routes that complemented maritime trade. Alongside their Yemeni neighbors, Omanis participated in the Red Sea trade by helping move goods toward Ethiopia, Somalia, and Egypt, and thus into North Africa and the Mediterranean. Across the Gulf, Omanis helped pave land routes connecting Iraq and Persia, opening Gulf commerce to Fars, Khurasan, and present-day Afghanistan. Whether by trekking south from there or by sailing almost directly east from Oman's mainland, Omanis accessed South Asia and the Indian subcontinent.

Omanis benefited from certain structural advantages, such as the geographic security of Oman's harbors. "I don't know of any place that I have ever visited that would afford so fine a subject for a painting as the harbor of Muscat," Charles Putnam described. He continued: "It is almost entirely shut in from the sea. The entrance is very narrow, and the harbor not very large in extent, though there could lay at anchor here the whole American navy with perfect security and ease, the water being deep and the shore bold."[10] As ships sailed along the coast into the harbor, the water was so crystalline that sailors could see the coral-laced seafloor in depths up to nearly fifty feet.[11] These harbors, their shores naturally protected from land attacks, facilitated Muscat's rise as a powerful center of trade in the Indian Ocean by the end of the fifteenth century.

Aside from Muscat, Oman had several other thriving ports, providing Omani leaders with a rich foundation for extending their imperial ambitions.[12] The port of Sohar, farther up Oman's coast from Muscat, was known throughout the Indian Ocean as a commercial and political powerhouse since at least the seventh century AD. A tenth-century Muslim scholar, in a geographic encyclopedia of the known world at the time, concluded that it would be difficult to find a more prosperous or cosmopolitan city.[13] Later, a thirteenth-century geographer echoed this sentiment: "Sohar is filled with people of upstanding morality, flourishing with affluence and commerce. Her fruits are more splendid than Zabid or Sanaʿa, or even the other marvelous markets and opulent cities spread throughout the seas."[14]

Omanis and other Indian Ocean peoples had great reverence for the sea. "Upon the sea 'tis true is boundless gain," lyricized the thirteenth-century Persian poet Saʿdi. Saʿdi's popular verse echoed the Qurʾan, which described how God had created the sea so that humans could take to it on ships and reap its bounties.[15] Sources dating as far back as ancient Sumer describe the talents of Omani shipbuilders and sailors.[16] The port of Sur, farther south along Oman's coast, was home to a large shipbuilding industry, a magnet for the best shipbuilders, many of whom were from Kachchh in western India.[17] One classic ship built in Sur was the *Sohar*, named for the port. Sleek and slender, its flanks were sewn together using rope made from braided palm and coconut husks. It had a single tall mast. Though built in Oman, the ship flew no flag.[18] Built this way, it was like countless other traditional Indian Ocean ships, with many types generally categorized under the generic label dhow.[19]

One of the most descriptive accounts of these ships comes from Ibn Jubayr, the great Andalusian geographer and traveler. He described how dhows were sewn together, fastened without nails or bolts. The ships were rubbed with oil, the best of which was made from shark fat. This softened the flanks and made them supple enough to be run ashore without fear of damage.[20] Instead of being relegated only to spaces with deep harbors, these merchants could essentially travel anywhere around the ocean, no matter the geography.

Ships like the *Sohar* were one component of what historian K. N. Chaudhuri described as "emporia trade."[21] Emporia, he wrote, were the great port towns and caravan cities stretching from Muscat to Malacca. Indian Ocean emporia were deeply cosmopolitan, a theme central to their histories.[22] As one historian observed, however, cosmopolitanism remains underdefined.[23] Cosmopolitanism did not carry present-day notions of inclusivity or equity, but without question, many Indian Ocean places like Oman's coastal areas were *cosmopolitan*: including or containing people from many different countries. As the Omani Empire grew, its leaders took certain steps to preserve such cosmopolitanism and augment competition in its marketplaces. Indian Ocean cosmopolitanism meant preserving difference and living with it. One scholar working on the Red Sea port of Jeddah referred to such cosmopolitanism as like a form of hospitality, a system in which myriad peoples could participate, albeit not necessarily equitably.[24] The inclusion of different peoples especially in commercial activities in Omani domains was a part of Omani state policy. One example, as will be shown, was when the Omanis lifted the *jizya*, or tax required to be paid by non-Muslims. Such actions spurred steadily increasing Omani power throughout the Gulf and down the coast of East Africa because it reinforced incentives for people and their businesses to engage in exchange and productive activity.

Yet policies protecting outsiders were not distinctly Omani. In many ways, the formal embrace of outsiders in the trading communities of the Omani Empire was very East African; the mixing of different groups of peoples all coming together in the pursuit of wealth in a port oriented toward a wider oceanic world was precisely what defined the Swahili mercantile societies of East Africa. The coasts of East Africa provided a space in which people mixed and lived under local, decentralized governance, settling in places that allowed for their mobility in pursuit of maritime commercial goals. The gradual expansion of Omani sovereignty throughout East Africa did not fundamentally transform this; rather, this space and its people facilitated the emergence of new institutional arrangements that magnified the abilities of peoples in East Africa to accrue wealth.

Swahili society epitomized the nature of this Indian Ocean cosmopolitanism. As two specialists of Swahili culture and history showed, outsiders were dealt with and differences were tolerated as part of a larger commercial system of catalyzing the pursuit of wealth.[25] As the empire matured, for Omanis, as for South Asians, Persians, and, much later, Europeans and Americans, East Africa became the beating heart of their commercial aspirations. This was not only because East Africans produced things like ivory or gum copal. Perhaps even more, it was because of almost insatiable East African consumerism.

Omani migration to East Africa did not supersede East Africa's prominence in Indian Ocean politics and trade; it magnified it.[26] Many foreign traders, Omani or otherwise, went to East Africa and married, using marriage as a tool for incorporating themselves into flourishing East African communities. Marriage protected them and their interests as quasi-kin. In social terms, Swahili society was rooted in embracing traveling merchants, with certain social habits geared toward facilitating market participation.[27] In the fourteenth century, the famous Muslim scholar Ibn Battuta remarked that whenever a ship docked in an East African harbor, a group of people greeted its sailors with dishes of food, declaring them their guests and ushering them ashore.[28] It was critical for foreigners to ingratiate themselves within East African communities because commerce was regulated foremost by personal relationships, whether kinship networks or commercial partnerships. The basic operating unit in emporia was personal relationships, many of which extended from kin.[29] Though the concept of home might have been somewhat fluid, kinship ties were concrete fixtures forming networks of exchange across and around the ocean.[30] The personal nature of economy and society in the Indian Ocean magnified entrepreneurship. Family webs and community relationships would become important building blocks for using Europeans and Americans to create transoceanic, global trade networks.[31]

But many of the people moving around the Indian Ocean were not doing so of their own volition. Human trafficking was ubiquitous. When Ibn Battutah traveled around the Indian Ocean in the fourteenth century, he purchased, traded, and gifted enslaved humans as part of his journeys. The business of human trafficking catalyzed connections between all three sides of the Indian Ocean. Some of the most prolific traffickers were South Asian merchants and financiers. The roles of these South Asian merchants were critical to commerce in the Western Indian Ocean. South Asian firms, as Pedro Machado and others have studied, were pivotal in forging trade networks across the Indian Ocean. South Asian merchants and financiers built and maintained commercial networks rooted not only in human trafficking, but also in the African demand for large-scale textile production among weavers in Gujarat and the distribution of ivory to consumers in

Western India. Their commercial role in human trafficking also linked different parts of the ocean, trafficking enslaved humans to the French islands in the Mascarenes, the Arabian Peninsula and India, and even to Brazil.[32]

Before Zanzibar's rise, Mozambique was arguably the main center for human trafficking along East Africa's littoral. As Machado showed, South Asian firms were central to the functioning of Mozambique's oceanic marketplace of slaves, especially by helping forge it into a transoceanic marketplace, financing the trafficking of humans into Brazil and other parts of the Atlantic. Enslaved humans were trafficked through Mozambique to Madagascar or to French-claimed territories in the Mascarenes, but they were also routinely trafficked through Omani ports like Muscat, Sur, and Sohar. Yet humans were also trafficked south, down to Cape Town in South Africa for use by Dutch and English charter companies and their colonists. As Machado showed, by the middle of the eighteenth century South Asians, Africans, Arabs, and Europeans had already come together in the market of human trafficking in the Western Indian Ocean that connected to a broader transoceanic and global exchange for enslaved humans.[33] Increasing elements of Omani power in East Africa during the eighteenth century fit into this already thriving oceanic exchange for enslaved humans and were critical to the empire's ultimate rise.

Whether it was because of their ability to extend credit or their grip on human trafficking or both, South Asian family firms were some of the most successful in East Africa. Omani expansion down the coast of East Africa was predicated on the presence of these South Asian firms.[34] The increasingly formalized alliance between Omani leaders and certain South Asian family groups emanated out from Muscat to create a foundation for the consolidation of Omani power and influence around the Western Indian Ocean. From Muscat, South Asians financed Omani expansionism from its outset. The increasing presence of South Asian peoples in Omani domains was tied to the increasing presence of Europeans in the Western Indian Ocean, especially the Portuguese. Initially, when the Portuguese began arriving in Mozambique in large numbers, they were able to settle and build their presence because of access to capital provided by South Asians already there. The Portuguese, however, soon began extorting South Asian firms and imposing severe taxes on them. This was one factor pushing many South Asians to begin moving northward to Kilwa, Mombasa, and Zanzibar, in addition to residing more on Oman's mainland, especially in Muscat.[35]

THE AL-YAʿARIBAH DYNASTY

All beginnings are difficult to pinpoint, but an apt starting point for understanding the emergence of the Omani Empire is the beginning of the Al-Yaʿaribah dynasty's rule in Oman in 1624. The Yaʿrubi dynasty began what would become a process marked by setbacks but nonetheless of nearly uninterrupted imperial expansion continuing with its successors for the next two centuries. Saʿid bin Sultan epitomizes this process of imperial expansion, expropriation, and enslavement because he ruled during the apex of Omani power, but he did not set it in motion. Saʿid's reign in the first half of the nineteenth century fit within a longer arc of region formation emanating from the increasing strength and efficacy of Omani state power. If Saʿid would ultimately seek to incorporate Europeans through formal treaties and other means, like the power of his customs officials, his Yaʿrubi predecessors seemed to be more focused on evicting Europeans, especially the Portuguese, from their domains, or allowing them to stay if they acceded to strict state demands.

Following Vasco da Gama's arrival in Mozambique in 1498, the Portuguese were the first Europeans to establish a widespread presence in the Indian Ocean. Some of the first historians writing in the emerging field of Indian Ocean historiography argued that the Portuguese almost immediately transformed this space.[36] A subsequent generation of scholars challenged this position, but only its periodization, arguing instead that fundamental change did not begin until 1750 or 1800.[37] The emergence of Yaʿrubi power questions any of these periodizations and adds another layer of history to the ways scholars of East Africa and the Indian Ocean have demonstrated how the Portuguese in East Africa reconfigured rather than destroyed already existing patterns of East African politics, economy, and society.[38] Even among specialists of Omani history, there has been relatively little work done on this dynasty and period of history. The Yaʿrubi were part of a textured seventeenth-century Indian Ocean world in which many different groups and actors operated in a cluttered field of states, family firms, merchants, and military powers. This dynasty adds another layer to our understanding of the seventeenth- and eighteenth-century Indian Ocean, and other parts of the world, as an arena in which the European presence was one of competition, deference, and subordination rather than dominance.[39]

As they began arriving in the Western Indian Ocean after 1500, the Portuguese were rather astonished by the cosmopolitanism they encountered. When they sailed into ports like Bombay or Mombasa, they observed peoples from all around the Indian Ocean littoral and their connected lands. The court historian Gaspar Correia described, with a degree of confusion, how fleets of ships from as far away as Cairo regularly arrived in Calicut, one of the ocean's busiest ports. He noted that these Muslim traders were not only rich and powerful but were also friends and supporters of Calicut's Hindu king, the Samudri.[40] Amicable, or at least tolerable, commercial partnerships between merchants of different religions or ethnicities might have been customary for Indian Ocean peoples, but they were unsatisfactory for the Portuguese. On March 9, 1500, the king of Portugal dispatched a fleet of thirteen ships to Calicut with orders to "ask" the king of Calicut to expel all Muslims from his kingdom because they were ostensible enemies of Christianity, and thus of Portugal. When the fleet arrived, the Portuguese commander did not ask anything. The bombardment of Calicut, aimed at evicting or killing all Muslims there, lasted for two days.[41] Sacking Calicut was part of the Portuguese strategy to obtain a trade monopoly by military force. They required every ship trading in areas under their influence to obtain a license, or *cartaz*, from a Portuguese authority. All ships were thus required to dock in a Portuguese controlled port and pay customs duties. The Portuguese used the cartaz system as income for their kingdom and as a buffer against other threats, chief among whom were the Omanis.[42]

In 1505 Portuguese sailors and soldiers entered Muscat and other nearby harbors, where they remained in small, relatively innocuous pockets until the Omanis forced their total evacuation from the Gulf in 1650. The first leader of the Ya'rubi dynasty was Nasir bin Murshid al-Ya'aribah.[43] Rising to power in 1624, Nasir set in motion what would ultimately become a centuries-long process of Omani imperialism aimed at corralling disparate markets into a more coherent, singular marketplace. Like his successors, Nasir did this alongside, and in many cases in spite of, European powers. The consolidation of Ya'rubi leadership and the ensuing expansion of Omani power throughout the Western Indian Ocean reflects domestic, regional, and global transformations. Nasir came to power amid a devastating civil war in Oman rooted in disagreements over kinship and political authority. The Omani chronicler Al-Izkawi described how the country was being torn apart, people everywhere suffering from the "severest misery."[44] The Portuguese and the Persians exploited the civil war to encroach upon

Omani control of ports and important coastal enclaves in the Gulf. Nasir's first goal was thus uniting Omanis under his leadership to stop domestic feuding as a means for buffering the country against increasing foreign encroachment. According to Al-Izkawi, Nasir succeeded relatively quickly in settling the civil war and he used Portuguese and Persian threats to orient the attention of many Omanis toward maritime affairs.

Nasir used his power for commercial aggrandizement. He established policies to protect and privilege the positions of Omani merchants in the Gulf. That was not necessarily a new policy in Omani history, however. As early as the eighth century AD, Omani leaders were using revenues to build ships expressly for naval combat.[45] Nasir fit into this longer arc of Omani and regional history. He built one of the most powerful navies in the Indian Ocean and used that navy as an instrument of his state policy.[46] Though Nasir might have had some degree of strategic acumen, his success against the Portuguese was facilitated by certain factors outside his control and volition. From the viewpoint of the Portuguese, the Gulf remained important to their own imperial interests as a space for capturing revenue and commodities, but by the 1630s the Portuguese were diverting many of their resources toward South Asia because of increasing conflict there with the Dutch. Seizing upon this inter-European rivalry, Nasir launched a series of offensives against the Portuguese, knowing that most of their resources had been diverted from the Gulf.[47] Nasir's first assault was on the Portuguese positions in Muscat. The Portuguese had built a series of forts in the rocky outcroppings protecting the harbor. Muscat's unique geography helped make it a strategic chokepoint for policing trade through the Strait of Hormuz, and the Portuguese had sought to co-opt this. But the Omanis were victorious. In his telling of the battle, Al-Izkawi made a passing reference to one of Nasir's demands of the Portuguese as part of their surrender, a clue for understanding broader factors in the expansion and consolidation of the Omani Empire.

After sacking their defenses surrounding Muscat, Nasir demanded that the Portuguese, before withdrawing, restore to the Shiʿa inhabitants of Sohar and other Omani ports their property and possessions.[48] As a relatively small minority group, these Shiʿa Muslims had been easy targets for Portuguese plunder. They could have been Persian, but al-Izkawi was likely referring to a group of entrepreneurial Khoja merchants—subscribing to the Twelver branch of Shiʿa Islam—who had long resided in Oman after emigrating from Sindh. For centuries, these South Asian Muslims had migrated in and out of Oman's ports as merchants and creditors, integral to the webs of commercial reciprocity binding the Arabian Peninsula with South Asia. The Khoja came to Oman already with great wealth. Once they settled in Oman, no matter how temporary that settlement was, they used their wealth as creditors and investors in traditional Gulf industries like the pearl and date trades. They would have increasingly begun providing lines of credit for Omanis venturing to East Africa. They were instrumental in helping forge circular commercial connections throughout the Indian Ocean, and Nasir seems to have understood this. Concluding his surrender terms, Nasir also stipulated that the Portuguese could remain as traders in Omani ports if they paid tribute to Oman and abided by Omani rules.[49]

Nasir's surrender terms for the Portuguese provide a portrait of the early modern Indian Ocean that would come to characterize the Omani Empire throughout Sa'id's reign in the nineteenth century. Nasir had contained a European power as one actor among others and then sought to use those Europeans for augmenting the positions of local peoples whom he ruled. Protecting the positions of the minority merchants in Muscat and other Omani ports helped maintain diverse portfolios of commodities being traded for both production and consumption. It was almost a form of antimobility: protecting certain groups of people so that they would establish and maintain commercial roots and leverage in Omani domains. This marked one beginning point of Omani imperial aspirations being entwined with the success of the peoples who lived in Omani domains. It was an example of using state power to ensure that certain demands were met as part of tying together the oceanic marketplace connecting parts of the Indian Ocean in a new age of Omani imperialism.

The rise of Omani power under Nasir did not stop there. Following the Portuguese surrender in Muscat, Nasir's army defeated the Portuguese in 1643 at Sohar. Retaking Sohar and reducing the Portuguese presence in the Gulf even more allowed the Omanis to begin increasing their trade flows with other Europeans, especially the English. Nasir began using revenue from trade with the English to finance his expeditions against the Portuguese. After driving the Portuguese from Sohar, Nasir welcomed the English, cultivating commercial ties with them to deprive the Portuguese of Omani markets. By the time he died in 1649, Nasir had diminished the Portuguese presence in Oman from controlling nearly five hundred continuous miles of coastline to a small pocket in Muscat, with little actual control of the market or the local people.[50]

Nasir's policies protecting legal and commercial rights of minorities in Oman would have enormous consequence during the reign of his successor, Sultan bin Sayf. When he came to power upon Nasir's death, Sultan's primary goal was defeating the last remaining Portuguese holdouts near Muscat. Nasir's previous victory there had seriously diminished their strength, but he had not been able to force their complete withdrawal. Because of the rugged landscape in which the Portuguese had entrenched their defensive fortifications, Sultan would have been forced to resort to a protracted siege had it not been for a dispute between the Portuguese commander and a South Asian man named Narutem.[51]

Prior to Sultan's assault on the Portuguese in 1650, the Portuguese had employed Narutem as a sort of local agent; he managed all the Portuguese finances and oversaw the maintenance of their defenses and provisions for their soldiers. As the story in Omani chronicles holds, Narutem apparently also had a beautiful daughter. When the Portuguese commander learned of this, he summoned Narutem and demanded to marry her. Narutem declined, but the commander insisted, even offering to pay him to marry his daughter. Narutem again refused. This time, however, the commander threatened to kidnap the daughter; forcibly marry her; and ruin Narutem with fines, imprisonment, and likely death. The Portuguese commander's threats seem to have alarmed Narutem, spurring him to act.

Narutem knew that Sultan's armies were camped nearby, and he crafted a plan for an Omani surprise attack against the Portuguese. First, Narutem convinced the Portuguese that all their water and food reserves had been spoiled and had to be discarded. He also convinced them that their stores of gunpowder had been sullied with moisture and were thus useless. As the Portuguese were discarding their only provisions of food, water, and gunpowder, Narutem dispatched a secret messenger to Sultan. The messenger informed Sultan of Narutem's plan, encouraging the Omanis to attack at a specified time after the provisions and gunpowder reserves had been discarded. Sultan agreed to the plan, and on the specified date and time the Omanis attacked. Narutem's plan worked: the Omanis sacked the Portuguese and destroyed most of their ships. Their victory in Muscat with Narutem's assistance forced the total evacuation of the Portuguese from the Arabian Peninsula and the Gulf.[52]

The story of Narutem in the battle for Muscat is recounted in Omani chronicles and near-contemporaneous European sources. As recounted in the sources, it has some element of fantasy, almost like a fairytale. At the least, Omani chroniclers might have dramatized it. There is no way to corroborate whether Narutem did in fact have a beautiful daughter with whom the Portuguese commander was smitten. Narutem's secret plan hatched in coordination with Sultan might indeed be part of a romanticized and mythologized Omani remembrance of the battle for Muscat. But there were South Asians in Muscat, and the Omanis did prevail over the Portuguese, forcing their evacuation. Regardless of whether Narutem's story is fantasy, that it exists at all in the Omani literature reflects the existence of these South Asian minorities in Omani domains and the important roles they played in facilitating the rise of Omani power and influence. The role of Narutem in aiding the Omani victory over the Portuguese, however fantasized, remains something of a clue for understanding Sultan's first policy after the battle. After the Portuguese withdrew, Sultan issued a decree lifting the mandate requiring Narutem, a Hindu, and all other non-Muslims to pay the jizya, the tax technically required for non-Muslims to pay while living in Muslim domains.

Since Islam's revelation, Muslim leaders had used the jizya as a critical source of state revenue. It had always provided a high revenue stream because Islam, from its revelation in Arabia, spread so quickly throughout the Indian Ocean and Asian lands, places with high numbers of peoples who were not Muslim. Sultan did not leave writings indicating why he chose to abolish the jizya. On its face, however, his act might seem counterintuitive: given the relatively large population of non-Muslims living in Omani domains at the time, abolishing the jizya would have deprived Sultan of an important source of income for his budding expansionist ambitions. It seems to have been part of a broader strategy, with some degree of long-term thinking, aimed at cultivating ties with myriad peoples in Omani domains and legally protecting their positions as minorities in those domains. Abolishing the jizya is not the only act Sultan took in protecting these peoples after his victory in Muscat. Sultan also issued formal legal rights protecting Hindus in Oman. New laws guaranteed their rights to build temples, to keep sacred cows, and to otherwise practice their faith as they wished in Omani domains.

Sultan's policies formalized arrangements that were already in place. South Asian peoples had been migrating in and out of Omani domains, especially Muscat, as they left other places in the Arabian Peninsula that had become increasingly oppressive. Many Gujarati merchants left Mocha and Aden, where they had been involved in the southern Red Sea's coffee trade for centuries, because of oppressive policies enacted by Yemen's rulers. Some of these South Asian merchants left for Muscat, and others left for Mozambique. In other parts of the Arabian Peninsula, oppressive policies applied to minority communities had proved relatively disastrous. About one hundred years before Sultan's rule, the governor of Jeddah on the Red Sea coast had ruined the port's economy, causing it to be nearly abandoned because of oppressive taxes he instituted on Hindu merchants.[53] Omani society remained stratified and separated according to different tribal, ethnic, and religious communities, but formal legal protections for minority peoples quickly began attracting even more peoples to Omani domains. The rapid growth in the numbers of merchants from South Asia after the Portuguese evacuation was a critical factor in rejuvenating Oman's economy after the troubles it had faced under Portuguese control.

The Omani chronicler Ibn Ruzayq described how the country blossomed under Sultan. In the characteristically understated fashion of many Arab chroniclers, he then listed in passing three reasons for this prosperity: prices were cheap, traveling from place to place was again safe, and merchants made profits (using a form of the word *ribh*, meaning profit).[54] Many scholars have used a translation of Ibn Ruzayq's chronicle by the English scholar George Percy Badger. In this passage, Badger translated the phrase *wa ṣaluḥati al-asfāru* as "the roads were safe," but it is not just that roads were safe. In the context of the passage, Badger's translation misses a larger point. Ibn Ruzayq was describing how Omani economy and society grew in this time because peoples were once again able to be mobile. Sultan's reign facilitated and protected mobility, and this mobility was a critical component in bringing about low prices and high profits. Low prices and high profits were linked with mobility.

Ibn Ruzayq's father worked for Saʿid's grandfather, the first ruler of the Al Bu Saʿid Dynasty, so this source was written at some point in the nineteenth century. Ibn Ruzayq's chronicle can be rather triumphalist, celebrating Bu Saʿidi power. This passage, however, is especially intriguing. That it was written about two centuries after Sultan's rule can be seen as its most illuminating strength. It gives us a window into how Omanis like Ibn Ruzayq and the Omani rulers his family was connected to thought about their economy and society. The pursuit of profit and the linking of certain state policies with facilitating mobility in pursuit of high profits is not strictly a historian's interpretation of what shaped this period of Omani history. This casual sentence in Ibn Ruzayq's chronicle is a look into Omani markets: Omani and other protected merchants moving around under the safety of state protection in pursuit of profit, or *ribh.*

The pursuit of profits was not new to peoples in this part of the world, but under Sultan that pursuit became increasingly central to the extension of Omani state power. Indeed, Sultan used much of the income generated from the revivification of Omani commerce to invest in his navy and ransack Portuguese positions wherever Omani sailors could find them in the Western Indian Ocean. The Portuguese had rushed away from the Gulf, but they remained in parts of South Asia and East Africa. Sultan ordered his sailors to follow them and attack them at will. The Portuguese suffocated under this Omani onslaught. Compounded by imperial troubles elsewhere, they struggled to maintain any position in the Western Indian Ocean. In 1651, a year after withdrawing from the Gulf, the Portuguese viceroy wrote to the king, warning that the Omani navy was so lethal that the Portuguese had to dramatically increase their naval forces or risk having the Omanis follow them all the way to East Africa.[55] Other sources corroborate the viceroy's concerns. As one French sailor observed, by the 1660s the Omanis had become "masters of all the navigation and commerce" in the area.[56]

For the Portuguese, maintaining a position in East Africa—especially the Mozambique channel—was vital because it provided them with entrepots for human trafficking. They used enslaved humans for labor, but they also profited from their trafficking, using that revenue to help sustain their presence in the Indian Ocean. By forcing the Portuguese out of Muscat and following them all the way to India and Mozambique, Sultan was thus depriving the Portuguese of both slaves and revenue, diminishing their ability to maintain force anywhere in the world.[57] One stronghold in East Africa for the Portuguese was Mombasa, where they had built the formidable Fort Jesus overlooking the sea. In 1660 Sultan laid siege to the fort and forced the Portuguese to withdraw. Although the withdrawal was temporary, it spotlighted the declining power of the Portuguese, while also highlighting growing Omani imperialism. The Omani siege of Mombasa in 1660—the first of many over the next two centuries—also marks a beginning of Omani leaders projecting their state power in East Africa.

Sultan died in 1679. His successor, Bel'arab, continued reaping the profits of Omani commercial superiority. Like his predecessors, he also used these profits to strengthen the navy. By the 1680s the Omani navy had become so large and effective that the Omanis began filling vacancies in their fleets by hiring English or Dutch sailors as navigators and gunners, even purchasing weapons and ammunition from them. Europeans who witnessed this frequently commented on Omani superiority. "The Muscatters daily increase their Naval Forces, and prevail against them [the Portuguese] incontestably at Sea by fitting out against them Ships of Burthen and Strength" observed one English sailor in 1689, who noted that many of the Omani ships were built in India, weighed more than one thousand tons, and carried more than one hundred cannons.[58] In fact, the Omanis were so successful at sea that they commonly referred to the Portuguese as "the chicken-hearted."[59] As John Wilkinson wrote, Omani maritime violence was so merciless that "even the Europeans, no sluggards themselves at buccaneering, began to look askance at their behavior."[60]

By the early 1690s, under the reign of Sayf bin Sultan (Sultan's son), the Omanis had cemented their position as the superior maritime force in the Western Indian Ocean. Under Sayf, the Omanis ravaged Portuguese forts in Diu, Bassein, and Bombay in India.[61] The Omanis were certainly not seeking to liberate local peoples from the Portuguese. Their attacks in South Asia or East Africa were aimed at market penetration and control, removing one major competitor from their sphere of commercial and political influence. In forcing the Portuguese to withdraw from their last remaining strongholds in the Western Indian Ocean, the Omanis not only facilitated easier mobility for merchants and others, but also gained a stronger footing in markets in South Asia. Omani leaders began having ships built for their navy in places like Bombay. As state revenues increased, Sayf invested in building new forts, constructing water aqueducts in mainland Oman, and investing in building larger date plantations. In its ability to project power, the Omani navy had become by the time of Sayf's reign an instrument of a national policy of commercial aggrandizement.[62]

Sources for understanding certain components of Omani economy and society during the Yaʿrubi dynasty are exceptionally sparse and incomplete. Using Omani chronicles, however, John Wilkinson highlighted how especially under Sayf Omani, commercial aggrandizement became increasingly tied up with enslavement and human trafficking. By using state violence to protect the movements and positions of Omani merchants in the Western Indian Ocean, Sayf was facilitating their ability to engage in commerce, and one of the main forms of commerce for Omanis but also for others in this time was human trafficking. Certain capital projects required a relatively larger number of enslaved humans as coerced labor. Wilkinson claimed that Sayf personally owned at least two thousand slaves, whom he used as labor on his date plantations and for building and maintaining state infrastructure projects, especially water aqueducts (*aflaj*). In a practice that would continue beyond Ya'rubi rule into Sa'id's reign, slavery also became central to Oman's ability to project force throughout the Western Indian Ocean. Not all those humans enslaved in Omani domains were coerced into labor; some had relatively larger degrees of autonomy and held key positions as mercenary soldiers, sailors, and local governors.[63]

The potential for accruing wealth in human trafficking was a primary factor pulling Omanis to East Africa. For centuries Omanis and others had gone to East Africa to trade in ivory and other commodities, but neither the ivory trade nor any other part of the economy or society in the Western Indian Ocean could be separated from enslavement and human trafficking. The deeply entwined nature of these trades, combined with a rising consumer demand for them—whether products in the form of enslaved humans or ivory tusks—is demonstrated more in subsequent chapters, but the tremendous profits to be gained from engaging in these trades were probably a factor prompting Sayf to more formally exert Omani sovereignty in East Africa, especially in Mombasa.

In 1696 an Omani fleet of seven warships and three thousand mercenaries sailed into Mombasa's harbor and laid siege to Fort Jesus, the formidable Portuguese fortress. The siege lasted until 1698, when the Omanis sacked the fort.[64] In some ways, the Portuguese defeat in Mombasa heralded a new era of Omani imperialism. The Omanis established a garrison there and at Kilwa, Zanzibar, and Pemba.[65] These garrisons allowed the Omanis to consolidate their grip on human trafficking and to funnel revenue back to mainland Oman. The Portuguese briefly returned to Mombasa in the 1720s, but the presence of these Omani garrisons and the removal of Portuguese impositions began shifting northward the focus of East African trade, especially human trafficking and ivory, away from Portuguese-influenced, Mozambique-centered routes. In other ways, however, Omani imperial expansion in East Africa reflected continuity in an oceanic pattern of the rise and fall of different sea powers.[66] Just as the Portuguese did not bring immediate change in the areas they controlled, the Omanis did not bring about immediate change in East Africa—nor did they seek to. The growing presence of Omani traders combined with increasing numbers of South Asians provided new opportunities for East Africans to augment their positions as both discerning consumers and prolific exporters. Omani sovereignty in East Africa was based on maintaining local rulers and customs. The Omani imperial difference, however, would ultimately become the practice of funneling trade directly to Zanzibar. This practice, as the French diplomat Édouard Loarer observed, would ultimately forge the different markets of the East African coast into a "single state" centered on Zanzibar, a state whose economy boomed not only because of its production but also because of its consumerism.[67]

By 1698, when the Yaʿrubi seized Mombasa from the Portuguese, there was already a significant presence of Omani settlers there. The most powerful group were the Mazruʿi family, whom the Yaʿrubi appointed as their proxies. The extent to which the Mazruʿi were subject to Yaʿrubi or, later, Busaʿidi sovereignty would remain contested until the late 1830s, when Saʿid had the family's leaders imprisoned and killed. Contests over power and autonomy between the Mazruʿi in Mombasa and Omani leaders in Muscat reflected the increasing nature of Omani imperialism, yet nearly every instance of the Mazruʿi seeking to amplify their autonomy revolved around one thing: not sending customs duties or other taxes to Muscat.[68] There are different perspectives in the sources from this time regarding the ways that sovereignty emanating from the Yaʿrubi in Muscat influenced the Mazruʿi and other proxy rulers in East Africa. Contemporaneous European observers tended to use moments of Mazruʿi autonomy as much for depicting the ostensible weakness of the Omani state as for stereotyping the Mazruʿi as warlike, blood thirsty Orientals.[69] Omani chroniclers tended to depict this period in rosy hues, as one of uncontested Omani expansion and enlightenment throughout East Africa.[70] Shaykh Al-Amin, a member of the Mazruʿi family, spoke of his predecessors' "rule" (*mulk*) and their "influence" (*nufūdh*); however, he also acknowledged that Sayf bin Sultan was known by the Mazruʿi and other peoples in East Africa as "*qayd al-arḍ*."[71] There are different ways to interpret this title in English. It basically means master or ruler of the land, or a piece of territory. The Arabic word *qayd*, however, has a rich vocabulary of meanings. It is a noun coming from a verb that means to bind together, to stipulate, or to restrict. The title applied to Sayf bin Sultan was an expression of a growing understanding among peoples in East Africa that they lived under a degree of sovereignty emanating from Sayf bin Sultan in Muscat. That the debate over varying interpretations of Mazruʿi autonomy exists at all reflects the emergence of a new political and commercial framework for lands with Omani garrisons and proxy rulers. Countless groups of Omanis, East Africans, and others had always moved between parts of the East African coast. That certain peoples began to refer to a single ruler as *master of the land* highlights a growing sense of empire. Though the extent or nature of Omani state power was unsettled and would continue to be questioned, there was an understanding by 1698 with the fall of Fort Jesus to Sayf bin Sultan that increasing Omani state power now emanated far beyond Oman's mainland in Arabia and the Gulf to parts of East Africa.

Omani chroniclers suggested that Sayf held this title because he established stability and tranquility in Oman and extended Omani sovereignty to East Africa.[72] Sayf unleashed the Omani navy and sacked one Portuguese holdout after another. But Sayf did not just evict the Portuguese from Arabia, the Gulf, and much of East Africa and South Asia. In evicting them, he and other Omani leaders began using their withdrawal combined with the ever-increasing strength of the Omani navy to establish new political hierarchies for centralizing markets from Mombasa to Muscat into a discernibly Omani sphere of influence. This was war capitalism in its purest sense: ruthless assertion of maritime violence and dominance to expand into new territories while expropriating land and local peoples to control markets. Omani expansion throughout East Africa came in a particular form: funneling customs duties and taxes from market hubs like Mombasa to a central place. Under Sayf, those customs duties were funneled to Muscat.[73] Sayf used those customs duties to invest in capital, such as larger, better armed ships, larger date plantations, and more water aqueducts, all things that formed a foundation for the empire's continued growth after his death.[74]

Sven Beckert developed the concept of war capitalism to show the entwined forces of military expansion and commercial aggrandizement. War capitalism, as he put it, had an "intimate connection to European imperial expansion."[75] The history of the Yaʿrubi dynasty's increasing projection of power throughout the Western Indian Ocean highlights a connection to European imperial expansion that is not often stated. For Beckert, the connection was the European subjugation of non-European peoples. Omani war capitalism uncovers a different picture: the faltering of Europeans in the face of Omani expansion. Under the Yaʿrubi, time and again the Omanis checked European expansion, forcing them to leave or acquiesce. Such patterns foreshadowed events driven by the Yaʿrubi's successors, the Al Bu Saʿid.

THE AL BU SAʿID DYNASTY

Omani scholars often divide Omani history into three phases: the first beginning with Islam's spread to Oman, the second beginning with the

Ya'rubi, and the third beginning with the Al Bu Sa'id. The first leader of the Al Bu Sa'id dynasty, which continues to lead Oman today, was Ahmad bin Sa'id. Ahmad came to power at some point around 1750, though no sources agree on which year.[76] As the Omani scholar Ahmad Al-Isma'ili noted, however, these phases are debatable, with overlapping elements of continuity and change between them. Because of this, Al-Isma'ili suggested dividing Omani history (and all history) according to different "structural arrangements" (*al-nasaq al-bunyawī*) and "systems of thought (*manẓumat al-fikrīyah*)."[77] In some ways, the Busa'idi dynasty reflected long-refined patterns in both structural arrangements and systems of thought. Especially by the nineteenth century, however, life in Omani domains would come to look tangibly different. The center of Omani politics followed Sa'id to East Africa, where his Busa'idi predecessors had increasingly monetized economic relations and standardized mechanisms of exchange with the explicit goal of incorporating European and American visitors into their commercial orbit. There was also a definitive change in scale of commercial exchanges. The style and scale of these transformations and commercial exchanges fit within similar changes taking place around the world in this time, what Fernand Braudel referred to as a global shattering of "restrictions, obstacles, structures, proportions and numerical relationships that had hitherto been the norm."[78]

Across the first three decades of the eighteenth century, the Ya'rubi dynasty faltered, family rule falling to factionalism and domestic turmoil. This turmoil gave rise to Ahmad's rise to power.[79] Ahmad came to power by gathering an army of thirty thousand men to put down the quarrels raging in Oman. Some sources estimate that nearly ten thousand of his soldiers died in the fighting.[80] Ahmad was a very wealthy coffee merchant. His personal life and career before taking power were thus imbued with considerations of maritime commerce and security. The trade of coffee that he staked his career on involved commercial exchanges between the Gulf and Red Sea but also across the Arabian Peninsula. Establishing and maintaining security and order was thus among his first considerations. When he came to power, he at once began reorganizing his military, consolidating government institutions, and further expanding the navy.[81] He delegated authority to deputies responsible for different government functions: in Muscat, one deputy managed taxes, another managed shipping, and another managed customs duties.[82] Aside from these government reforms, Ahmad was most known for pacifying warring factions within Oman—putting to rest the quarreling that had ended Yaʿrubi rule. Doing so paved the way for Omanis to cast their gaze more toward international commercial affairs.[83]

Ahmad sought to consolidate his authority throughout East Africa. He did so by strengthening political, social, and commercial ties with South Asian merchant communities already living there. When Ahmad sent a delegation on his behalf to Mombasa and elsewhere in East Africa on a diplomatic and commercial mission, the delegates sailed aboard ships borrowed on credit from South Asian tycoons residing in Muscat. Ahmad might have been wealthy, but his wealth stemmed from the mostly seasonal coffee trade. He did not have generational wealth in vast capital reserves like many South Asians in Muscat. After Carsten Niebuhr, a German scholar and explorer serving the Danish court, spent two weeks in Muscat in 1765, he asserted that there were more Indian Hindus there than in any other part of the Muslim world outside South Asia. Niebuhr also noted how in Oman those Indian Hindu communities were legally protected, allowed to bring their wives to settle there and to otherwise freely practice their religious traditions.[84]

By the latter half of the eighteenth century, many South Asians had begun migrating to Zanzibar. Zanzibar had not previously been a major center of trade in the Western Indian Ocean. As South Asians began settling there, they used their wealth to exploit a largely unstructured political and economic situation, allowing them to monopolize the slowly emerging trade there and extort and exploit other merchants. In response to this, Ahmad appointed a member of his family to serve as his governor in Zanzibar, giving him command as well of a mercenary security force.[85] Ahmad died around 1778, and his son, Saʿid bin Ahmad, succeeded him.[86] Saʿid bin Ahmad quickly became unpopular; in the mid-1780s, domestic challenges to his rule forced him to withdraw from public life and assign responsibility for governing to his son, Hamad.[87] Hamad made several important foreign and domestic policy changes. He moved the capital from Rustaq to Muscat, where he had more access to maritime commerce. He introduced a flat 6.5 percent customs duty for all foreign traders, regardless of religion.[88] In 1786 he established diplomatic relations with Tipu Sultan, ruler of the Kingdom of Mysore in India.[89] He also established direct trade routes between Oman and the Kalat state of Balochistan, projecting Omani power across the Gulf.[90] Hamad died of smallpox in 1792, and his uncle, Sultan bin Ahmad—Saʿid's father—succeeded him.[91]

Sultan remains one of the most pivotal rulers in Omani history, remembered for his political cunning, strategic thinking, and bravery.[92] Sultan further developed the government bureaucracy by appointing a governor for

Muscat and a commander for his army there. As foreign traders began flocking to Muscat and other Omani ports in unprecedented numbers, he established a police force and new policies for tax collection. He invested heavily in the navy. All this allowed him to expand Oman's imperial orbit, incorporating Gwadar in present-day Pakistan; Chahbahar, Hormuz, Bandar Abbas, and Qeshm in Iran; and Bahrain.[93] Oman now commanded both sides of the Gulf, controlling the entry and exit of every ship sailing through the Strait of Hormuz.

To augment Omani maritime control of the Gulf, Sultan established a pass system requiring all non-Omani vessels—European or otherwise—to anchor in Muscat and pay customs. Once a captain paid the required duties, an Omani convoy sailed with the ship to its destination, ensuring its safety.[94] Economy and society in the Western Indian Ocean were thus beginning to reflect new institutional arrangements rooted in state power. As their rigid pass system indicates, markets were "free" to competition so long as that competition played by Omani state dictates. The distinguished Indian Ocean historian Abdul Sheriff once characterized Indian Ocean ports as being like "beads in a rosary, each forming a distinct entity, and yet threaded together by maritime communication and a common culture."[95] Under these Omani imperial institutions, we might add another bead to Sheriff's rosary of connectivity: state-sanctioned violence.

By the final decade of the eighteenth century, Muscat was dominating trade in the Western Indian Ocean.[96] At least half of all commerce between the Arabian Peninsula and India passed through Muscat.[97] The policies of Yarubi and Busaʿidi leaders—whether flat customs taxes, the strategic protection of minorities, or the pass system—catalyzed Oman's ability to control Gulf commerce and project force. But Oman's continued rise across the eighteenth century was complemented by other geopolitical factors, some of them political and others environmental, factors outside of any one person's control or volition. Persian trade in the Gulf had already been disrupted in the first half of the eighteenth century because of repeated invasions from peoples in present-day Afghanistan. These invasions were not merely disruptive. They helped bring about the fall of Persia's Safavid dynasty. The disruptions stemming from the Safavid's fall led to profound domestic unrest throughout Persian lands.[98] This unrest was perpetuated and compounded by a flea-borne plague that ravaged parts of present-day Iran and Iraq in 1772 and 1773, killing millions. The plague unsettled the region, helping spark a series of civil wars in Persia in the century's final two decades. The wars and the economic downturn from the plague dampened the regional influence of Basra, Bushehr, and Bandar Abbas, all of which contributed to a decline in specie throughout Persia and Turkish Iraq. While Persia had for at least a century been a menace to Omani ambitions, by the conclusion of the eighteenth century it was unable to exert significant influence in the Gulf or beyond in the Western Indian Ocean.[99]

Stemming from social transformations taking place oceans and continents away, a new global factor was also facilitating Oman's continued rise. Across the seventeenth century, many people in Europe and the lands of the Ottoman Empire began drinking coffee and reshaping entire social worlds around it. Some of the best coffee in the world was cultivated in Yemen, and local, regional, and global demand skyrocketed throughout the seventeenth century.[100] There were other competing producers and traders, however. Both the Dutch and the British employed agents from their respective trading companies in Yemen, where they had been granted permission to begin trading between 1618 and 1620. By a century later, Yemen's coffee industry was challenged by Dutch cultivation of coffee at Java and by the French in the Mascarenes, but neither the French nor the Dutch could keep pace with the Yemeni trade. The trade and consumption of coffee began remaking social life in Oman, as in other parts of the world in this time. A leading theologian, attuned to the enormous profits the coffee trade was bringing his fellow Omanis, lifted a traditional religious ban on coffee as a mind-altering substance.[101] In addition to Ottoman-controlled networks, Yemen exported much of its coffee through Omani merchant networks.

In the eighteenth century, Yemen was annually producing fifty million pounds of coffee—more than three times the amount produced by the Dutch and French combined. When one European visited Basra in 1774, he observed nearly the entire coffee trade being brought there on armed Omani ships.[102] Omani influence in the contested commercial world of Yemen's coffee trade increased in the following decade, and in the 1790s the volume of coffee passing through Omani hands doubled.[103] The Omanis developed an armed convoy system for protecting ships laden with coffee sailing from the Red Sea to the Gulf. This reduced the threat of European plunder and augmented Oman's ability to control markets within its sphere of influence.[104] While the Omanis moved coffee from Yemen to Muscat and protected it from loot, South Asians helped finance it.[105]

Just as Sultan was cementing his hold over the Gulf, he was also exerting more influence in East Africa. Omanis' influence in the region was tied to the numbers of humans they enslaved and trafficked. The steady rise in Omani migration to East Africa and influence there throughout the century was predicated on the success of South Asian migrants in the region. When they arrived, Omani migrants, merchants, and government officials relied on these South Asian entrepreneurs to advance capital, giving them the resources and time necessary to ingratiate themselves into preexisting East African commercial networks, especially those involved in human trafficking. The Omanis were among the leading traffickers in the Western Indian Ocean. They became especially involved in trafficking with the French, who, by 1800, had established sugar plantations on the islands of Isles de France (Mauritius) and Bourbon (Réunion).

Across the eighteenth century, increasing Omani migrations throughout East Africa and more formalized connections with South Asian firms in the region began to remake the commercial hierarchy of East African ports. Until the 1780s, Kilwa had been the central market for human trafficking.[106] French traders preferred to traffic enslaved humans in Kilwa because they could avoid Omani duties there, as opposed to Mombasa, another leading center, where the Omanis had more powerful customs officials and proxy rulers. The increasing presence of Omanis in the region, however, began to shift market forces away from Kilwa. According to Chhaya Goswami, in 1785 the Al Bu Saʿid appointed a Gujarati tycoon, Shivji Topan, as the customs manager in Zanzibar.[107] Appointing the Shivji family to manage customs at Zanzibar strengthened a process in which Zanzibar began to emerge as central to the Western Indian Ocean, and a part of interoceanic commerce. At the root of this imperial expansion were tangible, reciprocal connections binding the Shivji family with the Al Bu Saʿid. Until long after Saʿid's death in 1856, the Al Bu Saʿid remained deeply in debt to the Shivji family, relying on them not only for credit in terms of fast cash, but also for capital advances for things like ships for outfitting military campaigns. While the Shivji family held great influence over the Al Bu Saʿid, the Omanis also held sway over the Shivji family firm, which relied on the successes of Omani imperial adventures for their own commercial prosperity and longevity.[108]

These global, regional, and local transformations tied up with Omani imperialism had social ramifications throughout Omani domains, whether in Arabia and the Gulf or in East Africa. Some of the most dramatic consequences of Omani imperialism and the destruction of social worlds expropriated by Omani expansion were in Zanzibar. Growing Omani influence in Zanzibar and elsewhere in East Africa fortified rigid social hierarchies.[109]

In Oman's mainland and in East Africa, this hierarchy was almost like a caste system. By 1754 there were reportedly around four hundred Omani merchants in Zanzibar.[110] Drawing capital advances on their homes or borrowing money from South Asian firms in Zanzibar, Omanis on the island began expropriating peoples already living there, primarily the WaTumbatu and the WaHadimu. As Thomas McDow has shown, increasing Omani migration to Zanzibar and the growing commercial nexus between the Al Bu Saʿid and the Shivji firm there pushed those local peoples from their historic lands and stripped them of their own traditional sources of work and income.[111] The increasing presence of Omanis and South Asians in Zanzibar exacerbated economic inequalities. Granted, small numbers of Zanzibari and other East African elites leveraged their private wealth to ally with Omani settlers. Some of these elites were able to leverage the Omanis' rapacious demand for human trafficking to participate in it, growing their own incomes to maintain some semblance of power.[112] Despite this, however, Omanis brought with them to East Africa engrained notions of racial and religious hierarchy. In Zanzibar and elsewhere, Omanis referred to local peoples as *makhadim*, meaning those who are subordinate or servile.[113]

Omani racial attitudes in East Africa were bolstered by entwined political and economic transformations taking place in mainland Oman. More than a century of expansion, expropriation, and enslavement had consolidated tremendous amounts of wealth in the hands of a few elites.[114] Economic disparity was a consequence of the previous centuries of expansion, and as John Wilkinson put it, the disparity led to a veritable social revolution in Oman. It empowered a privileged class of merchants and landowners at the expense of people who became parts of lower classes.[115] For centuries in Omani history, there had been an accepted prestigious class of theologians and jurists, but by 1800 wealthy merchants had become ensconced alongside their scholarly counterparts as part of an almost untouchable elite, favored by the state. When Hamad had died in 1792, for example, his successor invited to the state-sanctioned funeral celebrations Oman's elites: notable guests like members of the family, jurists, and theologians, but also Muscat's leading merchants.[116]

Aboard their dhows, Omanis went to East Africa with commercial aspirations entwined with this social hierarchy. Omani state policy in Zanzibar and neighboring places was one of divesting indigenous peoples of their fortunes and prospects. With some exceptions, Omanis forced East Africans, whether they were technically enslaved or not, into positions of subservience—cogs in the wheels of a vast, transoceanic process of economic integration that unfolded on a plane above any single individual, but inevitably shaped every person's life. The increasing presence of Omanis in East Africa relegated many local peoples to things like fishing, small-scale agriculture, or a coastal carrying trade, because the business of the most profitable things—ivory, cloves, and enslaved humans—was becoming monopolized by Omanis and South Asians. Ironically, by finding themselves anew amid Omani imperialism in things like the small-scale coastal carrying trade or fishing, many East Africans were helping fuel the very structural, commercial changes that were divesting them of their historical roles as oceanic merchants.[117]

Looking back over the period of Omani expansion beginning with Nasir bin Murshid Al-Ya'aribah in 1624, we see that Omani leaders co-opted the presence of myriad peoples within their domains. South Asian minorities and Muslim minorities were legally protected in Oman, but this legal protection did not lead to any notion of social equity. In fact, it fomented social and economic stratification, attracting and then protecting a class of financial and commercial elites. The long history of Ya'rubi and Busa'idi rulers guaranteeing the protection of Shi'a and Hindu minorities facilitated their emergence as wealthy, elite classes with capacity to monopolize markets, not just to compete in them.[118] The position of elites in maritime-oriented places like Muscat or Zanzibar was especially important because their capital reserves and protected status preserved the near constant circulation of commodities and people between ports. As Fernand Braudel described, the farther goods traveled the more the prices of those goods increased. The strategic cosmopolitanism—the presence of peoples from many different countries—embraced by a string of Omani leaders can be seen as actually fortifying stratification by guaranteeing that there would be a monied, elite class in ports throughout Omani domains with the wealth and capital necessary for purchasing goods, outfitting voyages, paying customs duties, and thus setting off perpetual circuits of exchange. By the final decade of the eighteenth century, this was evident to those who passed through Muscat. A British report on Muscat in 1790 noted: "Commerce is a never failing source of Wealth and it has rendered Muscat a more rich and a flourishing Sea Port than any of those bordering on the Persian Gulph."[119]

Yet neither Muscat's rise nor the sovereignty of Omani leaders were unidirectional or without challenges. In 1804 Sultan bin Ahmad was at the height of his reign, his domains stretching across the Gulf and south to East

Africa.[120] Sultan had also maintained Omani power in places he did not directly control, like Basrah, by enforcing the collection of an annual tribute paid to him.[121] In 1804 Sultan prepared for his annual trip to collect that tribute by placing a trusted deputy in charge of Muscat for his brief absence. He arrived in Basrah, collected the tribute, and boarded his ship *Al-Badry* for the short voyage back home to Muscat. It was a routine trip, and Sultan sailed with only a few slaves and deputies.

Around midnight, as the *Al-Badry* passed through the Strait of Hormuz, Sultan and his small crew were accosted by three ships belonging to a neighboring Arab confederacy, the Al-Qawasim, who ruled mostly out of Ras Al-Khaimah in the present-day United Arab Emirates. The Al-Qawasim's political and economic positions in Arabia and the Gulf had been seriously troubled by the rise of Omani power. Lit only by the moon, the ships bobbed beside each other, and one of the Qasimi men yelled out, demanding to know who was aboard the Omani vessel. Sultan defiantly answered, announcing his identity. The Qasimi sailors responded that they were seeking his death and challenged him to fight at sunrise. The next morning's combat was searing. Amid arrows, swords, and javelins, one Qasimi man aimed a musket into the melee and fired. The round struck Sultan in the face, killing him.[122] Sultan's death paved the way for his son, Saʿid, to seize power in 1806.

CONCLUSION

On the morning of February 3, 1840, Zanzibar's harbor was especially abuzz. For centuries this East African island had been one port in a coherent maritime arena connecting Africa, the Middle East, and Asia. By 1800 it had gained newfound prominence under Omani rule as a center for human trafficking and related trades, like ivory, gum copal, and animal hides. On this day, however, the *Sultanah*—the first Middle Eastern ship to arrive in the United States—was about to depart. At 6:30 in the morning when the *Sultanah* pulled up anchor, it was already 85°F, and as the crew pointed its sails toward New York City, the sky was clear and the sea was calm.[123]

For weeks before the ship's departure, enslaved East Africans had prepared it for the voyage. They loaded and organized the cargo of Omani dates, Persian rugs, Zanzibari cloves, and Yemeni coffee. They even built stables for several fine Arabian horses, each a gift from Saʿid to US president Martin Van Buren.[124] Some of those enslaved East Africans remained as part of the crew during the transoceanic voyage. With them were Indian sailors, a Portuguese cook from Goa, two French passengers, two English passengers, an East African captain, and an English navigator. Presiding over everyone on board was one of Saʿid's chief envoys, Ahmad bin Naʿaman. Ahmad had been born in the Gulf—perhaps in Bahrain—but lived much of his life in Zanzibar as he traveled on Saʿid's behalf to America, Europe, Cairo, and Canton.[125]

Three months later, newspapers throughout the northeast United States covered the *Sultanah*'s arrival in New York with great pomp. "The arrival in our harbor of the first Arabian man-of-war that ever crossed the Atlantic is a matter of much interest," heralded the *New York American*.[126] The New Yorkers who greeted the ship were enamored of the captain. "Captain Ahmed bin Naman, the commander of the Arabian corvette Sultanah, is a great man," proclaimed New York's *Morning Herald*.[127] Residents were also struck by the ship itself. "There is a great curiosity in New York now, in the shape of an Arabian ship," recorded the *New Hampshire Sentinel*. "She is a fine vessel of about 400 tons, built in Bombay of Teakwood."[128]

The *Sultanah* and its voyage to New York illuminate elements of both continuity and change in the Indian Ocean as a stage for the unfolding of modern world history. Built by South Asians in India, the ship's flanks were bolted together for carrying a tremendous surplus of goods and for withstanding large-scale naval combat. It carried fourteen cannons and could sail with more than three hundred tons of cargo.[129] Though built in India, it belonged to Saʿid, an Arab from Oman, who made Zanzibar in East Africa the capital of his empire. The horses carried on the ship as a gift to President Van Buren from Saʿid's own personal stock were part of a diplomatic strategy for strengthening commercial ties, but they were also bound up in broader global dimensions in which Africans, Arabs, and Asians stitched the relatively new Atlantic into their far longer-standing world.

For centuries Omanis had sailed ships across oceanic spaces in the pursuit of wealth. In this sense, there is little surprising about Saʿid dispatching the *Sultanah* to New York. Seen from the broader contours of world history, however, the ship's arrival in New York highlights the relatively late emergence of the Atlantic world as an important commercial space, and reflects how the Atlantic, rather than being a platform allowing Europeans to dominate non-Europeans, provided Indian Ocean peoples with new markets for satisfying their own pursuits of wealth and new imports for satisfying their own rapacious consumerism.

Though perhaps the most famous of Sa'id's ships, the *Sultanah* was neither his largest nor his best armed. The *Caroline,* among his favorites, was built in Bombay in 1814 and could stow 575 tons of cargo. But even the *Caroline* was dwarfed by the colossal *Liverpool.* Built in Mumbai in 1826, its 150-man crew managed its seventy-four cannons and eighteen hundred tons of cargo. In 1833 Sa'id presented the ship as a gift to British king William IV, who changed its name to *Al-Imam,* in honor of Sa'id. Though not as large, among Sa'id's most heavily armed battleships were the *Shah 'Alam,* carrying fifty-two cannons; the *Piedmontese,* carrying thirty-six; and the *Victoria,* carrying forty.[130] In addition to having ships built in India, Sa'id also purchased ships from Cochin, China, and the United States.[131] Each of these ships and their counterparts in oceans around the world were like juggernauts fueling the rise of modern capitalism.[132] In the context of the Western Indian Ocean, Sa'id's fleet reflects Omani ambitions dating from at least as early as the seventeenth century, simultaneously with other states elsewhere in the world, of reallocating naval power from "military-defensive to commercial-offensive purposes."[133]

Ships just like these were central to a profound, interrelated set of economic institutional arrangements: expansion into new lands; expropriation of indigenous peoples and their reorientation toward new markets; and transoceanic, interhemispheric commerce—all manifestations of a planned accumulation of wealth beyond historical limits. These ships were emblems of wealth, state power, and commercial connections, but they also reveal something else. The laborers who built those ships, whether in Bombay, Sur, or elsewhere, lived in squalor. Some of them might have earned wages, but never enough to transcend expectations of poverty. As historian Janet Ewald demonstrated, countless unnamed and unrecognized enslaved men worked on ships and played vital roles in sustaining an Indian Ocean world at the fore of an emerging global economy.[134]

On the morning of its departure, the *Sultanah* would have been surrounded by hundreds of more traditional Indian Ocean vessels, just like its precursor, the *Sohar.* In fact, most of Sa'id's fleet, and the greatest number of vessels throughout the Indian Ocean, were dhows.[135] Neither the Omani Empire nor any other empire vanquished this ostensibly "traditional" vessel and its trade.[136] In fact, the commodities the *Sultanah* carried to New York—such as rugs, dates, coffee, and cloves—all presupposed the continued existence of the dhow trade. Docked in Zanzibar harbor beside countless African, Arab, and South Asian dhows, the *Sultanah* was a concrete manifestation of capitalism's abstractions, especially the concept of scale. It was built to carry more goods across greater distances and at the fastest velocities ever in human history. And that the ship was built by South Asians in Bombay for an Arab person leading an empire based in East Africa and carrying commodities to New York City prompts historians to think of global capitalism and world history in terms of cocreation. Anchored in Zanzibar harbor alongside European and American men-of-war and countless African, Arab, and South Asian dhows, the *Sultanah* also highlights the comingling of the old with the new—change as continuity within a longer historical arc.

THREE

Contesting the Gulf

INTRODUCTION

Upon seizing power in 1806, Sa'id bin Sultan declared war. Two years earlier, the Al-Qawasim, a powerful confederation based mostly in Ras al-Khaimah, had killed his father at sea. Sultan's killing was not an isolated act; it was part of an especially turbulent period in Gulf history across the first two decades of the nineteenth century in which many groups, including emerging states, were competing for maritime supremacy and autonomy. The Omani chronicler Ibn Ruzayq recorded a letter Sa'id wrote in 1806 to his uncle Qais, then governor of Sohar. There was no way to avoid war with the Qawasim, Sa'id reasoned. Their leader, Sultan bin Saqr, had been attacking Omani shipping—he had made himself their enemy, Sa'id stated. Remarkably, Sa'id's letter to his uncle contained no mention of his father's killing, but he did mention the broader agenda of violence and political contestation the attack on his father had been part of. Sultan bin Saqr was an enemy, Sa'id stated, because he had "corrupted" the seaways (*afsadda ṭarīq al-baḥr*). He and his followers "forcibly" plundered ships belonging to Omanis, whom Sa'id labeled his subjects. Sa'id then drove home his point, concluding that Sultan and his followers were enemies of Oman because their goal was to corrupt the sea by means of plunder and murder (*fasād al-baḥr bi-an-nahb wa-al-qatl*).[1]

Yet Sa'id's war against Sultan bin Saqr was unconventional; his enemy soon became his ally. Sultan did not remain Sa'id's enemy for long. The Omani campaign against the Al-Qawasim was a war of protracted negotiations and political machinations as much as it was a war of violence on land and on sea. A decade later, Sultan bin Saqr was firmly within Sa'id's imperial orbit. Saʿid's evolving dynamics with Sultan bin Saqr were not unique. Saʿid built Omani power in the Gulf and Arabia through both force and negotiation, and with other local elites as well.

One of those other local elites was Rahmah bin Jabir, leader of another powerful group, the Al-Jalahimah.[2] The Al-Jalahimah family were one family that comprised the Al ʿUtub confederation, which had migrated from Najd, an area in the center of the Arabian Peninsula, at some point in the late sixteenth century. Alongside the families that came to establish the present-day states of Bahrain and Kuwait, the Al-Jalahimah resettled themselves along Arabia's coasts and almost immediately "took to the seas," reinventing themselves in maritime commerce.[3] The complicated interplays between Saʿid bin Sultan, Sultan bin Saqr, and Rahmah bin Jabir delimited the Omani Empire but were also part of the emergence of other states in the area, including the First Saudi State. The First Saudi State was centered on Al-Diriya in the Arabian Peninsula, and its emergence was part of entwined political, theological, social, and commercial factors affecting the region in the second half of the eighteenth century and beginning of the nineteenth.[4] In their political negotiations and discerning uses of violence, Sultan bin Saqr and Rahmah bin Jabir were like political entrepreneurs, navigating new spaces of contestation in the Gulf and Arabia opened by Omani imperialism, the emergence of other Arab states, and the increasing British presence in the Gulf after the East India Company signed a treaty with Oman in 1798 and another in 1800.[5] Sultan and Rahmah provide a glimpse of local agency beneath the veneer of empire, whether Omani or British: they reached the heights of their power *because* of Omani expansion, shrewdly navigating themselves within the Omani orbit and becoming part of a new order in the Gulf.

The British routinely branded Sultan bin Saqr and the Qawasim as pirates. At first, Saʿid labeled Sultan an enemy and described his forcible seizure of cargo, killing of seamen, and destruction of ships as reasons for that. Though piracy is a ubiquitous theme in the British sources from this period, the British used a more convoluted vocabulary when dealing with Rahmah bin Jabir. The British understood Rahmah's reputation for violence. The journalist working for the East India Company, James Silk Buckingham, spent time with Rahmah when they were both in Bushehr, and afterward characterized him as "the terror of the Gulf . . . the most successful and the most generally tolerated pirate, perhaps, that ever infested any sea."[6]

Buckingham's description of Rahmah as a tolerated terror has a deeper layer of history. Rahmah—and Sultan bin Saqr, as well—were political actors who had to be worked with, rather than merely cast aside. As Charles Davies demonstrated in a study of Gulf maritime violence at this time, diving deeper beneath the stigma of piracy reveals highly discriminatory acts of maritime violence, entwined with landed affairs. Acts of maritime violence might have at times been highly idiosyncratic; nonetheless, they can be read in this time and space as part of political agendas of emerging states. Rahmah and Sultan became formative actors in the unfolding of a new political and social hierarchy in the Gulf across the first half of the nineteenth century. As political entrepreneurs, they were more than mere pirates; they helped shape the entwined political, economic, and social dimensions of imperial transformations in the Gulf in the early nineteenth century.[7]

Interpreting persons like Rahmah or Sultan as political entrepreneurs illuminates a different mobility than the type of commodity-following mobility that is characteristically traced in Indian Ocean histories. As they sailed the seas, Rahmah and Sultan also sailed between friend and foe, remaining malleable and dynamic as they navigated social and political ruptures in the Gulf around the turn of the eighteenth century. This interpretation helps temper triumphalist narratives of empire in this time and space. First, it challenges the notion of the Indian Ocean being or becoming a British lake. Equally important, however, it provides a more nuanced understanding of how Saʿid fortified his position as an imperial sovereign. Although Saʿid used force—sometimes in dramatically violent ways—his sovereignty and the function of his empire were also forged by protracted negotiations with some local groups, aimed not so much at exterminating them as rivals as at swinging them into his commercial orbit.

Rahmah may never have called himself a political entrepreneur, but he embodied the role.[8] He began his career fighting against Bahrain. In the first decade of the nineteenth century, Rahmah bet on the success of the First Saudi State's rapid rise and allied with it to plunder Omani shipping. By 1813 he was working with the British, agreeing not to attack their ships in hopes they would seize Bahrain—forever his archenemy.[9] By 1816 Saʿid had the initiative against the Saudis, and Rahmah denounced his previous alliance and joined the Omanis.[10] In turn, he soon joined the Omani-British campaign against certain factions within the Qawasim confederation. By 1819 his fortunes had shifted, and he began working for the Persian governor of

Fars, again focused on sacking Bahrain. In 1820 Rahmah was in Bushehr, and the British resident there asked him to sign onto a newly written treaty for the suppression of maritime violence in the Gulf. He declined, haughtily proclaiming that he was no longer interested in helping the British. He was, as he declared, now a servant of the Persian emperor.[11]

Embodied in Rahmah bin Jabir and Sultan bin Saqr are entire local and regional histories bound up with global transformations. As much as anything done by Saʿid or his government officials, Rahmah and Sultan also helped clarify the boundaries of empire. Establishing maritime security in the Gulf was a ruthless process of connection by means of disconnection and reconnection. And in this process, Saʿid contained the British as one actor among others.[12] Saʿid co-opted the British, getting some British officers to even eschew standing British policy and assist him in his own military goals. Nearly all the sources available for understanding the Gulf in the first two decades of the nineteenth century are British East India Company records. We can complement our understanding of this period with Arabic-language chronicles and some travelers' memoirs, but the British archival sources give us the most fine-grained details of daily circumstances. But those British sources can be used to challenge some conventions of the archive itself. Combining records from multiple continents and reading them against the grain and in conversation with Arabic chronicles opens a window into a period in which the British understood themselves to be reliant upon Saʿid bin Sultan as an imperial sovereign, and perhaps the dominant actor in the Gulf at that time.

Saʿid's maneuvering highlights a shift in Western Indian Ocean power dynamics. A century earlier, a British traveler had called the Omanis a "Terrour to all the trading People in India."[13] With the consolidation of Saʿid's reign, however, the Omanis came to increasingly dictate who was considered a maritime threat, and the British allied with the Omanis in often subordinate ways to deal with those threats. As one British official observed in 1820, the Omanis had left other Gulf peoples with no choice but to accept "a new order of things."[14] Persons like Rahmah and Sultan, by creating trouble for agents of empire, helped forge the very order of things that restructured their lives, reconfiguring their ambitions for taking advantage of imperialism and imperial competition. Dissent and disruption were manifestations of empire, and in the end, the very act of dissent ultimately strengthened that which was dissented against: the empire and its control over the marketplace.[15]

The Qawasim were an extended family confederation living along the coasts north of Oman, mostly in the present-day United Arab Emirates.[16] Historically, they were prolific maritime merchants and sailors involved in the pearl and date trades. By the beginning of the nineteenth century, the Omani pass system and its armed convoys had marginalized many factions within the Qawasim. When Saʿid seized power in 1806 the Qawasim were already storming the seas, using violence as a means for preserving their commercial fortunes and challenging Omani expansion.[17] Their violence at sea was one iteration of a global trend in modern world economic and social history in which economic disruptions created disequilibria between newly transformed maritime markets and long-established societies.[18] By 1800, parts of the Qawasim confederation had formally allied with the First Saudi State to plunder Gulf shipping.[19] The previous century, in 1744 a roving spiritual reformist, Muhammad Ibn ʿAbd al-Wahhab, had agreed to a pact with Muhammad bin Saʿud, a local political leader in Arabia's interior region. Their pact catalyzed a new political entity emanating from Al-Diriya, a thriving oasis town in Najd. This entity has been called the First Saudi State. By 1800 the First Saudi State had expanded throughout much of Arabia, exerting influence over its Red Sea and Gulf coasts. When Saʿid came to power, Saudi expansion along his land borders would have been a primary concern, one closely tied to defending Omani shipping at sea from Qasimi plunder. Saʿid would have understood the link between Saudi expansion and Qasimi maritime violence. His predecessors had fought the Qawasim since at least as early as his grandfather Ahmad's reign, just as they had also found different ways to resist increasing Saudi encroachments into Oman.[20]

In 1800 the British sent Sir John Malcolm, future governor-general of Bombay, on a diplomatic mission throughout the Gulf. An anonymous member of Malcolm's delegation kept a log of the voyage. Sailing north through the Strait of Hormuz, the author called upon one of the Arabs sailing with Malcolm and inquired about the country they were sailing past on their left. "With apparent alarm," the Arab sailor replied that they were sailing by the homes and forts of the Qawasim, who were "a sect" of the Wahhabi and whose "occupation" had become marauding commercial vessels at sea.[21] The Arab sailor's statement was somewhat misleading, in that many factions within the Qawasim confederation continued their work in the pearl trade and other regional trades, but it also demonstrates how widely known the alliance between the Saudis and the Qawasim had become at the time.

The Saudis and Qawasim allied, leveraging land and sea power to their mutual advantage. The Qawasim were powerful at sea, and the Saudis could marshal relatively large armies. Each of them, moreover, needed capital: the Qawasim needed it to survive, and the Saudis needed it to expand. The emergence of the First Saudi State was, from its inception, tied up with commercial affairs; it was not only an evangelizing theological movement.[22] Some elements of Wahhabism can be interpreted as a hostile reaction to the strategic cosmopolitanism and international trade fueling the Omani Empire, but the Saudis did not want to end that international trade; they wanted to reorient its revenue to their own coffers.[23] A major theme of two primary early Wahhabi chronicles, those of Ibn Ghannam and Ibn Bishr, is the importance for the Saudis of seeking power and influence over eastern Arabia's Gulf ports. The Saudis sought these ports to secure revenue streams and to project force.[24] Arabia's eastern coasts were prime targets for the Saudis because they were home to many of the region's wealthiest merchants, many of whom were from Najd. The political goal of reorienting capital and wealth was inherent in their theological tenets.

As Ibn Ruzayq recorded, the Saudis sent the Omanis a treatise detailing their beliefs during the reign of Saʿid's father. The treatise warned the Omanis to renounce their ways or face invasion and death. As they explicated in the treatise, they viewed any persons, even other Muslims, who did not embrace Wahhabism and ally with the Saudi state to be *mushrikīn*, or polytheists; understood as such, the Wahhabi claimed that they could legally be killed and their forms of wealth (*māl*), like ships or date groves, be seized. The concept of *shirk*, idolatry or polytheism, was thus at the heart of Saudi-Wahhabi discourse, and it can be read as running parallel to the Saudi state's concern for obtaining new streams of wealth for sustaining its own reformist and expansionist agenda.[25] According to Ibn Ruzayq, most Omanis ignored the treatise. "The treatise contained a mass of incoherent sentences quite inconsistent with the truth," he claimed, "and no one took any notice of it."[26]

Ibn Ruzayq's claim contains a degree of Busaʿidi triumphalism. Most Omanis certainly did regard Wahhabi doctrine as egregious. Like most Muslims everywhere at the time, the Omanis scoffed at the theological arguments. But the Saudi-Wahhabi accusation that the Omanis were mushrikīn whose wealth could legitimately be seized caused profound alarm. The author of the treatise and the founder of Wahhabi ideology, Muhammad Ibn ʿAbd al-Wahhab, had argued, perhaps in a nod toward the Omanis, that certain mushrikīn were worse than others. The worst offenders, he submitted, were those persons who claimed to be Muslim, yet lived alongside non-Muslims, associated with them, and formed partnerships with them.[27] These partnerships and associations were irreconcilable with Wahhabi doctrine, which required its followers to actively distance themselves from and scorn those who were not Wahhabi, if not kill them. They even forbade their followers to travel to non-Muslim countries.[28]

Such theological decrees were not always followed, of course.[29] On one occasion, in either 1811 or 1812 a Saudi envoy visited the British Residency in Bushehr off the Persian Coast and attempted to begin negotiations for establishing "mutual amity and commercial relations" between the Saudis and the British in the Gulf.[30] In 1814, as Saʿid and his navy squeezed the Qawasim at sea, a Saudi envoy again went to Bushehr, bearing letters from Saudi and Qasimi leaders, proposing to the British that they would cease their maritime plunder if they could in turn receive restitution "of certain specific property."[31] The British spurned both proposals, but the Saudi attempts at even considering such political moves reflect the malleability in the Gulf of both persons and states seeking commercial viability.

In the context of Arabian Peninsula economy and society in this time, the Wahhabi declaration that non-Wahhabi were mushrikīn legally permitted to be killed, with their property seized, was an expression of their own expansionist needs for wealth. Ibn Ruzayq recalled that he was present at a meeting between prominent Omani theologians, Saʿid's brother Salim, and a shaykh who had fled the Saudi state for refuge in Muscat. At the meeting, Salim implored the shaykh to provide insight into the Saudis' arguments regarding *tashrīk*—declaring persons mushrikīn. The shaykh confirmed that they viewed any non-Wahhabi as a polytheist worthy of death. He also described how, in addition to legalizing the seizure of so-called polytheists' property and wealth, the Wahhabi had legalized the enslavement of their offspring and their wives. Rather than being driven by mere zealotry, however, the shaykh suggested that there was a shrewd economic strategy behind these political-theological doctrines. The driving factor behind those zealous theological tenets, the shaykh proclaimed, was a relatively simple goal: the acquisition of māl.[32]

The veracity of the shaykh's statement was apparent to Saʿid. In 1809 he wrote to the British explaining the nuances of the increasingly hostile relations between the Omanis and the Saudis. He declared that things were dire, and that there would need to be major military actions taken against the Saudis and their Qasimi allies. In Saʿid's estimation, the situation was clear: he and his subjects could either be "reduced" to Wahhabism, "or remain merchants."[33] In one sense, Saʿid was wrong. From their home in Najd, a desert plateau area in present-day Saudi Arabia, many of the people who became the first Wahhabi were, like Saʿid, maritime-oriented merchants, just as many peoples living in Najd always had been. They intermingled and did business with foreign traders in the Arabian Peninsula, just as they traveled throughout the lands of the Western Indian Ocean and Mediterranean littorals while buying and selling spices, ivory, and other highly profitable goods.[34]

Read another way, however, Saʿid's dichotomy reveals what he perceived to be at stake in this historical period. The conflict was not a mutually exclusive battle between Wahhabis and merchants. It was a battle for who controlled those merchants and who refereed the rules of the markets in which they traded. Though both the Saudis and the Omanis had their own ingrained racial and religious hierarchies, the Omanis sought to control the marketplace by attracting certain foreign merchants, regardless of religion or ethnicity. The violence that followers of Wahhabism and subjects of the First Saudi State used against minority groups was a threat to the multinational and multiconfessional marketplace at the core of the Omani state. In fact, when Saʿid wrote this letter to the British in 1809, Saudi agents were apparently already disrupting commerce in Muscat and other coastal cities in Oman. That year, there were six Wahhabi evangelists in Muscat. At prayer times, they would patrol the city streets, reportedly forcing merchants out of their shops and to the mosque, all as a way of spreading their messages and laying a bottom-up foundation for converting Omanis to their side and accessing their ports, revenue streams, and capital stores.[35]

Saʿid's push for maritime security reflected his imperial ambitions and his personal ambitions as a merchant. It was one iteration of a long-term trend in which Omani leaders preserved difference for diversifying markets. The Italian physician Vincenzo Maurizi, Saʿid's personal doctor, and, later, one of his field commanders against the Saudis, described Indian Hindus as the "great Bankers of Arabia," minority entrepreneurs providing capital to facilitate the commercial ambitions of merchants traversing the entire Western Indian Ocean world. Maurizi described, moreover, how during Saʿid's reign, "[p]eople of all nations and all religions may arrive and depart without molestation."[36] Maurizi's account aligns with numerous other reports.

When he visited Muscat around 1800, the journalist and agent of the East India Company James Silk Buckingham estimated that Indian Hindus comprised about 10 percent of the population. Buckingham also stated that, living in Muscat and legally protected, were "Parsees from Bombay; Sindians and Belooches from the coast of Mekran; Persians from Bushehr; Arabs from Bahrein; and Jews from Bussorah."[37]

Omanis might have scoffed at being called polytheists because of their business associations or even their religious beliefs, but they understood that the other side to the Wahhabi accusation of polytheism—the seizure of māl—was a threat to their fortunes and their futures. This threat became especially apparent for the Omanis when the Saudis formally allied with the Qawasim around 1800. The Saudi commander who received the Qasimi vows made the strategic goal clear: while the Saudis would focus their armies on laying siege to the Omani interior, the Qawasim were to plunder the seas, massacring anyone who was not allied with them and seizing their ships to be reappropriated as part of a new, de facto Saudi-Qasimi navy.[38] One British diplomat stationed in the Gulf described how Wahhabi-allied Arabs, after seizing merchant ships in the Gulf, would tow them back to their home ports before refitting them for their own uses.[39] The Wahhabi chronicler Ibn Bishr, in hundreds of pages explicating theology and paying homage to Wahhabi leaders, also provided a veritable index of Saudi battles and raids on Arabia's coasts.[40] Those raids were important for seizing cargoes, but also because the ships augmented their own maritime forces. As the Saudi-Qasimi navy grew, Saʿid began protracted negotiations with its leaders, seeking to stitch them within an Omani-dominated regional marketplace, or, to borrow wording from Pekka Hämäläinen, flip them into his orbit.[41]

FLIPPING LOCAL ELITES

The Saudi-Qasimi alliance began a decade of Saudi expansion in the Arabian Peninsula and a proliferation of violence at sea.[42] Saudi-Qasimi troubles ultimately led to the apex of Omani maritime power in the Gulf, which Saʿid achieved using force and shrewd political negotiations. Many historians have assumed that maritime security was achieved in the Gulf because of British power. Abdul Sheriff, whose work paved the way for studying the history of the Omani Empire in the broader context of Indian Ocean and world history, claimed that by 1800 Oman had "sacrificed" its autonomy to the British "altar of commercial profit," with Saʿid's naval campaigns being mere attempts at finding "new niches in what had become a British Lake."[43] Sheriff's position cannot be written off as outdated. More recent waves of distinguished scholarship have also departed from this basic presupposition, casting the British as the primary actors in Gulf history in the first two decades of the nineteenth century, using their position as masters of the seas to "severely limit" Oman's role in Gulf affairs.[44] While local Gulf peoples might certainly have resisted this unidirectional rise of British power, this general narrative holds that the British were nonetheless able to mold local peoples and their politics and economies into conduits for serving their ostensibly outside capitalist economy.[45]

Despite challenges, Saʿid steadily expanded Omani power in the Gulf. The Omanis used the British, whose resources only allowed for them a small presence in the area, in a supporting role. British naval officers readily admitted this. "Any one now visiting the Red Sea, the East Coast of Africa, and the Persian Gulf," declared one naval officer in 1877, "would fail to realise the fact that, up to within the latter half of this century, the British flag was seldom seen in these waters."[46] The British flag was there in the Gulf, to be certain. But the British understood their relative weaknesses; at most, they operated from a position of parity with Saʿid. This was evident to the British in commercial terms, as well – not just in terms of naval forces. In 1804 a group of British merchants in Bombay reported with alarm that Omani shipping by tonnage greatly exceeded British shipping in that port. They noted how frequently the Omanis extorted Bombay merchants, controlling the market and bending it to their own ventures. "We shall soon find," they proclaimed, "the Arab shipping to be to our Indian commerce what the Dutch was to our European."[47]

The British formalized their commercial ties with Oman in treaties signed in 1798 and 1800. These treaties marked the beginning of formal Omani-British commercial relations, with the British beginning to trade almost exclusively with the Omanis. The treaties thus contributed to the disenfranchisement of the Qawasim by removing the British as potential trading partners for them. An unintended consequence of the treaties was thus a concerted upsurge of Qasimi attacks on British shipping. The first documented case of a Qasimi attack on a British ship was in 1797, but the number of attacks increased after 1800. By 1809, the Qawasim captured and plundered six more British ships.[48] This is an astonishing number when one considers that, in 1802, the British had only sixteen ships in the entire

Indian Ocean, a space comprising more than twenty-seven million square miles.[49] Even as late as 1858 the entire Indian Navy consisted of thirty-one ships.[50] Moreover, as Saʿid would tell them, the ships they did have were ill-equipped for the Gulf's geography and the aggression of the Qawasim. As one British historian lamented, "The Government, in sending to the Persian Gulf wretched little craft . . . not one-third the size of the ordinary Joasmi [Qasimi] war dhows . . . positively invited the loss of their ships, and, still worse, of the crews."[51]

In fact, the British relied on the Omanis in the Gulf because they had two distinct advantages in expunging the Qasimi threat. First, Saʿid commanded a powerful navy, which he used to control a relatively confined geographic space. The American merchant and diplomatic envoy Edmund Roberts concluded that Saʿid had the most powerful navy anywhere from the Cape of Good Hope to Japan.[52] Aside from size, the Omani navy was powerful because its sailors understood the Gulf's social and environmental landscape. The Gulf was ideal for the proliferation of maritime asymmetric threats because it was "studded with little islands, indented with narrow, twisting creeks, protected with treacherous sand banks, and jagged coral reefs . . . often only a few feet below the water level."[53] Saʿid commanded large ships of war, but he also had at his disposal countless numbers of dhows, whose bottoms would not shatter when run aground on the Gulf's banks and creeks. Larger ships of war required marines to disembark several miles from the coast and climb down rope ladders onto rowboats; conversely, dhows could simply be run ashore or at least into very shallow water. Saʿid and other Omanis understood this, but they also understood the more fundamental reasons for the Qawasim resorting to maritime violence.

Time and again, however, Sultan bin Saqr, as leader of much of the Qasimi confederation, frustrated the Omani and British imperial agendas in the Gulf. Sultan had come to lead most of the Qawasim confederation in 1803, ruling from his main base in Ras al-Khaimah. Ras al-Khaimah was a vital port city with a strategic location. Situated in a rich pearling area, it provided a potential chokepoint over the Strait of Hormuz and a door through which Saudi armies could pass when invading Oman. In fact, nearly every successful land invasion of Oman in its history had passed through Ras al-Khaimah. Ras al-Khaimah had always been a flourishing center for maritime commerce.[54] One reason Ras al-Khaimah flourished is something that is largely absent in the sources from this time: the presence of countless numbers of enslaved Africans. Arabs in Ras al-Khaimah trafficked enslaved Africans and used them to sustain the interregional trade in pearls and other local commodities, such as dates. Enslaved Africans were used as divers for the pearls and also took part in the actual shipment and trade of pearls and dates.[55]

The Qawasim and other neighboring confederations also relied on enslaved Africans in the Gulf as the core of their military and security forces—whether as more conventional land-based security forces or as fighters in maritime plunder. One scholar claimed that most seamen who fought on behalf of Rahmah bin Jabir were enslaved Africans.[56] A European observer noted that the majority of Qasimi seamen plundering shipping off the coast of western India were enslaved Africans. James Silk Buckingham concluded that enslaved Africans comprised more than half the men defending Ras al-Khaimah.[57] The degree to which enslaved Africans imbued the politics, society, and economy of Ras al-Khaimah mirrored other similar ports in the Gulf, and the ability of local Arab peoples to rely on enslaved persons lent Ras al-Khaimah a regional prestige: slaves were perhaps the most demanded form of wealth in the Gulf and the domains forming the Omani Empire.

After Sultan bin Saqr rose to power in Ras al-Khaimah, he would have used these enslaved Africans while leading a vicious campaign, marauding Omani and British shipping and using the revenue from that plunder for tasking other groups of slaves with strengthening Qasimi defensive fortifications. By the end of the first decade of the century, however, he had grown wary of his Saudi overlords. There are no precise details in any sources, but at some point toward the end of the first decade of the century, Sultan shifted his political calculations in favor of allying with Saʿid, rather than the Saudis. Sultan was also aware of the advantages coming to peoples in Oman from the formal Omani-British commercial treaty.[58]

Around 1808 Sultan thus embarked on a new strategy. He wrote to Saʿid and proposed a secret alliance. On paper, Sultan would remain allied with the Saudis, but the secret alliance would create a backdoor through which Saʿid and Sultan could communicate to decrease Qasimi attacks on Omani shipping and thus end Omani attacks against his Qasimi subjects. Saʿid agreed, but the alliance did not remain secret. Sultan's uncle, Hasan bin Rahmah, somehow discovered the ploy. Hasan notified a Saudi commander, who summoned Sultan to the Saudi capital, where they stripped him of his authority and threw him in prison.[59] But even a Saudi prison did not prevent Sultan from his political machinations. From prison, Sultan negotiated a deal with the Saudis, promising that he would ransack Omani and

British shipping even more than he already had done if they released him. The Saudis acquiesced. When they released Sultan, he fled to Yemen, hastily boarded a ship in Mocha, and sailed for Muscat. There, Sultan went straight to Saʿid. He explained that he had fled the Saudis. Pleading for Saʿid's protection, Sultan acceded to all Saʿid's demands.[60]

Sultan's escape from the Saudis and asylum in Muscat began Saʿid's process of weaving factions of the Qawasim into an Omani commercial web. By negotiating with Sultan, Saʿid was implicitly acknowledging the limits of his navy—and any navy—in dealing with asymmetric threats like attacks on shipping. He was also augmenting his own sovereignty and the power of his state by demarcating a new political and social hierarchy in the Gulf. Like his strategy of maritime plunder, Sultan's appeal to Saʿid for protection was an attempt to preserve Qasimi legitimacy in a space undergoing profound transformations caused at least in part by increasing Omani dominance in the Gulf. Yet Sultan's appeals to Saʿid were also sparked by fracturing within the Qawasim, which was never a monolithic entity. By 1809, with Sultan no longer in power, the Qawasim confederation was rupturing from internecine feuds. Essentially, it split in half between two new leaders: one ruled from Ras al-Khaimah, the other from Rams, a small adjacent port community that is today part of Ras al-Khaimah.[61] After Sultan reneged on his alliance with the Saudis, the Qawasim began a new wave of marauding Omani and British shipping, and the Saudis launched new land invasions against Oman's northern ports.[62]

With threats multiplying, and seemingly impatient with waiting on Saʿid, the British set out in 1809 on their first major expedition against Ras al-Khaimah.[63] The expedition was almost entirely a failure from the outset. Less than twenty-four hours after leaving Bombay, the entire bottom fell out of one ship, causing the explosives on board to detonate. Everyone on board died, and the ship sank. Poor weather slowed the expedition, and the sailors and marines began running out of water. When the fleet finally arrived in Muscat, the British officers in charge pleaded with Saʿid to rally his navy and assist in the attack. Saʿid agreed to provide drinking water, but he otherwise refused to cooperate because, as he told the British, their fleet was insufficient. The British fleet consisted of 1,358 sailors and marines. Saʿid advised the British that they would need at least ten thousand to subdue the port. Presciently, he warned the British that their canon would be useless because the shallow waters would prevent the ships from getting close enough for the canons to reach their targets on land.[64]

The British did not heed Sa'id's counsel. When they arrived at Ras al-Khaimah, they faced one thousand Qasimi vessels reportedly manned by twenty thousand fighters, all backed on shore by a Saudi army. The British warships, in fact, could not sail closer to shore than three miles, rendering their cannon useless. The British landed their troops anyway and faced ferocious resistance. The Saudi-Qasimi defenders maintained a withering fire as they melted into the rocky crags and canyons surrounding the port. As the Qawasim slipped away, the British burned Ras al-Khaimah and upward of fifty ships. Though the town was largely destroyed, the British were unaware that most of the Qasimi fleet had hidden from the British in the bays and inlets surrounding the port and was thus left unharmed.[65]

The 1809 British attack on Ras al-Khaimah emboldened the Qawasim. It catalyzed even more maritime plunder of British ships. Throughout the next decade, the British began appealing more to Sa'id for Omani cooperation. They asked Sa'id to use his navy for protecting their merchant vessels in the Gulf. In 1811, still reeling from the British defeat two years earlier, the British resident in the Gulf described how successful Sa'id was at maintaining security in the Gulf. He had sent ships from Bushehr, his residence, to Muscat, and he was shocked to announce that they had not encountered any threats. He concluded that the situation in the Gulf was more secure than it had been for decades, "owing in a great measure to the active part the Sultan of Muscat has taken against the [Qawasim], who he has attacked both by sea and land with very great success."[66]

In this decade of heightened tensions, both Sultan bin Saqr and Rahmah bin Jabir emerged as especially cunning entrepreneurs. While living in Muscat under Sa'id's protection, Sultan had tried convincing Sa'id that were he to be restored as leader of the Qawasim, he would halt attacks on Omani and British shipping. That Sultan was appealing in this way to Sa'id at all is remarkable. Though they had been at war with each other, by 1813 Sa'id had brought Sultan into his orbit to the extent that he convinced the British to engage Sultan as a new ally—under his supervision. Sa'id proposed a treaty between the British and Sultan, arguing that they could use him as a security bulwark against other Saudi-Qasimi threats. The British resident in the Gulf considered Sa'id's plans and then met with Sultan to discuss them. There are no details of the meeting. Soon after it, however, the resident wrote to his superiors that he would "be happy to enter into any engagements Government may wish and which I think there is little doubt of his [Sultan's] standing by."[67] Once an enemy, Sultan was now Sa'id's imperial agent. By flipping

Sultan, Sa'id had removed most of the Qawasim confederation as competition. Doing so allowed Sa'id to more carefully detect which Qasimi factions remained threats as he continued uniting competing factions within the Arabian Peninsula and Gulf into a more integrated marketplace.

Despite the success with Sultan, maritime security in the Gulf remained troubled. As he was dealing with Sultan, Sa'id had to manage rumors of a Persian invasion of Bahrain, an island he claimed as part of Omani jurisdiction but was never able to fully control. As rumors swirled, Sa'id wrote to the British warning them against cooperating with the Persians. "It will not become you to consent to act against me on this," he cautioned the governor-general in Bombay.[68] The Persians did not end up invading Bahrain. With the rumors of a Persian invasion of Bahrain quelled, in 1813 Sa'id launched his own attack on Ras al-Khaimah. The attack failed, prompting Sa'id to plan another campaign. He reported feeling more confident a second time because this time Sultan bin Saqr would be assisting him, helping bring down the Qasimi threat from within.[69] Part of the Omani strategy was thus exploiting and manipulating family splits within the Qawasim confederation—a strategy Sa'id would use in coming decades in consolidating his power in East Africa. Sa'id pressured certain Qasimi factions, such as those loyal to Sultan who had disavowed the Saudis, to take a more strategic approach by making certain political changes aimed at ensuring longer-term commercial prosperity. He convinced Sultan and his followers to temporarily relinquish their claims to Ras al-Khaimah and instead move to nearby Sharjah.[70] This made it easier for Sa'id to differentiate between Qasimi factions and delineate threats to Gulf commerce.

The British never fully grasped the intricacies of Gulf politics. First, they viewed the Qawasim as a monolith. Yet though they shared a family name, groups within the confederation had their own ambitions, loyalties, and goals. Maritime marauding was not an intrinsic characteristic of them as an ostensible pirate tribe; rather, it was an expression of how the Qawasim, as a confederation, were made up of smaller competing firms, united by a social lineage but each having its own political and economic agendas. Sultan bin Saqr once wrote to the British trying to explain this. He instructed the British on why it was illogical to categorically label the Qawasim as pirates. He noted how, in fact, the threats to their shipping came from one particular chief, his uncle Hasan bin Rahmah. He explained that Hasan was acting on orders from the Saudis, whom Sultan had long since disavowed, and confirmed his commitment to his standing alliance with the Omanis and the British.[71] In an unconnected yet serendipitous twist, at almost the same time the British resident received a letter from Rahmah bin Jabir, who also pointed out that Hasan bin Rahmah, under Saudi orders, was ordering attacks at sea. The resident considered both letters and combined the information with other sources. He then wrote a letter to Hasan.

Hasan was livid when he received the letter. He excoriated the British resident for speaking to him on behalf of Rahmah bin Jabir. "You speak to me on the authority of Rahmah bin Jabr [*sic*]," Hasan opined, demanding, "You certainly will not by any means cite his assertions in evidence against either friend or foe." He continued, explaining his hatred for Rahmah: "First because he reverted from the true faith to the worship of Idols, and secondly because he is a man of no Character, full of deceit and treachery, performing wicked actions and attributing them to others to remove the imputation of guilt from himself, and his heart too is filled with Enmity to the truth and its professions."[72] Hasan's declarations illuminate in real time the ruptures of entwined political-theological divisions within Gulf society as new institutional frameworks ordering life were taking root. In scorning Rahmah because he had turned toward "idols," Hasan was extending the basic Wahhabi tenet of accusing all non-Wahhabis as polytheists, to be not only shunned but also killed. His allegation that Rahmah was a "man of no Character" reveals how, by that time, Rahmah had turned away from his previous alliance with Hasan and the Saudis and was now focusing his allegiances elsewhere.

As represented in Hasan's letter, the Qawasim and other Gulf peoples fractured in this time according to calculations they made about political and economic legitimacy: Hasan remained allied with the Saudis, while Rahmah disavowed his previous alliance and focused his powers elsewhere. Yet perhaps more importantly, Hasan's letter prompts us to think more deeply about *how* connections were forged. It amplifies the violence inherent in connections, many of which were predicated foremost by lethal disconnections. Rooted in transnational flows of supply and demand for coffee, dates, pearls, slaves, ivory, and more, the Gulf marketplace thrived in this time *because* of violent disconnection.

In fact, Rahmah had been reveling amid the fracturing Qawasim confederacy, happily marauding at his leisure. He picked his targets carefully, however, always accommodating the Omanis and their British partners. Rahmah's campaign of selective rule breaking in this decade provides another ground-level look into the fractured complexities of Gulf politics and economy. Like Sultan bin Saqr, Rahmah had deftly navigated relationships with Oman and Britain. On one occasion, for example, the Persian vessel *Ahmad Shah* was sailing in the Gulf under the command of a British officer and therefore under British colors. Rahmah was nearby, and when he spotted the *Ahmad Shah*, he sailed toward it.

The British officer ordered his sailors to fire upon on Rahmah, but seeing the British flag, Rahmah did not respond. The *Ahmad Shah*'s sailors missed, and the ships came abreast one another. To the British officer's surprise, Rahmah appeared on deck, welcomed him aboard, and introduced him to a top deputy of the khan of Bushehr, whom Rahmah was escorting home. Rahmah knew that Bushehr was the headquarters of the British Residency for the Gulf; in the presence of the khan's deputy, Rahmah assuaged the British officer's anxieties, sneering that he would not attack any British ships since they "were only to be considered as the servants of the King of Persia."[73]

Rahmah confounded the British. For his part, Saʿid remained relatively aloof from their relations with him. In the British view, Rahmah was most definitely a problem, but he was not attacking British ships.[74] He once seized a Basran ship and, after boarding, saw that it was carrying horses belonging to the British. He at once brought the ship to shore and, knowing that his own ships were far less likely to be attacked, instructed his sailors to bring the horses directly to Bombay.[75] Already by 1810, the British had debated what to do about him. That year, the Persians had attacked Rahmah. Fighting alongside his Qasimi allies, however, Rahmah defeated the Persian fleet. Because the British residency was in Bushehr, the British resident at the time "strongly advocated" that they punish Rahmah for attacking the Persians. The Bombay government dismissed the resident's argument because Rahmah had never actually attacked a British vessel and, moreover, was at the time allied with the Saudis, with whom the British wanted to avoid conflict.[76] Yet by 1814 Rahmah had soured on his relationship with the Saudis and was trying to fortify his relationship with the Omanis and the British. In August that year, he asked the British for a formal "Pass and Certificate" to sail to Bombay and visit none other than the governor-general there. The British consented and granted him an audience in Bombay.[77]

Rahmah's appeals to the British were part of a larger strategy for courting Saʿid. After writing to the British in August 1814, in December he went to Muscat to discuss an alliance with the Omanis. Saʿid welcomed Rahmah but was also cognizant of his fickle allegiances. An Omani agent in Muscat noted that Rahmah's overtures seemed dubious, arguing that he would not abide by any alliance longer than was convenient.[78] In fact, the agent's assessment bore some truth. While in Muscat, Rahmah noticed a ship anchored in the cove under British flag. Rahmah knew the ship and insisted that it was owned by an Arab he regarded as an enemy. He vowed to Saʿid that if he were to meet that ship at sea, he would attack it, while simultaneously telling him not to worry because "if he took her, the English property and subjects onboard would be carefully forwarded to their places of destination."[79] Despite the continued strengthening of the Omani state and its closer ties with the British in the Gulf, Rahmah maintained his enterprising autonomy. Saʿid understood that Rahmah could be worked with and sometimes even allied with if he was given avenues for maintaining sources of revenue for his followers. The British struggled to understand that. "This conduct of Rahmah's appears very extraordinary," confessed the British resident, "and I am at a loss how to account for it."[80]

Until then, Rahmah had still not plundered any British-owned ships. The British assumed that their flag-based shows of sovereignty, which might have held purchase in the landed politics of Europe, would translate to the Western Indian Ocean. But the politics and economy of empire at sea were more fluid and porous than they understood, and Rahmah exploited that reality. Only a few months after concluding his alliance with Saʿid, Rahmah attacked a vessel belonging to a merchant from Basra flying under a British flag. The British resident was exasperated. "His proceedings lately appear as if he no longer stood in awe of our Power to annihilate him if we pleased," he vented. The British were furious that their bluff had been called; it seemed to them that Rahmah knew they struggled to marshal naval forces in the Gulf in any definitive capacity. "[Rahmah] seems to have forgot that his being in existence at present is owing to our forbearance," the British resident continued.[81]

Yet for all this frustration, the British still would not act against Rahmah or his followers. In January 1815, Rahmah seized the *Darabee*, a ship he recognized as the property of one of his Qasimi enemies. As in the previous incident, when Rahmah boarded the ship, he discovered its cargo was owned by the British. He confiscated all of it, loading it onto his own ship and taking it to Muscat, where he sent a dispatch to the British resident in Bushehr, telling him that the cargo would be waiting for him in Muscat, where he could go get it if he wanted it. He added that he would be keeping the *Darabee* as his own.[82]

Rahmah's boldness extended from his alliance with Saʿid, which gave him a great advantage. He began sailing throughout the Western Indian

Ocean under Saʿid's flag and pass, essentially immunized from any threat.[83] In 1817 he took the grand step of moving his own headquarters to Bushehr, adjacent to the British Residency. Rahmah had become a crucial ally for the Omani imperial order in the Gulf, and despite the protests of British officers in Bushehr, they were ordered to treat Rahmah with utter deference. One order instructed the British resident to provide him with "personal attention and friendship."[84] This infuriated the British, whose frustration grew as they watched Saʿid and his allies continue to consolidate their own interests throughout the Gulf.

SACKING RAS AL-KHAIMAH

Omani naval campaigns in the Gulf and throughout the Western Indian Ocean were certainly marked by failures. Nevertheless, numerous sources note how successfully the Omanis defended their own commercial interests against Saudi and Qasimi threats. Saʿid often personally led attacks against his enemies, suffering wounds on several occasions. The reputation of Omani aggression at sea was legendary. Once, in 1818, a British ship sailing under the protection of an Omani armed convoy stopped what the British thought was a Bahraini vessel to inspect its cargo. Upon inspection, the British realized it was an enemy Qasimi ship, and so the senior British officer turned the vessel over to his Omani counterparts in the convoy. The Qasimi sailors were so terrified of being taken prisoner by the Omanis that many of them jumped overboard to their deaths.[85]

The British, conversely, did not begin to seriously consider augmenting their naval presence in the Gulf until 1818, after settling violent uprisings in India in the Gurkha War of 1814–1815 and the Maratha War of 1817–1818.[86] By 1817 they had become fully aware of their relative weaknesses in the Gulf, and ordered all British ships in the Indian Ocean that were not otherwise engaged to sail for the Persian Gulf "for the protection of the Trade against the depredations of the Joasemees [Qasimis]."[87] As their forces grew, they began planning a major offensive against the Qawasim at Ras al-Khaimah, whose inhabitants, they alleged, were "deserving of the most exemplary punishment."[88]

The end of the second decade of the century was opportune for a new campaign against Ras al-Khaimah because the British had freed up resources and because the Saudis had been decimated by Egyptian-Ottoman invasions. The First Saudi State had mostly crumbled. The Ottomans had captured its leader, Abdullah bin Saʿud, and taken him to Istanbul, where they publicly executed him. Against the backdrop of the First Saudi State's decreasing power, British planning for the second major assault on Ras al-Khaimah was from its beginning a joint venture with Saʿid. The British did not begin planning anything until they first obtained Saʿid's cooperation and counsel. Saʿid contributed his own ships, sailors, and soldiers, and all necessary provisions, the most important being drinking water. Saʿid agreed to send three ships of war, countless more traditional armed dhows, and four thousand soldiers. To back the naval assault, Saʿid agreed to provide one thousand camels and more soldiers, not only for attacking Ras al-Khaimah by land but also for moving equipment and provisions during and after the battle.[89] More important than providing this materiel, however, Saʿid also convinced Rahmah bin Jabir and his followers to join the attack.[90]

Yet as determined as the Omanis and the British were to finally sack Ras al-Khaimah and force the surrender or subjugation of the Qawasim, both knew that managing the latter after the conflict and incorporating them into the new Omani-dominated commercial world of the Gulf was the more difficult mission. Ensuring Omani oversight of majority-Qasimi coastal areas was especially important for Saʿid. Though he benefited from the Egyptian-Ottoman victory over the Saudis, he continued to express concern that the Saudis might rebuild and continue to try to encroach upon Oman, by land or by sea. Saʿid and the British agreed that, should their attack be successful, Saʿid would administer the rebuilding of Ras al-Khaimah and managing the political and social affairs of its inhabitants.

The joint Omani-British assault was devastating. Nearly every building was razed; nearly every ship was burned. Only cattle remained standing.[91] Afterward, the *Bombay Courier* confirmed the ruin: "Houses, walls and towers have all been levelled with the dust; and the scattered fragments of buildings lie in all directions, exhibiting a most perfect scene of destruction."[92] The destruction of Ras al-Khaimah marked a new social and political order in the Gulf. After the battle, Hasan bin Rahmah submitted his unconditional surrender to the Omanis and to the British, who then began debating who was the best person to lead Ras al-Khaimah under Saʿid's supervision. Saʿid favored Sultan bin Saqr, but the British tried to cajole Saʿid into taking direct, personal control over the entire coast. Saʿid balked, most likely because he was by now casting his gaze more fully toward East Africa. The British had reasons to be concerned with placing Sultan bin Saqr back in a position of power. As they described him when debating what to do with Ras al-Khaimah after the attack, Sultan was a "much more sanguinary monster" than any other Qasimi chief. But he also, by then, was like an agent of Saʿid, and Saʿid exerted a significant degree of leverage over him. They thus agreed with Saʿid's plan to place Sultan back in charge of the port city, under Saʿid's management.[93]

Beginning with Sultan, by the end of 1820 each of the leading Arab chieftains on the coasts near Ras al-Khaimah, except for Rahmah bin Jabir, had surrendered and acceded to the British-authored General Treaty of Peace. The treaty, which called for "a cessation of plunder and piracy by land and sea," enforced a new set of rules and norms for commerce and society in the Gulf. Under the new provisions, no Qasimi peoples would be allowed to maintain vessels armed for war, and their forts were dismantled. Stipulated in the treaty, however, was that Indian ports under British control would remain open to Qasimi traders, a provision aimed at maintaining their "spirit for Commercial pursuits."[94] The treaty required all Qasimi vessels to fly under a new, clearly identifiable flag; to carry a register for identifying every vessel; and to carry a clearance pass noting the details of the vessel's itinerary.

The treaty and the violence leading up to it had ramifications beyond Arabia's coast, extending into the peninsula's interior and across the Gulf into Persia. The port of Linga, just north of the Strait of Hormuz on the Persian coast, had for nearly a century facilitated Omani-Persian commerce. It was a depot for maritime commodities but also a central node in moving peoples and their goods from Persia into the Arabian Peninsula, and from the Peninsula into Persia and Central Asia. In the years leading up to the 1819–1820 campaign against Ras al-Khaimah, many Qawasim staged their attacks from Linga. With the fall of Ras al-Khaimah, the British, from their residency in Bushehr, appealed through Persian imperial channels for greater control over Linga, but the bureaucracy in Tehran had limited power there. With the Qawasim now acceding to the 1820 Treaty of Peace and fully part of the Omani commercial orbit, Linga began losing some of its prominence as a commercial center because the Omanis funneled maritime trade away from Linga and through the nearby Persian port of Bandar Abbas, which Saʿid rented for an annual tribute from the Persian Empire.

The restructuring of social, political, and economic life in the Gulf had ramifications within Oman's mainland, as well. Just after the 1820 treaty was concluded, the Bani Bu Ali confederacy from one of Oman's interior regions began plundering Omani shipping. Their plundering of fellow Omanis was a manifestation of long-simmering disagreements over Omani dynastic rule.[95] The leaders of the Bani Bu Ali confederacy and many of their constituents had embraced Wahhabism and allied with the Saudis to augment their opposition to Saʿid. Like other Saudi allies, the Bani Bu Ali began marauding international shipping in the Gulf.[96] Their attacks were not random. As one British intelligence report indicated, the Bani Bu Ali's maritime campaign was part of a "regular and preorganized" strategy for commercial gain and political leverage.[97] Capitalizing on momentum from the recent expedition against Ras al-Khaimah, Saʿid pressured his British partners to now assist him in ending Bani Bu Ali resistance. He wrote to British forces stationed in Persia, describing how the Bani Bu Ali were in open rebellion.[98] For decades, British policy had been to abstain from involvement in landed affairs in the Arabian Peninsula. Despite this, local British officers ignored their own orders from the Crown and Foreign Office and agreed to assist him. Saʿid deliberated with his deputies on how to proceed. They decided to first send a messenger on Saʿid's behalf to the Bani Bu Ali, demanding that they end their rebellion or face a combined Omani-British invasion. The Bani Bu Ali were not cowed. They murdered the messenger, cut his body into pieces, and left them in full view as a message to Saʿid.[99]

News of this event strengthened Omani and British resolve. Certain British officers argued that despite their orders to remain uninvolved in landed affairs, the Bani Bu Ali's attacks on Omani shipping warranted their involvement because they were beginning to harm British commerce in the region. "The most ready way of accomplishing the objects of the British Government," declared one official, "would appear to be cooperating with the views of His Highness [Saʿid]."[100] The Omanis and British quickly gathered a force and mounted an attack, but they were routed and forced to retreat. In the retreat's chaos, the British field commander, Captain Thomas Perronet Thompson, saw Saʿid from a distance on the front line and rode toward him, finding that he had been wounded while saving the life of a British artilleryman. "One of the enemy fired at him so close," Thompson recalled, "that the powder entered the wound."[101]

When news of the attack's failure reached Bombay, officials were dismayed. Thompson insisted that he had joined Saʿid's expedition against the Bani Bu Ali because of their maritime violence, but Bombay officials chastised him for acting merely as an "instrument of Saiyid's internal policy."[102] The governor-general was infuriated with what he called Thompson's "disastrous expedition."[103] The British were supposed to be building their own empire, he asserted, not helping strengthen Sa'id's. He wrote to Thompson, blaming him for the failure and relieving him of duty. Thompson was ordered back to Bombay, where he faced a court-martial.[104] Despite his anger, the governor-general acknowledged that British success in the Gulf was predicated on Omani success. Though furious with Captain Thompson, the governor-general conceded that cooperating with Sa'id was "indispensable for maintaining the advantages of our success in the Gulph."[105] The British thus agreed to support Sa'id once more in attacking the Bani Bu Ali. Sa'id and the British were eager to make this second assault a devastating show of force that would deter further destabilizing actions throughout the Gulf. The attack decimated the Bani Bu Ali and ruined their village. Those who were not killed were taken prisoner; Sa'id reportedly let them starve to death in prison.[106] Before he withdrew, Sa'id issued scorched-earth orders. He commanded his troops to destroy the Bani Bu Ali's date groves—a primary food source and revenue generator—and even to divert their water canals in another direction.[107]

Sa'id reduced the Bani Bu Ali to refugees in their own homeland. After two years, the British thought they had suffered enough, having by then taken to heart the seriousness with which Sa'id regarded Gulf security. In 1823 the Court of Directors ordered the Bombay government to try to convince Sa'id to help rebuild their homes, date groves, and water canals, acknowledging the "extremity of want and misery" Sa'id had brought upon the Bani Bu Ali.[108] After initially refusing, Sa'id finally consented under pressure, while maintaining his refusal to pay for the rebuilding.[109] The British government thus agreed to pay the Bani Bu Ali a sum of 2,500 German Crowns to repair their homes, agriculture, and infrastructure.[110] As one British historian later described, however, the Bani Bu Ali were never able to recover the position they had once held in Oman.[111]

CONCLUSION

Rahmah bin Jabir never tired of his ultimate mission: subjugating Bahrain and the Al Khalifah family. By 1822 he had apparently worn out his welcome with Sa'id, who exiled him from Muscat. Sa'id sent Rahmah to the British with a letter stating that he would no longer associate with him or be answerable for his actions.[112] Rahmah found an uneasy refuge along the Persian coast, where he maintained some semblance of association with the

British. Yet in 1826, now nearly seventy years of age, mostly blind and covered in wounds, he turned on his Persian hosts.[113] He went to the British Residency and petitioned officials to assist him in fighting the Persians and, through them, the Bahrainis.

The British spurned him and, furious, Rahmah stormed from the residency. He boarded his ship the *Ghatrusha* and sailed to Bahrain, where he fired a round of cannons over the island. Bahrain mobilized its entire fleet in response. Soon a Bahraini vessel caught up with the *Ghatrusha*. The ships collided, their flanks shattering and their sails collapsing. The crews jumped aboard each other's ships, armed with anything they could find. The combat was so intense that blood ran down the decks, staining the churning sea. More Bahraini ships arrived, and Rahmah's men were overpowered. The Bahraini commander called for Rahmah and demanded his surrender. Rahmah did not answer. Carrying his eight-year-old son and accompanied by his favorite slave, Rahmah had snuck below deck. As the Bahrainis above called his name, he lit a torch and plunged it into a barrel of gunpowder. Fire burst from the ship and, when the pall of smoke lifted, everyone was dead.[114]

Rahmah's death and the troubles caused by groups like the Qawasim or the Bani Bu Ali foreshadowed similar resistance movements that would plague Sa'id in East Africa. In the Gulf as in East Africa, the troubles caused by political entrepreneurs unwittingly helped forged the Omani Empire and honed the edges of its sovereignty. Eviscerating the Bani Bu Ali for their intransigence and corralling the Qawasim into an Omani sphere of commercial and political influence had regional and global ramifications. Groups like the Qawasim had been marginalized and labeled as pirates by global historical transformations ultimately outside their control. The centralization of Omani authority in Muscat under the Al Bu Sa'id dynasty was one part of a process taking place around the world characterized by the more vertical integration of previously decentralized market spaces. "Rendering the violence and excesses of piracy concrete and recognizable, and therefore something to be shunned," concluded one historian, "was an important part of the maturation of imperial political administration."[115]

Political entrepreneurs like Rahmah bin Jabir and Sultan bin Saqr were like "many-headed hydras," resisting—and by means of resisting, ultimately strengthening—increasingly hierarchical and imperial forms of commercial and political organization.[116] Looking at the Gulf through their eyes allows us to think in more nuanced ways about empire and the inequalities inherent in the formation of capitalism. Older style histories cast expropriated peoples as without agency, eliding their resistance and, most of all, blurring how many peoples throughout the world used empire for augmenting and preserving their own pursuit of wealth.[117] More recently, however, historians have begun challenging approach, seeking to redefine empire not as a system of top-down power but rather as a continued process of negotiating dissent and managing trouble.[118] In this conceptualization, the structures and institutions of the marketplace become at once more concrete and more nebulous.

Scaling in on single interactions between Rahmah, Sultan, Saʿid, and others in this time and space illuminates fine-grained contestations over local political disputes and regional affairs. Scaled furthest out, the individual interactions traced in this chapter can be seen as parts of the far broader whole of the makings of international law: of new laws and norms being used as instruments of imperial orders, both Omani and British, in the Gulf. The Gulf marketplace after 1820 was one in which ships carried specific port clearances and cargo registries and also sailed under clearly identifiable flags. The marketplace and the social landscape of the Gulf had been violently reconfigured by joint Omani and British military expeditions. Saʿid's interactions with the British as allies in the first decades of the nineteenth century were a critical part of how the British made sense of an emerging and dynamic global system, a system in which both the Omani and British Empires came to meet in the Gulf.

Saʿid's negotiations and uses of force as well as those of the British were parts of a legal formation most completely manifest in the 1820 treaty that used law as an instrument of imperial sovereignty. While the emerging imperial sovereignty of both the Omani and British Empires ran against persons like Sultan bin Saqr or Rahmah bin Jabir, these individuals show that local circumstances and indeed personalities continued to shape an emerging international order in the first half of the nineteenth century. As Lauren Benton and Lisa Ford have shown, notions of international order across the first half of the nineteenth century ultimately stemmed from disorder, a complicated and at times haphazard process of machinations, negotiations, violence, destruction, and construction of new norms and laws like the carrying of passes, registries, and flags for all Gulf shipping.[119]

Those passes, registries, and flags became so important precisely because of the market's hydras, those peoples who caused it trouble, smuggling and marauding across the seas, bringing the market's margins to its very core.[120] The connections that characterize the broader Indian Ocean world are in part manifestations of natural structures like monsoon winds or relatively shallow coastlines. But connections are also actively forged, and as this chapter has demonstrated, the connections that were forged under Saʿid in the first decades of the nineteenth century, as in similar instances at the same time around the world, came about by the calculated, purposeful fragmentation of social existences and local structures of authority for better suiting new, market-driven imperial agendas. Through Rahmah bin Jabir or Sultan bin Saqr, we witness capitalism's "creative destruction" in action: the deliberate dismantling of established norms and systems aimed at opening new vistas of a more systematized accumulation of capital and pursuit of wealth.[121] Peering into the Gulf through the eyes of these individuals illuminates the makings of an imperial space as it unfolded in a world of paradoxes that were not necessarily contradictory; a world characterized as much by integration as by disintegration, a strengthening of ties that bind by means of that which divides.[122]

FOUR

Moving to Zanzibar

INTRODUCTION

In 1827 the American merchant Edmund Roberts was nearly destitute. As had other New England merchants in the early nineteenth century, Roberts had taken enormous risks trading in the Caribbean Sea, but each of his franchises there had failed—his ships were plundered by Spanish and French pirates. Seeking a new space of opportunity, Roberts obtained a loan to charter a vessel and sail for the Indian Ocean.[1] In October he dropped anchor in Zanzibar harbor. He had planned to stay for only ten or twelve days before returning to the United States loaded with luxuries like ivory or tortoise shells. He also sought more useful things, such as animal hides, but most especially gum copal, a product extracted from certain East African trees and used by American furniture makers as a finishing varnish. His time in Zanzibar, however, was disastrous. He was detained by local agents, who seized his goods and extorted him. He was once again on the verge of bankruptcy, yet this time he was thousands of miles from home.

In January the following year, Roberts was still stuck. Fortuitously, however, Saʿid had just arrived on the island. Commanding a war fleet, Saʿid had recently left Muscat and sailed for Mombasa, where he began what would become a decade-long siege to end resistance there to his rule. It was fortuitous that the two men were on the island at the same time. Exasperated, Roberts sent a letter to Saʿid, confessing that he was "truly overwhelmed" and in a condition of "utter ruin" from the "gross deceptions and impositions" he had suffered in Zanzibar.[2] Upon receiving the letter, Saʿid met with Roberts, addressed his grievances, and reequipped him for his return voyage to the United States. Even after returning home to New Hampshire, however, Roberts was still fuming. He had been one of the first Americans to sail the East African coast, and he wrote a letter to his senator about the experience. As he explained, the region had a thriving economy but was brimming with obstacles precluding "profitable" opportunities for Americans.[3] Many years after his initial voyage, he recalled that commerce had been "on a most precarious footing, subject to every species of imposition which avarice might think proper to inflict."[4]

By 1850 Atlantic merchants like Roberts found Zanzibar transformed. This tiny island—less than 650 square miles—was by then home to three foreign consulates, a magnet for merchants and mariners from around the world. The Omani-Zanzibari chronicler Al-Mughairi was neither incorrect nor exuding bias when he claimed that Saʿid presided over the founding of a "new Zanzibar."[5] Indeed, by 1850 Zanzibar had become a center of global oceanic commerce and the most important commercial center in East Africa. Driving this transformation were Omanis, South Asians, and some East Africans who went to Zanzibar and transformed it from a densely forested island whose inhabitants generally led quiet lives of fishing and subsistence agriculture to a major commercial center where its elites had expropriated their ways to the "peak of luxury."[6] Zanzibar's rise was predicated by violent disconnections—changes beginning with the physical landscape of the island, whose inhabitants' bodies and lands were commodified as part of a new landed aristocracy.

Zanzibar had not been a significant center for Indian Ocean commerce until the latter decades of the eighteenth century and especially the beginning of the nineteenth century, when Omani leaders in Muscat appointed the Shivji family firm to manage trade and customs duties there. Three centuries earlier, when the navigator and expert on Indian Ocean geography and commerce Ibn Majid mapped out East Africa's coast, he stated that the best-known ports were Mogadishu, Barawa, Mombasa, and Mozambique.[7] He did not mention Zanzibar in his account. As David Bresnahan has shown, already by 1500 Mombasa was the most prosperous and powerful place along East Africa's coast, with powerful reciprocal relationships with inland areas as well.[8] The making of modern Zanzibar and its place in a global oceanic marketplace was affected by local, interregional, and global trends. Yet Zanzibar's rise and its place as the capital of the Omani Empire was sparked in the most immediate sense by Saʿid's initial failures in Mombasa and continued resistance to his rule there until 1837.

Once Saʿid had arrived in Zanzibar, however, its development into a transoceanic, interhemispheric center of global commerce was catalyzed by certain specific policies. After the French diplomat and naval officer Charles Guillain met with Saʿid in the 1840s, he wrote to his superiors in Paris describing "certain administrative and fiscal arrangements" Saʿid had made that, in only a matter of years, had launched Zanzibar onto a "far more" prosperous plane than any other place in the Indian Ocean.[9] The arrangements Saʿid made in Zanzibar were not necessarily new ideas, nor were they entirely his own. Each can be situated within a longer arc of Indian Ocean history. Though sparked by the agencies of individuals and energized by the increasing arrivals of European and American merchants, each arrangement nevertheless bore Saʿid's imprint.

As sovereign Saʿid presided over the establishment of a political system in Zanzibar, with ramifications that also shaped towns and ports throughout East Africa. This political system was rooted in mitigating risk to create incentivizing institutions for facilitating private enterprise and folding Atlantic merchants into the Omani commercial web. While Zanzibar's rise was due in part to structural forces—whether droughts in South Asia or Arabia that pushed people to East Africa or economic downturns in New England—it was also tied up with local political conditions of possibility emanating from state power delegated to Jairam, the expropriation of local Zanzibaris, and the enslavement of countless others.

As Roberts's miserable first experience in Zanzibar demonstrated, Saʿid, as a person vested with public power, had to establish and enforce certain norms and institutions more effective for transoceanic exchange. His first task was safeguarding Atlantic merchants from the hazards of opportunism. That meant using his power to enforce new modes of conduct for his own subjects. Roberts was not the only American entrepreneur to face trouble in East Africa. While Roberts was detained in Zanzibar, another American vessel was in Lamu when they encountered an Omani dhow from Sur. The Omanis boasted, without any fear of reprisals, that their intention had been to plunder the American vessel and a nearby French slaving vessel. As the American warned, everyone in the region had to "be on their guard" from Omani buccaneers.[10] Saʿid's first goal in Zanzibar was thus mitigating risk to incentivize more American and European investment in the region, but attracting foreign merchants was only one part of his strategic puzzle: Saʿid not only had to create an institutional framework for unifying his domains into a marketplace with defined and clearly understood rules, but he also had to facilitate the abilities of foreign merchants to make their return journeys home.[11] Looking at this process through Saʿid's eyes allows us to see how circulation—a culmination of journeys and return journeys—was forged through violence, strategic generosity, political cunning, diplomacy, and even a degree of gambling on the future. And at the core of this entire process and, in a sense, the entire worldwide historical moment, was the relatively new awareness that time itself had become money.

THE MOVE TO ZANZIBAR

Saʿid did not choose Zanzibar to be the empire's capital. The Mazruʿi of Mombasa chose it for him. For centuries, Omanis had migrated to East Africa, ingratiating themselves with local communities and their flourishing maritime-oriented markets. After 1698, when the Yaʿrubi vanquished the Portuguese in Mombasa, they installed the Mazruʿi, a distinguished Omani family, as their proxies there.[12] Having Omani proxies governing Mombasa increased the rate of Omani migration to East Africa, which began attracting the interest of others, especially South Asians. For Omanis, South Asians, and indeed many Africans, the coasts of East Africa were a "staging ground" for intertwined commercial and political aspirations.[13] Mombasa was not just an oceanic-facing port city; it was connected with East Africa's inland and non-Swahili-speaking East Africans, especially Mijikenda speakers. Over the past thousand years Mijikenda speakers in the environs surrounding Mombasa had acted as gatekeepers between the world of coast and interior, mediating the flow of profitable commodities like ivory and gum copal through Mombasa's port.[14]

Once installed in Mombasa, the Mazruʿi were part of a broad process whereby much of East Africa's trade—especially human trafficking—began shifting north from Mozambique toward Mombasa and then to Zanzibar. Saʿid began his siege of Mombasa to end Mazruʿi resistance to his rule in 1827, but the Mazruʿi had for more than a century been relatively autonomous. The negotiations and disputes between the Mazruʿi in Mombasa and the Al Bu Saʿid in Muscat were part of the empire's manifestation. The divergent goals and actions of peoples like the Mazruʿi—and as David Bresnahan showed, their Mijikenda-speaking counterparts—contained options for Omani expansion and forced Saʿid to look elsewhere for a capital in East Africa.

By the time Saʿid arrived in Mombasa harbor with his fleet of warships in 1827, Mombasa was ensconced as a commercial powerhouse. The Mazruʿi were there, perched in their domineering Fort Jesus, atop a global transformation in which African markets and peoples, including the enslaved, were becoming even more central to the world economy. Consumer demand throughout the Atlantic for products from Africa like gum copal or ivory was skyrocketing, but so too were East African demands for things like American cotton and brass wire. As more people in England and New England began building pianos with ivory keys or spicing their fruit cakes with cloves, Africans, Arabs, and South Asians began reformulating the lives of enslaved humans and routes for human trafficking to sustain, on a global scale, these commercial and social changes. Saʿid was a part of this moment, and he gave it a more tangible political shape.

Bresnahan illuminated how laying siege to and ultimately absorbing Mombasa into the Omani imperial orbit was not merely absorbing the port city itself. Mombasa was fundamentally interconnected with significant expanses of inner regions of East Africa, not only in commercial networks but also in terms of social and cultural practices. Seizing Mombasa did not give Saʿid total control, but it allowed him to more thoroughly channel trade through Zanzibar, centralizing customs revenue. The consolidation of Omani sovereignty in East Africa was thus not so much about holding clearly demarcated territory as it was geared toward using Omani-appointed Indian customs officials to corral already existing individual markets into a centralized marketplace. Swinging these East African markets into the Omani commercial orbit was done through a mixture of coercion and cajoling. In the first decades of his rule, nearly every Omani settler community in East Africa opposed Saʿid, each seeking in its own way to carve out its autonomy and capitalize on the region's surging importance for global trade.[15] Yet by the time Saʿid arrived in Zanzibar in 1828, he and his sailors and soldiers had such a reputation for brutality in warfighting that sometimes negotiations were not necessary. In 1828, as Saʿid and his fleet sailed back to Muscat from Zanzibar, they ransacked Mogadishu. In the fighting, a senior Omani officer was killed. Guillain later reported that the people of Mogadishu were so fearful of Saʿid's response to the death of one of his senior officers that they immediately dispatched a messenger to him volunteering their unconditional surrender.[16]

The situation in Mombasa was different from that in Mogadishu, however, because it was ruled by Omani proxies, who had for many years been exploring the limits of their own political entrepreneurship, testing the boundaries of Saʿid's power. In 1814 a new Mazruʿi governor, Abdullah bin Ahmad, came to power. According to several local sources, he sent a package to Saʿid in Muscat containing a coat of chain mail armor, gunpowder, and musket balls—apparently a challenge to Saʿid, daring him to fight.[17] The Mazruʿi continued flaunting their autonomy into the next decade. In 1823, while Saʿid's attention was still predominantly fixed on Gulf security, they appealed to a visiting British officer, Captain William Owen, betting that they could pit the British against Saʿid and establish their autonomy under British protection.[18] They convinced Owen that Mombasa would be the ideal headquarters for British interests in the region, and in 1824 Owen raised the British flag over Fort Jesus. When the news reached Muscat, Saʿid was irate. In protest, he skipped over the entire Bombay government and wrote directly to the king of England. He insisted that the British had breached his trust, a potentially unforgiveable offense because it flouted his sovereignty in a key area of Oman's historical sphere of influence.[19] The king instructed the British resident in the Gulf to immediately "endeavor to remove any bad impression which that affair might have produced on the mind of His Highness the Imaum of Muscat [Saʿid]."[20] The Bombay government stripped Captain Owen of his post and essentially forced him to retire.[21]

Saʿid allowed the British to evacuate Mombasa while he planned his siege. His plan centered on Shivji Topan, a Gujarati tycoon living in Muscat. Shivji agreed to provide ships and to finance Saʿid's campaign, a move that cemented a relationship that would, in only a few years, become pivotal to Zanzibar's flourishing.[22] Armed now with Shivji's assistance, Saʿid admitted his feeling that "mild measures" would never compel the Mazruʿi to accept his sovereignty. The British—themselves no strangers to violence—feared what Saʿid would do. "I am seriously apprehensive that the Imaum of Muscat will forcibly take possession and put to the sword the whole of the Inhabitants," professed one official.[23] In1827 Saʿid sailed for Mombasa, arriving in its harbor with a fleet including the colossal seventy-four-gun *Liverpool* and the sixty-four-gun *Shah Allam*, meaning, in Persian, "King of the World." Saʿid's fleet was a display of overwhelming force given the relatively meager defenses of the Mazruʿi. Yet despite Saʿid's fleet and the Mazruʿi's lack of offensive capabilities, Fort Jesus was virtually indomitable. By no measure did Saʿid have a monopoly on force. He had kept his plans secret, therefore, to surprise the people of Mombasa and add to the shock of his arrival.[24]

When the fleet arrived in the harbor below Fort Jesus, Saʿid did not bombard the fort. Instead, he dispatched a negotiator who brought the Mazruʿi leaders four possible conditions for their surrender, asking them to choose one.[25] The first condition stipulated that the Mazruʿi could evacuate Fort

Jesus and hand it over to Saʿid but continue residing in Mombasa as local authorities collecting revenues. The second stipulated that Saʿid would pay the Mazruʿi 10,000 rials annually for them to resettle elsewhere. The third and fourth conditions stipulated that, should they leave Mombasa entirely, Saʿid would grant them authority to govern the nearby islands of either Pemba or Lamu. Saʿid concluded his overture by confirming that, should the Mazruʿi evacuate the fort and agree to one of his conditions, "enmity will never exist between you and us." Should they reject his overtures, however, Saʿid declared that, just as his predecessors had defeated the Portuguese, he would vanquish the Mazruʿi.[26]

The Mazruʿi were uncowed. They refused to hand over Fort Jesus, beginning a decade-long siege of the port. Saʿid assaulted the fort several times during the following decade, but each attack failed. In fact, when Mombasa did finally fall in 1837, it was not because of anything having to do with Saʿid and his navy; rather, it was mostly because a plague had spread through Mombasa and neighboring communities, decimating the populations. Certainly the siege compounded the stress of the plague, and by 1837 the Mazruʿi family had broken into quarreling factions. One faction, devastated at the loss of their commercial prosperity, sailed to Muscat and met with Saʿid. They apprised him of the dire situation in Mombasa and convinced him to once again assault the fort. In secret, they planned with Saʿid that, before his assault, they would place some of their own faction's loyalists inside the fort to offer its surrender. After taking Mombasa, Saʿid gathered the leading men of the Mazruʿi, threw them aboard one of his ships, and took them to the Gulf, where he left them to die in prison.[27]

Imprisoning and killing the Mazruʿi might have opened Mombasa and related ports such as Lamu, Kilwa, and Pemba to Saʿid's sovereignty, but Saʿid had to establish policies to motivate cooperative behavior among different parties for participating in a unified commercial system, from Mombasa north to Muscat. For centuries Mombasa had been home to thriving mercantile communities, and Saʿid's primary goal was thus reviving their roles in a mutually dependent commercial arena. Aside from the leaders of the rebellion he imprisoned and killed, Saʿid allowed the people of Mombasa to keep their own local leaders and administrative systems, even sending them judges and jurists to interpret legal matters according to their own customs.[28] In proclamations to the people of Mombasa, Saʿid stressed a collective, shared nature of what it meant to be "in obedience" (*fī ṭāʿa*) to him.[29]

Being in obedience to Saʿid meant partaking in a shared set of rules that bound the empire into an oceanic marketplace. The seizure of Mombasa reflects an intensification of these connections and a manifestation of those rules. In his usual poetic language, Saʿid expressed to the Mazruʿit that a single, ostensibly isolated act of resisting a local edict in Mombasa, such as not paying a required duty to the Omani-appointed customs master, could affect the entire marketplace. One person's act in Mombasa could prevent an Atlantic merchant in Zanzibar from making a deal and thus also influence commercial flows across the world. Not paying a customs fee in Mombasa would not just deprive the Omani Empire of revenue for things like maintaining a navy, it could also hurt the entrepreneurial interests of peoples connected across oceans, from African caravan leaders and wage workers who gathered products like gum copal, to American entrepreneurs like Edmund Roberts acting as minority middlemen, to woodworkers in Boston who used it as a varnish.

As Saʿid stressed to the people of Mombasa, then, in this emerging oceanic marketplace, people had to bear in mind the collective. Here, connectivity was not a scholar's abstraction but was actually spelled out in Saʿid's proclamations to the Mazruʿi. Private wealth was not entirely private. In his proclamations to the people of Mombasa, Saʿid articulated this reality. He spoke in terms wealth—*māl*—and alluded to the interconnected social, legal, political, and commercial chains of interactions that constituted wealth in the first place: something that happened in one part of the empire's orbit would inevitably affect other parts; *māl* in one corner of the empire was ultimately tied up with *māl* everywhere else in the empire and, indeed, the world.[30]

Saʿid was generally uninterested in involving himself in local administrative matters, whether in Muscat or Mombasa, instead turning his eyes more toward cultivating global commercial partnerships. In 1837 he wrote to the people of Mombasa, declaring that they would remain "representatives of their people." He continued, in his lyrical Arabic:

> And no one may infringe upon their status, so long as we live, so long as their children live, and the children of theirs. Their taxes remain as before. If one of their own commits a crime, they alone are responsible for justice—not my representative there (*wālī*). And anyone who follows them will be safe, and their capital (*amwālahum*) secure. Anyone who is hostile toward them is also hostile toward us. They are responsible for policing their own and for pardoning their own. In local affairs, my representative is equal to them.

And if my representative ceases to remain in their favor, they may dismiss him, and I will not object.[31]

Saʿid's proclamation illuminates, however implicitly, an understanding of connectivity and the places of relatively autonomous communities within a larger, connected entity. Abstaining from becoming overly involved in local, landed affairs was not so much an innovation as it was a magnification of long-running trends in Indian Ocean economy and society, where states generally did not intervene in the administration of mercantile communities so long as the general structures of a commercial system remained intact.[32] The nature of Saʿid's sovereignty was thus bound up with the success of his customs officials and other agents throughout his domains, who collected duties and funneled revenue and trade to Zanzibar. This strategy fomented the emergence in Zanzibar of a monied elite who commanded the market and benefited from demanding the highest prices from Atlantic merchants. The establishment of this system by means of both violence and negotiation reveals a complicated imperial structure, one not necessarily rooted in a monopoly on violence, no matter how violent it was. It helps us see past triumphalist notions of empire—Omani or otherwise—and bring to light how empire was characterized as much by trouble as by success. As one historian writing about a similar empire continents away put it, some empires, like the Omani Empire, were social, political, and economic structures woven by "complex webs of cooperation, coercion, extortion, and dependence."[33]

Saʿid's declarations for the people of Mombasa highlight even more about the empire's structures of power and dependence. His relatively deferential tone to the people of Mombasa can be interpreted as an acknowledgment of the power East African peoples had held for centuries over oceanic commerce in the Western Indian Ocean. His statements are part of a longer arc of region formation, a deeper contour of political, social, and economic history in which East Africans—coastal or interior peoples—significantly influenced interregional Indian Ocean affairs. One reason the Portuguese had struggled to maintain a footing in Mombasa was not only the Portuguese Empire's own political problems, overstretched resources, or the efficacy of Omani naval onslaughts, but also because the Portuguese had never learned to enculturate themselves into East African economy and society. In many ways, when Saʿid negotiated with the leading tribes of Mombasa or the Mazruʿi, he was also negotiating with the peoples who were connected to Mombasa through tributary relationships, such as Mijikenda speakers.

Through political affiliations and commercial relationships, wrote Bresnahan, Mijikenda-speaking peoples and others "helped establish the legitimacy of governing authorities in Mombasa and other coastal towns."[34]

One component in East African society that foreign peoples—whether traders or Omani leaders seeking to exert suzerainty—had to abide by to be successful was a long-refined set of social and economic rituals known as *heshima* in Swahili or *eshima or ishima* in Mijikenda languages. As Bresnahan wrote, heshima is an Arabic loanword in Swahili. In its original Arabic, it meant diffidence, timidity, or shame. But adopted in Swahili, heshima referred to tributary practices of gift giving and tribute tied to understandings and manifestations of political power and autonomy. Saʿid did not use the word *heshima* in his proclamations to the people of Mombasa, but this shared Arabic and Swahili concept can be read alongside Saʿid's lesson for Guillain that began this book—that there was a particular way in this Indian Ocean world of arriving at any object desired. Indeed, this was a lesson that many Europeans and Americans learned as they conducted their affairs with East African peoples. When the German missionary Johan Ludwig Krapf arrived in Mombasa in 1844 to begin a trek throughout East Africa's interior regions, he witnessed this firsthand. The ritual performances tied to heshima that he witnessed were something "all the great merchants" adhered to because if they did not properly "honor" local East African peoples, they were "liable to be robbed" or killed.[35] To be clear, in his proclamations and style of governance with the people of Mombasa Saʿid was not doing heshima. But he was reflecting an understanding of broader political and social realities whereby various parts of the empire, especially in East Africa, remained generally autonomous and in positions of influence so long as they abided by certain commercial stipulations, most especially by paying required customs duties. Indeed, whenever foreign powers arrived in Mombasa or its connected environs, they adopted existing practices of various forms of tribute to cement their relationships with the mainland.[36]

Although Mombasa was Saʿid's primary choice for his East African capital, Zanzibar had its own advantages. By the late eighteenth century, Zanzibar had been growing in commercial importance almost exclusively because of French demand for enslaved humans. The Omanis had capitalized upon this situation by appointing a governor in Zanzibar to begin remaking the island into a waystation for human trafficking, especially for the French. When Saʿid began focusing his attention on Zanzibar after 1828 and made it his capital in 1832, he sought to open trade there by means of restricting it.

It was this control over the Zanzibari market, and the monopoly held by his customs master, that propelled Zanzibar's rise as a fulcrum in nineteenth-century global commerce. From Muscat, Omanis already exerted some degree of suzerainty over Zanzibar in the first decade of the nineteenth century. In 1804 a French naval officer responsible for trafficking enslaved humans to Bourbon visited the island. He described how the island was under the ultimate sovereignty of the "Prince of Muscat," but that administration on the island was divided between different deputies—who were slaves themselves—responsible for the island's defenses, civil affairs, and commercial affairs. The commercial governor in charge of customs, an enslaved man named Yaqut, frequently allied with a settlement of powerful Omanis from the Al-Harthi confederation to extort foreigners, especially the French.[37] In 1807, at only sixteen years of age, Saʿid was already aware of the importance Oman's monopoly on human trafficking with French consumers; one of his first diplomatic acts was signing a treaty for regularizing this trade with Ile de France.[38]

While Saʿid was aware of Zanzibar's commercial potential, structural factors also contributed to Zanzibar's rise. As leisured, monied classes emerged in the Atlantic, their worlds became increasingly entwined with the Indian Ocean because of their newfound obsession with ivory and cloves. Consumerism in the Atlantic ran parallel to consumerism—and production—in the Indian Ocean. The Gulf's dates and pearls remained important, but more and more global consumerism was driven by East Africa.[39] These changes were not mere abstractions; Saʿid, like others, was aware of them. Around 1833 he explained to one of his deputies that the British were pressuring him to remain in the Gulf to maintain security. As he described, however, things had become "very different" for him, and for many other Omanis as well. He noted that his revenues in Muscat were small compared to his expenses, and explained that he would soon leave Muscat behind and set out for East Africa.[40]

Saʿid did not name Atlantic consumerism for ivory and dates as a factor pushing him to resettle in East Africa, but his migration there, alongside countless other Arabs, South Asians, and others, was part of this oceanic shift. But it was not just Atlantic consumerism. As more Americans began arriving in East Africa, East Africans spurred a thriving economy for buying American products, like cotton textiles and brass wire. East Africans' demands for American goods added to human trafficking and the export of products like cloves and ivory to make the East African commercial space a center of the transoceanic economy at the time. Saʿid's emigration to Zanzibar was different from seasonal, monsoon-based voyages of the past. Saʿid was a settler in Zanzibar. Mobility was thus not the end, it was the means for ultimately settling. This is not to say that he or his fellow Omanis never returned home, nor that they necessarily became East African; rather, it hints at a different element of this historical moment. As will be shown, Indian Ocean peoples like Saʿid were using wealth to act upon the privilege of being immobile, of putting down roots and transcending the environmental rhythms of historically monsoon-based commerce and becoming aristocrats in a new land, as shown in chapter 6.

Some of the structural factors pulling peoples like Saʿid toward Zanzibar were environmental. Oman's mainland is generally arid. For centuries the Omanis had maintained an intricate system of water canals (*aflaj*) for drinking and irrigation; however, as successful as the *aflaj* system was, it sustained modest relatively modest economies and lifestyles. Many Omanis went to East Africa as they were pushed out of their homes by severe droughts that struck Oman in the first half of the nineteenth century.[41] Structural factors also influenced the emigration of South Asians to Zanzibar. Political turmoil ravaged the Kachchh region for the first two decades of the century. Western India was also struck by droughts, leading to widespread crop failures. The drought in Kachchh was so disastrous that in just one year, 1823, 20 percent of the region's population fled.[42]

As Omanis and Kachchhis emigrated to Zanzibar, the island's geography facilitated their success. Naturally deep and sheltered, the harbor provided a safe anchorage point for ships in every month of the year, unlike other Indian Ocean harbors whose waters often fluctuated based on monsoons and other environmental factors. The island was self-sufficient in drinking water and many food staples, especially fruit, vegetables, and grain. Perhaps most important, ships could regularly traverse the narrow stretch between Zanzibar and the mainland anytime, without having to rely on monsoon winds. Saʿid and his web of governors, mercenaries, and customs officials could funnel international trade through the island, fostering the emergence of Omani, African, and South Asian elites to monopolize the greatest returns from newly arriving European and American entrepreneurs.

Zanzibar was also physically attractive. Though some Europeans and Americans complained about what seemed to them a chaotic layout of certain parts of Zanzibar town, the weather was advantageous for their health. Many Atlantic peoples struggled in Muscat; the British could barely keep their officials alive. Edmund Roberts recalled of Muscat: "The heat is excessive. . . . Every one complained of its suffocating effects, the perspiration poured from the body like rain, and the strength was at once prostrate."[43] Conversely, for many foreigners—Omani or otherwise—Zanzibar was an ideal space for pursuing their growing commercial aspirations. The natural beauty and relative ease of life were often the first things foreigners commented on when arriving.[44] One young American sailor from Salem, having recently departed the island, reminisced in a letter to his family: "I have often wished myself back in Zanzibar. To tell the truth, I never felt so lonesome or homesick as I did on leaving that place."[45] This sailor was not alone. A popular verse recited in Zanzibar in the nineteenth century effused: "She has but one flaw / that is, she makes a foreigner forget of home."[46]

FIXING CUSTOMS

It became easier for foreigners to forget home in Zanzibar because, under Saʿid, it became a space for people to transcend expectations of modest lives. This was especially true for Omanis, particularly those from the interior. In the 1770s there were about three hundred Omanis in Zanzibar. By 1819 there were about one thousand, and by 1850 about five thousand.[47] These Omanis served as brokers and portfolio managers for webs of family and commercial networks emanating from Zanzibar deep into the African continent. But underwriting their success and indeed sustaining it was neither Saʿid nor any other Omani, but rather enterprising tycoons from Gujarat in western India.

"Of all classes connected with the trade of East Africa," concluded a British official in 1873, "there is none more influential than the natives of India.[48] This official was not overstating things. The position of South Asian merchants and financiers in Omani domains had been fostered by Omani state policies legally protecting them as minorities. Over the past two centuries, Omani leaders had fostered the emergence of an elite Indian merchant class acting as financiers, merchants, and imperial bureaucrats. As they arrived in East Africa, many Indians focused on Zanzibar, where they became especially wealthy from trafficking enslaved humans to the French. Indians used their private equity and intergenerational wealth to leverage political influence with the Al Bu Saʿid. Saʿid was not the first Omani leader to rely on Indian financiers for outfitting his military expeditions in East Africa.

In the 1780s, when Ahmad bin Saʿid sought to evict the Portuguese from their last remaining holdouts, he borrowed capital and credit from an Indian firm in Muscat. Ahmad's successors continued to rely on Indians in East Africa. Saʿid formalized the Omani-Indian financial relationship in Zanzibar. By the midpoint of the nineteenth century, the British explorer Richard Burton was thus confidently able to claim that sure profits were "commanded only by the Banyan [Indian] system."[49]

As Saʿid signed commercial treaties with the United States, Britain, and France, he formalized the Omani-Indian nexus even more, not only by fixing customs at a certain rate to be paid exclusively to one firm, but also by including certain provisions that encouraged those Atlantic merchants to do almost all their business in Zanzibar. This meant that a cadre of Atlantic merchants was there, ready to purchase East African exports. It also helped establisha central place that voracious East African consumers could go to purchase the Atlantic commodities they demanded for sustaining their own consumer tastes and preferences. Having made Zanzibar his official capital in 1832, Saʿid moved his royal court and family there in 1840. By that time the Indian entrepreneur Jairam Shivji was Saʿid's customs master and held significant influence over Saʿid. Jairam was a Bhatia, a mercantile community and caste coming primarily from Gujarat, Sindh, and Punjab. Jairam was born in 1792 in the port of Kachchh in Gujarat, a province in present-day western India. His father, Shivji Topan, had moved his family firm from Kachchh to Muscat in the previous century. Shivji had sailed with Ahmad bin Saʿid in 1785 to reassert Omani influence in East Africa, providing Ahmad with fast cash for settling political disputes, paying mercenaries, repairing and outfitting ships, and more.

For Shivji, the region was bursting with potential. The Omanis were gradually asserting firmer control, mitigating risks to property, lines of credit, and personal safety. Omani leaders maintained protections for religious and ethnic minorities carrying on business in the empire. Perhaps most important for Shivji, however, was East African consumerism. East Africans had voracious and discerning demands for certain commodities such as beads and textiles. They used these products to augment cultural norms and practices, especially for delineating identities and socioeconomic statuses. With increasing numbers of Atlantic merchants arriving in East Africa, Shivji seized the moment and moved his family to Zanzibar. By 1804 when Saʿid's father died, the Al Bu Saʿid family was deeply in debt to Shivji's firm. Saʿid leaned into this debt, continuing like his predecessors.

The full weight of this debt would be neither tallied nor renumerated until after Saʿid died.[50] As with Saʿid's own debt, each of the political acts that formalized commerce in the Omani Empire carried Saʿid bin Sultan's name, but signing his name was predicated on the existence of a commercial web already woven, to a large extent, by the Shivji family and their compatriots in East Africa and the Gulf.

Saʿid's meeting with Edmund Roberts in Zanzibar in 1828 was fortuitous. It was also a strategic boon. It prompted the letters Roberts wrote to his senator that would culminate in his mission to ratify a treaty with Saʿid, but it also provided a great deal of information for Saʿid to better understand the frustrations of international merchants in Zanzibar and the rest of East Africa. For several decades prior to that meeting, most commercial transactions in Zanzibar were handled by an Omani-appointed local governor. The most notable Zanzibari governor was an enslaved man named Yaqut.[51] Though nominally subservient to Saʿid, Yaqut capitalized on the absence of Omani leaders in the arena and the relatively weak degree of control they could exert from Muscat. He extorted visiting merchants at will.[52] When Saʿid moved his capital to Zanzibar, among his first policy decisions was to remove commercial transactions from the realm of the governor and instead give control of them, including customs, to a private family firm. Referred to as "tax farming," this practice was not Saʿid's innovation, but it was part of transforming the thriving yet disparate oceanic markets stretching from Zanzibar north to the Gulf into a single coherent marketplace.

In 1835 the Shivji Topan family firm won the contract for farming customs in Zanzibar. Under this establishment, the Shivji firm, by then run by the eldest son Jairam, was entitled to all profits from customs paid in Zanzibar, and in turn paid an annual sum of 84,000 Maria Theresa dollars (MTDs) to Saʿid, who used this annual sum for administering the empire.[53] Saʿid established a fixed customs fee of 5 percent to be paid by all merchants selling their goods at any port throughout the Omani Empire.[54] Saʿid thus expected Jairam to place his own deputies at ports along the coast for collecting these fees and funneling them back to Zanzibar. By all accounts, this made Jairam tremendously powerful. It also cemented a commercial partnership between Saʿid and Jairam as a pivotal layer in the empire's foundation. Jairam's prestige was not just rooted in the social capital he accrued from having been appointed by Saʿid. It was also rooted in the fact that Saʿid was deeply in debt to him. Saʿid's power as leader of the Omani Empire stemmed from his abilities to negotiate between factions, to marshal force when needed, and to provide opportunities for peoples within his domains to improve their own economic status; it did not come from his own wealth. In fact, aside from the stipulated annual amount he was required to pay Saʿid in return for his position to farm the customs, Jairam controlled much of Saʿid's access to cash and credit. Thus the British consul was not overstating the case when he wrote to his superiors that Saʿid was "entirely dependent on his [Jairam's] good-will for any money he requires" and that "scarcely a dollar reaches His Highness [Saʿid] or any of his family except through him [Jairam]."[55]

Before this arrangement, customs fees differed between ports; often, they even differed within the same port, as different local traders sought to extort foreigners. Roberts recalled, for example, how American ship captains had been forced to pay 7.5 percent on both imports and exports, in addition to docking fees and other bribes.[56] Fixing the customs fee was vital for mitigating risk and for creating incentive. Instead of keeping cash for paying bribes and arbitrary fees when sailing to the Indian Ocean, Atlantic merchants could instead invest that cash in more commodities for selling upon arrival. Once they arrived, rather than a few actors taking their funds through extortion, with fixed customs fees Atlantic merchants had more funds generally available for catalyzing exchanges among local African, Arab, and South Asian consumers and for purchasing their exports. Enacting a fixed fee incentivized more Atlantic merchants to bet on the success of what remained a dangerous transoceanic journey. At least once merchants and goods arrived in East Africa, Saʿid was aware of those dangers, and they were something he actively sought to mitigate. Doing so provided him and other elites more commercial opportunities, which were all tied up in a pretext for him to further consolidate his authority throughout the empire.

Though customs were delegated to Jairam, Saʿid still needed to maintain supervision, often by projecting force.[57] On one occasion in 1839, the American consul Richard Waters was preparing for a trading voyage from Zanzibar to Barawa, in present-day Somalia. Saʿid dispatched a message in advance to the people, instructing them to "respect and look out for him, and assist him in everything in your power." He declared: "Take notice: you must not demand anything [extra] on account of duties, and if you do take anything, I will hold you responsible."[58] This was not an empty threat. Two years later, in response to local traders there refuting his orders and extorting visiting merchants, Saʿid launched an attack against people living near Barawa with several ships of war and nearly five thousand soldiers.[59]

Saʿid and Jairam worked in tandem. Their entwined roles structured the empire and created political conditions of possibility by acting like a reserve bank. Jairam had license to place deputies from Zanzibar north to the Gulf, and those deputies were tasked with funneling customs revenues back to Zanzibar. As the second American consul in Zanzibar, Charles Ward, observed, Jairam's contract to farm the empire's customs "embraces Zanzibar and the whole extent of his [Saʿid's] domains in East Africa. The Custom master [Jairam] has his revenue officers in every town and village and the duties on the coast are regulated by him, and is all included in the Zanzibar district."[60] Using varying combinations of force and guile, Saʿid used state power to ensure that the institution of Jairam's customs firm remained strong. Yet neither Jairam nor Saʿid was trying to ensure equitable competition. They were both commanding competition, consolidating the positions of elites in the empire at the apex of the trading hierarchy. Saʿid's appointment of Jairam and the increasingly close bonds, in the very literal sense of debt and capital ventures, that held them together were manifestations of connected regional economies becoming part of a globally oriented marketplace.

The more wealth Jairam and his deputies accrued, the more established his firm became in Zanzibar. Jairam's success ensured for Saʿid a steady annual revenue. Jairam used his position to form a vast business intelligence network, fostering his ability to command the market with firsthand knowledge of shifting currents in supply and demand.[61] Like a central bank, he could almost single-handedly affect prices throughout the Western Indian Ocean. Refuse to comply with Jairam's terms, noted one American merchant, and "with doing little or nothing" he would drive one from the market.[62] Jairam could bend the market to his whims because he had the most liquid assets for extending near-instantaneous lines of credit. Having so many people indebted to him allowed him to gather and store the finest grades of ivory, copal, tortoise shells, animal hides, and other commodities. He helped negotiate the best prices for local East African consumers for the commodities they wanted, especially American beads, cotton cloth, brass wire, and muskets. Acting in conjunction with Saʿid's overall imperial parameters, Jairam established the daily rules of the commercial game.

Jairam and his firm were understood this way in this time by those doing business in the Omani Empire. Jairam was known throughout the Western Indian Ocean. "His fortune and his position give him immense credit," described Guillain, "which, in turn, make him the supreme regulator of the country's commercial transactions."[63] Jairam's prestige and capacity for affecting commerce throughout the Omani Empire flipped the market on its conventional head. As Braudel argued, marketplaces were not necessarily forged through equitable competition.[64] This marketplace was forged by commanding competition, by so completely controlling capital and wealth that foreign merchants had no choice but to play by Jairam's rules. Jairam made this clear. He understood his role in this way. He once remarked to Guillain that although the customs duties themselves brought him immense profits, his real wealth came from the position his firm had in dominating the Omani Empire's commerce, allowing him to monopolize competition and drive prices as high as he wished, with little concern for a drop in demand.[65]

Augmenting Jairam's position as East Africa's apex creditor, financier, and merchant was part of Saʿid's political strategy. Saʿid and Jairam created a political-commercial nexus that funneled capital, merchants, and wealth directly to Zanzibar. After Roberts returned to the United States in 1828, news of his visit with Saʿid spread throughout New England, and American merchants began sailing in greater numbers for East Africa. The surge of Americans in East Africa attracted the gaze of European merchants, including the French, British, and people from present-day Germany. Some Americans had sought to skirt Zanzibar and trade instead on the East African coast, where they attempted to demand higher prices for their cotton cloth and brass wire and not pay customs duties. Saʿid and Jairam took notice. As he began more intense treaty negotiations with Europeans, Saʿid sought to prohibit European and American traders from going directly to ports along East Africa's coast, known as the *mrima*, instead demanding that they do their business in Zanzibar. Because any deals in Zanzibar bore the scrutiny of both Jairam and Saʿid, this helped ensure that proper customs duties were paid, but it also helped keep the market tilted in favor of the local population.

No Atlantic trader was above this. The American consul Richard Waters once sought to curry favor with Saʿid and skirt protocol by unloading some cargo consigned to him directly in front of his seaside residence, rather than at Jairam's customs house. Saʿid prohibited this. "You know that you and all foreigners must send their inward and outward cargo to the Customs house," Saʿid instructed Waters. "This is what I do myself."[66] All traders, whether from the Atlantic or Indian Oceans, were thus required to unload their cargoes in front of the Customs House, where Jairam and his men would inspect them and charge the necessary duties. When Atlantic vessels unloaded their cargoes, local traders could then take these goods and ferry them free of fees throughout the empire, reaping enormous profits from East Africans' notoriously particular tastes and demands.

Loarer aptly described Saʿid and Jairam's attempts to control commerce along East Africa's coast as the "Mrima monopoly."[67] Despite their attempts, the monopoly was never entirely controlled. The British and French treaties stipulated that their citizens must do all their business in Zanzibar and not on East Africa's shores, but such a stipulation had not been written into the American treaty. Nevertheless, the attempt at establishing a system that corralled all Atlantic merchants in Zanzibar helps explain an ostensibly offhand comment by one Omani commercial agent when he referred to Jairam with the adjective *muḥibbuna*: "our dear Jairam."[68] Jairam and his firm, as Fahad Bishara pointed out, mediated the flows of capital that ran through the Omani Empire's veins. Perhaps even more than Saʿid, Jairam stood at the nexus of empire and commerce in the Western Indian Ocean.[69]

The positions of Jairam and Saʿid as privileged elites—politically and financially—were manifest by elements of structure and of agency. Each of them made certain decisions to augment their positions, but their decisions were caught up in a vast rising tide overtaking the world of changes in consumer tastes and preferences. Indians like Jairam and Omanis like Saʿid might have been drawn to Zanzibar because of environmental factors or because of troubles caused by rebels like the Mazruʿi, but structural economic factors helped keep them there beyond the seasonal monsoon. Every time a piano was built in New Orleans, an ivory comb was carved in Paris, or a clove-spiced fruit cake was baked in Boston, Saʿid and Jairam grew wealthier. And more than anything else it was cloves—a fragrant, thorny spice barely the size of a pencil eraser—that wove the Atlantic and Indian Ocean worlds together.

CLOVE MANIA

When Saʿid sailed to Zanzibar from Mombasa in January 1828 and met with Roberts, he did more than set in motion a treaty with the United States and begin taking stock of how to fix customs. While there, he also confiscated tracts of land from Zanzibaris and commanded Omani elites to begin transforming that land into clove plantations. By the following decade, the confiscation of indigenous land was official state policy. Clove cultivation remade Zanzibar's physical, political, and commercial environment.

The global trade in cloves, almost entirely centered on Zanzibar, would bring unprecedented wealth to some by means of devastating entire human communities.

We do not know what exactly prompted Saʿid to stake so much on clove cultivation or to order landholders in Zanzibar to remake their land for it. When he arrived on the island in 1828, cloves were already being grown in small numbers. As Abdul Sheriff noted, when the French traveler Francois Albrand visited Zanzibar in 1819, a decade before Saʿid's visit, he saw clove trees already fifteen feet high. This height indicated that they had been planted roughly ten years earlier. Even before Saʿid's treaty with the United States was ratified, American merchants were purchasing cloves in Zanzibar. In 1830 one American vessel purchased 127 *fraselas* of cloves from the Zanzibari governor, earning a profit of 10 MTD per frasela.[70] Historians have debated how exactly cloves were introduced to the island and by whom.[71] What is certain, however, is that their ascendance by 1840 to Zanzibar's primary export—making Zanzibar one of the world's most vital commercial centers—was in fact a bet. Almost immediately upon visiting in 1828, Saʿid ordered large landowners in Zanzibar to purchase and plant three bushels of cloves instead of any other crop. If they did not have the space for those cloves, they were ordered to clear whatever they were already growing to make room. Those who refused these orders risked having their land seized by Saʿid's deputies and being exiled from Zanzibar.[72]

Certain British agents working with Saʿid counseled him against his policy to expand clove production. Cloves were not native to Zanzibar; they were native to the Moluccan Islands in present-day Indonesia. No one in Zanzibar had any significant experience growing them. The British pleaded with Saʿid to halt his move toward cloves and instead focus on sugar production. Given their shared imperial agendas rooted in maritime security, having a steady supply of sugar in the region would have been of great benefit for their soldiers, sailors, and diplomats. As the British started focusing more on East Africa, their officials were often dismayed at how little attention Saʿid gave their attempts at cajoling him into focusing on sugar. The first British consul in Zanzibar, Atkins Hamerton, could not understand Saʿid's focus on cloves when, he noted, the sugar grown in Zanzibar was "as fine as any in the world."[73] Later, Hamerton's successor summarized British frustration: "Cotton and sugar cane grow in great perfection in the islands of Zanzibar and Pemba, but the Arabs are too indolent to cultivate them for exportation."[74]

Yet the Arabs who flocked to Zanzibar under Saʿid did not spurn sugar and cotton because of indolence. Saʿid had, in fact, tried to increase sugar production in Zanzibar. He had partnered with an English entrepreneur, working out a deal whereby the Englishman would provide machinery if Saʿid would provide land and enslaved laborers. Saʿid's plan was to ship the raw product for refining in the United States. When Americans in Zanzibar heard of this, however, they told Saʿid that the US government would not import his sugar, fearing that it would allow the British greater penetration into their continental sphere of influence. At the same time, the British banned the importation of sugar from any slaveholding state. Zanzibari sugar was thus deprived of both the American and British markets.[75] For elites on Zanzibar and in the surrounding region, the question of sugar production barely registered. Zanzibar's elite readily took to Saʿid's orders to cultivate cloves, and the spice quickly became so profitable that a visiting French official, Édouard Loarer, described the entire island as being overtaken by a "clove mania."[76] As elites began clearing their land for cloves and expropriating more land from indigenous peoples, things like sugar and rice came to be viewed as relics, no longer profitable investments.[77]

With its ample rain, sun, and fertile soil, Zanzibar's environment was naturally suited for cloves. Cloves became one of the Atlantic world's most sought-after commodities, used for spicing baked goods, beverages, meats, and other things. By the time Saʿid died in 1856, he had purchased or confiscated forty-five clove plantations, each run by enslaved humans. In 1840 Saʿid's plantations annually produced between five and six thousand fraselas, or two hundred thousand pounds, of cloves. By the end of that decade, he alone was producing between twenty and thirty thousand fraselas of cloves, or more than a million pounds. But Saʿid was only one among what became by the end of the 1840s a class of landed aristocrats. Each of his children, concubines, and eunuchs had their own plantations. Hasan bin Ibrahim, an Omani naval officer who also helped manage the commercial portfolios of American traders in Zanzibar, owned a plantation with twelve thousand clove trees; he named it Salem after the home port of his American trading partners. Indians also became part of Zanzibar's landed aristocracy. Jairam and his brother Ebji each owned plantations. In fact, by 1845 those outside Saʿid's ruling family were outproducing the royal family by two to one.[78]

In 1840 Zanzibar exported 315,000 pounds of cloves; just sixteen years later it exported nearly 5,000,000 pounds.[79] By all measures, Zanzibar's economy was roaring. In 1810 the total annual revenue from the empire's

East African dominions totaled 40,000 MTD. By 1819 it had doubled, to 84,000 MTD. It doubled again in the 1840s, and by the end of the 1860s totaled 310,000 MTD: "a phenomenal, nearly seven-fold growth" over just half a century.[80] Zanzibar's economy dwarfed even that of Aden, one of the British Empire's prized ports. In 1858 Zanzibar imported 908,911 British pounds of goods, Aden only 594,635. The same year, Zanzibar exported 753,666 pounds of goods, and Aden only 312,268.[81] By 1860 the British consul in Zanzibar was thus able to confidently claim that Zanzibar was "the chief market in the world for the supply of ivory, gum copal, and cloves."[82]

Propelling this commercial rise was a transformation in the institutional framework of using land, a process at once imbued with notions of financial capital, cultural capital, and racial hierarchy. Like other Swahili societies, Zanzibaris tended to view land communally. Land might change hands, but no people could be permanently alienated from it; moreover, even when it did change hands, it did so in a way that provided for use and advantages of the land short of destroying it or permanently and entirely expropriating it from others. Indigenous peoples used land that had been cleared for agricultural use, *kiambo* land, as part of a communal tenure system in which ownership was shared by all who were patrilineally descended from the man who originally cleared the land. In an understatement, Sir John Gray, chief justice of Zanzibar in the twentieth century, described how the nineteenth-century expropriation of indigenous peoples in Zanzibar "would have born scrutiny in a court of law."[83] Increasingly under the influence of Omani elite rule, land in Zanzibar and throughout East Africa became privatized—whether by confiscation or by private sales backed by dynamic Muslim legal frameworks.[84]

Omani-led expropriation of indigenous peoples changed the fabric of Zanzibari society, in addition to other parts of East Africa, such as Pemba, an island about sixty miles from Zanzibar. As had Zanzibar, Pemba had always been a rich agricultural island, naturally abundant with grain, fruit, and vegetables. It had historically been populated by relatively small farming communities who made their living on small-scale exports, especially grain, to Mombasa. Some grain was also sent north to the Arabian Peninsula. Saʿid's state-mandated spread of clove cultivation on both islands had dramatic environmental, social, and economic ramifications. So much land was appropriated for cloves that the self-sufficiency of both islands was seriously undermined, forcing most of the islands' native populations, already close to subsistence living, into deeper levels of poverty. According to a visiting

French official, in less than a decade, by 1849 two-thirds of Pemba's native forests had been destroyed to make space for clove plantations.[85] Enslavement and other forms of servitude were embedded in the flourishing of Zanzibar and Pemba. When the British explorer and linguist Richard Burton visited Zanzibar in 1858, he observed that Omanis referred to Zanzibaris as *makhadim*, meaning helots or serviles. Burton's observation is corroborated by an earlier report from Atkins Hamerton, who in 1841 told his superiors in Bombay, "The whole of the Native inhabitants of the Islands of Zanzibar and Pemba are considered by the subjects of His Highness as slaves."[86]

Enslavement was fundamental to the Omani Empire, but not every indigenous person in Zanzibar or East Africa was enslaved, as Hamerton had suggested. While in the strictest sense Hamerton's observation is misleading, it alludes to the emergence of a new phenomenon tied up with changing social, commercial, and geographic landscapes in the Omani Empire: a form of indentured servitude. Many Zanzibaris participated in clove cultivation as laborers who were legally free but commercially subservient to newly arriving elite overlords.[87] Inherent in the emergence of "clove mania" was the radical remaking of Zanzibar's social fabric and the physical layout of the island's population. Religious and ethnic minorities were protected by law and guaranteed the right to practice their respective religions, but this legal protection was nonetheless subsumed within a deeply engrained racial hierarchy. This hierarchy was rooted not just in social attitudes but also in the actual physical layout of the island and its capital, Stone Town, as it is known today.

As Zanzibar's connections with other parts of the Indian Ocean and Atlantic worlds intensified, so too did the disconnections between peoples and their daily lifestyles on the island. Though everyone on the island would have congregated near the Customs House and at the seafront, the actual spaces where different peoples on the island lived were quite segregated, in location but also in style or architecture. Saʿid and other elites, including visiting Europeans or Americans, lived in relatively ornate houses. Most people on the island, however, lived in more typical wattle-and-daub style houses. "The surface of Zanzibar town is in a great measure covered by small square mud huts which are occupied by the more numerous and poorer portion of the population," observed one American visitor. "They are thatched with leaves of the cocoa tree and have very low doorways."[88]

The island's security forces, comprised partly of enslaved Africans and partly of Baloch mercenaries earning monthly wages, lived with their families basically atop one another inside the island's main fort, steps away from the Customs House and Saʿid's seaside residence. Americans and Europeans lived in an exclusive part of town named Baghani in upper-scale homes given to them free of rent by Saʿid. Arabs and Indians lived separated, but near one another, in another exclusive part of town. Their homes exhibited their elite status, being multiple stories and made of expensive timber and coral. Most of the main town, like the rest of the island, was home to the island's indigenous and enslaved persons, who lived in houses made mostly from coconut fronds and mud; in Zanzibar town, their quarters were physically separated from the elites by a canal that would fill with the rising ocean tide.[89]

As manifested in its social divisions, every aspect of Zanzibar's rise was due to a parallel rise in enslavement and human trafficking and the physical delineation of people according to elite status and racial hierarchy. Enslaved humans were used to work on clove plantations but also in other trades, such as ivory and copal, which brought local people tremendous wealth. As seen in the physical transformation of Zanzibar island, that wealth was used to set people apart from one another. Omanis went to Zanzibar and other parts of East Africa not only because they could get rich, but because they could use that wealth to refashion themselves as privileged elites. This was true also for certain groups living in East Africa. Some East African communities capitalized on increasing demands for human trafficking to similarly refashion themselves as elite commercial actors, changing social structures and political hierarchies in East Africa. Certain East African confederations, like the Yao and Nyamwezi, actively worked alongside Omanis in establishing caravan routes for trafficking enslaved humans to Zanzibar, where they were either kept as slaves on plantations or trafficked elsewhere in the Indian Ocean.[90]

Diving under the surface of the lines penned by Édouard Loarer when he wrote of "clove mania" thus illuminates an entwined mania for enslaving humans and racial and social hierarchy. The destruction of human communities forced into enslavement and human trafficking was requisite to Zanzibar's commercial rise and the waves of profits that emanated from it throughout the Atlantic and Indian Oceans. When discussing large-scale historical dynamics like changes in consumer tastes and preferences, or intensification of market connections, or treaties facilitating these connections, it can be easy to occlude just how jarring the reality of life on the ground in Zanzibar was for the people who were in the most immediate instance responsible for catalyzing that clove mania: the enslaved.

For instance, Zanzibar island is only forty-five miles long and about fifteen miles wide—less than seven hundred square miles. In 1850 its population was estimated at three hundred thousand persons, two-thirds of whom were enslaved, or about two hundred thousand enslaved persons.[91] One American sailor passing through Zanzibar observed that there were as many enslaved humans on one acre of land in Zanzibar as there were in the United States on six.[92] New England's clove-studded holiday hams and England's clove-spiced tea thus came from a place where every square mile of land was packed with more than two hundred enslaved humans, in addition to the tens of thousands who were annually trafficked through the island, their fates mostly unknown, bound for other parts of the Indian Ocean.

VELOCITIES OF CIRCULATION

Zanzibar's rise as a global commercial center and capital of the Omani Empire was rooted in a multifaceted process by which velocities of circulation between vast stretches of East Africa's interior and its coasts increased, but it would be an overstatement to suggest that the Omani Empire connected these spaces. East Africa's inner regions had for centuries been connected with its coasts in reciprocal relationships, with interior East African peoples exerting varying degrees of influence over oceanic commercial and social affairs.[93] The Omani Empire shifted the energy of its commercial flows through a central station, Zanzibar. As Zanzibar emerged as a world fulcrum, peoples might have revolved around it with greater frequency, but they were not entirely forging new routes.[94] Related to the increasing rates of circulation, a new element of this history was that people living and working in the Omani Empire began acting upon the explicit understanding that time had become synonymous with profit. Saʿid geared his policies not just toward facilitating the number of journeys taken by merchants and caravan porters, but toward constantly increasing the velocities at which those journeys and return journeys were concluded.[95]

One way Saʿid sought to increase velocities of circulation within the Omani Empire was introducing a new form of small-unit currency, the copper pice. The myriad currencies used in the Western Indian Ocean during Saʿid's reign, and for at least a century before it, reflect its fundamentally global nature. Maria Theresa thalers, or dollars, were first coined in 1741 in present-day Austria, but were used throughout the Indian Ocean. These coins served as currency, as a reference for weighing goods, and even, by wealthy Omani women, as jewelry. Spanish dollars were also popular, in addition to British pounds, Indian rupees, French dollars, and German crowns.[96] Loarer observed how there were sometimes difficulties throughout East Africa's smaller mainland ports in having thalers and other large currencies accepted.[97]

The Maria Theresa dollar (MTD) was useful for procuring large volumes of commodities or other needed goods, but especially along caravan routes, smaller forms of currency were often needed for procuring various smaller items needed on a daily basis. Perhaps in response to these difficulties, at some point in the 1840s Saʿid sent a deputy to India to purchase five thousand units of copper for minting new, small-unit coins in Bombay bearing the image of two lions.[98] He called this new currency the pice. One pice equaled forty-six Indian rupees; in turn, one Indian rupee equaled twelve sterling pounds. Sixty-four pice equaled one-half MTD.[99] In introducing the pice, Saʿid would not have been trying to replace the MTD or any other larger-unit currency. As a small-unit currency, rather, the pice complemented those currencies by facilitating more mundane transactions necessary for supporting commerce, especially along the caravan trails emanating from Zanzibar.

The people who led caravans or worked for wages as caravan porters were perpetually on the move. Their journeys took months, sometimes years. Along the way they needed to purchase basic goods necessary for maintaining daily sustenance. Prior to the pice, the smallest coin in circulation was one-quarter of an MTD. Transactions involving amounts less than this were typically concluded by payment in kind, or bartering.[100] A bartering system was not as efficient as a monetized system. The pice was meant to standardize and make faster smaller transactions fundamental to the realities of the caravan trade. Small, seemingly mundane transactions along the trail mattered; they might have often made the difference between whether a venture was successful or arrived at its destination in a timely enough manner to be profitable.[101] Showing his usual shrewd insight, Loarer observed a straightforward result arising from the abilities of persons in East Africa to choose from different currencies: "greater ease of circulation."[102] Caravans would have continued to be financed mostly by foreign credit, but the pice was one small part of trying to facilitate greater efficiency during the journey, one part of what Bresnahan termed the "capitalization of commerce."[103]

Although the pice never overtook the MTD as the dominant form of currency, its introduction magnified an important part of this historical moment. Most persons moving about the Western Indian Ocean world as part of the global intensification of transoceanic market connections were not elites and would not have had access to large sums of currency or capital.[104] Whether by introducing the copper pice or centralizing customs, these economic policies had profound effects within Africa, not just on islands like Zanzibar. They allowed both Arab and African caravan traders to be better equipped, to be more powerful, and thus to grow in number. When Burton and other European explorers began traveling deeper into Africa in the second half of the nineteenth century, they did so on trails that Omanis, in the first half of the century, had already formalized with waystations, depots, customs houses, and security forces, all geared toward funneling caravans in and out of Zanzibar.[105]

By Saʿid's death in 1856, Omanis were frequently found living in outposts as far inland as the Great Lakes. "It is certain," concluded Coupland, "that during his reign the whole system of inland trade was extended and elaborated far beyond the more or less casual operations in which the Arabs of the coast had been engaged for ages past."[106] The pice was one part, perhaps a small one, of a process that tethered the caravan trade to Zanzibar. Caravan leaders and porters who used the pice had to purchase the coins in Zanzibar. The currency allowed those on caravan journeys to make faster transactions, no longer having to rely on bartering and negotiating for basic goods. The caravan trade, however, was not just about bringing commodities and enslaved humans to Zanzibar. Caravan traders also went to Zanzibar because that is where they could most efficiently purchase the things East African consumers wanted, especially American cotton cloth and Arab beads.[107]

While the pice was one part of a broader moment in which circulation became more efficient, the forceful, state-backed centering of circulation on Zanzibar and through Omani imperial coffers had destructive effects on many East African peoples. Already in the first half of the nineteenth century the consolidation of Omani sovereignty in Zanzibar and the policy of funneling all customs through Jairam's customs house in Zanzibar began marginalizing many inner East African peoples within their own communities and economic worlds, as well as within the global oceanic commercial system Zanzibar was part of.[108] Loarer might indeed have witnessed an increase in the ease of circulation because of the pice and other policies, but scaling out, commercial success in East Africa increasingly came to hinge upon whether a person was able to procure a line of credit from Jairam Shivji.

"The best and only certain way of obtaining a supply of cash for immediate service is by getting it from the Imam's Customs Master," declared the British consul in Zanzibar Atkins Hamerton. He continued: "From the Customs Master Jairam Sewjee I can get in a few hours notice any reasonable sum even to the extent of five thousand dollars."[109] Hamerton's observation reveals insight into the way he and his counterparts in Zanzibar thought about their commercial activities. The need for cash to take "immediate" advantage of something was a very tangible expression of the market's abstractions. Markets fluctuate; buyers and sellers must seize opportunities. Obtaining vast sums of cash "in a few hours notice" would have been critical for a merchant's ability to respond to news of price fluctuations or beating out a competitor. And the fact that Hamerton, who was always one for specificity, noted that Jairam was the "only certain way" of obtaining cash, points to the increasing centralization and monopolization of the marketplace as the empire further consolidated its norms and institutions across the first half of the century.

But Hamerton's taking out a line of credit in hard cash from Jairam does more than just illuminate the importance of debt, credit, and buying time for striking the best deals. Persons like Hamerton were bound together in a particular historical moment in which they were attempting to shrink time itself by using wealth, or capital, to act upon opportunity as immediately as possible. The immediacy of seizing opportunities was so important that Jairam often extended credit on behalf of other persons—even on behalf of Saʿid. On one occasion, the American consul in Zanzibar, Richard Waters, wrote to Saʿid, who was actually a favored trading partner to many in Zanzibar, requesting a loan of US$8,000—the equivalent of nearly US$300,000 in 2025.[110] Shortly afterward, Saʿid responded. "Your letter arrived, and your friend understood it," he conventionally began. "You mention wanting eight-thousand dollars for a certain time. I have ordered Jairam to do it, and to deliver to you the money."[111]

The readiness and immediacy with which Saʿid took a line of credit from Jairam to lend Waters a vast sum of money highlights yet another element to this social and commercial system and broader world historical moment. As do many of Saʿid's letters, this one ended with a classical Arabic phrase essentially telling the recipient that if he had any need, to please let him know so he could take care of it.[112] In one sense, Saʿid's closing was merely proper and conventional Arabic *adab*, or etiquette, from the time. It helps corroborate how nearly every written description from European or American visitors to his domains highlighted his apparent generosity.

Saʿid might certainly have been generous to foreign visitors, but that ostensible generosity can be interpreted as a clue to understanding broader and deeper contours of the modern, transoceanic economic world in the making. It was, in many ways, a calculated strategy of commercial aggrandizement. And this strategy worked: people were acutely aware of Saʿid's personal touch in catalyzing commerce. Loarer made this clear when he described how Saʿid, though always generous, shrewdly linked that generosity with economic considerations.[113] This remained a deeply personal period of history. Although Saʿid's strategic generosity attracted merchants to Zanzibar, getting them there was only one part of the puzzle. Saʿid was trying to facilitate the abilities of Atlantic merchants not just to sell their commodities in Zanzibar, but also to quickly make their return journeys home—to close the circuit.[114] Saʿid's decisions and actions, beginning with helping the destitute and stranded Edmund Roberts in 1828, helped guarantee not just that foreigners would come to Zanzibar, but that they would be taken care of while there and would quickly be sent back on their return voyage, all the more likely to keep repeating the circuit in perpetuity.

In fact, European and American merchants frequently needed assistance, and for things that can mistakenly be regarded as insignificant. In January 1842 Richard Waters called upon Saʿid, notifying him that an American vessel near Zanzibar had lost its best anchor. Waters described how the ship's captain and crew had been trying for several days to retrieve the anchor, and under dangerous conditions. The crew had even hired local divers, but stormy conditions precluded its retrieval.[115] Two days after Waters wrote to Saʿid, the American vessel was underway, sailing back to New England with one of Saʿid's own anchors.[116] This was one among countless incidents in which Saʿid used the prowess of local divers and sailors for rescuing American and European visitors. On another occasion, in September 1843 a British vessel was sailing to Zanzibar with a cargo of 365 tons of goods and a crew of thirty-one men. The vessel was shipwrecked and stranded on a small island; days later, the sailors had made their way to Muscat in emergency rowboats. When Saʿid found out, he housed them aboard his frigate the *Maurphei*, complete with rations, while he arranged for them to be sailed back to their home port. The British captain afterward recalled that he had "received every kindness from His Highness [Saʿid]."[117]

These acts of strategic generosity were part of a calculated political agenda. The generosity was not categorical; recall, for example, when Saʿid prohibited Richard Waters from flouting the rules by unloading cargo directly in front of his residence rather than at the Customs House. As Loarer indicated, Saʿid's generosity was linked with a broader commercial goal: the capitalization of commerce. When negotiating his treaties with the Americans and, later, with the British, Saʿid insisted on legally enshrining this strategic generosity in the treaties. Edmund Roberts, sent to negotiate the treaty with Saʿid in 1832, recalled that Saʿid had only objected to one of his proposals—a clause stipulating that the US government would be legally required to compensate Saʿid for his assistance in saving shipwrecked seamen and, after recovering them, outfitting them for returning to the United States. "The article he wished so altered," Roberts later described, "as to make it incumbent upon him to protect, maintain, and return them to their own country, free of every charge."[118]

Replacing lost anchors, fixing damaged ships, and even extending cash loans were important because they allowed merchants to remain mobile and to make their return journeys home. They closed the deal. The idea of a return voyage—a closed circuit—might easily be taken for granted from the perspective of the twenty-first century, but in this historical moment it was part of a very tangible, concerted effort by merchants to mitigate risk and to make their return voyages as swiftly as possible. "It is very desirable to have vessels return as quickly as they can, and bring full Cargoes," wrote one leading Salem tycoon in 1841 to Richard Waters in Zanzibar, "and we shall not be wanting in dispatching them [back] to you."[119] This statement is like countless others in the records of American merchants doing business in Zanzibar. All sides in this emerging commercial system had to do their part. Merchants in Salem had to take certain steps for loading their vessels bound for Zanzibar with the choicest cotton cloth, but ultimately the return journey was up to the efficiency of the system Saʿid oversaw in East Africa. By farming out customs to Jairam, introducing the cotton pice, and ensuring a perpetual supply of cloves alongside other coveted things like ivory, Saʿid was lessening the need for transoceanic merchants to involve themselves in the logistics of their own mobility.

CONCLUSION

Structural elements of the past, like the formation of an interregional and transoceanic marketplace, are based on seemingly mundane, easily overlooked events, such as replacing lost ship anchors. In the first half of the nineteenth century, having the ability to retrieve a lost anchor was the difference between taking the risk to cross entire oceans or not. It made mobility possible. Yet just as replacing a lost anchor or introducing the copper pice made it easier for merchants to increase their velocities of circulation, mobility was just one part of the broader goal. One aspect of the oceanic marketplace in the Omani Empire was that it facilitated the ability of certain persons to choose to be immobile—to stay in place. This was true of Saʿid himself: once in Zanzibar, he returned to Oman on only a few occasions, and for only the most pressing matters. No sources indicate whether he ever traveled through East Africa's mainland.

In Zanzibar and elsewhere, the privilege of choosing to be selectively immobile—to delay the return voyage—became a calculated commercial strategy. In 1837 Richard Waters wrote home from Zanzibar to his family in Salem, reminding them how torn he felt by his extended stay there, acknowledging that, in the immediate term, he was leaving them with "but little money." But he assured them that things would get better if he remained in Zanzibar. "I am willing to work hard for a few years if I can acquire a necessary portion of riches," he wrote. "Not that I mean to make gold my God, but feel that I am in the performance of duty, while engaged in an honest business acquiring riches."[120]

The commercial system in Zanzibar centered on the nexus between Saʿid and Jairam facilitated merchants' abilities to selectively choose between being mobile or being immobile.[121] Saʿid could remain in Zanzibar because of those revenues, just as the countless persons who borrowed from Jairam could use that credit to strike out on the caravan trails or possibly wait in Zanzibar for better market prices. The wealth that merchants living in Zanzibar accrued was frequently used not to be more mobile but rather to stay put as part of a newfound existence as elite commercial actors, spending wealth to delegate commercial tasks for establishing caravan waystations or plantations. Richard Burton once observed, "The more a man spends the more he is honoured."[122]

Ostentatious displays of wealth came to characterize a settled, landed aristocracy in Zanzibar, as more fully demonstrated in chapter 6. Deeds from estate sales of British citizens who died while living in Zanzibar reflect ornate houses full of fine textiles, exotic furniture, and the world's finest oils and spices.[123] Even the middle classes of society, people like ship captains that Richard Waters would have employed for conducting his business, became wealthy. By 1840 a ship's captain in Saʿid's merchant fleet—many of whom were British contractors—could expect as much as US$70 per month in pay.[124] This was far more, by comparison, than many American ship captains made.[125] They even earned bonuses for incentivizing their crews.[126] Indian merchants in Zanzibar became legendarily wealthy; a British visitor once remarked how astonished he was to see an Indian merchant with so much ivory that he had to store extra tusks under his bed.[127] The countless numbers of transactions in land and plantations, or *shambas*, that remain are expressions of how people used accrued wealth in this period for the privilege of being immobile, putting down roots, and transcending expectations of modesty by *not* following the monsoons.

Commercial policies in Zanzibar and the politics of the Saʿid-Jairam commercial monopoly were aimed at exploiting and controlling fortune. Viewing him in this way helps reorient our understanding of him. Saʿid's decisions and actions in helping establish the commercial system in Zanzibar are emblematic of a larger, more global portrait of changes shaping the emergence of our modern world. Saʿid's attempts to use state power to connect local agricultural production (cloves) with wider, outside economies are not unique in modern world history. They are similar to how Genoese merchants began cultivating sugar in Sicily in the fifteenth century; or how entrepreneurs in Bordeaux and Burgundy began distilling grapes into wine and satisfying palates around the world; or how Egyptians began exporting cotton, the Algerians began exporting grain, and Palestinians began exporting cotton, textiles, and even olive oil.[128]

Zanzibar was one great entrepreneurial port flourishing in the same way and in the same time as other similar ports like Baltimore, London, and Marseilles. Looking into this process in the Western Indian Ocean brings to light the same sort of spirit of enterprise that allowed capitalism to take root in other parts of the world, recasting Indian Ocean peoples as actors unto their own ends, not merely recipients of a unidirectional, ostensibly European modernity. Looking back, Saʿid's fiscal and political arrangements in Zanzibar stand as great historical leveling agents, in which we can see the simultaneous polyphony of causes that go into any global historical moment. His decision to fix customs and legally enshrine the duty of his government to equip American merchants for their return journeys had as much to do with his own aptitude as it did the demands of East African consumers and even the Spanish and French pirates who ransacked Roberts's ships and spurred him to sail for East Africa. Attracting American and European merchants to Zanzibar and facilitating their rapid return voyages was one step in stitching the nascent Atlantic world economy into the broader Indian Ocean. Seen in this way, the Omani-Zanzibari historian Al-Mughairi was perhaps unintentionally contributing to a broad world historical debate when he noted that East Africa in many ways sustained the emergence of the modern world as a space integral to linking the Atlantic and Indian Oceans.[129] Al-Mughairi was careful in his choice of words. He used the Arabic verb *tadurr*. Broadly, this verb connotes flowing abundance or the bestowing of riches; more precisely, however, it denotes a mother providing nourishment for her baby. It reflects the provision of sustenance: that which is needed to survive. In the increasingly global conditions of the long nineteenth century, the Omani Empire provided crucial sustenance for the linking of the Atlantic and Indian Oceans.

FIVE

Politics of the Marketplace

INTRODUCTION

On May 30, 1834, US president Andrew Jackson informed the US Senate of a secret mission. In a letter, Jackson explained his conviction that the United States had to look beyond European markets and invest more in countries "bordering the Indian Ocean." Jackson then explained that he had appointed Edmund Roberts as a "Special Agent" of his administration. Under utmost secrecy, he had tasked Roberts with traveling to three places in the Indian Ocean—present day Oman, Thailand, and China—to negotiate commercial treaties for "securing additional advantages to our trade in that quarter." Jackson then declared Roberts's success in concluding a treaty with the "Sultan of Muscat," ensuring that American trade in his empire, "which had been previously embarrassed by serious disadvantages and obstructions," was now "placed upon a footing with that of the most favoured nation."[1]

The Senate ratified the treaty the following month and dispatched Roberts once more to Oman to ratify it with Saʿid. One member of the American delegation, Dr. William Ruschenberger, later described the ratification ceremony. The Americans met Saʿid in his Muscat residence. Gathering on his verandah overlooking the sea, a space graced with Persian rugs and Chinese chairs, Ruschenberger described how he had noticed two prints hanging prominently above the chairs Saʿid reserved for himself and his visiting dignitaries. The prints depicted scenes of American naval victories over the British in the War of 1812.[2] These American victories had humiliated the British. An article published in the *London Times* soon after one of the battles reflected the scorn with which the British regarded their fast-emerging American rivals. "It is not merely that an English frigate has been taken," the author asserted, "but that it has been taken by a new enemy, an enemy unaccustomed to such triumphs, and likely to be rendered insolent and confident by them."[3]

Roberts secretly completed his mission, and the treaty was made public. Upon learning of it, the British were cautious, but they remained relatively confident. A year after the treaty was signed, in 1834, one British official harped that despite the new treaty, "the trifling trade which they [the Americans] may carry on in their small vessels" would not interfere with the Crown's or Company's ambitions for the region.[4] By the next decade, however, Britain's commercial subordination in Zanzibar was clear, as was its relatively small degree of political influence over Saʿid in East Africa. In 1841, when Atkins Hamerton moved to Zanzibar as Britain's first consul to Saʿid, he professed to his superiors: "I am sorry to inform Your Excellency, that our influence at Zanzibar is in the lowest possible scale, there being a strong party in favor of the French and American interests and more particularly the latter."[5] This statement was among the first dispatches Hamerton sent to his superiors in the British government upon assuming his duties in Zanzibar. In it, he was already signaling his frustration. He went on to describe how, on his first day in Zanzibar, he visited Saʿid in his seaside residence. They met in a room reserved for diplomatic receptions, and Hamerton noticed two paintings in "richly gilt frames." Hamerton griped in his letter about how the paintings portrayed American naval victories, with the American flag being hoisted above resigned British sailors, pleading for mercy as their great ships sank.[6]

In 1840, when Saʿid moved his family from Muscat to Zanzibar, he had taken the prints from the wall of his Muscat residence and sailed with them back to Zanzibar. As in Muscat, he hung them in his reception area for visitors to see. Saʿid certainly might have simply found the prints to be nice decorations. There are no sources indicating when or how he obtained them. The prints, however, aptly reflect a veritable international chess match of commercial and political affairs in the nineteenth century in which the Omani Empire was a leading player. Amid the geopolitical rivalry in Zanzibar between the British and Americans, Saʿid maintained a system in which Arab, African, and Asian merchants could carry on their business on their own terms and unto their own ends, absorbing newly arriving Atlantic merchants. Well into the second half of the nineteenth century, the United States remained the superior Atlantic commercial actor in the Western

Indian Ocean, beating out the British at nearly every turn. In fact, the British in this time were aware of their own commercial subordination, unable to compete with American merchants. As this chapter shows, Americans not only brought with them items for trade that East African, Arab, and some South Asian consumers demanded the most, but they also had a consul who more effectively situated the country's trade within the framework of the market in Zanzibar.

The Americans trounced the British commercially, but they were not the dominant actors. The dominant political and commercial actors in the Omani Empire during the reign of Sa'id remained Arab, African, and Asian peoples. These Indian Ocean peoples were not mere mediators between an ostensibly prepackaged Euro-American capitalism and peripheral Indian Ocean markets.[7] The relatively recent arrival of Europeans and Americans in the Indian Ocean world did lead to certain changes—socially, geographically, politically, and economically. These changes, however, were driven as much by local Indian Ocean peoples as they were by peoples from the Atlantic; the former co-opting the latter, in many ways, to maintain and augment their own pursuits of wealth. From a longer world historical perspective, then, and while acknowledging certain changes to the Indian Ocean world, the co-optation of Atlantic merchants into this world can be seen as continuity with a long Indian Ocean history of different factions coming together and actively reconciling with each other while driven by the pursuit of wealth.

Peoples in the Omani Empire were active participants in shaping the long-term, complicated process of melding the Atlantic and Indian Oceans together into a shared oceanic marketplace, one part of a global system of capitalism. They were not just part of an antique world of the bazaar that was shaped by Europeans and Americans.[8] In terms of nineteenth-century world affairs, Sa'id actively exploited and manipulated the British-American rivalry to ensure the continued agency of his subjects. European and American capital and capitalists expanded in the Indian Ocean, as in other parts of the world, by accommodating Indian Ocean peoples and their commercial networks and business practices, acceding so that they could succeed. In this, the British were almost entirely shut out from commerce in the Omani Empire, especially in East Africa, while Americans succeeded because of a conscientious strategy of acquiescence and assimilation to the commercial demands of Arabs, Africans, and Asians in the Omani Empire.[9]

Americans and Britons approached the Omani Empire differently, their distinct agendas shaping their interactions with Saʿid and his subjects. These differences were evident to Saʿid, and he exploited them to augment the agency and commercial gains of local peoples. Regarding the British in this time and space, there might have been somewhat divergent general agendas between the East India Company based in Bombay and the home government based in London. But British interests in the Omani Empire were represented by Atkins Hamerton, the consul after 1841, who represented both the Company and the Crown and was assigned personally to Saʿid bin Sultan. Whether he was acting on orders from London or from Bombay, for Hamerton commercial relations in the Omani Empire were important to the extent they helped abolish human trafficking, a policy the British pursued for strengthening their own imperial agenda.

Few Britons conducted business in East Africa, and they were aware of their subordination. In 1838 a British intelligence report began by highlighting the importance of the Omani Empire for regional and global affairs, but lamented how British merchants and agents had struggled to enculturate themselves into the Omani Empire. The report then stated that Saʿid was "a Commercial Ally of no contemptible importance" to Britain's fastest-growing rival, the United States. The author of the report noted the value Saʿid placed on his alliance with the Americans, and the remarkable "gratitude of that Country [the United States] for the advantages rendered to it by H.H. [Saʿid] and which in a Commercial relation certainly exceeds that asked for or extended to Great Britain, which is certainly our own fault, by not adopting that kind, conciliatory, & complimentary intercourse which has been carefully attended to by the American Govt."[10]

The British approached the region in the pursuit of ending human trafficking.[11] "No doubt the extension of commerce in Africa is an object to be aimed at," wrote an official in a different government report, "but I am inclined to think that such extension will be the effect rather than the cause of the extinction of the Slave Trade."[12] The Americans, conversely, were foremost interested in private enterprise, though of course there were political implications of this. When President Andrew Jackson sent Edmund Roberts to Muscat to ratify the treaty with Saʿid, the US secretary of state had instructed Roberts to highlight these differences: "You will studiously inculcate upon all those with whom you have intercourse . . . that although we are a powerful nation . . . we desire no colonial possessions. . . . You will point out, where it may be necessary, the difference which exists between ourselves and other nations in these respects; and endeavor to remove the fears and prejudices which may have been generated by the encroachments or aggressions of European Powers."[13]

Roberts did not have to do much inculcating. Saʿid was already aware of the potential for commercial relations with the United States. In fact, Saʿid had already made overtures to the US government outlining his desire for a treaty before he met Roberts in 1828, and during that meeting Saʿid made clear his ambitions for a treaty. When Roberts returned in 1832 to Muscat to negotiate the treaty, Saʿid went to every expense in courting the Americans. Roberts and his delegation were showered with gifts. Even before Roberts was able to anchor his ship and row ashore, Saʿid dispatched a boat to greet him, laden with fruit, goats, sheep, and letters congratulating him on his arrival and "expressing himself highly flattered" to receive the official American delegation.[14] The following day, Saʿid and Roberts quickly agreed on the treaty's framework. The agreement stipulated that Americans had the right to trade at any "port" in Saʿid's dominions, pay a fixed duty of 5 percent on goods they imported into those ports, and pay no duty on goods purchased as exports, and it guaranteed that Americans would not face arbitrary taxes or other impositions. The treaty also authorized the president of the United States to appoint a consul to manage commerce in the Omani Empire, thus establishing the first foreign consulate in Saʿid's domains.

The stipulation that Americans would not pay customs duties on exports —any goods purchased in Zanzibar or other Omani-controlled ports for importing back into the United States—augmented the positions of local peoples in the empire as producers and consumers, most especially East Africans. Exempt from paying export duties, Atlantic merchants purchased East African commodities in greater volumes. Granted, certain commodities, such as cloves, might have brought profits mostly to Omani and Indian elites who owned most of the clove plantations in Zanzibar and Pemba—but some wealthy East Africans owned plantations, as well. Purchasing large amounts of things like ivory, animal hides, or gum copal, however, had entwined economic and social ramifications stretching deep into Africa's interior. The profits earned by East African, Omani, and Indian entrepreneurs in Zanzibar created a complex system of wage labor that sustained the caravan trade, which around the midpoint of the nineteenth century, reached across the continent. The caravan trade was not strictly a means for making a living. For many, it was an enterprise for accruing wealth, transcending expectations of merely getting by.[15]

The flourishing of American trade in Zanzibar was rooted in East African consumerism. As Jeremy Prestholdt put it, "Through demand, perhaps more than through production, East Africans leveraged global commercial relationships during the nineteenth century."[16] East African consumerism was rooted in more than the pursuit of monetary wealth. East Africans used American commodities purchased in Zanzibar or transported from there to manifest individual and group identities, fortifying their cultural agency in a historical period of African history that has often only been looked at for the beginnings of colonialism. Peoples throughout East Africa used different American textiles and jewelry made with American brass wire to conspicuously set themselves apart from one another.[17] Dropping the duty paid by Americans on goods purchased in Zanzibar to carry back to the United States facilitated the ability of more East Africans from the interior to participate in the marketplace. Not having to pay that duty made it more amenable for Americans in Zanzibar, as well, corralling them in the island where Jairam could ascertain that they would not be extorted or bribed, and where Saʿid could ensure a speedy return voyage.

The politics surrounding the treaty's negotiation reflect how shrewdly Saʿid played the Americans and British against each other. Beginning with their meeting in 1828, Saʿid implored Roberts to keep their discussions secret, apparently "anxious the English government should not know his designs."[18] Saʿid told Roberts the Americans should frame their treaty to be like the one he had with Britain. Apparently neither Edmund Roberts nor anyone in the US government was aware that Saʿid, in fact, did not have a commercial treaty with Britain. Saʿid had leveraged the idea of a treaty with the Americans' rival to spur them into action. He did the same thing to the British. Despite telling Roberts to keep their negotiations secret, Saʿid sent a letter to the British resident in the Gulf, describing his plans for concluding a commercial treaty with the United States, unless the British would like to conclude one first. He asked the British resident for his opinion on this but did not wait for a response before concluding the treaty with Roberts.[19]

The British were outraged. Granting the Americans "immunities and advantages of trade with a factory at Zanzibar" was "very inimical to our Interests," decried one official.[20] The British at first sought to determine whether there were any preexisting arrangements precluding Saʿid, as a naval ally, from entering a treaty with another state. There were none. The British then moved to formally lodge their protest with Saʿid, but could not do so because he had just left Muscat, sailing for Zanzibar. Until 1841 the British did not have any government officials in Zanzibar or elsewhere in East Africa. In 1832 the Bombay government sent an officer, Captain Henry Hart, to meet Saʿid in Zanzibar and gather intelligence regarding American influence in the region. When Hart arrived, Saʿid immediately began playing down the importance of his treaty with the United States. He assured Hart that he was actually "anxious" to break the treaty and instead sign one with Britain.[21] Saʿid followed this up by writing a letter for Hart's superiors describing the treaty as nothing more than a "trifling affair," barely deserving further mention.[22] He gave a copy of the letter to Hart, promising that he had no "intention of injuring or forgetting his best friends the English." Of his time discussing international affairs with Saʿid, Hart later recalled: "As for the Americans he cared nothing for them, they were nothing to him, his attachment was to the English."[23] Saʿid was fooling Hart. He convinced Hart that, despite the treaty, he had no interest in furthering the aims of Americans in his empire. He described Roberts as coming to him as a mere pauper, calling him "an old, fat, blustering man" and apparently promising Hart that he had only signed the treaty to "get rid" of Roberts and the American delegation, not thinking the treaty would ever hold any importance.[24]

Roberts's account of the treaty negotiations with Saʿid is strikingly different. Roberts described how he had been "received by His Highness as though I was his dearest friend, who had long been absent."[25] Saʿid ensured the Americans that entering into a commercial treaty with him reflected the young country's "great wisdom."[26] Roberts confirmed Saʿid's graciousness toward the American delegation. "My reception was everything that humanity, benevolence, and brotherly feeling could dictate," he recalled.[27] Based on everything we know about Saʿid's personality—and more broadly, the etiquette and decorum of Arab culture—it is unlikely that he had disparaged Roberts to Hart in the way Hart described. Hart was most likely dramatizing events in hopes that his superiors in Bombay would take greater notice.

Regardless, Saʿid clearly played the Americans and British off each other. He had followed similar tactics before. In 1809, for example, when Saʿid was courting the French, he assured the British that they were relatively unimportant to him, and that he would break with the French altogether if it would guarantee more British support for his campaigns against the Wahhabi.[28] As before, just as he was telling the British that he would break his new treaty with the Americans should they desire it, Saʿid was secretly sending a different message to the US government. In a letter to Andrew Jackson, he confirmed his desire to build a commercial partnership with the United States. Saʿid wrote to Jackson that Roberts's visit had made him "supremely happy," ensuring Jackson that the treaty would be followed by himself and his successors "as long as the world endures." In his typically lyrical rhetoric, Saʿid told Jackson that he would forever hold the president dear to his heart, offering him his entire and devoted services.[29]

THE CONSUL-CAPITALIST

For Hart and for anyone else who passed through Zanzibar, American commercial success was clear. During his stay in Zanzibar of less than one year between 1833 and 1834, Hart saw thirteen ships arrive from the Atlantic: four were British; the rest were American. More important, however, Hart observed how each of the American ships was already on its second voyage to Zanzibar.[30] Upon meeting some of the American sailors, Hart questioned them, apparently challenging their commercial position and telling them that it would be only a short time before the British began driving them from the region. Haughty from success, one of the American sailors responded: "Well, if we have lost the Trade, we have had it for these last fourteen years, whilst the English were too stupid to find it out, they never thought a Yankee could do so."[31]

Americans had indeed been trading in East Africa for more than a decade before the ratification of the treaty. Neither Jackson nor Saʿid initiated American commerce in East Africa. Rather, they both used their respective positions of power to amplify a trade that had already begun.[32] The degree to which Americans had ingratiated themselves into Indian Ocean networks was evident to Britons like Captain Hart. In the first half of the nineteenth century, Britons along East Africa's coast or in the Gulf had no presumptions that this oceanic space was a British lake, nor that it was anywhere near the cusp of becoming one. In his report, Hart detailed that Americans faced no competition from other Atlantic peoples in East Africa. They were free to trade, as he put it, in "a ready market for any stuff they choose to take out, and have carried it on at an enormous profit for fourteen years."[33] American trade in Zanzibar dwarfed that of any Europeans. Between September 16, 1832, and May 26, 1835, thirty-two American ships docked in Zanzibar with cargoes totaling 5,497 tons. In the same period, seven British ships docked, with cargoes totaling 1,403 tons.[34] The trend continued. In 1859, only one British ship docked in Zanzibar, carrying 493 tons of cargo. Seventeen ships from Hamburg docked with 4,428 tons of cargo; twelve French ships docked with 3,066 tons; nine Arab ships docked with 3,430 tons; and three Spanish ships docked with 680 tons, as well as one Danish ship and two Portuguese ships. That same year, thirty-five American ships docked in Zanzibar carrying a total of 10,890 tons of cargo.[35] The year 1859 was not an exception. In the combined four preceding years, eleven British ships docked in Zanzibar, carrying less than 4,000 tons of cargo; in the same period, 119 American ships unloaded almost ten times that, with cargo totaling 37,800 tons.[36]

One reason American trade flourished in Zanzibar is that the American consul, Richard Waters, was a career merchant. After beginning his duties in 1837, his first years were marred by dramatic trouble.[37] After about two years, however, Waters had ingratiated himself with local traders and their networks, beginning foremost with Jairam Shivji. The role Waters played as consul and the nature of his duties in Zanzibar were unique. Other American consuls in important commercial places such as Mauritius, Batavia, Canton, Manila, or Honolulu held duties relegated almost exclusively to social functions.[38] But Waters's role was different. The French naval officer Charles Guillain, after meeting Waters when he went to Zanzibar to negotiate a French treaty with Saʿid, remarked upon this. Guillain noted that Waters had a "triple job": he was at once consul, manager of his own private trading firm, and consignee of American shipping to Zanzibar.[39] As consul, Waters was responsible for diplomatic affairs with Saʿid, but he was also responsible for managing the entire portfolio of American commerce in East Africa. As consignee, his own success as consul was predicated upon the success of American commerce in the region.

American commercial success in East Africa was never unidirectional. To strike the best deals for his American counterparts, Waters first had to act as something of a representative for East Africans, Arabs, and Indians who wanted American commodities. After an initially turbulent period, Waters formed deep commercial ties with Jairam Shivji, monopolizing the market alongside him. Jairam and Waters worked out deals that allowed Jairam first access to American shipping and gave Waters key advantages. To keep American cotton, brass wire, muskets, and more flowing steadily into East Africa, Jairam helped Waters navigate the several ways local merchants sought to dupe Americans and Europeans. Despite the Americans' insistence that they were interested only in commercial matters, Waters's triple job shows just how political commerce remained. He suffered through enormous setbacks in his first years as consul while ingratiating himself with local communities. No matter how legalized or formalized commerce became, politics still mattered, and American commerce succeeded in East Africa—to the benefit of local peoples as much as Americans—because Waters used his political skills, alongside Jairam, Saʿid, and others, to weave the interests of people across oceans into a more coherent commercial web.

This process was not seamless. Americans were painfully aware of the risks involved. Far from home, Americans were compelled to use foreign weights, measures, currencies, and languages. American merchants, including Waters, were in every way subordinate to local peoples.[40] American merchants practically begged Waters to use his connections with local tycoons like Jairam or Saʿid to give them an advantage in the Zanzibar market. Merchants in Salem, Zanzibar's primary American trading partner, implored Waters to help them maximize their profits. In 1840 one Salem merchant wrote to him asking for $3,000 in "good Zanzibar Gum Copal at the lowest price you can obtain it."[41]

At first glance, this request seems relatively innocuous: wanting to pay the lowest price for something is so obvious as to seem unimportant. The merchant's request to Waters, however, opens a window into an entire world of on-the-ground diplomacy and politics, a protracted series of wrangling negotiations that would have occurred between Waters and Jairam for getting just that: the lowest possible price. For Waters to obtain commodities at the lowest possible price, he would have had to work closely with Jairam, checking in with him at the Customs House almost daily. Prices were never truly fixed; they were negotiated. While supply and demand across continents and oceans affected general patterns of increases or decreases in prices, prices were also very tangibly affected by negotiations between merchants at the apex of the trading hierarchy. And no matter how successful American commerce was, or how much East African consumers demanded their products, they remained cognizant of its inherently tenuous nature. "This being an experiment with us," concluded the merchant in his letter to Waters, "the success of which will determine whether we shall enlarge our orders or stop with this experiment."[42]

Beneath the surface of the Salem merchant's letter to Waters was a situation that highlights the tenuous position of Atlantic traders in the Indian Ocean. The Salem merchant implored Waters to avail himself of every "opportunity and advantage" in selecting the best copal in terms of purity.

In fact, local merchants—often with Jairam being fully aware—were masters of duping their Atlantic counterparts for maximizing their own profits. Waters used his position to try to help Salem merchants avoid these risks, acting as a cross between a veritable quality control manager and a business intelligence analyst. The risk Atlantic merchants took trading in the Omani Empire was part of the vocabulary of their official transactions and correspondence. To lessen the risk, Americans relied on Waters, but they also used other strategies. One was to essentially pool funds among a group of merchants to charter and outfit ships to make the dangerous voyage from New England to Zanzibar. This decreased the total risk of loss any one person would face if the vessel were damaged or lost at sea. The strategy of commercial crowdsourcing augmented the standing of American merchants in Zanzibar because it allowed enormous quantities of American commodities to be shipped there. It also allowed American ships to keep returning in perpetual loops at faster velocities than any other nation.

One representative Salem vessel left for Zanzibar with several hundred thousand pounds of cotton cloth, East Africans' most demanded product, and umbrellas, brass wire, candles, muskets, rocking chairs, chandeliers, and jewelry. The entire cargo was supplied on a joint account invested in by four Salem merchants.[43] The master of this ship was John Waters, the consul's brother. The largest investor in the ship's journey was David Pingree, one of the wealthiest merchants in Salem. Pingree wrote to John Waters, instructing him to first stop at Mozambique, then "without delay" stop at Majunga, before proceeding "with as little delay as possible" to Zanzibar, where the greatest sales would be. Pingree closed his letter by instructing John Waters to fill the ship at Zanzibar to its maximum capacity before returning to Salem "with as little delay as possible."[44] Other ports, like the ones in present-day Madagascar, remained important for American merchants, but Zanzibar was understood to be the prize: that is, after all, where the American government had placed their consul, and by all accounts Zanzibar received the highest volume of American shipping. Pingree's instructions to John Waters amplifies how clearly merchants at this time had understood the extent to which time was synonymous with profit. The letter reveals the other side—the receiving end, so to speak—of Saʿid's policies in East Africa for facilitating return journeys. These merchants had an unceasing ambition to get to Zanzibar as quickly as possible, without delay, before returning to Salem and making the voyage again.[45] They wanted their ships to sail between Salem and Zanzibar as often and as quickly as possible.

Thus, one reason American merchants crowdsourced the capital for outfitting ships bound for Zanzibar was that it increased the rates and velocities of their shipping to Zanzibar. By crowdsourcing, they did not necessarily have to wait for any one person to accrue enough capital to outfit an entire voyage. Saʿid's policies for facilitating return journeys worked reciprocally with American merchants' impatience with idle time. Saʿid's fixed policy on imports and exports was a major draw for Americans in funneling their trade to Zanzibar. In another letter, Pingree wrote to Waters in Zanzibar, pondering whether he should cease all business interests in Madagascar because of the "heavy duties on exports and imports" and instead focus his business entirely in Zanzibar.[46] Aside from the fixed customs, having a consul-capitalist in Zanzibar like Richard Waters was a great advantage for American merchants, who leaned on Waters to sway the market in their favor. "Hope you will be able to control the Copal Market at Zanzibar," wrote two of Salem's wealthiest men to Waters. "If so we can make a good business of it here."[47]

Despite all of Richard Waters's skills as a merchant and a diplomat, the greatest reason American commerce flourished in East Africa was East African consumerism. Waters was able to capitalize on East African consumerism and maximize demand for American goods because he ingratiated himself within the networks demanding it. Already in 1835—before Waters arrived in Zanzibar as consul—Edmund Roberts had observed that one of Saʿid's deputies, Hasan bin Ibrahim, managed nearly all business on behalf of American merchants.[48] The importance of these local actors was readily apparent to American merchants as the only sure way to success. Leading Salem merchants instructed their traders in East Africa on the importance of solidifying their ties with local actors, most especially Jairam and other South Asian merchants and tycoons. "Keeping the Banians in your debt will give you an advantage over others," instructed one of Salem's most successful merchants, referring to Indian merchants and financiers in Zanzibar.[49]

As consul, Richard Waters understood the primacy of Jairam and his influence over East African and thus world markets. In January 1840, when Waters was preparing to take leave from Zanzibar, he instructed his temporary replacement that the most important thing to do when any American vessel arrived in Zanzibar harbor was to "hold a conversation with Jeram bin Seva [Jairam Shivji], the Custom Master," before adding: "[A] more safe & expeditious business can be done with Jeram, than all the other merchants put together in Zanzibar."[50]

Jairam was a lifeline for American commerce because his private equity allowed him to extend lines of credit, whether to Americans or local merchants seeking to do business with Americans—like Saʿid. But his position as customs master also provided him with the best and most immediate knowledge of changing tastes and preferences among East African consumers. With their discerning demand, East Africans affected commodity prices, and those market fluctuations flowed directly through Jairam, onto American ships, and back to the wharves of Salem and Boston. By remaining in Jairam's debt—literally and figuratively—Americans were not able to control those fluctuations, but they were able to maintain something of a privileged position for navigating them, rather than merely being cast aside. But Waters's instructions to his temporary replacement deserve more pause. Having a conversation with Jairam was important precisely because the market was not guided by a hidden hand; it was actively shaped by what East African, Arab, and Indian consumers wanted at any particular time. And the hand that manifested those changes, making them tangible in written business transactions, was Jairam's.[51]

THE BRITISH TREATY

The British had been mostly absent from East Africa while Edmund Roberts and Richard Waters were there formalizing commercial relations with Saʿid. American commercial success in East Africa was driven foremost by East African demand for American products, especially cotton cloth and brass wire. New England merchants could barely supply enough cotton cloth to satiate East African demand, with consumers there preferring New England cloth over that from any other country. No matter how many Arabs, Indians, Americans, or Europeans arrived in East Africa, East Africans maintained their demand for what they wanted and refused to settle for inferior or otherwise secondary products, like British cotton.

Soon after Edmund Roberts's first trip to Zanzibar in 1828, the British grew increasingly alarmed at the degree to which local consumers were scoffing at them throughout the Omani Empire. The disregard for British merchants increased after Saʿid formalized economic relations with the United States between 1833 and 1835. Already by the time Waters had arrived, however, local consumers were spurning British attempts at selling their own cotton, trying to dislodge the Americans from the market. The British faced several disadvantages. First, they had no consul, and they had essentially cornered themselves in Saʿid's arena of maritime security in the Gulf. There were single-digit numbers of British merchants who went to East Africa to trade, and when they did go there, they could not miss the insatiable East African demand for American cotton cloth. A few British merchants tried to manipulate this and exploit East Africans by stamping their own cloth with American brands, a ruse East Africans quickly discovered. "It is in vain the British endeavor to imitate our fabric by stamping their own with American marks," observed one member of the Roberts delegation, "for the people say, the strength and wear of the American goods is so superior, that, lest they be deceived, they will no longer even purchase from Englishmen."[52]

Until well into the 1840s, there were few, if any, British firms in East Africa, and the first British consulate was not established until 1841. Despite this absence, however, there had been a few voices within the Bombay government trying to highlight the importance of commerce in East Africa. In 1823, when Captain Owen had gone to Mombasa to meet with the Mazruʿi, he noted that Mombasa could be the ideal entrepot for ferrying British commerce in East Africa, linking with their factories and naval bases in South Asia and thus encircling the entire rim of the Western Indian Ocean. Owen had also wanted to establish a protectorate over Mombasa as an entry point for "civilizing" the continent by abolishing human trafficking.[53] Ultimately, Saʿid forced Captain Owen to evacuate Mombasa and stymied British influence in the region until the second half of the century, after Saʿid's death. Years after Owens's withdrawal, some British officials came to admit the loss of a commercial advantage. The British naval officer commanding the Africa fleet warned how "appeasing" Saʿid's "nefarious" demands not only had "moral effects" for the reputation of the British Empire, but, he warned, had also proven "injurious to the British trade in general" by depriving them of any harbor in East Africa.[54] In fact, the British had not easily acquiesced to Saʿid's demands that Captain Owen leave Mombasa. They tried resisting it diplomatically, even offering to compensate Saʿid with territory elsewhere or in cash if he allowed them to remain there.[55] The British clearly had an interest in the region, but Saʿid prevented them from capitalizing upon it because those commercial interests were so clearly linked with abolition, as discussed more in chapter 6.

By the time Saʿid had ratified his treaty with Edmund Roberts in the mid-1830s, British officials in the Foreign Office were keenly aware of their subordinate position in East Africa. They would have studied Hart's intelligence report from Zanzibar demarcating the strength of local actors in shaping the market and the finesse with which American entrepreneurs were weaving themselves into East African commercial networks. News of Saʿid's treaty with the United States had prompted concern, and many officials began lodging impassioned protests. Captain Owen, though no longer formally part of the British government, wrote to Lord Palmerston, governor-general of Bombay, in 1834. He decried how the British had lost their "footing in East Africa" for opening "new sources of wealth" for Her Majesty's "interprize [*sic*] and industry."[56] For a decade, Owen had watched as his government lost every opportunity in East Africa. He fumed in his letter to Palmerston: "Shall we still refuse to reopen to our fair enterprise those countries which aforetime furnished even to Solomon his Ivory, his Pearls, and his Gold?"[57] To his chagrin, Owens's calls went unanswered.

By the close of the 1830s there was only one British merchant residing in Zanzibar, and no government officials. That single British resident in Zanzibar, Robert Norsworthy, wrote to Bombay describing how visiting British traders, though few, faced special obstacles in conducting their business and forging longer-term social, political, and economic ties with locals because they did not have a consul to represent them and assist them. He contrasted this with the Americans, who, he observed, had "the manifest and valuable advantage of having a resident and consul at Zanzibar."[58] Another British official prodded Bombay to establish a consulate in Zanzibar, arguing that it would help "do away with the opinion of American supremacy."[59] From Saʿid's perspective, business was so good in Zanzibar that there was no need for him to discuss a commercial treaty with the British. By the end of the 1830s, cloves were already taking off on the island, and the Americans were purchasing them by the ship load. And East African demand for New England textiles was so high that merchants from Salem, Boston, and New York could barely send enough ships fast enough.

Unlike in his numerous overtures to the Americans, Saʿid never approached the British for a commercial treaty. In fact, he preferred to use them instead as a naval ally in the Gulf. The British caught on to this, realizing that they had been outmaneuvered. While Saʿid had left them to supervise the Gulf, the center of the emerging transoceanic economy had shifted to Zanzibar. After visiting the island, a British official returned to London in 1838 and described how "the good wile" of Saʿid was being actively and strategically cultivated by the governments of France, the United States, and even Russia. He noted that Saʿid had given the French, though they did not yet have a treaty, "exclusive advantages" of trade, arrangements rooted in the French demand for enslaved humans and indentured servants to work their plantations in the Western Indian Ocean. The United States, he wrote, had by nature of its treaty a commercial advantage over "every other state."[60]

By the end of 1838 the British had sent a representative to negotiate a treaty with Saʿid. They concluded their negotiations in 1839 and ratified the treaty the following year. The treaty's preamble illuminated distinct differences from Saʿid's treaty with the United States. Although all economic matters are in some way also political matters, Britain's political agenda was made explicit by connecting its commercial interests solely with abolition. According to the treaty, its goal was strengthening the commercial intercourse between the Omani and British Empires, but by means of "the perpetual abolition of the Slave Trade."[61] Otherwise, the treaty was like Saʿid's treaty with the United States, especially by establishing the first British consulate in Saʿid's dominions. Atkins Hamerton arrived in Zanzibar in 1841 as Britain's first consul. Unlike his American counterpart, Hamerton was a career soldier; he was not a merchant.[62] He viewed the world, and thus his affairs in Zanzibar, according to British geopolitical concerns with the French and to a lesser extent, the Americans. But most important among his duties was abolition. Hamerton described his own understanding of his duties as consul as "furnishing Government with information regarding the slave trade . . . and . . . inform[ing] Government of the nature of the aggressions of the French Nation in the territories of the Imam [Saʿid]."[63]

Soon after he arrived in Zanzibar, however, Hamerton realized that in terms of East African commerce, the French were relatively minor players compared with the Americans. He admitted in a dispatch to his superiors that "the whole trade of Zanzibar" was "monopolized" by Jairam and the Americans.[64] Hamerton was not exaggerating; in fact, this was a clearly articulated strategy for the Americans. John G. Waters once wrote to his brother, the consul Richard Waters, that their firm was sending another vessel to East Africa from Salem with one paramount goal: "to keep others out of the trade as much as possible."[65] The Americans did not have to worry much about British competitors. Robert Norsworthy, who ran the only British firm in Zanzibar, had for several years been suffering deficits between $80,000 and $150,000 annually. By 1837 Norsworthy closed the firm, admitting that its partners and investors had "tired of the trade."[66] Only two years after his arrival, Richard Waters was already transacting 90 percent of all American commerce through Jairam. Waters and Jairam had allied in the pursuit of monopoly, both realizing that controlling the market maximized their profits.[67]

They did not try to hide this. Hamerton quickly caught on, lamenting that "one and all" were "ill disposed" toward the British.[68] In July 1841 Americans in Zanzibar held a raucous Independence Day celebration. Amid fireworks and revelry, they hoisted giant American flags above their residences and ships in the harbor. In response, one British trader raised a flag printed with the words "No Monopoly." The celebration frustrated Hamerton, but he feared that the British trader's flag would offend Jairam or Saʿid. In fact, by the time the party ended and Hamerton went to meet with him about it, Saʿid had already ordered one of his deputies not only to go to the British trader's residence and remove the flag, but also to remove the entire flagpole.[69]

The American celebration foreshadowed a worsening of affairs for the British. Hamerton tried appealing to Saʿid in personal terms, before resorting to more formal diplomatic channels. Saʿid agreed to grant Hamerton a meeting. He listened to Hamerton's concerns about the poor treatment of British traders. Hamerton recalled that he had told Saʿid, "The people about him who advised him to treat or allow British subjects to be treated as they were at Zanzibar were not his real friends."[70] Hamerton did not record Saʿid's response to his appeal, but soon after the meeting Saʿid issued an order for Jairam to gather all the copal in the port and reserve it. Hamerton was overjoyed. He thought that Saʿid's reservation of the copal reflected how seriously he had taken his concerns, and that Saʿid was attempting to cajole Jairam into more equitably distributing the copal among vying merchants.

Hamerton soon realized, however, that Saʿid's order to reserve the copal was in preparation for the imminent arrival of an American ship, owned by a leading Salem merchant and consigned to Richard Waters. "And when Mr. Waters's ships arrive," Hamerton groaned, "all hands must wait until he is supplied."[71]

THE MARKET AT WORK

All hands, most especially Jairam's, waited for Richard Waters because he attempted to enculturate himself into Zanzibar's trading world. The path for Waters had been difficult. First, production in New England, especially in Lowell, could not keep pace with demand in East Africa.[72] Local persons in Zanzibar apparently had many reasons to be frustrated with Waters.

Shortly after his arrival as consul he was beaten, and locals frequently hurled stones at his house. At one point he wrote to Saʿid complaining that locals had stoned his house about twenty times in two months.[73] Adding to his troubles, stipulations in the commercial treaty between the United States and Saʿid did not, of course, preclude local merchants from seeking to extort Americans. Even Jairam caused profound trouble for Waters when he arrived. At first, Waters insisted that all American cargoes be unloaded in front his house. Jairam immediately ended that practice, with Saʿid's backing, telling Waters that all American ships would unload their cargo in front of the customs house. After the American treaty was ratified, Jairam tried to circumvent certain parts of it. He instructed Indian traders to pay him a 5 percent tax on all goods they sold to Americans, to compensate for the loss in revenue from the treaty's stipulation that no locals in Zanzibar would pay export duties. Saʿid ultimately stopped that practice, enforcing the treaty's stipulations, but navigating these troubles was made even more difficult for Waters because, for at least his first year in Zanzibar, local Arabic-speaking peoples refused to even help him by translating correspondence with Saʿid or anyone else on the island.[74]

American merchants conscientiously acceded to local commercial institutions. They understood that their own success was tied up with local commercial actors also being successful. On one occasion, Waters wrote to Ebji Shivji, Jairam's brother, notifying him how excited he was that Jairam was "making a great deal of money this year."[75] American success depended on prosperous local traders, like Jairam, because they sustained demand for American goods. Americans relied on local Indian Ocean peoples not just for sustaining business, but also for more practical requirements, like assistance weighing goods, translating languages, repairing and captaining ships, and more. The persons who provided those services for Americans demanded high prices for their skills.[76] American traders, for example, often relied on local dhow captains to transport their goods to different markets and bays surrounding a major port. These dhow captains charged for their time and even demanded extra when being forced to wait "over time" if the Americans did not have their cargoes ready.[77] One American admitted how critical these local peoples were for helping facilitate American commerce in the region—without them, admitted the American sailor, they "would not get along at all."[78]

The degree to which Richard Waters wove himself into the East African commercial world of the Omani Empire was made tangible in the written contracts he struck with Jairam and other local merchants. Most of these contracts bore Jairam's signature, either as a party to the contract or indicating that he had supervised the transaction and that necessary customs had been paid. When he issued his instructions for his temporary replacement in 1840, Waters did not just demarcate Jairam's importance; he also stated that any transaction must be drawn up as a written contract, with one copy to be retained by Jairam and another to be retained in the consular files. These written contracts often moved between English, Arabic, and Gujarati, depicting the transnational nature of business in the Omani Empire, as well as the extent to which merchants in this time and space transcended kinship-based ties in forming commercial networks.[79]

The degree to which Americans acceded to local conditions is evident in how they readily and knowingly resorted to paying higher prices than they often should have, just to maintain their position in Indian Ocean networks. Michael Shephard, a leading Salem merchant and financier, once wrote to his agent in Zanzibar that local traders "probably will force you to give higher rates, but as we consider that the least of two evils, you will have to submit to it."[80] Refusing to pay a price higher than standard market value would have been the greatest evil—it most likely would have resulted in that American agent being driven from the market. Even when they very clearly knew they were being dragooned by inflated prices, they still readily purchased the largest possible quantities of goods. In the same letter, Shephard instructed his agent that despite inflated prices, "the prospect for Copal the next year is good, so get all you can."[81]

This was not a world in which Europeans or Americans dictated terms or prices. Americans paid higher than market value—and did so at the largest possible volumes—because the local actors demanding those prices were the same people instrumental to their success in the region. But most important, Waters and the American merchants he represented in Zanzibar resorted to paying higher prices to protect their positions within these Indian Ocean networks, especially the position of merchants and firms from Salem. At times this led to some tension in Waters's role as American consul when he sometimes favored Salem commerce over other parts of New England. Waters once wrote to a counterpart that there was news of a new American ship soon to arrive from Boston. "You must do all you can honorably to prevent their contracting and thus getting a footing in Zanzibar," he instructed. "We must be willing to pay as high as they will if necessary and if it comes to the worst loose [*sic*] a few thousand dollars if by so doing we can keep the trade in the hands of those who now hold it."[82]

The footing held in East African commerce by Waters and other Salem merchants was often kept in place by certain local agents. Observing the business of Atlantic merchants in Sa'id's domains, Guillain recalled that one Omani-Zanzibari merchant, Khamis bin Uthman, worked as a business agent "for all foreigners." Because of his fluency in multiple languages, Khamis was known in Zanzibar as being "indispensable in all sorts of commerce."[83] Having a person like Khamis was instrumental for success. Khamis was indispensable because he would have helped Waters and other Americans settle business contracts. Entering into these contracts required foreigners to have someone translate through protracted negotiations; to understand local currencies, weights, and measures; and to understand the basic landscape of business firms and the best caravan porters. Khamis, fluent in multiple languages, would have helped Waters and other Americans move with ease between different languages and units in the same contract. For example, one contract declared: "It is agreed between Syed Sulleiman [*sic*] bin Hamed on one part and Richard P. Waters on the other part that the said Syed Sulleiman agrees to furnish the said Mr. Waters on his order two hundred frasillas of good dry cloves within three and a half months from this day, at $4.25/@ four dollars and one quarter per frasilla."[84]

While the US dollar is found as a unit of currency in many contracts, it never really caught on as a currency throughout the Omani Empire. The *frasilah*, however, became part of local vernacular in New England. The frasilah was a unit of measure equaling 35 pounds. Contracts for cloves, copal, coffee, dates, and other commodities were transacted in units of frasilahs, but the frasilah became so ingrained as part of American merchants' vocabularies that they used it in more informal, unofficial correspondence as well. Americans adopted the frasilah throughout the entire business cycle: when ivory, cloves, or copal arrived back in New England, they were advertised in local newspapers in units of frasilahs—not pounds.[85] In Zanzibar, traders moved between vernaculars in concluding their business. Bound by certain rules stipulated in treaties and the rules Jairam set for his customs house, traders from across oceans learned to understand one another.

When Jairam concluded a contract with Richard Waters for a quantity of cotton—an American product—the contract was stipulated in terms of bales, an American unit of measure. Similarly, when Waters signed contracts with any one of countless East African trading partners for copal—an East African product—the contract was concluded in units of frasilahs. Sometimes traders striking these deals moved between different units of measure

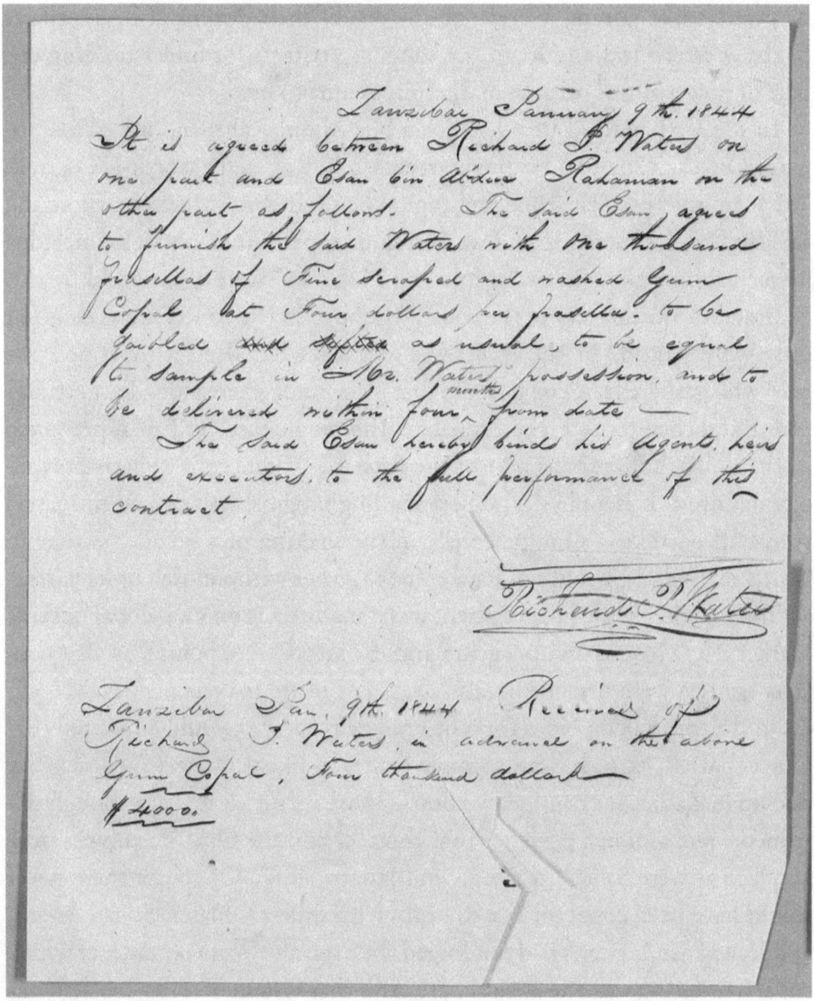

Zanzibar January 9th. 1844
It is agreed between Richard P. Waters on one part and Esau bin Abdue Rahaman on the other part as follows. The said Esau agrees to furnish the said Waters with One thousand frasillas of Fine scraped and washed Gum Copal at Four dollars per frasilla. to be garbled ~~and sifted~~ as usual, to be equal to sample in Mr. Waters possession, and to be delivered within four months from date —
The said Esau hereby binds his Agents heirs and executors, to the full performance of this contract

Richard P. Waters

Zanzibar Jan. 9th 1844 Received of Richard P. Waters, in advance on the above Gum Copal, Four thousand dollars
$4000.

FIGURE 3. Contract between Richard P. Waters and Esau bin Abdue Rahaman, January 9, 1844, for a sale of gum copal. This is a typical contract from the time, except that it is entirely in English, without any Arabic or Gujarati text. Richard P. Waters Papers, MH 14, box 2, folder 6. Courtesy of Phillips Library, Peabody Essex Museum, Rowley, MA.

in the same contract. In one example, Richard Waters concluded a contract with three Indian merchants in Zanzibar. Waters agreed to sell gunpowder to the Indian merchants, transacted in kegs. The Indian merchants agreed to pay for the gunpowder with ivory, transacted in frasilahs.[86]

These contracts were more than documents sealing business deals. They were manifestations of mutual dependence. These pieces of paper, created by persons like Jairam, Waters, or any one of their dozens of counterparts in the Western Indian Ocean, are tangible artifacts for understanding one part of how a global oceanic marketplace came to be.

In 1844 Richard Waters lent Esau bin Abdul Rahman, one of his primary Omani-Zanzibari trading partners, a line of credit worth US$4,000. The loan gave Esau the time and capital he needed to gather one thousand frasilahs of "fine scraped and washed gum copal." The contract concluded by mentioning that Esau's "agents and executors" were also bound by this contract for the delivery of the copal.[87] Imbued in the contract was thus not only Waters and Esau, the agents and executors, but also the unnamed persons who gathered the copal in the first place somewhere along East Africa's coasts and then ferried it to Zanzibar. This single piece of paper, preserved in the Phillip's Library as part of the Richard Waters collection, is polyphony manifest: it is a physical object making tangible named and unnamed voices all partaking simultaneously in the making of a broader whole, in which that whole would not have come together without each of its parts.

That single piece of paper, then, was a manifestation of a global oceanic marketplace. Just as Esau's agents and executors were bound by this contract, so too were persons oceans away. Furniture makers and woodworkers in Boston, Salem, New York, or Philadelphia who would have used that gum copal as a varnish were, through contracts like this one, fundamentally tied up in Zanzibar's commercial flows. Those furniture makers, though unnamed, were as much a part of that contract and the Omani Empire's marketplace as were Sa'id bin Sultan and Jairam Shivji. Of course there never would have been copal for sale to begin with unless Omanis, South Asians, and some East Africans had not forged the caravan system of trade, of which copal harvesting was one critical part. And that system of trade, in turn, was rooted in enslavement and human trafficking. Though they are not named in it, the contract between Esau and Waters illuminates the countless enslaved Africans whose kidnapping, buying, selling, and trafficking sustained the economies of both the Atlantic and Indian Oceans.

In a refrain to be followed by many historians, Fernand Braudel once remarked that the market was "equivocal": uncertain, imprecise, or ambiguous in nature.[88] When approaching economic and world history through a structural lens, the market certainly may seem so. The hand that shapes it and sustains it, after all, is ostensibly hidden. But dropping anchor in Zanzibar and wading ashore allows us to look at the market through the eyes of persons like Jairam Shivji or Richard Waters, in which the market crystallizes into literal manifestations of dependence tying together furniture makers in Salem with caravan porters in Bagamoyo, written down on that contract. Contained in this single, small piece of paper—the contract between Richard Waters and Esau bin Adul Rahman—was a transoceanic, intercontinental market in all its manifestations. This was a market of credit and of debt, of commodified time, of highly demanded products. It was also a market of agents and executors who would close out the deal should something happen to Esau.

Contained within that single document were distinct chains of a business cycle—the capitalists who struck the deal, the caravan porters and enslaved Africans who gathered and moved the copal likely in lands expropriated by Omani settlers, the merchants who sailed it to New England, the workers who turned the copal into varnish, the woodworkers who used the varnish, and the consumers who bought that furniture—all providing profits that would have catalyzed that same cycle in more voyages and return voyages.

That single piece of paper also represents the collapsing of distance, the bonds stretching across hemispheres united disparate markets into a global oceanic marketplace. An American entrepreneur from Salem, Massachusetts, was in Zanzibar off the coast of East Africa doing business with a person of Swahili heritage. At the center of the deal would have been Jairam Shivji, the Indian customs master from Gujarat, on India's western coast. The line of credit advanced to Esau would have given him the time necessary to gather a group of East African caravan porters and wage workers to trek into Africa's interior for gathering copal, before bringing it back to Zanzibar and unloading it in front of Jairam's customs house. From there, Richard Waters would have shipped it with all haste back to Salem, where it would have been sold throughout New England—all while the cycle was continuing back in Zanzibar, the capital of an empire ruled by a person from Oman in the Arabian Peninsula. Just as there were broad, structural international forces shaping the diplomatic negotiations surrounding the signing of British and American treaties with Saʿid, these structural forces were simultaneously shaping and being shaped by the very tangible ideas, actions, and goals of entrepreneurs in Zanzibar, like Richard Waters and Esau bin Abdul Rahman.[89]

CONCLUSION

The treaties Saʿid negotiated with the Americans and the British were parts of an oceanic marketplace in the making. As high-level bilateral negotiations, they were the consequence of transoceanic interrelations already in place and centered on Zanzibar. The treaties did not begin a historical moment, but rather encapsulated processes already underway, of capitalists from around the Indian Ocean, Europe, and the United States converging on Zanzibar. In his characteristically specific fashion, in 1844 Richard Waters summarized this historical moment in a letter to Sadick bin Barack, one of his favored Omani trading partners. "Our object is to do an honest business," he wrote, "and make all the money we can."[90]

From oceans apart, persons like Waters and Sadick went to Zanzibar in pursuit of wealth. Though this was never a unidirectional or smooth process, they formed ties transcending kinship, ethnicity, or religion. The ways Saʿid played the Americans and British against each other or the ways Jairam used Americans to monopolize trade in the Western Indian Ocean fortify the agencies of non-Europeans. Saʿid played the Americans and British to stymie the latter's attempts at curtailing human trafficking, thus facilitating the pursuit of wealth for the countless numbers of human traffickers moving about the Omani Empire. Likewise, Jairam monopolized trade with the Americans because local peoples, especially East Africans, demanded American goods more than those of any other country. Seen this way, this politics of the marketplace in Zanzibar amplifies the interests, ideas, actions, and goals of Arabs, Africans, and South Asians in the Western Indian Ocean and the world, despite an equation of global interfaces historiographically weighted toward the effects of Europeans' interests, ideas, actions, and goals.[91] Close readings of contemporaneous sources from this period in this space help deconstruct institutional and societal blocs rooted in the assumption of nineteenth-century British hegemony in the Indian Ocean especially in economic matters, an assumption that many historians continue to perpetuate without questioning its analytical points of departure.[92]

Interpreting this period of history from a point of departure rooted in polyphony, a more entangled historical picture, helps challenge the idea of British hegemony. In the Omani Empire, Americans—and to a lesser extent Britons and other Europeans—were minority middlemen helping connect local East Africans, Arabs, and Indians with the products they demanded to sustain their own pursuit of wealth, both monetary and sociocultural, according to their own institutions and rules. The international affairs surrounding Saʿid's treaties, combined with the actions of different persons in his domains, help enrich our understanding of the complex and fragile global order emerging in the first half of the nineteenth century, bringing to light a more multidimensional manner than has typically been portrayed. Amid this emerging global order, the interests of local peoples in the Omani Empire remained decisive. While the British Empire certainly was expanding in this period, it was also foundering against newly invigorated Atlantic competition in the Indian Ocean, the claims of the Omani Empire, and the evasive adaptations of entrepreneurs in the Omani Empire and its fluid commercial networks.[93]

The domains of the Omani Empire thus provide a helpful space for adding to our understanding of the "popular culture of enterprise" taking off in New England in the first half of the nineteenth century.[94] Far from New England, Indian Ocean persons like Esau bin Abdul Rahman, Sadick bin Barack, Jairam Shivji, or even Saʿid himself were helping facilitate that culture of enterprise in the United States by doing what present-day economists call *financial intermediation*. They were matching producers or holders of certain goods with people from around the world who had the capital to invest in those goods and facilitate their mobilities in perpetually circling carousels of trade.[95] Sailors in Zanzibar recognized the global nature of its marketplace. In 1850 an American captain looked out from the deck of his ship anchored in Zanzibar harbor and observed: "There is now lying here a larger number of foreign vessels than I have ever seen before. Just astearn of us was a French barque, on either side a Spanish . . . and ahead a Dutchman, and in the other part of the harbour a Frenchman, Arab, and Yankees."[96] Of course, surrounding those Atlantic ships would have been countless Indian Ocean dhows owned by Africans, Indians, Arabs, or perhaps even Persians and Armenians. That American ship captain's observation highlights the connected nature of this world. Yet connectivity as a motif in Indian Ocean histories has been somewhat taken for granted. Connectivity does not just exist. Inherent in the global nature of this marketplace and its connectivity was the unfolding of a process. Saʿid's protracted negotiations, the struggles Waters faced in ingratiating himself with Jairam, and the frustrations continually faced by the British in losing out on trade in Zanzibar all reflect how the idea of a marketplace need not necessarily be understood so much as a specific place or thing, but rather as "a process by which the economies of distinct marketplaces get folded into one another."[97]

Primary to this process was fostering the willingness of buyers and sellers to travel between marketplaces—surely something Saʿid understood given the steps he took in mitigating risk and increasing the velocities of circulation between Atlantic ports and his domains.[98] But even showing the process by which these connections were forged in the Omani Empire is only one part of the world-historical puzzle: the other, larger part of the puzzle is unscrambling the many different pieces that prompt us to question what those connections mean for understanding local, regional, and global elements in the making of the modern world. Most broadly, understanding the making of this marketplace as a continual process in which different parties borrowed from each other, but Indian Ocean institutions remained prominent, helps encourage seeing the Indian Ocean not merely as a place that absorbed Western-dominated modernity, but was rather constitutive of modernity itself.[99] Narratives of East Africa or anywhere else in the world being incorporated into a world economy presuppose that that world economy already existed, but the modern, capitalist world economy was, from its beginnings, fundamentally shaped by Indian Ocean actors taking part in different planes of interaction with modernity. Such a perspective is, in fact, more honest in terms of world history, for most of which Europe was a periphery, not a core.[100]

SIX

Enslavement and Human Trafficking

INTRODUCTION

The children had crossed the ocean before. In 1844 they were stewarded once more aboard a ship, this time bound east for Bombay. Upon their arrival, a British officer gathered them to record their testimonies.

Haleema went first. She said she was either sixteen or seventeen—she could not remember her birthdate. Born in Kirkuk, Iraq, she had been kidnapped as a toddler. Her kidnapper whisked her to Baghdad, where he sold her to a trafficker from India, who loaded her aboard a ship bound for Bombay. There, he sold Haleema to an Arab, who detained her for seven months before loading her on yet another ship bound for Muscat, selling her there.

Fatima said she was about sixteen. She was from a small village in India. She remembered that she had been kidnapped when very young—at what age exactly she did not know. Her kidnapper sold her to a man in Calcutta who worked as a store clerk. She most likely was forced to work as a domestic servant—at least on paper—but the man would rape her at his whim. When the man's wife found out, she beat Fatima, then took her to a slave market and sold her. Fatima's new owner loaded her among his cargo on a ship and sailed for Muscat.

Saʿadullah said he was about fourteen. He was from Hyderabad. He had been kidnapped at such a young age that he did not remember the names of his parents. His kidnapper had taken him to Bombay and sold him to an Arab, who took him to Sohar, in Oman. There, Saʿadullah was thrown in another slave market, sold again, and taken to Muscat.

Ghulam Hussain said he was about eleven. Born in Lucknow, he had no recollection of his father, and the only thing he remembered about his mother was watching her die. His kidnapper trekked him a thousand miles across India to Hyderabad, then on to Bombay, where he was sold to an Arab. From Bombay, the Arab trafficker stowed him on a ship and sailed for Muscat.

Haleema, Fatima, Saʿadullah, and Ghulam Hussain each shared the terror of being kidnapped, enslaved, sold, resold, and trafficked around the Indian Ocean. They also shared the experience of being enslaved together in the royal household of Saʿid bin Sultan.[1] We know the names of these children as recorded in their testimonies, but Haleema, Fatima, Saʿadullah, and Ghulam Hussain could each stand in for tens of millions of other enslaved humans from the Indian Ocean whose names and stories remain unknown, submerged beneath the historical disruptions and violence of empire and capitalism. This chapter deals mostly with enslavement and human trafficking in the Omani Empire's East African domains, but as Haleema, Fatima, Saʿadullah, and Ghulam Hussain show us, the entire Indian Ocean world was a whirlpool of slavery, with enslaved humans trafficked in all directions. As with other types of sources, relatively few testimonies from enslaved persons exist from the first half of the nineteenth century. These children's testimonies exist because the British took special interest in them as slaves to Saʿid and his family, their most stalwart ally in the Indian Ocean region.

Haleema, Fatima, Saʿaadullah, and Ghulam Hussain would not have been alone as slaves in Saʿid's royal household. Saʿid bin Sultan might very likely have been East Africa's most prolific human trafficker, alongside other privileged members of the Al Bu Saʿid family. But enslavement and human trafficking were not only for elites. Few historical claims are absolute, but this one is: slavery permeated every aspect of the Omani Empire. In the Omani Empire and in other parts of the Indian Ocean world, s slavery existed in many forms and degrees of servitude. Taking various forms over time, slavery has been an immovable layer in the foundation of this world, a fixed element in economy and society.[2] Under Saʿid, enslavement and human trafficking became more profitable than ever, underpinning the Western Indian Ocean economy. The numbers of enslaved humans trafficked between East Africa, the Gulf, South Asia, and Southeast Asia increased alongside the commercial flourishing of the Omani Empire because those persons worked in certain functions that buttressed the entire societal structure, not just constituting labor as one part of a cycle of capital accumulation.[3] Defining and holding together the Omani Empire was a system of coerced labor and human trafficking that facilitated the movements of commodities—like copal or ivory and enslaved humans—throughout the empire.

In the Indian Ocean, slavery was different from in the Atlantic Ocean. One reason is that many of the enslaved had legal personhood, with clearly delineated rights and certain degrees of autonomy. Nevertheless, in the Omani Empire markets, enslavement and human trafficking were inseparable, as they were in other parts of the world.[4] The exploitation and trafficking of kidnapped, enslaved, and trafficked humans no different than Haleema, Fatima, Saʿadullah, or Ghulam Hussain sustained the deals that culminated in fruit cakes, spiced hams, and billiard balls in new, leisured societies throughout the Atlantic. Although a vibrant system of free, wage labor–based caravan trade emerged in East Africa oriented around Zanzibar, the caravan trade was entwined with the movement of enslaved humans alongside ivory, copal, animal hides, cloves, and other commodities. In fact, British abolitionism did almost nothing to alter this; enslavement and human trafficking skyrocketed throughout the first half of the nineteenth century alongside the commercial flourishing of the marketplace, which was forged as much by enslaved humans as by consuls and capitalists.

In the Omani Empire, human trafficking increased exponentially well into the second half of the nineteenth century, despite the pressures of British abolitionism. The British threw the entire weight of Crown and Company into pressuring Saʿid to end it. From Atkins Hamerton to Queen Victoria, time and again the British insisted that Saʿid do everything in his power to stop the trade. Their attempts failed.[5] By 1840 the British were admitting this. That year the governor-general of the Bombay government put it succinctly: "All our attempts have failed."[6] Yet despite admitting failure, the governor-general urged his compatriots, "Relax in no exertions which our influence can command to put an end forever" to human trafficking.[7] Saʿid refused to diminish human trafficking, let alone end it. Nor did he ever feel inclined to do so; slavery was too lucrative, fueling both the empire and his personal wealth.

Especially when discussing enslavement and human trafficking, interpreting this history through Saʿid is instructive because it brings to light not only his private commercial interests as a merchant, but also his interests as an imperial sovereign of an empire that he understood to be connected with states and societies around the Indian Ocean the Atlantic. Like any other person in the empire at this time, Saʿid was caught up in global structural transformations in markets, commodity flows, and consumer tastes and preferences emanating from the hands of enslaved humans. Slavery was the blood that pumped through the arteries of economic relations that were stitching the Atlantic and Indian Ocean worlds together. As highlighted by a constellation of previously unused sources, Saʿid was aware of the globally enmeshed nature of the marketplace unfolding in his time. As he made clear to the British, to curtail slavery would risk eliminating entire markets and perhaps even new social and cultural norms around the world.

SLAVERY IN THE OMANI EMPIRE

The British political agent at Aden was not overstating things in 1841 when he observed: "From time immemorial the traffic in slaves on these coasts has been considered equally just with any other, and by far the most lucrative branch of commerce among these people; that their principal wealth is derived from this source."[8] For millennia human trafficking enriched Indian Ocean societies. With the Yaʿrubi dynasty, in Omani history it became central to imperial expansion. By the nineteenth century, one reason Zanzibar was part of the global economy was that the Omanis and their Indian commercial allies had molded it into a primary entrepot in the Indian Ocean for human trafficking, a trade entwined with the rising global demand for ivory, cloves, copal, and other commodities. Zanzibar's importance as a waystation for trafficking extended into the Atlantic world as well.[9] Spanish, Portuguese, French, and even some Armenian traffickers went to Zanzibar because it was known around the world for the "superior quality of slaves" in its markets.[10] The French were the most numerous traffickers in Zanzibar because decades of Omani pressure had corralled them to the island and away from other trade routes in the Mozambique channel where the Omanis had little to no influence.

By shifting trafficking to Zanzibar, the Omanis reaped great profits because of the coinciding influx of wealthy Indians who helped monopolize the market and force the French to pay nearly any price demanded. As Edward Alpers suggested, it is difficult to quantify the number of humans trafficked through Zanzibar before the American and British consuls began recording figures.[11] He concluded that scholars working on this earlier period most likely were incorrect in vastly inflating those numbers. Yet Alpers was not just quibbling with the veracity of certain numerical figures. As he argued, inflating the numbers of slaves *trafficked* through Zanzibar in the late eighteenth century and first two decades of the nineteenth century "obscures the importance of the market for slaves that was created by the rise of the colonial plantation economies of Zanzibar and Pemba in the decades after 1820."[12] In other words, a focus on trafficking, while critical, can obscure the rise of Zanzibar as not only a through-station but also a final destination for the enslaved. While the enslaved continued to pervade every aspect of the empire as local governors, security forces, ship captains, pearl divers, and domestic servants, a major interregional transformation in slavery in the Western Indian Ocean culminated with Saʿid's establishment of Zanzibar as the capital of the Omani Empire and the emergence of a plantation system. Though other forms of bondage did not end, Omani, South Asian, and some African elites increasingly began to use enslaved laborers for sustaining their newly refashioned lives as landed aristocrats presiding over plantations forged from expropriated indigenous land.[13]

As Zanzibar's role in trafficking grew, so did the number of enslaved workers on the island's plantations. In 1820 a British visitor noted that Zanzibar was already "the great seat of the slave trade" and described how a significant amount of Saʿid's state revenues derived from it. The British visitor probably did not know how prescient his next remark would prove to be. Because Saʿid's state revenues were so imbued with human trafficking, he concluded: "It seems beyond all hope that His Highness will be persuaded to put a stop to it."[14] Trafficking increased throughout Saʿid's reign and into the latter half of the century. As one scholar put it, in a statement echoed by many others: "In no other part of Africa, and at no other time, did slavery and the slave trade expand as rapidly as in nineteenth-century East Africa."[15]

The empire's success was inseparable from slavery, which permeated its economy, its society, and its politics. Slavery and human trafficking were each fundamental to what it meant to live in this part of the world. In Zanzibar, people understood enslaved humans to be things—objects bound in the pursuit and display of wealth—but differentiated between things that could speak (enslaved humans) and things that could not (inanimate objects). In the marketplace, traffickers and buyers approached an enslaved human as any other object, with a desire to employ the purchase or sale to further their own financial and social interests.[16] Yet while enslaved humans in the Omani Empire and Indian Ocean more broadly were understood as things, in other instances—if they were Muslim—they were also understood as legal persons. If Muslim slaves, they were not merely one type of disembodied property: they were persons with legal rights and certain degrees of autonomy. Around the Muslim world, some persons who were technically enslaved became powerful political rulers or military commanders, many others owned property, and countless more received an education and had other important social standing. From more powerful slaves acting as political deputies or military officers to the *watumwa wa mtumwa*, "slaves of a slave," enslavement and freedom had "multiple meanings depending on the social structures of the community, the status of owners, and the gender, age, and skill set of the enslaved."[17]

The differences between Atlantic Ocean and Indian Ocean slavery are reflected in scholarly debates. For example, one historian of the United States asserted—apparently without worrying about encountering disagreement—that no other question in American or Atlantic history has been debated as much as whether slave-owning plantation masters were capitalists, and thus whether slavery was part of a capitalist or precapitalist economy.[18] Rather than debating whether slavery was capitalist or precapitalist, or whether plantation owners were capitalists, Indian Ocean historians have instead sought to demonstrate that there is no single definition for what it meant to be a slave, nor is there a scholarly consensus on how enslavement manifested in economy, politics, and society. In the Omani Empire and throughout the Indian Ocean, however, being enslaved was simultaneously a legal status, a social status, and part of a complicated form of patron-client relationship.[19] As something embedded in every aspect of daily existence, enslavement existed along a spectrum of bondage. It did not always constitute a distinction between slave and free.[20]

Along this spectrum of bondage, slaves lived and worked at every level of society in the Omani Empire.[21] Some held relatively elite status, as crucial officials who helped run the empire. Before Saʿid made Zanzibar his capital in 1832, his governor there, Yaqut, was an enslaved man. The governor, in turn, relied on a force of about five hundred enslaved soldiers for maintaining port security.[22] Even after 1832, Saʿid relied on a slave to command his garrison at the fort overlooking the harbor between his palace and the customs house. Rebecca Wakefield, a British missionary working throughout East Africa, visited an enslaved man, a ship navigator, identified only as "Buckhett," and described his home as filled with vases, glassware, china, pictures, and mirrors from around Asia, Europe, and America.[23] Whether government officials, soldiers, sailors, merchants, carpenters, blacksmiths, pearl divers, or weavers, many enslaved men were educated and held positions of respect in society.[24]

Orlando Patterson argued that upon enslavement, a person could no longer belong in a new community and thus faced a "social death."[25] Such a conceptualization is especially apt in an Atlantic context, where enslaved humans had little, if any, participation in political, social, or commercial affairs outside the immediate confines of their bondage. In the Omani Empire, things were sometimes different for enslaved persons. Many African and South Asian persons were kidnapped, wrested from their homes, and trafficked around the Indian Ocean world, and many certainly would have endured Patterson's social death. Some enslaved persons, however, had a sort of social remaking and were able to exert certain degrees of agency and autonomy despite being enslaved. Slaves used varying degrees of autonomy and their abilities to accrue wealth to remake their statuses.[26] Some enslaved persons in East Africa were able to accrue wealth and establish themselves in society with varying levels of respectability according to their wealth and occupations. In addition to ship navigators like Buckett, whose expertise and abilities would have been irreplaceable, other enslaved persons held respected positions as commercial agents of their owners or as councilors.[27]

Buckett the ship navigator would not only have charged for his services, but he also would have likely bought and sold various commodities as he piloted ships to and from various ports. Many enslaved persons took on lines of debt—unto themselves or by associating themselves with their masters—and these lines of debt helped tie together Western Indian Ocean markets. Indian financiers commonly employed enslaved persons, and these slaves were especially important in leveraging their masters' capital reserves for engaging in commercial transactions. As a representative example, one leading Indian tycoon, who had for a time farmed customs in both Muscat and Zanzibar, referred to his slave as "the dearest, the most honorable, and the most respectable."[28] Atlantic visitors frequently remarked upon the pivotal role enslaved persons played in helping conduct business, employed in "the most trustworthy situations as supercargoes of ships, stewards, and superintendents."[29] Saʿid even employed slaves at his palaces to manage his stables and to teach his children equestrianism.[30] Other slaves worked on the plantations for cultivating cloves and as domestic servants; still others were part of the caravan trade for ivory, copal, and other goods from Africa's interior.[31]

The spectrum of bondage along which enslaved women fell is perhaps most illustrative of how embedded slavery was in the Omani Empire as a source of its existence. Slavery was intensely gendered.[32] In the Omani Empire, many enslaved women were household servants. Many were also concubines, especially those from present-day Ethiopia or the Caucasus—and some were the mothers of future sultans. Within the broader spectrum of enslaved status, concubines comprised their own spectrum.[33] Concubines were a form of wealth. Concubines reflected not only financial wealth—a man's ability to purchase them, house them, feed them, and so forth—but they also reflected social capital and status. Saʿid probably had the largest number of concubines of any person in the Omani Empire. The relative statuses and social perceptions of concubines highlight the complexities of this world. On one end of the spectrum were Saʿid's wives, all but one of whom were concubines. According to Saʿid's daughter Princess Salmah, her father had seventy-five "secondary wives" or concubines at the time of his death in 1856.[34] Salmah's mother was a Circassian slave, who apparently held great influence over Saʿid. Despite the horrific circumstances of her kidnapping and trafficking when she was a child, when she was brought to Saʿid's court she was taught to read and, as an adult, had a large social circle in the royal palace.[35]

Enslaved women who lived as concubines in the Omani Empire were constrained by patriarchal social norms and relegated to the royal harems. Within these spaces, however, they lived like royals. Every concubine had her own team of servants—themselves enslaved—who waited upon her at every hour. These enslaved royals had specially built lounging chairs that cradled their feet, legs, and arms, supporting the women while they reclined as their enslaved servants dressed them and adorned them with jewelry, henna, perfumes, or other ornaments.[36]

Not all women enslaved as concubines, however, lived in royal palaces. Any Muslim man who could afford it was legally entitled to possess concubines, and those enslaved by relatively poorer men hardly had the luxuries afforded to women enslaved in Saʿid's court. Many women in East Africa in the nineteenth century enslaved as concubines understood themselves as living within a social class defined by their status as enslaved humans. A popular song sung by enslaved women in Tanzania warned:

> A concubine is still a slave,
> Today the concubine is still a slave,
> Do not think about lying on a mattress,
> A concubine is still a slave.[37]

Just as the actual positions of enslaved persons were crucial to the empire, so too was their trafficking. Saʿid was among the most prominent traffickers and probably profited from human trafficking more than anyone else in East

Africa or the Gulf because he received a tax paid directly to him on every enslaved person sold in Zanzibar or trafficked through the island. Saʿid's family members were also among the most prominent human traffickers.[38]

In 1841 when Atkins Hamerton arrived in Zanzibar he was astonished by the extent to which human trafficking imbued daily life. "All, each, and every one, the subjects of His Highness the Imaum of Muscat are concerned in the Slave Trade," he declared in a briefing for his superiors. He added, moreover, that inhabitants of the Omani Empire were not just engaged in trafficking; they were also slave owners—"every person in proportion to his means," he said.[39] By the 1840s human trafficking had reached unprecedented levels. In 1842 Hamerton estimated that fifteen thousand humans were trafficked into Zanzibar annually. But that was only a partial figure, because any boat trafficking slaves to Zanzibar on behalf of Saʿid or his family did not have to pay the normal tax and thus would not be counted in any annual estimates. Saʿid's family, Hamerton noted, were the most prolific traffickers. "They are constantly bringing them over in some of [their] boats," he described in frustration, "as many as three and even four hundred" at a time. Two years later Hamerton revised his estimate, submitting that at least twenty thousand enslaved humans were trafficked through Zanzibar every year.[40]

The enslaved were trafficked to Zanzibar from throughout the eastern and central regions of Africa. Caravan leaders were usually Africans or Arabs. Along the caravan routes they maximized their profits by forcing the trafficked humans to carry other trade goods, like ivory or copal. The caravan leaders often shackled the enslaved men, in a line, to a massive tree trunk, which they were forced to carry on their shoulders, preventing them from escaping or fighting their traffickers. Arriving at the shore, traffickers loaded the enslaved in dhows for the trip to Zanzibar, where their treatment did not improve. Although Zanzibar is a relatively short distance from most of the major ports along the coast, the voyage could take several days, and the enslaved were rarely fed or given water. Countless numbers died before reaching Zanzibar.

It might seem counterintuitive that the high rate of death did not deter the traffickers from so terribly treating the enslaved—seemingly indifferently allowing to perish that which they were seeking to profit from. Because both price and demand for enslaved humans in Zanzibar were so great, however, the trade remained profitable for traffickers even if many of their prisoners died along the voyage. One young American sailor, Joseph Osgood, described this in the following verse:

What cares the merchant for that crowded hold
The voyage pays if half the slaves are sold!
What boots it in that dungeon of despair
How many beings gasp and pant for air;
How many creatures draw infected breath
And drag out life, aye, in the midst of death.[41]

There might have been some bias in Osgood's description of the trafficking. He might very well have been interpreting the trafficking through an Atlantic lens, with the horrors of the Middle Passage. The ships that would have ferried the enslaved from ports along East Africa's coasts to Zanzibar would not have been nearly as large as the Atlantic ships of the Middle Passage. Many of them were smaller and relatively simpler dhow-style ships, and the enslaved would have been onboard among other commodities and supplies, rather than shackled and isolated in certain holds beneath the deck. This was, in fact, one reason that Britons struggled to identify whether a ship was actually carrying enslaved humans as they began policing the ocean more.

When they did reach Zanzibar, however, the enslaved who survived their kidnapping and the trek to Zanzibar were unloaded at the Customs House, under Jairam's supervision, "in the same manner as a load of sheep would be."[42] Those who had died onboard were thrown into the ocean. Every trafficker was required to pay a tax of 1 MTD per enslaved human, which went directly to Saʿid. At the Customs House, they were fed a simple meal: typically uncooked corn or some other local, cheap vegetable, which they were fed "like horses."[43] Attached to the Customs House was a "wooden cage" in which the slaves were confined while their traffickers prepared to take them to the market.[44] Those who observed the ordeal surrounding the market often described it using animal metaphors.[45] The traffickers smeared the enslaved with oil, painted their faces with colorful designs to grab the attention of potential buyers, and also outfitted them with all kinds of gold and silver trinkets and ornaments.[46]

The market began around three or four in the afternoon. Traffickers divided the enslaved between male and female and then arranged them by age. The trafficker led them through the market, escorted by other slaves employed as armed guards. The trafficker, "in a sort of song," would chant the qualities of those for sale while suggesting prices. When a potential buyer called out, the trafficker stopped the whole solemn procession, calling for the interested party to come forth and inspect the shackled persons. It was, as one observer put it, an ordeal "not equalled in any cattle market."[47] The potential buyer would examine the slaves, running them through a series of tests to confirm their physical prowess and to check their hearing and speaking abilities. Perhaps because so many of them were bound to be household servants, a potential buyer would confirm that they did not snore or grind their teeth while sleeping. Slapping, prodding, and groping, the potential buyer inspected every part of the enslaved bodies, often forcing them to run or do other athletic movements. Those purchased were then stripped of the trafficker's ornaments and led off with the buyer.[48]

Whether they remained on the island or were trafficked elsewhere, those sold in Zanzibar fueled economies across the Indian ocean. In 1831 it was estimated that close to two thousand male and female slaves were annually trafficked from Zanzibar to Muscat. Three-quarters of them came from the Swahili coast of East Africa, with the remaining coming from present-day Ethiopia. At least three-quarters of those brought to Muscat were women, helping run the households of families predominantly involved in maritime commerce and used as concubines. The women trafficked to Muscat were generally in their teenage years. The most sought after were Ethiopian. In 1831 Ethiopian women sold in Muscat for between 35 and 150 German crowns, whereas Swahili women or women from other parts of East and Central Africa sold for far less, between 25 and 45 German crowns. Young men, castrated to be enslaved as eunuchs, were especially sought after by elites in the Gulf. They sold in Muscat for between 80 and 300 German crowns, with those who were well educated selling for the highest prices.[49] Yet Muscat was not the only slave market on Oman's mainland. Sur and Sohar had thriving slave markets, as did neighboring places around Oman in the Gulf and Red Sea, trafficking thousands of enslaved humans through their ports every year: Mitisiwa, Tadjoura, Zeyla, and Berbera on the coasts of present-day Eritrea, Djibouti, Somaliland, and Ethiopia; Mukalla, Mocha, and Hudeidah in Yemen; Jeddah in Saudi Arabia; Ras El Khaymah in the United Arab Emirates; Bahrain; Basra in Iraq; and Bushehr in Iran.[50]

From Zanzibar, human traffickers did not just sail north to the Gulf or Red Sea. Many also sailed east toward the Indian subcontinent, where there was a thriving demand for slaves in Kutch and Kathiawar, especially for males under the age of twenty.[51] Traffickers relied on many techniques for avoiding British suzerainty. In Bombay, for example, they would frequently claim female slaves were their wives. Arab traffickers did not even necessarily try to keep these techniques secret. Claiming female slaves as wives to avoid the British was a well-known practice throughout the Arabian Peninsula. The British agent in Mocha, Yemen, wrote to the Bombay government about it, describing for his superiors the ease with which traffickers avoided British patrols. He noted, in a moment of frustration, that Arab traffickers had become so adept at importing enslaved humans into British India that the only way to stop the practice would be to seize every single non-British vessel arriving along India's coast—obviously an impossible task.[52]

BESTING THE BRITISH

By the 1840s the entire Indian Ocean was a whirlpool of human trafficking at unprecedented volumes.[53] Saʿid could never understand why the British wanted him to try to stop this. In December 1821 Saʿid wrote to the British governor of Mauritius, telling him that it ought to be clear "as the Sun and the Moon" why he could never, and would never, end enslavement and human trafficking.[54] Coming off their joint victories against the Qawasim and Bani Bu Ali in the Gulf, the British sought to use this momentum and inkling of goodwill to cajole Saʿid into exerting greater control over human trafficking. In 1822 Saʿid met with the British resident in the Gulf at his palace in Muscat. The British had a new proposal for Saʿid. The resident tried appealing to Saʿid to see if he would perhaps end trafficking only to "Christian" nations involved in Indian Ocean commerce. The British had in mind their rivalry with the French but were also aware that human trafficking was helping to sustain small pockets of Portuguese and Armenian traders in the region. Saʿid immediately rejected their proposal. He explained how ending human trafficking in just those select countries would cause tremendous annual losses in revenue for his empire.[55] The British countered that they could perhaps subsidize this loss for him, an idea that never came to fruition partly because of simple logistics and bureaucracy, but also because Saʿid shrewdly began pushing the British in a new direction.

Saʿid would have understood that the formal declarations and treaties the British insisted upon would not entirely affect the daily lives, actions, and thinking of local peoples living and working throughout his domains. In certain select instances, he thus acquiesced to British pressure by signing various treaties for stopping human trafficking in the Omani Empire.

Beginning with the 1822 Moresby Treaty, he signed these treaties while placing the obligation of enforcement on the British. Under the treaty's stipulations, any attempts to suppress human trafficking would have to come from British hands, a task Sa'id knew was far too great for their relatively meager naval force in the Western Indian Ocean. While divesting his own deputies and agents of any responsibility for enforcement, Sa'id granted the British the right to establish consuls or agents throughout his dominions.[56] The ability to place a consul or agent anywhere they liked throughout the Omani Empire seemed a gift for the British. As they reasoned, it would allow them not only to thwart American and French rivals, but also to increase their ability to pressure Sa'id and his subjects to suppress the slave trade. At this same time, however, the British were caught up in their campaigns with Sa'id for maritime security in the Gulf, their troubles compounded by Sa'id's forcing the eviction of the only British official, William Owen, from East Africa. Although the treaty technically allowed the British to establish consulates anywhere in Sa'id's domains, they were unable to do so until 1841, thus essentially watching helplessly as slavery continually expanded throughout the empire.[57]

In fact, as the years went on, the British admitted their own inability to reduce human trafficking. In 1861 the British consul, Colonel Christopher Rigby, assessed information from the first half of the century and concluded that the export of enslaved humans from the interior of Africa through Zanzibar had "greatly" increased and, most importantly, was carried on in a far more "organized manner." Rigby noted that traffickers used Zanzibar as a port of departure for trekking further into Africa than ever before for kidnapping and enslaving humans to traffic around the Indian Ocean. There was an irony at the heart of British failures to reduce, let alone stop, human trafficking. Before it had become so systemized with Zanzibar as a waypoint, Arabs, Africans, and South Asians who kidnapped and trafficked slaves around the region did so on scales small enough that the enslaved would be placed aboard dhows in small numbers amid other commodities. Having a few enslaved humans aboard a dhow made it easier for the captains to evade British policing. By the midpoint of the nineteenth century, Rigby noted how this had changed, and now local Indian Ocean traffickers were dedicating ships solely to trafficking humans. Though it had become a more "distinct traffic," as Rigby described it, the British still mostly failed at stopping it. In 1840 one British official estimated that between four and five thousand humans were trafficked north from Zanzibar to the Gulf; Rigby, however, estimated that by 1860 the "smallest computation" would be ten thousand humans trafficked from Zanzibar to the Gulf every year. All this considered, Rigby concluded that "the experience of many years has proved" that British attempts at reducing human trafficking in the Western Indian Ocean had "met with very little success." Hoping to drive home for his superiors in the Bombay government just how subordinate the British position was, he added that local human traffickers "scarcely regarded" the risk of capture by British cruisers.[58]

Two decades after the Moresby Treaty, human trafficking had reached unprecedented levels in the Omani Empire and beyond in the Indian Ocean. More humans were being trafficked in and out of Zanzibar than ever before. Having received Hamerton's initial intelligence reports after his arrival in Zanzibar in 1841, Lord Aberdeen, British foreign secretary, wrote to Saʿid in 1842, expressing his resolute dissatisfaction. Aberdeen acknowledged that abolishing human trafficking would pose financial difficulties for Saʿid, but affirmed his wish that Saʿid would do so regardless. He tried convincing Saʿid that any loss in revenue would be temporary, arguing that it could soon be made up by establishing a "legitimate commerce" even more profitable than human trafficking for local peoples throughout the empire. Moreover, added Aberdeen, the British were now ready to entirely compensate Saʿid for any loss in revenue, not just for halting trafficking to Christian nations, but to any and every nation. To augment his case, Aberdeen included a similar letter from Queen Victoria, who also pressured Saʿid to stop the slave trade.[59]

Saʿid's response was unusually blunt. In every other letter across multiple archives, Saʿid's writings to foreign government officials adhere to a certain etiquette, full of flattery and blessings, ending only with inquiries about the recipient's health and proclaiming assurances that he would provide that person with anything they might ever need. In this response, however, Saʿid was speaking directly to a government whose strategy of abolition threatened the existence of his empire and his private wealth. He responded with similar letters to Queen Victoria, Lord Aberdeen, and Viscount Palmerston, who would soon become British prime minister. Addressing Lord Aberdeen, Saʿid was polite. He acknowledged British concerns that "the traffic in slaves by sea should cease and not continue." But he made his stance clear: human trafficking would not stop. If that were to happen, Saʿid declared, the societies comprising his empire would be "totally and entirely ruined, and no revenue nor any income, saving and excepting a trifle, will remain for me."[60]

Saʿid was balancing between maintaining some semblance of complying with his British allies and maintaining the ability for people in his domains not merely to make a living but to accrue enough wealth to transcend previous expectations of getting by. And he knew that every avenue toward wealth was somehow tied up with slavery. News of British attempts to stop the trade in slaves began to spread beyond the diplomatic receptions between Hamerton and Saʿid in his palace, and people throughout the empire began to turn even more against the British. "His Highness the Imaum is in the greatest possible alarm," wrote Hamerton in a dispatch to Aberdeen, "and all his people, in consequence of the wishes of the British Government to suppress the Slave Trade on the Coast of Africa, subject to His Highness's control." Hamerton went on, spelling out why such alarm was spreading: "The chief part of the Imaum's revenue is derived from the sale of slaves, and indeed the wealth of his subjects also."[61] Beginning with Saʿid, people throughout the Western Indian Ocean became increasingly wary of the British because they were not just seeking to reduce human trafficking, they were seeking its total end. Aberdeen made this clear. Her Majesty's government, he proclaimed to Saʿid, would never "rest satisfied with an imperfect execution" of complete abolition.[62]

The situation in Zanzibar and throughout East Africa was becoming so precarious that Saʿid was apparently not content with written statements to Queen Victoria and her senior counterparts in the British Foreign Office. He appointed a deputy, Ali bin Nasir, to travel to London with instructions about what he should impress upon the British. Saʿid instructed Ali that he should encourage the British to think in a deeper, more interconnected manner regarding the place of slavery in the economic relations binding the Atlantic and Indian Oceans. "It is necessary," Saʿid instructed, that the British "consider our condition, at present, and for the future." If the slave trade were to end, Saʿid insisted again, every person in his empire would suffer, with capital streams entirely disappearing. He explained why:

> First: They bring down Ivory from the Country of Quilwah [Kilwa] and the Coast, and they bring down the Ivory and the slaves together: so that if you prohibit traffic dealing in slaves, you will prohibit them from coming down and selling ivory.
>
> Second: They bring beads down from the quarters of Yemen and India. But if the bringing down of Ivory and the dealing in slaves be forbidden, they will cease to bring these articles.
>
> Thirdly: They come from Oman and from the upper Country and in this way most of them will cease to come and there will no longer remain any

purchasers for the goods which come from Europe such as Cotton Cloth for the people of Zanzibar are satisfied with little and if this takes place, there will no longer be any revenue at all.[63]

With this, however, Saʿid was still not done. Next he dismissed Aberdeen's offer of compensation for halting the slave trade, stating that the amount the British offered would hardly equal his total loss of revenue. As for compensation, Saʿid retorted, the British could instead take over Bahrain, contenting themselves with managing the different factions vying for power there—a task he knew the British would never be able to manage. He closed his letter by coldly telling Aberdeen that to explain all the reasons for his frustration with the British government, "a month would not suffice."[64] Saʿid was attempting to spell out how the already globally enmeshed economy was balanced on Zanzibar as one critical fulcrum, in which transoceanic producers and consumers were knotted together by mutually beneficial consumer demands. Those demands, as Saʿid delineated, were all predicated on enslavement and human trafficking. Ending slavery would have had disastrous global repercussions. As he alluded, to end slavery in his empire would mean there would be no fruit cakes spiced with cloves in Boston, or piano bars in New Orleans, or billiard halls in London. It would be, he proclaimed, like "the loss of the whole world."[65]

Saʿid's declarations to Queen Victoria and Lord Aberdeen are extraordinary and previously overlooked sources for seeing an oceanic marketplace in the making. In this letter, Saʿid was spelling out for the British a system of coerced, enslaved labor that supported the Omani Empire. Enslaved humans were not just important parts of the economy in the Western Indian Ocean because they could be bought and sold for profit. They comprised a labor system—a labor system that was fundamentally entwined with the commercial systems of the global trade for things like ivory and gum copal. As he spelled out, coerced labor was integral to the emergence and function of the Omani Empire and its commercial system that was bound up with consumerism and markets around the world, not only there along East Africa's coasts.

Saʿid was spelling out what historians have since spent decades concluding: there would have never been nineteenth-century capitalism without slavery.[66] Saʿid explicated how connected the ivory trade was with slavery.[67] Stopping the slave trade in Zanzibar or elsewhere in his domains would have had disastrous effects for communities in Eastern and Central Africa who had used enslavement and human trafficking as one means for helping create a complex, wage-based political, economic, and social system in Africa's mainland, but pointed toward Zanzibar. This caravan trade that emanated from Zanzibar was driven by a pursuit for income and profit, and while it gave rise to a new class of wage-earning, free caravan porters, it was, as Saʿid said, inseparable from slavery. Saʿid's comment on the entwined existence of the slave and ivory trades highlights the violent, brutal disenfranchisement of entire human communities subject to enslavement and trafficking.

At the same time, however, it also prompts us to dive beneath the colonial veneer. Certain groups of African peoples manipulated human trafficking and other commercial institutions bound up with the Omani Empire for augmenting their own agency, preserving their own political legitimacy, and lining their own pockets.[68] The process of enslavement opened entrepreneurial doors for other Arabs, Indians, and Africans who became landed aristocrats in Zanzibar and at new, settled communities dotted along caravan trails deep into Africa's Great Lakes region. Stopping the slave trade would thus have meant stopping or seriously damaging the ivory trade, and stopping the ivory trade would have removed the source of wealth for an entire class of local peoples, just as it would have damaged the commercial interests of merchants and consumers throughout the Atlantic. It would have stymied economic, political, and cultural transformations taking place simultaneously around the world. Elite women would have no longer had fine ivory combs; elite men would not have been playing billiards; and a growing American industry in the production of pianos could have ground to a halt.

The slave trade was also a fundamental part of cultivating cloves and harvesting copal, two primary commodities bringing Americans to East Africa as local people's most prolific trading partners. Damaging the trades in ivory, cloves, or copal would have risked driving American merchants from East Africa, thus possibly diminishing one of the great economic engines of the nineteenth century: East African consumerism. Already by the beginning of the century African peoples from the "interior" were actively trading in Zanzibar and other coastal areas, selling ivory and other goods not only to the increasing numbers of American entrepreneurs but, more importantly, to the increasing numbers of Indians, whose presence in Zanzibar was being fostered by Omani leaders. As much as by Saʿid's proclamations to seize native lands in Zanzibar and transform them into clove plantations, the process of indigenous expropriation was also driven by the increasing numbers of "interior" peoples coming to Zanzibar, like the Nyamwezi, who grew into the most voracious consumer class in the arena.

Saʿid's statement hints at this. Saʿid's last assertion that the people of Zanzibar—referring to local Zanzibaris, not Omani, South Asian, or East African settlers—were "satisfied with little" reveals the extent to which the consolidation of the Omani Empire and its oceanic marketplace in Zanzibar had led to new stratifications in East African society. Zanzibar was part of a new form of market, one that was transoceanic in scope. Expanding Omanis, alongside their counterparts from South Asia, had arrived in Zanzibar and, through violence, trickery, or a combination of both, expropriated land and traditional ways of living from indigenous Zanzibaris. Although a few patrician elites might have remained, almost all indigenous Zanzibaris became a human means of production, enslaved or indentured, for sustaining the machine of empire and the workings of the marketplace.

Saʿid was telling the British in surprisingly honest language that stopping the slave trade and thus also stopping the trades in the world's most coveted goods would have meant that the East Africans who became wealthy off those trades—whether in slaves, ivory, copal, or animal hides—would no longer have come to Zanzibar. And that would have left Atlantic traders, as with Omani and Indian traders, with only indigenous Zanzibaris to trade with. Left destitute and indentured by Omani imperialism, they would have been unable to purchase anything brought to Zanzibar by Atlantic merchants. Stopping the slave trade, then, would have ended the oceanic marketplace. And that, as he said, would be like the loss of the whole world.

Saʿid was not alone in resisting British pressure to end the slave trade. While Saʿid was writing to the British, his customs master Jairam was making dramatic changes in the market. Soon after Hamerton arrived, Jairam threatened any person in Zanzibar who cooperated with British agents there in suppressing the slave trade with "utter ruin" by refusing to allow them to buy or sell any goods anywhere on the island.[69] Soon after this, Jairam forced every Indian merchant in Zanzibar to sign a declaration that they considered themselves citizens of Zanzibar and were not subject to any sort of British suzerainty.[70] Indians working and living in Zanzibar readily acceded to Jairam's agenda; everyone on the island had turned against the British. In 1842 a senior British official visited Zanzibar and reported how unhappy Saʿid was with the British. He continued to note that British pressure for ending the slave trade had become a "byword" with everyone on the island, fostering a prejudice against the British government.[71] Hamerton confirmed just how deep that prejudice was. In one report he warned the Bombay government that locals had promised to murder every Briton and British subject (Indians) living in Zanzibar if the slave trade were ever to be ended.[72]

As Zanzibar's commercial prosperity skyrocketed throughout the 1840s, Hamerton maintained his pressure on Saʿid. By the end of the decade, however, he seems to have abandoned his efforts. The only thing that could stop human trafficking in the Indian Ocean, he lamented in 1849, would be "the interposition of the Almighty above."[73] Four months later, at the beginning of 1850, Hamerton made a final attempt to convince Saʿid to do something—anything—to suppress human trafficking. Saʿid granted him an official meeting, and Hamerton pressed his case. Saʿid listened carefully. He then gave a simple response: "Inshallah."[74]

THE NEW ARISTOCRATS

By the 1840s Zanzibar's position as the Indian Ocean's primary center for human trafficking had been solidified. Not all those trafficked to Zanzibar, however, were taken elsewhere; countless enslaved humans remained in Zanzibar as their destination. The number of enslaved on the tiny island increased every year in tandem with increasing reciprocal demand between the Atlantic and Indian Oceans. In 1839 there were about twenty thousand slaves in Zanzibar. By the 1850s that number had quintupled to about one hundred thousand.[75] "The people are growing rich," Hamerton observed, and therefore "able to buy more slaves to cultivate cloves."[76]

From root to harvest, the clove industry was built on slavery. Omanis who emigrated to Zanzibar and other parts of East Africa brought with them notions of racial and religious hierarchies. This entrenched racism facilitated the emergence of plantation agriculture, but the system was also driven by emigrating Omanis' attempts to find the most efficient means of production for a globally demanded product.[77] The transformation of Zanzibar into the world's center of clove production reflects elements of continuity and change in Indian Ocean and world history. Many Omanis who followed Saʿid to East Africa—and the countless numbers who preceded him—were from Oman's interior, where their family confederations for centuries had been settled agriculturalists, primarily growing dates.[78] Although the product they cultivated changed from dates to cloves, the patterns of settlement and cultivation by Omanis moving throughout the Western Indian Ocean reflect established patterns in Indian Ocean history of peoples alternating between mobility and rootedness for harnessing natural environments in pursuit of wealth. Cloves were new to Europeans and Americans, but peoples throughout the Indian Ocean had used them for thousands of years for incense, perfumes, medicines, and spices for foods and beverages. From a world historical framework, the introduction of cloves to European and American consumers was one important step in the incorporation of the new Atlantic world into its long-standing Indian Ocean counterpart.

Zanzibar was so naturally fertile and well-suited for cloves that they would have grown without plantations and with little attention. "Indications are everywhere that nature is by no means meager in the returns made to [the clove] industry," remarked an American visitor. "Indeed the cultivator's limited attention may be rewarded by a plentiful supply."[79] The construction of plantations, however, was a part of a particular historical moment when a "plentiful supply" was good, but nowhere near enough.[80] Supply had to be the absolute maximum that the earth and slaves who worked it could produce. Omani plantation owners exploited both people and nature for ever-increasing plenty. In this system, the slaves forced to work the plantations were like organic machines, the plantations like organic factories, churning out quantities of labor and products in unprecedented volumes.[81]

Expanding plantations began with expropriating land. This process required dramatic physical changes to the island's landscape, a process that had parallels throughout the world in the nineteenth century. As one scholar put it, part of the worldwide forging of modernity was "implacably" eliminating everything that interfered with the efficient production of key commodities.[82] Coconuts, bananas, jackfruits, oranges, lemons, and many other native fruits grew intermingled with the island's fauna as natural parts of the landscape. Clove trees, however, required the land to be stripped bare before planting. Reaching more than twenty feet in height by maturity, clove trees absorbed so many nutrients from the soil that any competitors for those nutrients had to be eliminated.[83] Clove seeds were planted in rows, each row comprising six to eight thousand trees on larger plantations. With his customary flair, Richard Burton described seeing clove plantations for the first time: "Those prim plantations which, from the offing, resembled Italian avenues of oranges, the tea-gardens of China, the vines of romantic Provence, the coffee plantations of Brazil, or the orange yards of Paraguay, were the celebrated clove grounds, and the largest, streaking the central uplands, were crown property."[84]

In 1835 Edmund Roberts and Dr. William Ruschenberger traveled to Zanzibar after they ratified the American treaty with Saʿid. In Zanzibar, Saʿid's deputy Hassan bin Ibrahim accompanied them on a visit to one of Saʿid's clove plantations. Leaving Zanzibar town on horseback, they followed a road through "gently undulating country, of a most pleasing aspect, well cultivated and well inhabited."[85] After several miles they reached Saʿid's plantation. At the end of the road was a large gate, and just beyond was a small one-story house. The front of the house had a large veranda with a pyramid-shaped roof, unusual in a part of the world where nearly every building had a flat roof. As the visitors stepped inside beyond the verandah, they passed several rooms lined with spacious windows. Roberts was struck to see how the windows had hinges to open and close them and even had blinds. Several glass chandeliers hung from the ceiling. The walls had carved niches displaying French stained glass, porcelain ornaments, and other decorations. In one corner of the house, the visitors watched several recently arrived crates being unpacked, containing large, imported mirrors. There was a fine mahogany table with cabriole legs and claw-style feet, likely English. The chairs beside the table were Chinese. The floor was solid marble, part of it covered by *chunam*, a type of polished and ornately decorated plaster made in India.[86]

The house itself was made of coral and situated in a manicured, breezy yard. As they went into the yard, Roberts and Ruschenberger walked past a garden brimming with rose bushes, citrus fruit, and nutmeg trees. Looking beyond the garden, "as far as the eye could reach . . . there was nothing to be seen but clove trees."[87] Amid all of this were thousands of enslaved Africans. They would have been in the clove fields cultivating and tending to the tiny fruits, caring for the gardens, cleaning the house, minding its décor, polishing its marble floors, cooking for Saʿid and his family, caring for the horses, and constantly carrying supplies from Zanzibar harbor. All this labor was integral to the emergence of "clove mania," but these enslaved humans also were a foundation for the emergence of a class of landed aristocrats in Zanzibar and throughout East Africa's "interior." The descriptions of Saʿid's residence and the plantation on which it was built are artifacts in the making of modern global capitalism. These descriptions, important as much for what they included as for what went unsaid, were manifestations of the rise of luxury, leisure, and consumerism, each a transformative force inexorably propelled by violence, enslavement, and human trafficking.

As the two American visitors walked beyond the garden and toward the unending rows of clove trees, they passed dozens of smaller buildings that were homes for Saʿid's slaves. The largest plantations, like those owned by Saʿid, had several thousand slaves.[88] If they were Muslim, these slaves had complete legal rights as persons; but regardless of religion, slaves in this time and space had varying degrees of autonomy, and few, if any, were regarded as mere chattel once they had been trafficked and sold.[89] They could come and go from the plantation, and they were allotted their own private land for harvesting food for their families. They grew cassava, rice, plantains, mangoes, and other vegetables, and ate a great deal of seafood. Many had their own homemade mills for grinding dried cassava into bread and other baked goods.[90] They could trade and manage their own business affairs, and some enslaved persons even had their own slaves. Most of their time, however, was spent cultivating cloves. As Roberts and Ruschenberger kept walking, they watched hundreds of slaves standing on makeshift ladders picking the tiny fruits, while others worked beneath them clearing the ground of dead leaves and sticks and collecting any cloves that had fallen. "The whole is in the finest order," recalled Dr. Ruschenberger, "presenting a picture of industry, and admirable neatness and beauty."[91]

The work to maintain such "neatness and beauty" was agonizing. The trees grew in an almost conical shape, with the branches growing out from the trunk at right angles, starting a few inches above the ground. Ruschenberger estimated that the plantation had four thousand trees—rather astonishing when one considers the relatively small size of Zanzibar island, and this was only one of many other plantations.[92] Saʿid and other elites wrung from the island every possible measure of production. In a good season, the plantation owner could expect to profit 100 MTD for each tree. On Saʿid's plantation, in a good season he could expect to produce 700,000 pounds of cloves. The actual cultivation of the cloves took place from around October to February, depending on the timing and duration of the monsoons. The slaves who worked the plantations faced countless difficulties. The equatorial sun, though scorching, was perhaps the least of their worries. They were always battling swarms of mosquitos and other insects. Reaching the delicate fruit required a person to needle through the tree's dense and sharp branches and leaves. Sometimes they could shake the trees or use tools to beat the branches, causing the fruit to fall to the ground that had been cleared, but they had to take great care to not damage it. The harvested fruit would be collected and taken to a central gathering place on each plantation, where it would be spread on a patch of leveled and cleared ground to dry in the sun. Any remaining blossoms on the trees or immature fruits were left until they grew to about an inch in thickness, at which time they fell off and were used to plant more trees around the island. Once the cloves had dried, the slaves processed them and organized them by quality. Many slaves became specialists in sorting cloves by grade and negotiating the best prices for them. The best cloves, as one observer put it, were characterized by their dark color, fragrant oiliness, "hot biting taste," and aromatic smell.[93]

The profits brought to plantation owners by the labor of their slaves did more than line pockets. The profits also helped structure new understandings of identity, status, and social relations in Zanzibar and parts of East Africa connected to Zanzibar. As Sarah Croucher wrote, clove plantations reflected not only a shift in the economy of Zanzibar, but also a social transformation: "They were institutions through which plantation residents came to understand their lives, through which social positions were often structured."[94] New avenues of wealth brought by transoceanic commerce, all revolving around slavery, magnified preexisting racial and religious tensions that Omanis brought to East Africa. Many Omanis learned Swahili; for children of Omanis born in Zanzibar, Swahili became a first language. While their identity in many ways became imbued with Swahili language and culture, Omanis displayed their differences in social ways, including how they dressed. Pure white robes for men (with a tassle, or *fareeka*, that was often scented with perfume), ornately woven headdresses, and *khanjars* or traditional Arabian daggers with ivory handles were all symbols in East Africa of being Omani. From their clothing to their housing, Omanis thus used their wealth to make tangible their internal assumptions about what set them apart from others. Plantations were expressions of a capitalist rationality, but they were also forms of cultural capital. As Hamerton observed, "A man's wealth and respectability in the dominions of the Imaum of Muscat is always estimated by the number of African slaves he is said to possess."[95]

Owning enslaved humans allowed elites to delegate work and business—slavery thus added to the hierarchy of trade. Slavery, which imbued the plantation economy as it did the caravan economy, provided means for elites to transcend the natural limits of trade. It allowed trade to become so efficient, high-volume, and fast-paced that elite merchants were no longer entirely bound by the monsoon or the earth's natural capacities. Because of slavery, these elites became like tycoons in a transoceanic business in which they could remain mobile but also had the privilege of choosing to be immobile, of putting down roots. Mobility was no longer a requirement for pursuing wealth; it was one option among many, and it was increasingly an option that was delegated to others lower in the hierarchy of trade. Tinged with Orientalist racism, Richard Burton claimed that no Arab in the Omani Empire "dreams of doing any sort of labour when he has once got together sufficient money to purchase a slave, or a number of slaves, after which he lounges about from place to place."[96] Burton's claim is at once misguided and illuminating. Many Britons of the time, as did other Europeans and Americans, frequently cast Arabs as idle and insolent. His observation, however, highlights the extent to which labor had become stratified in East Africa, with a class of leisured elites firmly ensconced at the top while delegating entire business cycles—from security, to logistics, to agricultural labor, to shipping—to subordinates, many of whom were enslaved.

The rise of this settled, leisured, tremendously wealthy aristocratic class was not relegated just to Zanzibar's plantations. It was fundamentally connected to social, economic, and political transformations tethered to Zanzibar but extending deep into the African continent, to the Arabian Peninsula and Gulf, and to South Asia. Fortune stemming from initial periods of mobility revolving around business in Zanzibar allowed wealthy persons to begin putting down roots in East Africa's "interior." One such person was Thani bin Amir al-Harthi.[97] Thani emigrated to East Africa in the early 1840s. He was from Nizwa, a city in Oman's interior of immense political and theological significance and formerly the Omani capital. Until he left, he had spent his life in Nizwa living modestly as a confectioner of *halwa*, a sweet, jelly-like dessert, still loved by Omanis today. By 1840, however, the tides of fortune had shifted. A drought devastated Oman, drying up water canals in Nizwa and other major cities and thus ravaging Omani date palm plantations. Like countless Omanis, Indians, and others, Thani seized upon the moment to leave, pushed from his home by drought but pulled to East Africa by Sa'id's economic policies and its local spirit of enterprise.

When he arrived in Zanzibar, Thani found steady wages in the caravan trade. By 1852 he had become a business partner with another caravan trader, Musa Mzuri, who had emigrated to the area from Surat in India for much the same reasons as Thani. The two men pooled their wealth and talents in helping establish Kazeh, a bustling caravan depot and waystation for commodities, enslaved humans, and merchants coming and going from

Zanzibar. Thani and Musa purchased or enslaved hundreds of Africans, whom they used to help settle Kazeh. The enslaved were builders, security personnel, agriculturalists, concubines, and other domestic servants. In Kazeh, Thani and Musa each put down roots: they built homes, established a well system for irrigation and drinking water, had flourishing gardens, and married local women. Kazeh was five hundred miles from Zanzibar—thousands of miles from Thani's former home in Oman and even farther from Musa's former home in India. Each man had the wealth to remain mobile and return to his original home if he had wished, but each acted on his privilege of being immobile. They kept a near constant cycle of porters headed for Zanzibar to sell slaves, ivory, animal hides, copal, and more. While they put down roots in Kazeh, they relied upon others for bringing them constant "supplies of merchandise, comforts, and luxuries from the coast."[98]

Although Thani, Musa, and countless other elites lived hundreds of miles away from Zanzibar as rooted, settled aristocrats in East Africa's interior, they were enmeshed in Zanzibar's oceanic marketplace through slavery. Thani and Musa had begun their enterprises in East Africa as caravan porters, or *mpagazi*. Many caravan porters were free, and they worked as porters because of an explicit search for income and profit.[99] These free, wage-working, entrepreneurial individuals were critical to the success of the nineteenth-century world economy. For the Welsh explorer Henry Morton Stanley, this was clear. Without the caravan porter, Stanley observed, "Salem would not obtain her ivory, Boston and New York her African ebony, their frankincense, myrrh and gum copal."[100] But Stanley's observation points to only one part of the nineteenth-century world economy. New England did not just consume African goods; New England produced goods for African consumers, maintaining their central role in shaping the world economy past the first half of the nineteenth century. Without the caravan porters, leading Salem merchants like David Pingree, Henry Fabens, or Richard Waters would likely have gone bankrupt because there would have been no consumers to buy the goods their agents produced. Historian Steven Rockel was referring to Africa when he stated that without porters, "nothing would have moved."[101] Rockel's claim, however, might be extrapolated. Richard Waters did not have to travel into East Africa's interior to sell Lowell-spun cotton cloth or Boston-made muskets, just as Jairam Shivji did not have to go to the coast to collect the copal or ivory he used as collateral, because they each had agents and porters doing it for them. As much as Saʿid or Jairam, African porters also stitched together these vast transoceanic connections that helped forge the modern world.

Though most caravan porters were free, there never would have been a caravan trade without slavery. Indeed, many of those free, wage-earning caravan porters were enslaving and trafficking humans as a critical source of profit. On nearly every page of his autobiography, the famous Omani-Zanzibari caravan trader Tippu Tip mentioned slaves and porters in the same breath.[102] The institution of slavery was ubiquitous in every aspect of life in the Western Indian Ocean, never an isolated sphere of activity, and always entangled in local, regional, and transregional economic, political, and social forces.[103] The emergence of new aristocrats like Saʿid, Jairam, Thani, Musa, and Tippu Tip was a consequence of both continuity and change in this history. Slavery provided both profit and an efficient means of production, as it had before, but these aristocrats accrued unprecedented levels of wealth because they absorbed new Atlantic markets into their economic world. During Saʿid's reign, the wealth accrued doing business in this new transoceanic marketplace afforded elites the privilege of being immobile and putting down roots. Mobility had become a tool used by elites to delegate to subordinates to augment their own means to their own ends, with those ends being a settled life of luxury.

Saʿid's campaigns for maritime security, fiscal policies in East Africa, and the politics of forging the marketplace had helped crystallize in political and strategic terms a world in which persons in the Omani Empire used wealth as a means for transcending the obligation of mobility. People like Thani bin Amir, Saʿid bin Sultan, and Jairam Shivji were part of a moment in a world historically characterized by mobility in which private wealth allowed persons to separate themselves from the logistics of the mobilities they profited from. They put down roots, with delegated functions that allowed them to live as privileged elites, untethering themselves from any obligation of "returning home."[104]

Perpetuating the institution of slavery was critical to maintaining this aristocracy and bestowing its privileges—in both financial and cultural capital—upon future generations. After ruling the Omani Empire for nearly half a century, in August 1850 Saʿid bin Sultan sat down with one of his trusted deputies who often acted as his scribe. On this occasion, the two men met to record Saʿid's will and testament. Now aged fifty-nine years, Saʿid had dozens of children among whom he needed to divide his property—including his slaves. Beginning with the example of the Prophet Muhammad, for more than a thousand years it had been convention for practicing Muslims who owned slaves to emancipate them at their death, if not before. Doing so was believed to be a sure way of earning God's grace. In his will, Saʿid donated considerable amounts of his wealth and property to others and delineated what various members of his family would inherit. Toward the end, he left instructions regarding his slaves. "For the sake of the Almighty God, and in the hope of His Mercy," Saʿid, writing in the third person, declared free "all the male and female slaves which shall remain in his possession after his death, *excepting those who are at his plantation*."[105]

That Saʿid freed all his slaves except for those working at his plantation confirms the extent to which he understood slavery as a fundamental component of a labor system that created and preserved wealth for himself, his family, and the empire. There were countless other plantations besides Saʿid's that were run by enslaved labor. Aside from plantations, even if enslaved humans were not providing the actual labor in something like procuring ivory, they would have been entwined with it, there along the trails and at the customs stations along the way to bringing the ivory to Zanzibar. By 1850 elites like Saʿid had come to regard slaves as permanent fixtures of the social and economic order, no longer merely as commodities, servants, or workers temporarily in their custody. This became true even for those enslaved as domestic servants. Visitors to Zanzibar commonly observed that it was considered disgraceful to sell a person enslaved as a domestic servant.[106] There were social and cultural underpinnings to this, but there was also a clear, capitalist rationale at work. Emancipating the slaves at Saʿid's plantation would have ended his profit, forcing his heirs to bear a financial burden of either purchasing several thousand more slaves or finding a different way to carry on the plantation's work.

The plantation represented intergenerational wealth. Saʿid died in debt; the continued success of his plantation was necessary for his sons to continue running the empire and for his family members to continue their aristocratic lifestyle. Saʿid's will, like his letters to the British government, reflects just how clearly he understood the central role slavery played in preserving his empire and the broader world economy of which it had now become a part. Saʿid's decision to emancipate all his slaves except those at his plantation brings to light the entwined forces of structure and agency. Saʿid was an individual, no different from any wealthy Muslim person in Zanzibar, acting upon his own agency to do certain things to obtain God's graces, but also trying to preserve his wealth. That he emancipated all of his slaves except those at his plantation situates that agency within a larger historical structure that he was aware of, and ultimately subject to. But it also suggests where Sa'id placed the most value on enslavement: a system of coerced labor at the core of the empire he oversaw.

CONCLUSION

Visitors to Zanzibar during Sa'id's reign almost always commented on the island's beauty. In 1845 as the American merchant vessel *Emily Wilder* anchored in Zanzibar harbor, one of its sailors, Joseph Osgood, recorded: "Its appearance is strikingly beautiful and picturesque, its moods being clothed in an untarnished mantle of luxuriant and perennial verdure."[107] One evening after completing his duties, Osgood went to the beach to stretch his sea-cramped legs. As he began his walk, Osgood did not know that he would be seeing a different Zanzibar, one underneath wealth's pretty veneer. As he strolled along the beach with the harbor behind him, Osgood began to see a stark juxtaposition. The white beaches were strewn with what remained of those who maintained the island's beauty. Everywhere he looked, he recalled, the beach before him was littered with "bleached and ghastly skeletons . . . peering here and there from the chambers of their graves which the washing tide keeps ever open."[108] Osgood had stumbled upon a section of the seashore near the main harbor where the corpses of the enslaved were thrown. Enslaved humans who died in Zanzibar were rarely, if ever, buried; leaving their bodies on the beach was regarded as "the least troublesome mode of disposal," as if one was just throwing away a broken part of a machine.[109]

Standing there that night, Osgood recalled a feeling of grave reflection wash over him. He noticed that one of the waves had separated a skull from a skeleton. He picked it up, pondering the memory of this human: "No village bell had tolled out its solemn knells. . . . [N]o dear friend had chisseled a tender inscription and erected a simple monument. . . . [B]ut the hoarse growlings of ravenous beasts had sounded their requiem; the ever moaning waves had followed it in long procession and buried it in its shallow grave in the sand, watched over and watered it with their spray."[110]

After taking a moment, Osgood nestled the skull back into the sand, his mind racing with "a hundred inquiring thoughts as to the name, nation, station and language it had held."[111] As an American, Osgood would have known of the horrific slavery in his own country. The cloth he had helped bring to Zanzibar was fashioned from cotton picked by slaves in the United States. In Zanzibar, he visited plantations where slaves harvested the cloves he would sail back with to New England. Just as New England consumers sustained the enslavement of persons throughout East Africa, Omani, Indian, and African consumers sustained the enslavement of persons throughout the American South. In many ways, Osgood was just one among hundreds or thousands of similar merchants, sailors, and entrepreneurs betting their fortunes and their futures on ever-strengthening ties between the Atlantic and Indian Oceans. But unlike Osgood, few left behind a piece of writing so vivid in its description of vast, global transformations as they played out in real time. That singular moment on the beach was one person's confrontation with the savage side of the global economic system he himself was helping forge.

Osgood's reflection on the beach that night in Zanzibar might be melodramatic. It is no doubt colored by his Atlantic biases for understanding enslavement and human trafficking. Scaling out, however, it is true on a global scale, and provides an intimate expression of how so many historians have sought in the craft of writing history to do what Osgood said: to erect historiographic monuments to the unnamed enslaved persons who have sustained entities like the Omani Empire and provided labor for the emergence of our modern world economy. The institution of slavery and the legacies of millions of enslaved humans united the world into an oceanic marketplace as much as, if not more, than anything else. In his log, Osgood left for historians a magnifying glass for expanding the plantation complex. The Omani Empire exemplified how the full range of free or enslaved humans, agendas, and products involved in the nineteenth-century global economy were not relegated to hemispheric scope. The creation and consolidation of plantation economies in regions like the West Indies or East Africa was from inception driven by multiple global factors operating simultaneously on different scales. New England merchants like Osgood were thus part not only of an American plantation complex, but also of an Indian Ocean complex and thus of a global system of slavery that was the bedrock of wealth in the world.[112]

Osgood's moment shines a light on something else, as well. The broader history of the modern world is not so much the resolution of tensions or contradictions, but rather the condition of living with them and exploiting them. Zanzibar's fertility and strategic location were exploited to transcending nature's limits. Transcending nature's limits allowed the emergence of a landed aristocracy whose wealth was derived from the subjugation of other humans. Holding the skull, Osgood confronted a truth historians later debated, then confirmed: nineteenth-century capitalism was built on slavery.

SEVEN

The Omani Empire in World History

HE SEEMED TO HAVE known it would be his last time home. On April 16, 1854, Sa'id boarded his beloved ship *Victoria* and sailed from Zanzibar to Muscat.[1] He was going there to settle some political disputes and to visit his mother. Accompanied by a small cadre of officials, Sa'id sailed north, passing the Omani Empire at its height. Whether Mombasa, Malindi, Manda, or Muscat, each passing port would have appeared familiar. Each had a large harbor, of course—large enough to cradle ships from Africa, the Red Sea, the Persian Gulf, Persia, South Asia, the Far East and Southeast Asia, Europe, and the United States. Immediately ashore would have been a customs house, perhaps with a small contingent of Baloch mercenaries guarding it. Though inconspicuous, the string of customs houses lining the shores of East Africa's coasts and dotting its caravan trails was the tangible manifestation of the Omani Empire and the oceanic marketplace it helped foment. A customs deputy, appointed by Jairam, managed each one, ensuring as best he could that duties were sent directly to Jairam in Zanzibar. Buzzing around the customs house would have been a coterie of carpenters, fishermen, masons, porters, weavers, traders, and more, each hoping to demand the best prices from arriving Atlantic merchants, whose own cargoes of cotton, brass wire, and muskets satisfied local people's rapacious consumerism. And undergirding all this—a ubiquitous part of any port they passed—were the human traffickers and the enslaved, trekked thousands of miles around East Africa and bound for destinations encircling the Indian Ocean.

Sa'id's stay in Muscat kept him longer than anticipated. It was not until two years later, in 1856, that he decided to sail back to Zanzibar, once again aboard the *Victoria*. British consul Atkins Hamerton sailed with Sa'id on the return. Hamerton recalled how Sa'id delayed their departure so he could visit his mother, Ghanee.[2] According to Hamerton, Saʿid told his mother it was his final goodbye—that he would not be returning home again. Even before saying goodbye to his mother, Saʿid had procured in Muscat several wooden planks and had his crew load them onboard the *Victoria*. He instructed his crew: if anyone was to die during the voyage to Zanzibar, they were to build a coffin from the planks, and under no circumstances was that person to be buried at sea.[3]

Shortly after departing Muscat, Saʿid began to complain of swelling and pain in his joints. He was struck with severe fever, cramps, and abdominal pain. On October 19, 1856, at 8:30 in the morning, Saʿid bin Sultan drew his final breath.[4] Six days later the *Victoria* arrived just outside Zanzibar harbor. While Zanzibar slept, Saʿid's son Barghash loaded his father's body onto a small boat and rowed to shore. The *Victoria* remained outside the harbor, veiling the secret. Under moonlight, Barghash crept ashore with his father's body and laid him to rest in a small family cemetery at his palace Bayt al-Sahel, House of the Shore, where he remains today, overlooking the sea.

Ironically, Saʿid chose burial on land, despite the sea being central to his life, his empire, and the global economy they both helped shape. We do not know why he chose instead to be buried at Bayt al-Sahel. As those in Zanzibar woke and news of his death spread, the entire island went into mourning. Business stopped, and black flags were hung from every house. When news reached Muscat, his grandson poetically wrote, there was such an outpouring of emotion that the hills shook with sorrow.[5] And as the news spread across the sea, world leaders sent his sons letters of condolence, including President James Buchanan of the United States and Emperor Napoleon III of France.[6]

Saʿid was one part of a broader period of history. He often followed ongoing trends, such as by looking to East Africa as a source of commercial potential or by continuing to use Gujarati tycoons to help manage the empire's customs. But as letters from James Buchanan or Napoleon III or any other number of sources indicate, he was understood by persons around the world in the first half of the nineteenth century to be the leader of a state that played a role in that period's international affairs. Saʿid's governance amplified the economic agency of those within the empire. All these peoples—whether Africans, Arabs, South Asians, or others—helped mold a political, social, and commercial space that forged interhemispheric, transoceanic commercial connections. By Saʿid's death, the empire had forged a cohesive marketplace from Zanzibar north to Arabia and the Gulf. And that oceanic

FIGURE 4. Painting of Zanzibar harbor and seashore, showing the flags of several consulates and an American ship in the harbor alongside many Indian Ocean vessels. Charles Porter Brown, 1855–1930, Zanzibar Harbor, 1878, oil on canvas, image 13⅛ × 24⅛ in. (33.34 × 61.28 cm), lent by Mrs. Nathaniel Saltonstall Howe Sanders, M5734. Courtesy of the Peabody Essex Museum.

marketplace was one space in a larger global process wherein relatively new Atlantic markets were incorporated into the enduring Indian Ocean world.

Since seizing power in 1806, Saʿid had aimed to consolidate the marketplace, and enmesh the Atlantic traders within it. Other governments and private merchants recognized this. There remained a deeply personal element to the grand structural transformations in this period of history. In 1844 Richard Waters in Zanzibar wrote to his superiors in the United States government urging them to "earnestly" make some "suitable and lasting acknowledgment of the deep sense of gratitude which we all owe him [Saʿid]."[7] That was not merely an expression of diplomatic etiquette. Private merchants felt the same. Leading merchants in New England implored their counterparts in East Africa to do everything possible to express gratitude to Saʿid and to further ingrain their budding commercial positions in Indian Ocean markets. These personal connections highlight the reciprocal relations that others, like Jeremy Prestholdt, have shown. East African and New England consumerism were intertwined: New Englanders craved Omani dates and Zanzibari cloves, while Saʿid delighted in New England apples and cheese. Richard Waters once wrote to a leading merchant in Salem, David Pingree, to notify him that Saʿid had a balance remaining on one of their accounts. Waters noted that Saʿid wanted it to be invested in "the best fine apples and cheese" to be shipped to him as soon as possible.[8] Pingree, responded: "I am always happy of an opportunity to return in any degree the favors we have received from His Highness."[9]

Pingree's response could easily be written off as nineteenth-century etiquette. But it can also stand for more. The fact that a leader of a transcontinental empire in the Indian Ocean was eating apples and cheese from New England, and that a merchant in Salem, Massachusetts, was doing everything he could to ingratiate himself within that empire, reveals a profound world historical transformation. This was a transformation stemming from the meeting of two oceanic worlds—two worlds that did not meet and spark a co-planar story of domination and subordination, but rather each served as part of a broader whole: a global interoceanic system in which parts of those oceans helped constitute and sustain the others. Prior to Saʿid's reign, there were zero exchanges between Salem and Zanzibar—not of apples, nor of cheese, nor even of letters, ships, or diplomats. Saʿid did not cause this transformation. Diving into it through his eyes, however, helps magnify a world in which Indian Ocean peoples remained in the driver's seat of their own worlds, rather than being recipients of an ostensible outside world's domination and direction.

By the mid-nineteenth century Zanzibar had become a global crossroads. Weaving the lives of persons like Edmund Roberts and Atkins Hamerton together with Saʿid illuminates that these actors were aware, at least to an extent, of what they were taking part in: a new global economic system that tied vast, interoceanic parts of the world so closely together that shipping something like apples or cheese thousands of miles across oceans and continents was not unthinkable, but was rather conceived now as a relatively routine component of the etiquette of economic participation. An Omani ruler living in East Africa guarded by Baloch mercenaries and relying on an Indian customs master to help import American apples and cheese underscores that the Indian Ocean was not merely a conveyor belt for an Atlantic economy; it was a world unto itself.[10]

Pingree, however, was wrong about one thing: Saʿid did not refer to himself by any royal titles, whether His Highness or sultan. Saʿid was the acknowledged leader of the Omani Empire, and he lived the life of a wealthy elite. He had multiple homes with décor from around the world, owned dozens of ships used as much for his private commercial interests as for state affairs, and owned thousands of enslaved humans. By all accounts, Saʿid exhibited an affable, humble persona, in personal terms but also in terms of how he ran the empire and usually governed his constituents.

A parable-like anecdote preserved by the Omani-Zanzibari chronicler Al-Mughairi reflects this. At some point during Saʿid's time in Zanzibar, a local man wished to lodge a complaint with him. The man went out and found Saʿid alone, riding one of his beloved horses—as he often did. Seeing the man approach, Saʿid dismounted and greeted him. They discussed the man's need and then parted ways. Later, the man remembered something else he needed. Once more he found Saʿid riding alone on the trails of Zanzibar, and the man called to him from afar. Saʿid dismounted and they spoke again. Al-Mughairi ended his narration of the story by stating: "And this happened three more times."[11] The story is simple because it likely would have been recited orally. For those who would have passed it down, it represented how Saʿid's governance helped create conditions of possibility for peoples living from Zanzibar north to Arabia. As with the makings of the modern world as a whole, those conditions of possibility for some were rooted in the social deaths of others, those humans who were enslaved and trafficked or, if not enslaved, forced into new modes of being, like the Bani Bu Ali or the Al-Qawasim in the Gulf.

Countless other sources corroborate Saʿid's style of governance and personal nature. The Scottish writer and artist James Fraser recalled an instance when they met with Saʿid as he was traveling with the British envoy to Persia. They had stopped in Muscat along their way through the Gulf. As the British delegation was settling down for the evening in their seaside residence, Saʿid appeared just offshore, rowing a small boat and attended only by his translator and his young nephew. Surprised, the British envoy helped Saʿid ashore and apologized that they were unprepared to welcome him in a way befitting his position. "He replied that he came not to see a fine ship, or fine accommodations, or to receive fine compliments," recalled Fraser, but rather "to see the envoy of a friend, and it was the same thing to him whether he were in a palace or in a corner (pointing to one as he spoke)."[12]

Saʿid's dress was unpretentious. Daily, he wore a plain white robe, or *dishdasha,* often with a scarf of blue checked cotton either around his waist or around his head, as Omani men typically did, and still do today.[13] He maintained two primary residences in Zanzibar.[14] The first was Bayt al-Mtoni, or house at the river: *bayt* being the Arabic word for house and *mtoni* Swahili for at the river. Nestled amid "a grove of magnificent coconut palms, mango trees, and other tropical giants," this residence was situated next to a river where it met the sea, and the area in which it was situated was known as Mtoni. Saʿid's second and larger residence was Bayt al-Sahel, or house at the seaside, *al-sāhel* being Arabic for coast, seashore, or seaside. It was built in the heart of Stone Town, at the front of the harbor, where it "commanded a glorious view of the water and the shipping."[15] Visitors to Zanzibar can still tour it today.

Life at Bayt al-Sahel was as bustling as the port surrounding it. "Well do I remember the enchanting scene," recalled Saʿid's daughter, Princess Salameh, of her life there. The living quarters were on the upper floor, each of which opened onto a grand veranda overlooking the harbor, graced by the sea's breeze. An elaborate balustrade stretched across the verandah, supported by large columns. The family kept numerous chairs on the veranda for their gatherings and decorated the space with colored lamps, "which by night lent the house an aspect of a fairyland."[16] Saʿid's residence in Zanzibar would have been similar to the homes of other elites, graced with Persian rugs; Chinese pillows; Indian, European, and American tables; French mirrors; Asian and European porcelain; European and American clocks; and more.[17]

Like the homes of other elites, Saʿid's residence reflected important elements of how he understood himself and his place in the broader world of which he was a part. One of the last sources from Saʿid's life before his death comes from the memoir of a French diplomat, Joseph Arthur De Gobineau. In 1856, when Saʿid was visiting Muscat just before his final departure, De Gobineau sailed into the harbor, his ship bearing honors as the representative of the emperor of France. An aristocrat by birth, De Gobineau was stopping in Muscat to meet with Saʿid as he returned to Paris from Tehran, where he had been the French ambassador to Persia. De Gobineau carefully recorded the meeting, which he found puzzling. He could not believe the relative simplicity of Saʿid's residence, far from the palatial opulence he had grown accustomed to while working in the Persian Empire. He was shocked by how modestly Saʿid was dressed, describing his attire as like that of any other Arab man in Muscat. He observed no royal guard or permanent military, instead describing how Saʿid was accompanied only by his sons.

De Gobineau was perhaps most puzzled that Saʿid worked, for private interests, outside the realm of his official position as a statesman. De Gobineau noted that he was especially invested in human trafficking and the sale of products cultivated by his slaves. Rather than having diplomatic missions in other countries, De Gobineau recalled, Saʿid instead had a network of "correspondents" stretching throughout East Africa and Asia, encircling the

Indian Ocean, each of whom was foremost a merchant.[18] Puzzling more over Saʿid and the nature of the empire, De Gobineau observed: "Commerce was his whole life. It preoccupied him much more than his royal position; or, better stated, the value of his royal position was that it had created for him a commercial position unique to the world. 'I am nothing but a *négociant*,' he said of himself, with a smile belying his success."[19]

Saʿid would have spoken through a translator with De Gobineau, from Arabic to French. Whatever Saʿid said through the translator, De Gobineau understood him as describing a négociant. Many scholars have drawn upon this quote to highlight Saʿid's commercial proclivity, translating the statement as Saʿid saying he was nothing but a "trader."[20] But De Gobineau did not use the French word *marchand*, a trader. In 1856 the French words *négociant* and *marchand* had distinctly different meanings and histories rooted in a particular period in history and the makings of the modern global economy. This difference, of course, would have been evident to De Gobineau.

A French-language dictionary from 1835 delineated this. A négociant was different from a merchant or trader by virtue of scale and scope. A négociant engaged in trade on a "grand" scale of international, long-distance scope.[21] Historian Fernand Braudel described the emergence of such persons—négociants—in world economic history, noting that they were like "wholesalers" who captured all the latest technologies and institutions of the day to engage in commerce at unprecedented volumes covering what were unprecedented distances. Conversely, a retail merchant—a marchand—sold smaller numbers of hand-crafted goods in a local setting, usually from whatever stock they could store in a private residence, distinct from wholesale merchants who would finance or purchase on credit volumes of goods to be managed and sold by deputies within their large, stratified commercial operation.[22]

Understanding Saʿid as a négociant, as De Gobineau did, helps illuminate the world of which he was a part. Aside from the public economic interests of maintaining the health of the empire he oversaw, Saʿid also had private commercial interests. He relied upon vast sums of credit and debt for purchasing huge volumes of goods, often in advance and sight unseen. In doing so, he relied on a web of deputies, as De Gobineau mentioned. As was previously demonstrated, he sometimes relied on Atlantic merchants as those deputies for his own interests. He would not generally have sold the goods himself, nor would he have stored the goods in his own private residence. He also would not have traveled with the goods. All these financial and logistical tasks would have been delegated to those in his employ.

But De Gobineau's statement, placed in conversation with others, like the description of Saʿid's domains from Edmund Roberts that begins this book, still tells us more. De Gobineau was surprised by Saʿid's relative modesty and the relative modesty of his residence and governance precisely because he was well understood by high-ranking European officials like De Gobineau as a leader of international significance of a vast political entity, a political entity that was one important actor on the world stage of the nineteenth-century globalizing economy. De Gobineau's recollection of his conversation with Saʿid reveals how frequently European and American visitors tried to make sense of Saʿid and the entity he led. De Gobineau was surprised not to see a vast military apparatus holding the empire together just as Edmund Roberts expressed some degree of surprise at the same. De Gobineau was shrewd in noting that Saʿid's "royal position" was unique; one of the reasons it was unique is that it was entwined with Saʿid's position as a commercial actor himself, not just a royal sovereign removed from the daily affairs of a vast bureaucracy he was perched atop.

As leader of the empire, Saʿid was also very much a part of it, a commercial agent as much as a diplomat, naval commander, or politician. The entwined nature of Saʿid's royal position with his commercial position coalescing, as De Gobineau wrote, into something unique in the world is exactly what manifested the Omani Empire: the empire was an oceanic marketplace stretching north from Zanzibar to the Gulf, encompassing ports and caravan waystations from East Africa to Arabia that funneled capital, commodities, and customs directly to Saʿid's deputy Jairam Shivji in Zanzibar, to whom Saʿid was deeply in debt when he died. From the seventeenth century, the Omani Empire expanded through conquest, trade, and enslavement, linking East Africa, Arabia, and the Gulf—united not only by the monsoons, but also by commerce and state power. As the French naval officer Édouard Loarer described it, this vast Omani Empire became a "single state."[23]

On his own and through his intersections with others, Saʿid embodied the making of the Omani Empire. Looking into this empire through Saʿid's eyes illuminates its global dimensions. In many ways, his life made tangible the polyphony of modern world history's unfolding, in ways that are not mere abstractions. This was evident to persons who interacted with Saʿid. Decades before Saʿid moved his capital to Zanzibar, in January 1819 the Scottish diplomat Francis Erskine Loch visited him in Muscat. Saʿid had only been in power for thirteen years; he was not yet thirty years of age. An Indian man named Ghulab greeted Loch and his small cohort upon their arrival on shore. Ghulab escorted the visitors through Muscat's byzantine streets. They passed the slave market, thronged with traffickers, and they passed another market with so many goods for sale spilling into the streets that Loch and his cohort had to walk tightly in single file, squeezing between stacks and heaps of items for sale.

When they arrived at Saʿid's residence, a guard opened the gate, and the men entered a room overlooking the sea. Loch, in his words, was astonished. Contrary to what Loch assumed to be "Eastern custom," Saʿid was seated upon a "European chair." The men conversed through an interpreter of Greek origin, named Adey. Adey's father, a banker who worked for the British Embassy in Constantinople, had sent him for his education to London, after which he found work in Calcutta before settling in Muscat. As the men conversed through Adey, enslaved Africans served them Yemeni coffee and Omani dates.[24] The "European chair" that Saʿid sat in was complemented by other global accoutrements in his residence: Chinese porcelain, French glassware, American textiles, Persian rugs, and South Asian plasters. The enslaved Africans who served coffee and sweets to Saʿid's guests—while unnamed in the sources—sustained Saʿid's life, his family, his empire, and the global structures forming the oceanic marketplace of which they were parts.

Interpreting this history through Saʿid's eyes and from the perspective of the period itself, rather than from the perspective of historical hindsight, helps reimagine the contours of modern world history so that the adjective *global* is not a mere euphemism for Western domination. Peoples from around the world, from both the Atlantic and Indian Ocean worlds, came together in this space to navigate imperial agendas, exploit enslaved humans, and maximize their pursuit of profit by means of uniting previously disparate markets into more coherent transoceanic and interhemispheric webs of exchange. Connections in world history, commercial or not, can be somewhat taken for granted as an explanatory factor rather than that requiring historical explanation and description as a process.

The history of the Omani Empire is one such process, one part of the world history of how global trade in the eighteenth and nineteenth centuries came to be. Like others, Loch's story about his meeting with Saʿid reveals that Africans, Arabs, South Asians, and other Indian Ocean peoples were not merely responding to ideas and institutions brought to their shores and their doors on the decks of Atlantic ships. The Omani Empire was a space in which Indian Ocean peoples used new transoceanic markets for pursuing wealth, not just as an end unto itself but also to remake values, class and racial structures, societal and individual behaviors, and political hierarchies.

The Omani Empire can prompt historians to interpret world history untethered from arbitrary European scaffoldings, but it can also help peel apart European scaffolding for the discipline of Middle East studies and other area studies paradigms.[25] Looking out from Oman to the sea and following the fortunes of people like Rahmah bin Jabir or Jairam Shivji as they carved out new horizons for themselves by subsuming Atlantic persons within their own commercial agendas allows us to question how most works in Middle Eastern history, Indian Ocean history, and world history have been written. Rather than using a supposed endpoint, such as European empire, and moving backward in time from there to explain the rise of that supposed endpoint, interpreting this history provides an alternative vision of how the modern world came to be, a vision different from one shaded with the hues of Eurocentrism and Orientalism. It remains an imperial vision, granted, but it is an imperial vision that challenges historians to think of the agencies of non-European peoples at the fore of creating our modern world economy from its inception, rather than merely as a framework of vernacular reactions of disruption and dissent to a European core. Acknowledging the Omani Empire as part of Middle Eastern history, and also part of Islamic history broadly conceived, extends the analysis of persons correcting older-style narratives of Middle Eastern and Muslim decline. Even in the nineteenth century, the ostensible apex of European power, understanding Arabia and its Asian connections in the Indian Ocean reveals a space marked less by decline than by economic expansion, institutional innovation, and cultural creativity.

The Omani Empire was fundamentally creole. It was rooted in interconnections, even if those interconnections were often forged through violent disconnection. Viewing world history from Zanzibar or Muscat reveals a global economy shaped by intertwined histories, not merely overlapping worlds. Persons like Saʿid bin Sultan, Jairam Shivji, and Rahmah bin Jabir represent often-forgotten lives that help produce global transformations.[26] These individuals and others like them were not idle in the "waiting room of history," whose agency manifest only to the extent they reacted to global transformations.[27] They help us see in very tangible ways how modern world history was a polyphonic, complex series of multicultural passages co-creating a world anew. A more organic world historical framework necessitates a truly global view that does not depart from a supposed European endpoint. Instead, it can be informed from its inception by the entangled agencies of local, regional, and interregional developments, and beginning with human beings, not just structures.

The Omani Empire's physical and demographic geographies reveal its polyphonic makings. Oman is considered part of the Middle East, but the country is geographically closer to the mouth of the Indus River than the Euphrates.[28] The Omani Empire was an Arab, Middle Eastern empire by nature of its ruling family, the Al Bu Saʿid. Yet like other Omanis still today, they used the South Asian word *daal* when they sat down to eat lentils, rather than the Arabic word *ʿadas*.[29] Many Omanis who settled in Zanzibar or other parts of East Africa came eventually to learn Swahili as their first language. The mothers of future Omani sultans were Ethiopian or Circassian. Many East Africans came to adopt Omani styles of dress, like the *dishdasha*, the *kumma*, or even the *khanjar*. East Africans, Arabs, and South Asians in the Omani Empire used American cotton not just in products but as a symbol of class and status. And the Omani Empire reached into the daily lives of countless Europeans and Americans, whether in the cloves they used to spice their fruit cakes and hams, the billiard balls they used in their saloons, or the coffee they served in their cafes. The Omani Empire thus stands as a platform not only for seeing enduring Asian connections, but also for seeing the multicultural agencies of the world's peoples interweaving throughout history as it unfolded, rather than interpreting history as if humans existed in watertight compartments. It challenges imperial area studies frameworks and the extent to which many historians of the Middle East continue to overlook Arabia's oceanic connections as fundamental to the Middle East itself.[30] Oman is part of the Indian Ocean world, and it is part of the Middle East. The Middle East is also part of the Indian Ocean world.

Imperial history, then, whether in the form of the Omani Empire or the British Empire, can be brought back in not as a framework for eliding the voices of those upon whom expansion, expropriation, and enslavement took place, but rather by showing the polyphonic processes and entangled histories of multiple human communities who made empire happen in the first place. Understanding the Omani Empire as an empire in which the adjective Omani fundamentally connoted multicultural participation does not necessarily make it stand as something unique in modern world history. Instead, it can encourage historians to rethink accepted conventions in world history and imperial history, like what exactly was British about the British Empire. Omanis were shaped by Britain, but Britain was also shaped by

Oman, whether in the geopolitical realm of relying on Oman for Gulf maritime security or in the more cultural realm of Zanzibari cloves and Omani dates with their daily tea.[31]

For any period after 1500, historians have tended to use the ostensible "brute fact of Western domination" as an explanatory factor in interpreting why certain things in history happened—or did not happen.[32] Even if history is not explicitly written to explain why or how certain societies were incorporated by the West, the idea of some sort of Western domination continued to color explanatory frameworks and perspectives.[33] The birth of the modern world beginning in 1780, as historian Christopher Bayly concluded, depended on interconnections between human societies but was nonetheless rooted in the ultimate rise of the West. In Bayly's influential framework, non-European peoples took part in the birth of the modern world and were neither passive recipients of "Western bounty" nor the West's "supine victims." They had agency, but the interpretation of that agency, according to Bayly, departs from the endpoint of their domination; put otherwise, they had agency in terms of limiting the extent or nature of their domination by the West, but domination-subordination nonetheless remains the infrastructure of modern world history.[34] Such frameworks are not necessarily wrong. Indeed, Europe and the United States came to physically dominate many states and societies. Yet until Saʿid's death there was not necessarily any indication that the Western Indian Ocean was on a path toward eventual Western domination. Things that had not yet happened in real time need not be used as inflection points for interpreting history backward. The history of the Omani Empire until 1856 reveals multifaceted and multiscalar processes of local Indian Ocean peoples coming together in the empire to pursue wealth and remake their lives in ways that benefited from the presence of Europeans and Americans and, in so doing, contained them as fellow actors on a bustling commercial stage, not as masters in the making.

After Saʿid's death, the Omani Empire was, ultimately, split between two capitals—one in Muscat and one in Zanzibar—and it eventually became a British protectorate.[35] That the empire was split up after Saʿid's death might surprise some. Yet every empire in world history has fallen and split apart. The legal formulation of making Zanzibar a protectorate influenced daily life for peoples in Zanzibar and Muscat, but it did not necessarily coopt their own agencies or send their agencies and aspirations into "reverse gear."[36] In fact, as Prestholdt showed, the reign of Saʿid's son Barghash from 1870 to 1888 might in fact have been the height of Zanzibar's prosperity and regional economic influence. Though on paper a British protectorate, Barghash installed public clocks; established a free public water system, electric lighting, and a mint; instituted a steamship line between Zanzibar and other Indian Ocean ports; and established a thriving printing press especially for works of Ibadi political theology. He also cultivated the arts, built museums, and vastly improved transportation and infrastructure, including telegraph stations, streetlights, carriages, steamrollers, and more. Barghash built a tower at the seafront that symbolized his aspirations for Zanzibar and reflected the wealth and continued importance of Zanzibar in the region. He placed four massive European-style clocks atop the tower. Yet those clocks were not set according to European twenty-four-hour notions of time. The clocks were set to Zanzibari time: the day began with sunrise and the clocks were readjusted every ten days to account for the length of the day's light.[37]

Jeremy Prestholdt masterfully demonstrated how the adoption of European things did not necessarily imply Europeanization—the rest becoming more like the West. Barghash's clock tower reflects a people's conscious remaking of local and regional worlds in response to changing global dynamics, remaking their world in their own ways and for their own ends, not for European or Western ends. More broadly, the rise of the Omani Empire on the world stage and the continued effervescence of Zanzibar after Saʿid's death raises questions about how historians craft world history, Indian Ocean history, and Middle Eastern history. One such question is interrogating the notion of British coloniality and the extent of its power. But more importantly, the question is whether an event that had not yet happened—like the division of the empire and the legal category of a protectorate—must be used as a causal factor for interpreting history. Any historical period can be understood from the perspective of that period itself. And in the end, a truly world historical interpretation of humanity as interconnected societies reveals that the period of high European colonialism was, in fact, relatively brief in terms of historical time. Moreover, a historical framework looking out from the realms of the Indian Ocean reveals that the world today might be coming to look more like the world in 1800 than in 1900, with social and commercial power once again becoming increasingly centered on Indian Ocean societies. The changes that took place in the Western Indian Ocean after Saʿid's death, including the breakup of the empire and the temporary increase in British power, can be interpreted as relatively familiar changes as continuity within the long arc of Indian Ocean–centered world history.

The modern global economy emerged not from the Atlantic world's dominance, but from its integration into the long-standing Indian Ocean world.[38] There remains an abyss between how peoples in the period of Saʿid's reign and before understood themselves, and how historians looking back on that period have depicted them. At least until Saʿid's death in 1856, neither Americans nor Europeans went to the Western Indian Ocean assuming a position of dominance enabling them to dictate terms, ideas, or practices. As they understood it, their success in the region was tied to the extent that they acceded to local practices and institutions. This is not to say that the process was unidirectional: Europeans and Americans did sometimes have outsized levels of power or advantage. It is, rather, to highlight how *all* peoples participated in polyphonic, multiscalar, and multicultural processes of political, social, and economic negotiation. Indian Ocean peoples, in turn, were neither apathetic nor static. They also sometimes acceded. Like Saʿid moving from Muscat to Zanzibar or Richard Waters pleading with his family to let him stay longer in Zanzibar, the making of an oceanic marketplace was a cocreation between peoples from previously disparate places in the world coming together to make a world anew and remain at the fore of this global process that was at once structural and abstract but also tangible, prompting persons like Saʿid bin Sultan, Thani bin Amir, and Edmund Roberts to take great risks in uprooting themselves and leveraging mobility to pursue wealth.

Europeans and Americans were not the only makers of the global. The stitching together of the nascent Atlantic Ocean world into its much older Indian Ocean counterpart was a complex, polyphonic process in which different parts came not only to intersect but also to interact. As Edward Said instructed, the great task of writing human history is understanding wholes and seeing how parts speak with each other in forming wholes.[39] The Omani Empire did not create the modern world, but it played a role in its making. When interpreting the makings of the modern world, historians have created bounded identities, shored up exclusivist genealogies, and created disciplinary and discursive borders that can often occlude interactive spaces like the Omani Empire.[40]

Saʿid's reign, enmeshed with the lives of those who lived and worked in the Omani Empire, provides a platform from which we can place Arabs, Asians, and Africans at the fore of a global process melding the Atlantic into the Indian Ocean world, bringing previously disparate markets into relation for serving their own interests, not merely for serving the interests of others. This history presents opportunities for continuing to rethink the craft of world history and its epistemological structures and assumptions—especially for rethinking how most humans, outside the academy, understand how the world came to be. The structures that inform our lives are the predetermined architecture we live in or against.[41] One of those structures is the discipline of world history: the books that line or do not line library shelves, the teaching plans in secondary school classrooms, the stories that tell us how the world came to be. Diving into the margins of human history to augment bottom-up style history especially for marginalized groups necessarily requires the concurrent restructuring of how we conceive of world history itself, with much more exciting work to be done on showing how Arabs, Africans, Asians, and others—men and women, free and enslaved, elite and impoverished—have been actors on the world stage, not just reactors.

NOTES

PRELUDE

1. The entire preceding is from INA, Foreign Department, Secret Committee, October 5, 1840, 44–45, Guillain to Said, August 11, 1840, ff. 21–36.

2. INA, Foreign Department, Secret Committee, October 5, 1840, 44–45, HH the Imam [Saʿid] to Guillain, dated August 11, 1840, ff. 37–39.

3. Sven Beckert also studied these three themes. See *Empire of Cotton: A Global History* (New York: Knopf, 2014), 37. Beckert's history seeks to explain how "enterprising entrepreneurs and powerful statesmen in Europe" ostensibly came to dominate on a global scale, co-opting Afro-Asian trading networks and muscling Indian and Arab traders out of intercontinental markets. For a challenge to this general framework see John M. Hobson, *Multicultural Origins of the Global Economy: Beyond the Western-Centric Frontier* (Cambridge: Cambridge University Press, 2021).

4. J. C. Sharman, *Empires of the Weak: The Real Story of European Expansion and the Creation of the New World Order* (Princeton, NJ: Princeton University Press, 2019); Alison Games, *The Web of Empire: English Cosmopolitans in an Age of Expansion: 1560–1660* (New York: Oxford University Press, 2008); Rajat Kanta Ray, "Asian Capital in the Age of European Domination: The Rise of the Bazaar, 1800–1914," *Modern Asian Studies* 29, no. 3 (1995): 449–554; C. A. Bayly, *Rulers, Townsmen, and Bazaars: North Indian Society in the Age of British Expansion, 1770–1870* (New York: Cambridge University Press, 1988); and Lakshmi Subramanian, *Indigenous Capital and European Expansion: Bombay, Surat, and the West Coast* (Oxford: Oxford University Press, 1996).

5. Omani historians acknowledge this frustration, as well. See Suleimān bin ʿUmīr bin Nāṣir Al-Maḥdhūrī, *Zanjabār fī ʿahd al-Sayyid Saʿīd bin Sulṭān: Dirāsat fī al-Tārīkh al-Iqtiṣādī, 1804-1856* (Muscat: Al-Nādī Al-Thaqāfī, 2014), 189; and

Sa'īd bin 'Alī Al-Mughairī, *Juhaynat Al-Akhbār Fī Tārīkh Zanjabār*, 5th ed., eds. Muḥammad bin 'Alī Al-Ṣalībī and Suleimān bin 'Amīr bin Nāṣir Al-Maḥdhūrī (Muscat: Wizārat al-Turāth wa al-Thaqāfa, 2017), 233.

6. Lawrence Stone, "Prosopography," *Daedalus* 100, no. 1 (1971): 46–79; and Rajae Ankoud, "Prosopography: An Approach to Studying Elites and Social Groups," *AlMuntaqa: Arab Center for Research & Policy Studies* 3, no. 1 (2020): 70–85.

7. Polyphony is a method of writing multivocal compositions in which each voice can be isolated and heard as a melody unto itself, but when combined, they are heard as a harmonious whole, a whole in which it is impossible to decide which voice has the most important task allotted to it, because each voice is necessary for the general effect. See "The Evolution of Polyphony," *Musical Times and Singing Class Circular* 36, no. 630 (1895): 509–12.

8. Wilson Chacko Jacob has similarly shown how elements of biography can illuminate richer pictures of transformations in state, economy, and society in modern world history. See Wilson Chacko Jacob, *For God or Empire: Sayyid Fadl and the Indian Ocean World* (Stanford, CA: Stanford University Press, 2019).

9. On memory and its strategic elision in contemporary Omani society, see Amal Sachedina, *Cultivating the Past, Living the Modern: The Politics of Time in the Sultanate of Oman* (Ithaca, NY: Cornell University Press, 2021). An Omani documentary by Al Jazeera World discussed this period of history without a single mention of slavery's central role in forging and sustaining the empire. See Al Jazeera English, "Oman: History, Power and Influence," video, 47:10, February 2, 2021, https://www.youtube.com/watch?v=uoGGKWbKPW8. In the Omani National Museum, there are no mentions of slavery. Some Arabic works that reflect this silencing are 'Abd Allāh ibn Ṣāliḥ Al-Fārisī, *Al-Būsa'īdīyūn: Hukkām Zanjabār*, 5th ed., trans. Muḥammad Amīn 'Abd Allāh (Muscat, Oman: Ministry of Heritage and Culture, 2015); Al-Maḥdhūrī, *Zanjabār*; and Ismā'īl Al-Amīn, *Al-'Umāniyūn: Ruwwād al-Baḥār* (London: Riad al-Rayyes Books, 1990). For discussion of discourses more broadly on slavery in Middle Eastern societies, see chapter 5 of Ehud Toledano, *Slavery and Abolition in the Ottoman Middle East* (Seattle: University of Washington Press, 1998).

10. On the East African diaspora in late twentieth-century Oman and the politics of race and slavery today, see also Nathaniel Mathews, *Zanzibar Was a Country: Exile and Citizenship between East Africa and the Gulf*, California World History Library (Oakland: University of California Press, 2024); and Nāḍir bin 'Abd Allāh Al-Riyāmī, *Zanjabār: Shakhṣīyāt Wa Aḥdāth, 1828–1972* (London: Dār al-Ḥikmah, 2009).

11. For more on such hierarchies in Oman and elsewhere in Arabia, see John M. Willis, "Azad's Mecca: On the Limits of Indian Ocean Cosmopolitanism," *Comparative Studies of South Asia, Africa, and the Middle East* 34, no. 3 (2014): 574–81; Mandana E. Limbert, "Caste, Ethnicity, and the Politics of Arabness in Southern Arabia," *Comparative Studies of South Asia, Africa, and the Middle East* 34, no. 3 (2014): 590–98; Fahad Ahmad Bishara, "The Many Voyages of Fateh Al-Khayr:

Unfurling the Gulf in the Age of Oceanic History," *International Journal of Middle East Studies* 52, no. 3 (2020): 397–412.

12. The structural, built-in privilege that is tied up with the implicit and explicit language of erasure goes beyond contemporary Omani politics and society or debates in the United States as to whether one uses the word *slave*. Note the striking language in the ostensibly authoritative Cambridge World History series: "Through that trade [the Atlantic slave trade], 12.5 million Africans *left* Africa" (emphasis added). Note elsewhere the passive voice: "The Middle Passage was especially horrible. Hundreds of terrified and naked Africans were sent to the Americas in tightly-packed, foul-smelling ships on a 4-6 week journey." Jerry H. Bentley, Sanjay Subrahmanyam, and Merry E. Wiesner-Hanks, eds., *The Construction of a Global World, 1400–1800 CE: Patterns of Change*, vol. 6.2, The Cambridge World History (Cambridge: Cambridge University Press, 2017), 263, 275. Historians using flawed Eurocentric frameworks routinely use the passive voice when discussing slavery. Joyce Appleby, as one example, wrote: "[C]lose to twelve million African men and women were wrenched from their homes and shipped to the New World." Joyce Appleby, *The Relentless Revolution: A History of Capitalism* (New York: W.W. Norton, 2011), 10.

13. For a look at some problems with the English word *slave* for Africanists and a review of coinciding literature, see Philip Gooding, *On the Frontiers of the Indian Ocean World: A History of Lake Tanganyika, c. 1830–1890*, Cambridge Oceanic Histories (Cambridge: Cambridge University Press, 2022), 170–92. See also Steven Feierman, "Africa in History: The End of Universal Narratives," in *After Colonialism: Imperial Histories and Postcolonial Displacements*, ed. Gyan Prakash (Princeton, NJ: Princeton University Press, 1995), 40–65.

14. James Robert Burns, "'Slaves' and 'Slave Owners' or 'Enslaved People' and 'Enslavers'?," *Transactions of the Royal Historical Society* 2 (2024): 371–88.

15. Here and elsewhere, when referring to *Atlantic* or *Indian Ocean* I am not referring to the bodies of water, but rather to the regions or worlds these bodies of water are part of and have helped form.

16. W. S. W. Ruschenberger, *Narrative of a Voyage Round the World During the Years 1835, 36, and 37; Including a Narrative of an Embassy to the Sultan of Muscat and the King of Siam* (London: Richard Bentley, 1838), 1:139.

17. For the latter see BNA, FO 84/425, Cogan to Forbes, October 28, 1842.

18. As one representative example, see Al-Maḥdhūrī, *Zanjabār*, 18.

19. Okawa Myuko, "The Empire of Oman in the Formation of Oman's National History: An Analysis of School Social Studies Textbooks and Teachers' Guidelines," *Annual Report of the Middle East Society of Japan* 31, no. 1 (2015): 104.

20. A *mizmar* is like a European oboe. For the proverb, see, as one example, Aḥmad Ḥammūd Al-Muʿammarī, *ʿUmān Wa Sharqī Ifrīqīyah*, 3rd ed., trans. Muḥammad Amīn ʿAbd Allāh (Muscat: Wizārat al-Turāth wa al-Qawmī al-Thaqāfa, 2016), 80.

21. There is a vast literature on microhistory and global microhistory, but for the keyhole metaphor and approach see Tonio Andrade, "A Chinese Farmer, Two

African Boys, and a Warlord: Toward a Global Microhistory," *Journal of World History* 21, no. 4 (December 1, 2010): 573–91; and Jan de Vries, "Playing with Scales: The Global and the Micro, the Macro and the Nano," *Past & Present* 242, no. 14 (November 2019): 23–36.

22. We know almost nothing about Bibi Moza aside from her critical role in orchestrating Saʿid's rise to power, which all sources agree on. See Ḥamīd ibn Muḥammad Ibn Ruzayq, *Al-Fatḥ al-Mubīn Fī Sīrat al-Sādah al-Būsaʿīdiyīn*, 6th ed., ed. Muḥammad Ḥamīd Ṣāleh and Muḥammad bin Mubārik Al-Salīmī (Muscat: Wizārat al-Turāth wa al-Thaqāfa, 2016), 2:397–435; Ḥamīd ibn Muḥammad Ibn Ruzayq, *History of the Imāms and Seyyids of ʿOmān: From A.D. 661–1856*, trans. George Percy Badger, Cambridge Library Collection (New York: Cambridge University Press, 2010), 261–92; Ḥāmīd bin Muḥammad Ibn Ruzayq, *Al-Ṣaḥīfah Al-Qaḥṭānniyah*, ed. Muḥammad bin Mubārik Al-Salīmī, Muḥammad Habīb Ṣāleḥ, and ʿAllal Al-Ṣadīq Al-Ghāzī (Muscat: Wizārat al-Turāth wa al-Thaqāfa, 2009), 5:355; Al-Mughairī, *Juhaynat Al-Akhbār Fī Tārīkh Zanjibār*, 220–21; Aḥmad bin Saʿīd bin ʿUbayd Al-Bādī, *Qiṣaṣ Wa Akhbār Jarat Fī ʿUmān Wa Zanjibār* (Al-Sīb, Oman: Maktabat al-Ḍāmirī li'l-nashr wa al-Tawzīʿa, 2019), 134–43; E. C. Ross, "Administration Report of the Persian Gulf Political Residency and Muscat Political Agency for 1882-1883: Outlines of the History of 'Oman from A.D. 1728–1883," in *Annals of Oman to 1728 of Sirhan Ibn Sa'id Ibn Sirhan* (Cambridge: The Oleander Press, 2013), 91; Richard F. Burton, *Zanzibar: City, Coast, Island* (London: Tinsley Brothers, 1872), 1:290–91; Rudolph Said-Ruete, *Said Bin Sultan (1791–1856) Ruler of Zanzibar: His Place in the History of Arabia and East Africa* (London: Alexander-Ouseley, 1929), 14–15; Ruschenberger, *Narrative of a Voyage Round the World*, (London: Richard Bentley, 1838), 1:138; BL, IOR/R/15/6/16, "Political," August 1, 1882–December 1, 1884, "Biographical Sketch of the late Seyyid Saeed bin Sultan Imaum of Muscat," ff. 76.

23. I am grateful to Ahmed al-Maazmi for this insight.

24. Ibn Ruzayq, *Al-Fatḥ al-Mubīn*, 1:397; and Ibn Ruzayq, *Imāms and Seyyids*, 292.

25. I use the idea of institutions as put forth most notably by Douglass C. North, *Structure and Change in Economic History* (New York: W. W. Norton, 1982); and Douglass C. North, *Institutions, Institutional Change and Economic Performance* (New York: Cambridge University Press, 1990).

26. The word *Oman* or *ʿUmān* has been used since at least the time of Islam's revelation for the area closely adhering to the present-day boundaries of the country. On this see John C. Wilkinson, "The Origins of the Omani State," *Arabian Peninsula: Society and Politics*, 1972, 67–88. For different interpretations of the move in Omani history away from the imamate see John C. Wilkinson, *The Imamate Tradition of Oman* (New York: Cambridge University Press, 1987), 2; C. S. Nicholls, *The Swahili Coast: Politics, Diplomacy and Trade on the East African Littoral, 1798–1856*, St. Antony's College, Oxford, Publications, No. 2 (London: George Allen & Unwin, 1971), 22; Amal N. Ghazal, "Islam and Arabism in Zanzibar: The Omani Elite, the Arab World and the Making of an Identity, 1880s–1930s" (ProQuest Dissertations

Publishing, 2005), 51; and B. G. Martin, "Notes on Some Members of the Learned Classes of Zanzibar and East Africa in the Nineteenth Century," *African Historical Studies* 4, no. 3 (1971): 526. For one accessible account of how Ibadi Omanis interpret this, see ʿAlī Yaḥyā Muʿammar, *Ibāḍism in History: The Emergence of the Ibāḍī School*, ed. Kahlān Al-Kharūṣī, vol. 1 (Muscat: Ministry of Awqaf and Religious Affairs, 2007). For overviews of Ibadi Islam see ʿAmr Khalīfah Ennāmī, *Studies in Ibāḍism: Al-Ibāḍīyah* (Muscat: Ministry of Endowments and Religious Affairs, 1971); and Valerie J. Hoffman, *The Essentials of Ibāḍī Islam* (Syracuse, NY: Syracuse University Press, 2012).

27. The word *sulṭān* comes from the Arabic word for power or sovereignty; it is a position denoting this. Omanis did not begin adopting the word for describing their leaders until the second half of the nineteenth century. In Omani history, the word *sulṭān* was often understood to mean a tyrannical ruler. Wilkinson, *Imamate Tradition*, 190.Unrest and rebellion continued well into the twentieth century disputing the forms of government Omani leaders pursued. For a discussion of these rebellions see, in addition to Wilkinson, the discussion throughout Fahad Ahmad Bishara, *A Sea of Debt: Law and Economic Life in the Western Indian Ocean, 1780-1950*, Asian Connections (New York: Cambridge University Press, 2017). The classic Omani work on these uprisings and history after Saʿid's life remains ʿAbdullah bin Ḥumayd Al-Sālimī, *Nahḍat Al-Aʿyān Bi Ḥurriyat ʿUmān*, 2 vols. (Sib, Oman: Maktabat al-Imām Nūr al-Dīn al-Sālimī, 2000). For other works by Omani historians see Ṭāriq bin Khamīs Al-ʿAlawī, *Al-ʿAlāqah Bayna al-Imāmah Wa al-Sulṭanah Fī ʿUmān* (Beirut and Damascus: Dar al-Farqad, 2014); and Jumʿah bin Khalīfah bin Manṣūr Al-Būsaʿīdī, *Al-Dawlah Al-Būsaʿīdīyah Al-Ḥadīthah Min Al-Imāmah Īlā Al-Sulṭānah* (Al-Sīb, Oman: Maktabat al-Ḍāmirī li'l-nashr wa al-Tawzīʿa, 2016).

28. In this book I have limited the extent to which I engage questions of religious history. The foregoing is in no way meant to satisfy those interested in questions of religious history. The purpose is to make a very limited effort to correct the mistaken labeling of Saʿid as either an *imam* or a *sultan*.

CHAPTER 1. WRITING OMANI HISTORY

1. PL, PEM, MH 94 Fabens Family Papers, box 2, folder 10. I am grateful to Lucy Hereford, associate reference librarian at the Phillips Library, for assisting me in trying to determine the origin of the sketch. We cannot determine who drew it, though it was almost certainly drawn sometime during or shortly after a voyage on a Fabens-chartered ship to Zanzibar from August 16, 1844 to July 4, 1848.

2. Jeremy Prestholdt, *Domesticating the World: African Consumerism and the Genealogies of Globalization*, California World History Library (Berkeley: University of California Press, 2008); and Joshua Sidney Chamberlain Morrison, "Cut from the Same Cloth: Salem, Zanzibar, and the Consolidation of the Indo-Atlantic World, 1790–1875" (PhD diss., University of Virginia, 2021).

3. Matthew S. Hopper, "The Globalization of Dried Fruit: Transformations in the Eastern Arabian Economy, 1860s–1920s," in *Global Muslims in the Age of Steam and Print*, ed. James L. Gelvin and Nile Green (Berkeley: University of California Press, 2014), 158–82.

4. For two overviews of Indian Ocean world historiography see, in addition to works cited throughout this book, Markus P. M. Vink, "Indian Ocean Studies and the 'New Thalassology,'" *Journal of Global History* 2, no. 1 (2007): 41–62; and Edward A. Alpers, "Indian Ocean Studies: How Did We Get Here and Where Are We Going? A Historian's Perspective," *Journal of Indian Ocean World Studies* 5, no. 2 (2021): 314–36.

5. Edmund Roberts, *Embassy to the Eastern Courts of Cochin-China, Siam, and Muscat: In the U.S. Sloop-of-War Peacock, David Geisinger, Commander, During the Years 1832–3–4* (New York: Harper & Brothers, 1837), 361.

6. David P. Bresnahan, *Inland from Mombasa: East Africa and the Making of the Indian Ocean World* (Oakland: University of California Press, 2024), 183.

7. ANOM, OIND 2, Édouard Loarer, Rapport commercial, 1 partie, ff. 5.

8. Antoinette Burton and Tony Ballantyne, *World Histories from Below: Disruption and Dissent, 1750 to the Present* (London: Bloomsbury Academic, 2016); Antoinette Burton, *The Trouble with Empire: Challenges to Modern British Imperialism* (New York: Oxford University Press, 2015); and Eric R. Wolf, *Europe and the People Without History* (Berkeley: University of California Press, 2010).

9. John Darwin, *After Tamerlane: The Rise and Fall of Global Empires, 1400–2000* (New York: Bloomsbury Press, 2008), 328.

10. Marshall G. S. Hodgson, *The Venture of Islam: Conscience and History in a World Civilization: The Gunpowder Empires and Modern Times* (Chicago: University of Chicago Press, 1974), 3:12.

11. Hodgson, *Venture of Islam*, 3:233.

12. According to one leading historian of the Indian Ocean, the history of this space in the nineteenth century is one of Zanzibar (and much of the rest of East Africa) being "reduced" to a "conveyer belt" serving an industrializing and developing West. See Eric Tagliacozzo, *In Asian Waters: Oceanic Worlds from Yemen to Yokohama* (Princeton, NJ: Princeton University Press, 2022), 121, 129.

13. Abdul Sheriff, *Slaves, Spices, and Ivory in Zanzibar: Integration of an East African Commercial Empire into the World Economy, 1770–1873* (Athens: Ohio University Press, 1987), 24.

14. Wilkinson, *Imamate Tradition*, 56. In another work, Wilkinson characterized it as a "trade empire," before referring to "Oman and its growing East Africa empire." He used the phrase "Omani empire," then, in relation to the division after Saʿid's death of his dominions between two sons, one based in Zanzibar and one based in Oman. See John C. Wilkinson, *The Arabs and the Scramble for Africa*, Comparative Islamic Studies (Sheffield: Equinox, 2014), 59, 117, 130–31.

15. M. Reda Bhacker, *Trade and Empire in Muscat and Zanzibar: The Roots of British Domination* (London: Routledge, 1992), 3, 180.

16. Jane Burbank and Frederick Cooper, *Empires in World History: Power and the Politics of Difference* (Princeton, NJ: Princeton University Press, 2010).

17. Durba Ghosh, "AHR Forum: Another Set of Imperial Turns?," *American Historical Review* 117, no. 3 (2012): 773.

18. Wilkinson, *Imamate Tradition*, 21.

19. Wilkinson, *Imamate Tradition*, 1, 5.

20. Sheriff, *Slaves, Spices, and Ivory*, 5; Bhacker, *Trade and Empire*; and Patricia Risso, *Oman and Muscat: An Early Modern History* (New York: Croon Helm, 1986).

21. Andrew Liu demonstrated how the comprador thesis is bound within larger twentieth-century notions of development and "idiosyncratic markers of Asian backwardness." See Andrew B. Liu, *Tea War: A History of Capitalism in China and India*, Studies of the Weatherhead East Asian Institute, Columbia University (New Haven, CT: Yale University Press, 2020), 8.

22. The Omani Empire fits into an established body of literature showing non-European resiliency and agency in the face of European expansion. For representative works see Lauren Benton and Nathan Perl-Rosenthal, eds., *A World at Sea: Maritime Practices and Global History*, The Early Modern Americas (Philadelphia: University of Pennsylvania Press, 2020); Jorge Flores, *Empire of Contingency: How Portugal Entered the Indo-Persian World* (Philadelphia: University of Pennsylvania Press, 2024); Sebastian R. Prange, *Monsoon Islam: Trade and Faith on the Medieval Malabar Coast*, Cambridge Oceanic Histories (Cambridge: Cambridge University Press, 2018); Seema Alavi, *Muslim Cosmopolitanism in the Age of Empire* (Cambridge, MA: Harvard University Press, 2015); James F. Warren, *The Sulu Zone: The Dynamics of External Trade, Slavery and Ethnicity in the Transformation of a South east Asian Maritime State, 1768–1898*, 2nd ed. (Singapore: National University of Singapore Press, 2007); Tonio Andrade, *Lost Colony: The Untold Story of China's First Great Victory over the West* (Princeton, NJ: Princeton University Press, 2011); and Joshua L. Reid, *The Sea Is My Country: The Maritime World of the Makahs* (New Haven, CT: Yale University Press, 2015).

23. Alison Bashford, "Terraqueous Histories," *Historical Journal* 60, no. 2 (2017): 253–72; Michael Christopher Low, "Introduction: The Indian Ocean and Other Middle Easts," *Comparative Studies of South Asia, Africa, and the Middle East* 34, no. 3 (2014): 505; Nile Green, "Rethinking the 'Middle East' after the Oceanic Turn," *Comparative Studies of South Asia, Africa, and the Middle East* 3 (2014): 561; Bishara, "Many Voyages," 5; and Isabel Hofmeyr, "Universalizing the Indian Ocean," *PMLA* 125, no. 3 (2010): 721.

24. Marshall G. S. Hodgson, *Rethinking World History: Essays on Europe, Islam, and World History*, ed. Edmund Burke III (New York: Cambridge University Press, 2002), 99. See also R. J. Barendse, *The Arabian Seas: The Indian Ocean World of the Seventeenth Century* (London: Routledge, 2015), 202. Andrea Felber Seligman has shown how certain East African communities contained the Portuguese by developing mostly peaceful and mutually beneficial commercial ties with them. See Andrea

Felber Seligman, "Wealth Not by Any Other Name: Inland African Material Aesthetics in Expanding Commercial Times, ca. 16th–20th Centuries," *International Journal of African Historical Studies* 48, no. 3 (2015): 449–69.

25. Ina Baghdiantz McCabe, Gelina Harlaftis, and Ionna Pepelase Minoglou, eds., *Diaspora Entrepreneurial Networks: Four Centuries of History* (Oxford: Berg Publishers, 2005), xix.

26. Prestholdt, *Domesticating the World.*

27. Prestholdt, *Domesticating the World*, 35.

28. Thomas F. McDow, *Buying Time: Debt and Mobility in the Western Indian Ocean*, New African Histories (Athens: Ohio University Press, 2018), 34. Pedro Machado, similarly, called it an "expansionist empire." See Pedro Machado, *Ocean of Trade: South Asian Merchants, Africa, and the Indian Ocean, c. 1750–1850* (Cambridge: Cambridge University Press, 2014), 11.

29. McDow, *Buying Time.*

30. Bishara, *Sea of Debt*, 1–3.

31. Bishara, *Sea of Debt*, 18.

32. Pekka Hämäläinen, *The Comanche Empire*, The Lamar Series in Western History (New Haven, CT: Yale University Press, 2008), 2. Hämäläinen also notes that the Comanche, like other empires, spread their language and culture across expropriated places. I do not engage this part of the Omani Empire's history, though the Omani historian Al-Maḥdhūrī has done so, in addition to Randall Pouwels. See Al-Maḥdhūrī, *Zanjabār*; and Randall L. Pouwels, *Horn and Crescent: Cultural Change and Traditional Islam on the East African Coast, 800–1900* (Cambridge: Cambridge University Press, 1987).

33. See Karl Jacoby, "Indigenous Empires and Native Nations: Beyond History and Ethnohistory in Pekka Hämäläinen's The Comanche Empire," *History and Theory* 52 (2013): 60–66. He was also criticized for taking an "enormous historiographical and conceptual leap," a leap that is not so enormous in the Omani case given how many specialists have already identified it as some form of empire, but also because, as stated, empire as the expansion and expropriation of lands under one ruling house is a recurring part of Arab and Islamic history, as in European history. For this criticism see Gerald Betty, "Reviewed Work: The Comanche Empire by Pekka Hämäläinen," *American Historical Review* 113, no. 5 (2008): 1470–72.

34. Marshall Hodgson introduced the term *gunpowder empires*; it has become a central tenet of early modern and modern Middle East and Islamic world history. See Hodgson, *Venture of Islam*, vol. 3. Of these three, there has been debate on whether the Safavids qualified as an empire. See Rudi Matthee, "Was Safavid Iran an Empire?," *Journal of the Economic and Social History of the Orient* 53 (2010): 233–65.

35. Craig Calhoun, Frederick Cooper, and Kevin W. Moore, eds., *Lessons of Empire: Imperial Histories and American Empire* (New York: New Press, 2006), 3; and Matthee, "Was Safavid Iran an Empire?," 239.

36. Norman Robert Bennett and George E. Brooks, eds., *New England Merchants in Africa: A History through Documents, 1802–1865* (Brookline, MA: Boston University Press, 1965), 385.

37. PL Log 992, Cherokee (Brig) Seaman's Journal.

38. LOC MMC 3263, reel 3, box 4. Also cited in Roberts, *Embassy to the Eastern Courts*, 361.

39. I use *commercial networks* as Markovits conceptualized them: "a structure through which goods, credit, capital and men circulate regularly across a given space which can vary enormously in terms of both size and accessibility." Claude Markovits, *The Global World of Indian Merchants: Traders of Sind from Bukhara to Panama, 1750–1947*, Cambridge Studies in Indian History and Society (Cambridge: Cambridge University Press, 2000), 25. As a correction to Markovits, however, I add that women were also integral parts of these networks, even if they were enslaved women being circulated by traffickers across the ocean, as I demonstrate more in chapter 6. Admittedly, the present book does not engage questions of gender history, which I am not trained in, and I likely would not do the topic the justice it deserves. For anyone interested in writing a gendered history of the Omani Empire, I offer all my sources, from every archive.

40. Burbank and Cooper, *Empires in World History*.

41. For more on how oceanic peoples manifest connections and differences in everyday life, see Dilip M. Menon and Nishat Zaidi, eds., *Cosmopolitan Cultures and Oceanic Thought* (London: Routledge, 2023).

42. Salamah bint Said, aka Emily Ruete, *Memoirs of an Arabian Princess from Zanzibar*, trans. Lionel Strachey (New York: Doubleday, Page, 2016), 27. For an examination of women in Sa'id's family and their places in the empire, see Patricia W. Romero, "Seyyid Said Bin Sultan BuSaid of Oman and Zanzibar: Women in the Life of This Arab Patriarch," *British Journal of Middle Eastern Studies* 39, no. 3 (2012): 373–92.

43. Harald Gustafsson, "The Conglomerate State: A Perspective on State Formation in Early Modern Europe," *Scandinavian Journal of History* 23 (1998): 194–95; and J. H. Elliott, "A Europe of Composite Monarchies," *Past & Present* 137 (1992): 52–53.

44. Other Indian Ocean historians have challenged geographic area studies frameworks as well. For two representative examples see Sunil S. Amrith, *Crossing the Bay of Bengal: The Furies of Nature and the Fortunes of Migrants* (Cambridge, MA and London: Harvard University Press, 2013); and Eric Tagliacozzo, *The Longest Journey: Southeast Asians and the Pilgrimage to Mecca* (Oxford: Oxford University Press, 2013).

45. Sir Richard Burton, *The Lake Regions of Central Africa: From Zanzibar to Lake Tanganyika*, Historical Adventure and Exploration Series 33 (Santa Barbara, CA: The Narrative Press, 2001), 1:12–13.

46. Bishara, "Many Voyages."

47. Allen James Fromherz, "Introduction: World History in the Gulf as a Gulf in World History," in *The Gulf in World History: Arabia at the Global Crossroads* (Edinburgh: Edinburgh University Press, 2020); and Allen James Fromherz, *The Center of the World: A Global History of the Persian Gulf from the Stone Age to the Present* (Oakland: University of California Press, 2024). See

also Arang Keshavarzian, *Making Space for the Gulf: Histories of Regionalism and the Middle East*, Worlding the Middle East (Stanford, CA: Stanford University Press, 2024).

48. One of the first historians to write about Oman in English, Patricia Risso, had to point out in her preface that there was more to Omani history than oil production and contemporary geopolitical strategic concerns. See Risso, *Oman and Muscat*, xv–xvi. One respected textbook mentions Oman only in the context of the "smaller Gulf states" and in explicit reference to "the Petroleum Era." See William L. Cleveland and Martin Bunton, *A History of the Modern Middle East*, 6th ed. (Boulder, CO: Westview Press, 2016), 413. See the leading synthetic works of Middle East history, each of which ignores Oman except for minor references to it in relation to petroleum: James L. Gelvin, *The Modern Middle East: A History*, 5th ed. (New York: Oxford University Press, 2020); Albert Hourani, *A History of the Arab Peoples* (Cambridge, MA: Belknap Press, 2002); and Eugene Rogan, *The Arabs: A History* (New York: Basic Books, 2017).

49. Bhacker, *Trade and Empire*.

50. Fahad Ahmad Bishara, "Paper Routes: Inscribing Islamic Law across the Nineteenth-Century Western Indian Ocean," *Law and History Review* 32, no. 4 (2014): 798 (emphasis added).

51. In using the concept *cocreation*, I am inspired by Richard White, though I do not submit that there are direct parallels between his concept and its application in the Omani Empire. See Richard White, *The Middle Ground: Indians, Empires, and Republics in the Great Lakes Region, 1650–1815*, 20th anniversary ed., Studies in North American History (Cambridge: Cambridge University Press, 2011), 1.

52. In his chapter on slavery, Prestholdt makes explicit his focus on the second half of the nineteenth century. See Prestholdt, *Domesticating the World*, 117–46. Similarly, Elisabeth McMahon focuses on slavery in Pemba in the late nineteenth and early twentieth centuries, when the sources are far more numerous. See Elisabeth McMahon, *Slavery and Emancipation in Islamic East Africa: From Honor to Respectability* (New York: Cambridge University Press, 2013), 27.

53. Stephen J. Rockel, *Carriers of Culture: Labor on the Road in Nineteenth-Century East Africa* (Portsmouth, NH: Heinemann, 2006), 38.

54. McDow, *Buying Time*, 44, 51.

55. Hämäläinen, *Comanche Empire*, 13. Hämäläinen was drawing upon Richard White. See White, *Middle Ground*, xxx.

56. Frederick Cooper, "What Is the Concept of Globalization Good For? An African Historian's Perspective," *African Affairs* 100, no. 399 (2001): 196. Other historians have made similar points. Richard Roberts, for example, revealed how African interests effected the French presence in West Africa, that West African history was not merely a unilinear trajectory of French domination and West African subordination. See Richard Roberts, "West Africa and the Pondicherry Textile Industry," in *Cloth and Commerce: Textiles in Colonial India*, ed. Tirthankar Roy (Thousand Oaks, CA: Sage Publications, 1996), 142–74; and Prestholdt, *Domesticating the World*, 61.

57. Sharman, *Empires of the Weak*, 14–15. As another scholar put it, studies adhering to this framework use "the past to ratify the present." Michael N. Pearson, *Port Cities and Intruders: The Swahili Coast, India, and Portugal in the Early Modern Era*, The Johns Hopkins Symposia in Comparative History (Baltimore, MD: The Johns Hopkins University Press, 1998), 9–10. Yet another scholar showed how many Indian Ocean studies "assume uncritically the foundational moment of colonialism and work backward to study it." See Rila Mukherjee, "The Indian Ocean in the 'New Thalassology': Review Essay Based on Sugata Bose, *A Hundred Horizons: The Indian Ocean in the Age of Global Empire*," *Archipel* 76 (2008): 295. In an eloquent phrase Blumi calls this the "corrupting influence of hindsight." See Isa Blumi, *Foundations of Modernity: Human Agency and the Imperial State*, Routledge Studies in Modern History (New York: Routledge, 2012), 4, 7.

58. Tonio Andrade, "A Chinese Farmer, Two African Boys, and a Warlord: Toward a Global Microhistory," *Journal of World History* 21, no. 4 (December 1, 2010): 574; see also Jan de Vries, "Playing with Scales: The Global and the Micro, the Macro and the Nano," *Past & Present* 242, no. 14 (November 2019): 31.

59. See William H. Sewell Jr., *Logics of History: Social Theory and Social Transformations* (Chicago and London: University of Chicago Press, 2005), 124–51; and McDow, *Buying Time*, 9n15.

60. Carlo Ginzburg, "Clues: Roots of a Scientific Paradigm," *Theory and Society* 7, no. 3 (May 1979): 273–88; and Maria Lucia G. Pallares-Burke, ed., *The New History: Confessions and Conversations* (Cambridge, UK: Polity Press, 2002), 185.

61. See the interpretive frameworks, among many others, in C. A. Bayly, *The Birth of the Modern World: Global Connections and Comparisons, 1780–1914* (Malden, MA: Blackwell, 2004); and Hobson, *Multicultural Origins*.

62. On conventional statements about European domination of the Indian Ocean, see Kenneth McPherson, *The Indian Ocean: A History of People and the Sea* (Oxford: Oxford University Press, 1993), 198; and Michael Pearson, *The Indian Ocean*, Seas in History (London: Routledge, 2003), 191. For some representative challenges to this periodization, see Prange, *Monsoon Islam*; Sanjay Subrahmanyam, *Improvising Empire: Portuguese Trade and Settlement in the Bay of Bengal, 1500–1700* (Delhi: Oxford University Press, 1990); Tonio Andrade, *The Gunpowder Age: China, Military Innovation, and the Rise of the West in World History* (Princeton, NJ: Princeton University Press, 2016); and Andre Gunder Frank, *ReORIENT: Global Economy in the Asian Age* (Berkeley: University of California Press, 1998).

63. Sujit Sivasundaram, *Waves across the South: A New History of Revolution and Empire* (Chicago: University of Chicago Press, 2020), 2.

64. Bose rooted his arguments in the assumption of "European economic and political domination *by the first half of the nineteenth century*" (emphasis added). See Sugata Bose, *A Hundred Horizons: The Indian Ocean in the Age of Global Empire* (Cambridge, MA: Harvard University Press, 2009), 12. A as one reviewer concluded, Bose's work can be interpreted as depicting "a strangely lifeless, albeit very imperial Indian Ocean; an ocean that remains, despite his claims, a British lake." See Mukherjee, "Review Essay," 293.

65. Sivasundaram, *Waves across the South*, 39, 333.

66. Sivasundaram, *Waves across the South*, 123.

67. Kenneth Lipartito, "Reassembling the Economic: New Departures in Historical Materialism," *American Historical Review* 121, no. 1 (February 1, 2016): 101; Paul Cohen, *China Unbound: Evolving Perspectives on the Chinese Past* (London: Routledge, 2003), 5; Sven Beckert et al., "Interchange: The History of Capitalism," *Journal of American History* 101, no. 2 (2014): 506; and Timothy Mitchell, *Questions of Modernity*, Contradictions of Modernity (Minneapolis and London: University of Minnesota Press, 2000).

68. See chapter 4.

69. Throughout his three-volume *Venture of Islam,* Marshall Hodgson used the term *Islamicate* for the complex, creative, and cosmopolitan overall societies and cultures of the Afro-Asian world associated with the religion of Islam but not necessarily defined by it.

70. Prestholdt, *Domesticating the World*, 45.

71. Liu, *Tea War*, 12.

72. Immanuel Wallerstein, *The Modern World System*, 4 vols. (Berkeley: University of California Press, 2011). Wallerstein's thesis prompted a large body of literature. Some scholars responded by arguing that there was a world system, but it was Asia-centered, not European. See Janet L. Abu-Lughod, *Before European Hegemony: The World System A.D. 1250-1350* (London: Oxford University Press, 1991); Andre Gunder Frank, "A Plea for World System History," *Journal of World History* 2, no. 1 (1991): 1–28; and Frank, *ReORIENT.*

73. Peter Gran, *Islamic Roots of Capitalism: Egypt 1760–1840* (Syracuse, NY: Syracuse University Press, 1998), 187.

74. For one overview of the literature on capitalism and the modern Middle East, see Omar Youssef Cheta, "The Economy by Other Means: The Historiography of Capitalism in the Modern Middle East," *History Compass* 16 (2018): 1–14.

75. Gran, *Islamic Roots.*

76. Kenneth Cuno, *The Pasha's Peasants: Land, Society and Economy in Lower Egypt, 1740–1858* (Cambridge: Cambridge University Press, 1992); and Beshara Doumani, *Rediscovering Palestine: Merchants and Peasants in Jabal Nablus, 1700–1900* (Berkeley: University of California Press, 1995). For a powerful overview of this literature, see Kylie Broderick, "Middle East and Moral Dilemmas: The Problem of Studying Capitalism," *Epoch Magazine*, December 2020, https://www.epoch-magazine.com/broderickmoraldilemma.

77. Donald Quataert, *Ottoman Manufacturing in the Age of the Industrial Revolution*, Cambridge Middle East Library 30 (Cambridge: Cambridge University Press, 2002).

78. Jairus Banaji, *A Brief History of Commercial Capitalism* (Chicago: Haymarket Books, 2020), 126–28. See also K. N. Chaudhuri, *Trade and Civilisation in the Indian Ocean: An Economic History from the Rise of Islam to 1750* (New York: Cambridge University Press, 1985), 209, 214. For another discussion of this and the corresponding literature, especially that of Abraham Udovitch, see Aslanian's

material beginning in Sebouh David Aslanian, *From the Indian Ocean to the Mediterranean: The Global Trade Networks of Armenian Merchants from New Julfa* (Berkeley: University of California Press, 2011), 122. This literature is also discussed throughout Bishara, *Sea of Debt*. See also the discussion in Prange, *Monsoon Islam*, 58–78.

79. Al-Sarakhsī as cited in Banaji, *Brief History of Commercial Capitalism*, 128.

80. Ibn Khaldun as cited in Banaji, *Brief History of Commercial Capitalism*, 129.

81. In addition to the works of Marshall Hodgson, see especially André Wink, *The Making of the Indo-Islamic World: C. 700–1800 CE* (Cambridge: Cambridge University Press, 2020); and André Wink, *Al-Hind: The Making of the Indo-Islamic World*, 3 vols. (Leiden: Brill Academic, 1990).

82. This section draws on Banaji, *Brief History of Commercial Capitalism*, especially pages 125–38; Jairus Banaji, *Theory as History: Essays on Modes of Production and Exploitation* (Chicago: Haymarket Books, 2011), 262–68; Pamuk Şevket, "Institutional Change and Economic Development in the Middle East, 700-1800," in *The Rise of Capitalism: From Ancient Origins to 1848*, ed. Larry Neal and Jeffrey G. Williamson, 2 vols., The Cambridge History of Capitalism (Cambridge: Cambridge University Press, 2014), 1:193–224; and Maxime Rodinson and Roger Owen, *Islam and Capitalism*, trans. Brian Pearce (London: Saqi Books, 2007).

83. Even after writing thousands of pages, Braudel has been criticized for "vagueness in terminology." See M. C. Howard, "Fernand Braudel on Capitalism: A Theoretical Analysis," *Historical Reflections/Réflexions Historiques* 12, no. 3 (1985): 469–83. Similarly, Becket has been criticized for not providing a clear definition of what capitalism is or is not. See Shubham Sharma, "Capitalism and Its New Historians: A Review Essay," *Studies in People's History* 7, no. 2 (2020): 221–27; Charles Post, "Reviewed Work: Empire of Cotton: A Global History by Sven Beckert," *Journal of the Civil War Era* 5, no. 4 (2015): 581–83; and John J. Clegg, "Capitalism and Slavery," *Critical Historical Studies* 2, no. 2 (2015): 281–304. For more on how historians have grappled with the problematic of capitalism, see Lipartito, "Reassembling the Economic," 101–39.

84. Seth Rockman, "What Makes the History of Capitalism Newsworthy?," *Journal of the Early Republic* 34, no. 3 (2014): 439–66.

85. Jonathan Levy, "Capital as Process and the History of Capitalism," *Business History Review* 91 (2017): 483–510.

86. See chapter 3.

CHAPTER 2. THE EMERGENCE OF EMPIRE

1. PL, PEM, Log 992 Cherokee (Brig) Seaman's Journal. Putnam was born in Danvers, Massachusetts, in 1825. After retiring from his career as a mariner, Putnam married and moved to Manchester, New Hampshire, where he served as mayor from 1881 to 1888, and died in 1888.

2. Al-Amīn, *Al-ʿUmāniyūn: Ruwwād al-Baḥār*, 11.

3. Tomé Pires and Armando Cortesão, *The Suma Oriental of Tomé Pires: An Account of the East, from the Red Sea to Japan, Written in Malacca and India in 1512–1515* (London: Hakluyt Society, 1944), 1:228.

4. Pires and Cortesão, *Suma Oriental of Tomé Pires*, 2:287.

5. Of note is the western coast of India, particularly Gujarat, whose economy remained robust throughout the eighteenth century and in many ways was strengthened by the arrival of the East India Company. For more on this see Ghulam A. Nadri, *Eighteenth-Century Gujarat: The Dynamics of Its Political Economy, 1750–1800* (Leiden: Brill, 2009).

6. Quoted in Tillman W. Nechtman, "A Jewel in the Crown? Indian Wealth in Domestic Britain in the Late Eighteenth Century," *Eighteenth-Century Studies* 41, no. 1 (Fall 2007): 73.

7. "Muscat the Harbour," exhibit, Bait al-Baranda Museum, Muscat, Oman, October 19, 2017.

8. PL, PEM, Log 992, Cherokee Seaman's Journal.

9. John C. Wilkinson, "Oman and East Africa: New Light on Early Kilwan History from the Omani Sources," *International Journal of African Historical Studies* 14, no. 2 (1981): 275–76.

10. PL, PEM, Log 1005, Bark Emily Wilder, First Mate's Journal (Mixed Material, 1851, 1850).

11. NRS, GD1/633/3, Francis Erskine Loch in Persian Gulf and India, ff. 99.

12. There is a rich literature on how to conceptualize such ports. For a review of this literature see Prange, *Monsoon Islam*, 25–91.

13. Abu Isḥaq Ibrāhīm bin Mūhammad Al-Fārisī Al-Iṣṭakhrī, *Kitāb Masālik Al-Mamālik* (Leiden: Brill, 1870), 25.

14. Yāqut Al-Hamawī, *Mu'jam Al-Buldān* (Beirut: Dar al-Sadr, 1977), 3:393–94. In fact, here Al-Hamawī is directly quoting the equally renowned medieval geographer Al-Bashārī al-Maqdisi (d. 1000). Zabid was the capital of Yemen from the thirteenth through the fifteenth centuries; Sana'a is Yemen's capital today. Sohar was also an important intellectual center. An important sixteenth-century manual on the principles of navigational theory was completed there by the Yemeni scholar Suleimān al-Mahrī in 1740. See Suleimān ibn Aḥmad ibn Suleimān Al-Mahrī, "Tuḥfat al-Fuḥūl fī tamhīd al-uṣūl fī 'ilm al-biḥār" (unpublished manuscript, Sohar, Oman, September 7, 1740), 5, BL.

15. As cited in Prange, *Monsoon Islam*, 207; see Qur'an 14:32.

16. Abdul Sheriff, "The Swahili Coast: Africa's Window on the Indian Ocean," in *Oman and Overseas*, ed. Michaela Hoffmann-Ruf and Abdulrahman Al-Sālimī, Studies on Ibadism and Oman 2 (Hildesheim, Germany: Georg Olms Verlag, 2013), 80.

17. Chhaya Goswami, *The Call of the Sea: Kachchhi Traders in Muscat and Zanzibar, c. 1800–1880* (New Delhi: Orient Blackswan, 2011), 56.

18. "Model of Sohar," *Omani Vessels: Boat Building*, exhibit, The National Museum of the Sultanate of Oman, October 13, 2017. For more on Indian Ocean ships and maritime technology, see David Parkin and Ruth Barnes, eds., *Ships and the*

Development of Maritime Technology in the Indian Ocean (London: Routledge, 2002); and Dionisius A. Agius, *Classic Ships of Islam: From Mesopotamia to the Indian Ocean*, Handbook of Oriental Studies 92 (Leiden: Brill, 2008).

19. Indian Ocean vessels came in many forms. For a detailed contemporaneous study of these vessels, see François Edmond Paris, *Essai Sur La Construction Navale Des Peuples Extra-Européens Ou Collection Des Navires et Pirogues Construits Par Les Habitants de l'Asie, de La Malaisie, Du Grand Océan et de l'Amérique Dessinés et Mesurés Par M. Paris, Capitaine de Corvette, Pendant Les Voyages Autour Du Monde de L'Astrolabe, La Favorite et L'Artémis*, 2 vols. (Paris: Arthus Bertrand, 1841).

20. Muhammad Ibn Ahmad Ibn Jubayr, *The Travels of Ibn Jubayr, 1183–1185*, trans. R. J. C. Broadhurst (London: Jonathan Cape, 1952), 65; Pearson, *Indian Ocean*, 64; and Abdul Sheriff, *Dhow Cultures of the Indian Ocean: Cosmopolitanism, Commerce, Islam* (New York: Columbia University Press, 2014), 79–106.

21. Chaudhuri, *Trade and Civilisation*.

22. Philip Curtin described these as trade diasporas, the word *diaspora* coming from the Greek for scattering, "as in the sowing of grain." See Philip D. Curtin, *Cross-Cultural Trade in World History*, Studies in Comparative World History (Cambridge: Cambridge University Press, 1984), 2.

23. Ned Bertz, "Indian Ocean World Travellers: Moving Models in Multi-Sited Research," in *Journeys and Dwellings: Indian Ocean Themes in South Asia*, ed. Helene Basu (Hyderabad: Orient Longman, 2008), 32.

24. Ulrike Freitag, *A History of Jeddah: The Gate to Mecca in the Nineteenth and Twentieth Centuries* (Cambridge: Cambridge University Press, 2020).

25. Mark Horton and John Middleton, *The Swahili: The Social Landscape of a Mercantile Society* (Malden, MA: Blackwell Publishing, 2000), 89.

26. Bresnahan, *Inland from Mombasa*; and Gooding, *On the Frontiers*.

27. Horton and Middleton, *Swahili*, 90–91.

28. Said Hamdun and Noël King, eds., *Ibn Battuta in Black Africa*, expanded ed. (Princeton, NJ: Markus Wiener Publishers, 2010), 16.

29. On family firms as inherently translocal units see Hollian Wint, "'From Desh to Desh': The Family Firm as Trans-Local Household in the Nineteenth-Century Western Indian Ocean," *Journal of World History* 34, no. 2 (2023): 187–216.

30. In her study of Aden and its role in the Indian Ocean trade, Roxani Eleni Margariti noted that the shipping business "relied first and foremost on the family unit" and that "family ties" were a "major organizing principle for the conduct of business." See Roxani Eleni Margariti, *Aden and the Indian Ocean Trade: 150 Years in the Life of a Medieval Arabian Port*, Islamic Civilizations and Muslim Networks (Chapel Hill: University of North Carolina Press, 2007), 148–49. See also Engseng Ho, *The Graves of Tarim: Genealogy and Mobility across the Indian Ocean* (Berkeley: University of California Press, 2006). Margariti's depiction coincides with Hodgson's conceptualization of "Islamicate contractualism." See Marshall G. S. Hodgson, *The Venture of Islam: Conscience and History in a World Civilization: The Expansion of Islam in the Middle Periods* (Chicago: University of Chicago Press, 1974), 2:342, 346. See also Barendse, *Arabian Seas*, 182.

31. Overlooked in much of the literature is the labor of women, which made the seasonal movement of men possible. On this argument see Nidhi Mahajan, "Of Those on Shore: The Dhow Trade and Mobility in the Indian Ocean," in *Cosmopolitan Cultures and Oceanic Thought*, ed. Dilip M. Menon Menon and Nishat Zaidi (London: Routledge, 2023), 137–51. See also Holliann Wint, "Keeping It in the Family? Her- and His-Stories among Gujarati Business Communities in the Nineteenth Century Indian Ocean," in *Perspectives of Female Researchers: Interdisciplinary Approaches to the Study of Gujarati Identities*, ed. Sharmina Mawani and Anjoom A. Mukadam (Berlin: Logos Verlag, 2016), 173–88. For an overview of Gujarat and Gujarati traders in the Indian Ocean world, see Edward A. Alpers and Chhaya Goswami, eds., *Transregional Trade and Traders: Situating Gujarat in the Indian Ocean from Early Times to 1900* (New Delhi: Oxford University Press, 2019).

32. Machado, *Ocean of Trade.*

33. Machado, *Ocean of Trade*, 208–9. See also Richard B. Allen, *European Slave Trading in the Indian Ocean, 1500–1850*, Indian Ocean Studies Series (Athens: Ohio University Press, 2014).

34. Christine Dobbin demonstrated how many empires relied on Asian entrepreneurial minorities in fomenting the modern world economy. See Christine Dobbin, *Asian Entrepreneurial Minorities: Conjoint Communities in the Making of the World-Economy, 1570–1940*, Nordic Institute of Asian Studies 71 (Richmond: Curzon, 1996).

35. Bhacker, *Trade and Empire*, 12–13.

36. According to Chaudhuri, the Portuguese "abruptly ended the system of peaceful oceanic navigation that was such a marked feature of the region." See Chaudhuri, *Trade and Civilisation*, 69. Abdul Sheriff, Chaudhuri's student, claimed that the Portuguese began "a new process that in the long run undermined and subverted the Dhow Culture of the Indian Ocean." Sheriff, *Dhow Cultures*, 5.

37. Michael Pearson noted that the only major structural break in Indian Ocean history was later than Chaudhuri placed it, around 1800. This historical division reflects the time when "many of the deep structure elements" that defined the Indian Ocean as a coherent arena, such as monsoons, currents, and land barriers were "all overcome by steam ships and steam trains in the service of British power and capital; the Indian Ocean world [became] embedded in a truly global economy and for the first time production, as opposed to trade, [was] affected." Pearson, *Indian Ocean*, 11–12. See also Bose, *Hundred Horizons*, 272–73.

38. Bresnahan, *Inland from Mombasa*; Machado, *Ocean of Trade*; Jeremy Prestholdt, "As Artistry Permits and Custom May Ordain: The Social Fabric of Material Consumption in the Swahili World, Circa 1450–1600," in *Working Paper*, Evanston, IL: Program of African Studies, Northwestern University, 1998), 3:1–49; Jeremy Prestholdt, "Portuguese Conceptual Categories and the 'Other' Encounter on the Swahili Coast," *Journal of Asian and African Studies* 36, no. 4 (2001): 383–406; and Andrea Felber Seligman, "Wealth Not by Any Other Name: Inland African Material Aesthetics in Expanding Commercial Times, ca. 16th–20th Centuries," *International Journal of African Historical Studies* 48, no. 3 (2015): 449–69.

39. Sharman, *Empires of the Weak*, 2. Alison Games refers to this, in the English context, as dissimulation and cultural accommodation. See Games, *Web of Empire.* This corrects Joyce Appleby's conclusion, which speaks to her overall flawed framework, that "Portugal achieved naval supremacy in the Indian Ocean after defeating an Egyptian fleet in 1509." See Appleby, *Relentless Revolution*, 34. The Ya'rubi Dynasty adds another layer to one historian's conceptualization of this time and space as an "age of contained conflict." See Sanjay Subrahmanyam, *The Political Economy of Commerce: Southern India, 1500–1650*, Cambridge South Asian Studies (Cambridge: Cambridge University Press, 1990), 252.

40. Gaspar Correa, *Lendas Da India*, ed. Rodrigo Jose de Lima Felner (1858, Lisbon; Liechtenstein, 1976), 1:75; and Chaudhuri, *Trade and Civilisation*, 67–68.

41. William Brooks Greenlee, ed., *The Voyage of Pedro Alvares Cabral to Brazil and India: From Contemporary Documents and Narratives* (London: Hakluyt Society, 1938), 84–85; and Chaudhuri, *Trade and Civilisation*, 68.

42. Neither the *cartaz* system nor the subsequent Dutch or English "company" systems were entirely new to the Indian Ocean. Non-European peoples, especially the Omanis, had similar institutions since long before Europeans arrived. See Wilkinson, *Imamate Tradition*, 47.

43. Ibn Ruzayq, *Al-Fatḥ al-Mubīn*, 2:113; Ibn Ruzayq, *Imāms and Seyyids*, 53; Sirhān b. Sa'īd b. Sirhān, *Kashf Al-Ghumma* [Annals of Oman], trans. E. C. Ross (Calcutta: G. H. Rouse, Baptist Mission Press, 1874), 46; Sirḥān bin Sa'īd Al-Izkawī, *Kashf Al-Ghummah: Al-Jāmi'a Li-Akhbār al-Ummah*, ed. Hassan Muḥammad 'Abd Allāh Al-Nabudah (Beirut: Dar al-Kotob al-Ilmiyah, 2016), 2:850. R. D. Bathurst's doctoral dissertation from 1967 is the only English-language work on the Ya'rubi Dynasty, and it remains unpublished. I am grateful to Fahad Bishara for sharing his copy. See R. D. Bathurst, "The Ya'rubi Dynasty of Oman" (PhD diss., Oxford University, 1967), Bodleian Library (Department of Western Manuscripts).

44. Sa'īd b. Sirhān, *Kashf Al-Ghumma*, 45; and Al-Izkawī, *Kashf Al-Ghummah*, 2:849–50.

45. Al-Izkawī, *Kashf Al-Ghummah*, 2:736–37; and Sa'īd b. Sirhān, *Kashf Al-Ghumma*, 15. Similarly, the Omani jurist and scholar Nūr Al-Dīn Al-Sālimī recounts one of the most significant examples of Oman using its navy for enforcing state policy: toward the end of Imām Al-Ṣalt bin Mālik's reign (851–855), the Imam dispatched one hundred ships full of armed soldiers to end an insurrection against Omani influence over Socotra island, off the coast of present-day Yemen. See Nūr Al-Dīn 'Abd Allāh bin Ḥummayyid Al-Sālimī, *Tuḥfat Al-A'yān Bi-Sīrat Ahl 'Umān*, ed. Ibrāhīm bin Aṭfayish Al-Jazā'irī, 2nd ed. (Cairo: n.p.,, 1931), 1:139. See also Wilkinson, *Imamate Tradition*, 47.

46. This challenges Barendse's claim that Indian Ocean merchants were not "actively supported by their states, which generally remained aloof from conducting trade themselves, and did relatively little to protect the position of their own merchants." Barendse, *Arabian Seas*, 8. Abdul Sheriff came to a similar conclusion: "The Indian Ocean before the coming of the Portuguese was a *mare liberum* where continental states rarely tried to control maritime matters." See Sheriff, *Dhow Cultures*, 7.

It is therefore incorrect to claim that the Europeans introduced the "novel concept that sea-power was an instrument of state policy." Chaudhuri, *Trade and Civilisation*, 207; Abdul Sheriff and Engseng Ho, eds., *The Indian Ocean: Oceanic Connections and the Creation of New Societies* (London: Hurst, 2014), 31.

47. Bathurst, "Ya'rubi Dynasty," 85.

48. Al-Izkawī, *Kashf Al-Ghummah*, 2:862; and Sa'īd b. Sirhān, *Kashf Al-Ghumma*, 51. This is also recounted in Abū Suleimān Muḥammad bin 'Āmir bin Rāshid al-Ma'walī Al-Afawī, *Qiṣaṣ Wa Akhbār Jarat Fī 'Umān*, ed. Sa'īd bin Muḥammad bin Sa'īd Al-Hāshimī, 2nd ed. (Muscat: Wizārat al-Turāth wa-al-Thaqāfah, 2014), 238.

49. Ibn Ruzayq, *Al-Fatḥ al-Mubīn*, 2:130–31; and Ibn Ruzayq, *Imāms and Seyyids*, 65. Ibn Ruzayq was apparently drawing his information from eyewitnesses to the war between the Omanis and Portuguese.

50. Bathurst, "Ya'rubi Dynasty," 109–10.

51. Indian merchants had lived and worked in Oman for centuries before the Portuguese occupation. In addition to works subsequently cited, see Calvin H. Allen Jr., "The Indian Merchant Community of Masqaṭ," *Bulletin of the School of Oriental and African Studies* 44, no. 1 (1981): 39–53. There is a large historiography on the places of Indian merchants in the Indian Ocean. See Bishara, *Sea of Debt*, 7 n12.

52. Ibn Ruzayq, *Al-Fatḥ al-Mubīn*, 2:148–56; Ibn Ruzayq, *Imāms and Seyyids*, 79–87; Nūr Al-Dīn 'Abd Allāh bin Ḥumayyid Al-Sālimī, *Tuḥfat Al-A'yān Bi-Sīrat Ahl 'Umān*, 2 vols. (Cairo: Maktabat al-Istiqāmah, 2013), 2:69–72. As Allen pointed out, Al-Sālimī provided basically the same account, though shorter, and said that Narutem was the agent of another Indian merchant named Sakabila. See Calvin H. Allen Jr., "Sayyids, Shets and Sulṭāns: Politics and Trade in Masqat under the Āl Bū Sa'īd, 1785–1914" (PhD diss., University of Washington, 1978), 102–3, esp. n21. The earliest published account of this event was Carsten Niebuhr's work in 1765. Niebuhr contended that the Portuguese commander stole Narutem's daughter, prompting him to act. See Carsten Niebuhr, *Travels through Arabia and Other Countries in the East*, trans. Robert Heron (Edinburgh: G. Mudie, 1792), 2:115–16.

53. On Jeddah see Sanjay Subrahmanyam, "Of Imarat and Tijarat: Asian Merchants and State Power in the Western Indian Ocean, 1400–1750," *Comparative Studies in Society and History* 37, no. 4 (October 1995): 762. On the movement of South Asians away from Aden and Mocha to Muscat, see Bishara, *Sea of Debt*, 29–30; on their movement to Mozambique see Machado, *Ocean of Trade*, 20–24.

54. Ibn Ruzayq, *Al-Fatḥ al-Mubīn*, 2:157; and Ibn Ruzayq, *Imāms and Seyyids*, 89. The phrase in Arabic is *wa rakhuṣati al-as'āru, wa ṣaluḥati al-asfāru, wa rabbaḥati al-tujjāru.*

55. Quoted in Bathurst, "Ya'rubi Dynasty," 113.

56. François Martin, *Mémoires de François Martin, fondateur de Pondichéry (1665-1696)*, ed. A. Martineau, Bibliothèque d'histoire coloniale (Paris: Société d'éditions géographiques, maritimes et coloniales, 1931), 1:215.

57. Malyn Newitt, "The Portuguese in East Africa and the Omani Reconquest of East Africa," in *Oman and Overseas*, ed. Michaela Hoffmann-Ruf and

Abdulrahman Al-Sālimī, Studies on Ibadism and Oman 2 (Hildesheim, Germany: Georg Olms Verlag, 2013), 132.

58. John Ovington, *A Voyage to Surat in the Year 1689*, ed. H. G. Rawlinson (London: Oxford University Press, 1929), 125–26.

59. Ovington, *Voyage to Surat*, 254.

60. Wilkinson, *Imamate Tradition*, 48.

61. Charles Guillain, *Documents Sur l'histoire, La Géographie et Le Commerce de l'Afrique Orientale, Publiès Par Ordre Du Government*, ed. Arthur Bértrand (Paris: Societé de Géographie, 1859), 1:520.

62. The use of naval forces for pursuing national policies of commercial aggrandizement is similar to how John Brewer conceptualized the rise of British state power in this time, as well. See John Brewer, *The Sinews of Power: War, Money, and the English State, 1688–1783* (Cambridge: Harvard University Press, 1990), 11.

63. Wilkinson, *Imamate Tradition*, 220.

64. Al-Izkawī, *Kashf Al-Ghummah*, 2:878. The Portuguese would not leave the area entirely until 1729.

65. Nicholls, *Swahili Coast*, 25.

66. Pearson, *Port Cities and Intruders*, 46.

67. ANOM, Aix-en-Provence, OIND 2, Édouard Loarer, Rapport commercial, 1 partie, ff. 5.

68. Nicholls, *Swahili Coast*, 48–49; and Risso, *Oman and Muscat*, 121.

69. Lyne, for example, described their "warlike" propensities and "tyranny"; Pearce wrote of the "turbulent Mazrui"; and Owen colorfully described one Mazruʿi leader as "an old dotard who has outlived every passion but that of avarice." See Robert Nunez Lyne, *Zanzibar in Contemporary Times: A Short History of the Southern East in the Nineteenth Century* (repr., New York: Negro Universities Press, 1969), 30; F. B. Pearce, *Zanzibar: The Island Metropolis of Eastern Africa* (New York: E. P. Dutton, 1920), 109; W. F. W. Owen, *Narrative of Voyages to Explore the Shores of Africa, Arabia, and Madagascar* (New York: J. & J. Harper, 1833), 1:369; and Shaykh Al-Amin bin ʿAli Al-Mazruʿi, *The History of the Mazruʿi Dynasty of Mombasa*, trans. J. McL. Ritchie, Union Académique Internationale Fontes Historiae Africanae, Arabica XI (London: Oxford University Press, 1995), 7.

70. The classic example of this is Al-Mughairī, *Juhaynat Al-Akhbār*.

71. Al-Mazruʿi, *History of the Mazruʿi*, 22, 29. For the original Arabic see pages 6–7 and 14 of the Arabic appendix.

72. Al-Izkawī, *Kashf Al-Ghummah*, 2:877n3; and Al-Sālimī, *Tuḥfat Al-Aʿyān* (1931), 2:105, 107.

73. Wilkinson, *Arabs and the Scramble for Africa*, 24.

74. Bathurst, "Yaʿrubi Dynasty of Oman," 205–6.

75. Beckert, *Empire of Cotton*, xvi.

76. Al-Sālimī, *Tuḥfat Al-Aʿyān* (1931), 2:161. Omani sources disagree on the date Ahmad was elected Imam and came to power. Al-Sālimī dates it 1753. Ibn Ruzayq dates it 1741. See Ibn Ruzayq, *Imāms and Seyyids*, 152. Note that Ibn Ruzayq's father worked directly for Ahmad, which might lend credence to his choice of 1741.

See Ibn Ruzayq, *Imāms and Seyyids*, 158–59. Al-Mughairi places it in 1741 as well. Said's grandson places the date in 1744. See Said-Ruete, *Said Bin Sultan*, 3. Guillain dates it to 1744. Guillain, *Documents Sur l'histoire*, 1:539. For more on this see C. F. Beckingham, "The Reign of Aḥmad Ibn Sa'īd, Imam of Oman," *Journal of the Royal Asiatic Society of Great Britain and Ireland* 3 (n.d.): 257–60. In 1941 the British were planning a bicentennial event to celebrate the Al Bu Sa'id dynasty and the centuries-long partnership between the British and Omanis. British government correspondence notes their confusion in determining the proper date from Omani sources. Ultimately the British appealed to Sultan Sa'id bin Taimur, Oman's ruler, who admitted: "It appears that it is not possible to trace the correct Hijri date of Saiyid Ahmad's election as Imam." See BL, IOR/R/15/6/216, f. 66. In Zanzibar, the British celebrated the bicentenary in 1944, placing Ahmad's inauguration of the dynasty in 1744. See ZNA AB10/53 and AB10/201.

77. Aḥmad Al-Ismā'īlī, "'Aqlana al-Tārikh al-'Umāni (Conceptualizing Omani History)," *Nizwa*, January 17, 2018, 6, http://www.nizwa.com/عقلنة-التاريخ-العماني-الاجتماع-السيا/.

78. Fernand Braudel, *The Structures of Everyday Life: The Limits of the Possible*, trans. Siân Renolds, Civilization and Capitalism, 15th-18th Century (New York: Harper and Row, 1981), 1:69–70; and Chaudhuri, *Trade and Civilisation*, 221.

79. For more on this period of turmoil, which some scholars call a civil war, see Risso, *Oman and Muscat*, 39–52.

80. Risso, 45.

81. *Tārīkh Al-Dawla al-Busaidi*, exhibit, Bait al-Baranda Museum, Muscat, Oman, 2017.

82. Ibn Ruzayq, *Al-Fatḥ al-Mubīn*, 2:264–65; and Ibn Ruzayq, *Imāms and Seyyids*, 165.

83. Al-Sālimī, *Tuḥfat Al-A'yan* (1931), 2:165.

84. Niebuhr, *Travels through Arabia*, 2:116; Goswami, *Call of the Sea*, 80; and Allen, "Sayyids, Shets and Sulṭāns," 103.

85. Guillain, *Documents Sur l'histoire*, 1:547; and Nicholls, *Swahili Coast*, 26.

86. Again, Omani sources do not agree on the date. Ibn Ruzayq notes that Ahmad died in 1775. Ibn Ruzayq, *Imāms and Seyyids*, 188. The Omani National Museum places the date at 1783. Al-Sālimī places it at 1781. Al-Sālimī, *Tuḥfat Al-A'yān* (1931), 2:165.

87. Ibn Ruzayq, *Imāms and Seyyids*, 192, 201; and Ibn Ruzayq, *Al-Fatḥ al-Mubīn*, 2:313; and Al-Sālimī, *Tuḥfat Al-A'yān* (1931), 2:166-168. For more context see Risso's discussion of these sources beginning at *Oman and Muscat*, 96.

88. Bhacker, *Trade and Empire*, 26.

89. Wilkinson, "Oman and East Africa," 51.

90. Allen, "Indian Merchant Community," 42.

91. Ibn Ruzayq, *Al-Fatḥ al-Mubīn*, 2:333; and Ibn Ruzayq, *Imāms and Seyyids*, 213. Note that here again "Sultan" is a first name.

92. Ibn Ruzayq, *Al-Fatḥ al-Mubīn*, 2:333–34; and Ibn Ruzayq, *Imāms and Seyyids*, 213–14.

93. Ibn Razīq, *Al-Ṣaḥīfah Al-Qaḥṭānniyah*, 5:345; and *Tārikh Al-Dawla al-Busaidi*.

94. Bhacker claimed that some Muslim Indian Ocean societies had protective pass systems dating to at least as early as the twelfth century. See Bhacker, *Trade and Empire*, 33, 214n19.

95. Sheriff, *Slaves, Spices, and Ivory*, 8.

96. Risso, *Oman and Muscat*, 83–85.

97. Wilkinson, "Oman and East Africa," 53.

98. Risso, *Oman and Muscat*, 80.

99. J. G. Lorimer, *Gazetteer Of the Persian Gulf: 'Oman, and Central Arabia* (Calcutta: Superintendent Government Printing, India, 1915), 1:163; Goswami, *Call of the Sea*, 81; and Risso, *Oman and Muscat*, 53–74.

100. There is a very large literature on coffee, whether its trade or its incorporation into society and culture. On its place in Yemeni society and history see Nancy Um, *The Merchant Houses of Mocha: Trade and Architecture in an Indian Ocean Port* (Seattle: University of Washington Press, 2009). For one global overview see W. G. Clarence-Smith and Steven Topik, eds., *The Global Coffee Economy in Africa, Asia, and Latin America, 1500–1989* (Cambridge: Cambridge University Press, 2003).

101. Wilkinson, *Imamate Tradition*, 52; and Bishara, *Sea of Debt*, 10.

102. Risso, *Oman and Muscat*, 78.

103. Bhacker, *Trade and Empire*, 26.

104. Wilkinson, *Imamate Tradition*, 52. Here I am challenging Risso's claim that in the final decades of the eighteenth century, Oman was barely "involved in shaping Gulf politics or even in protecting its own interests." See Risso, *Oman and Muscat*, 65.

105. Wilkinson, *Imamate Tradition*, 65.

106. Nicholls, *Swahili Coast*, 84.

107. Goswami, *Call of the Sea*, 133. See also Bishara, *Sea of Debt*, 6–9, 24–57.

108. McDow, *Buying Time*, 48.

109. As Bishara demonstrated, this social hierarchy was not just imagined; it was inscribed in law. See Bishara, *Sea of Debt*, 66–79.

110. Edward A. Alpers, *Ivory and Slaves: Changing Pattern of International Trade in East Central Africa to the Later Nineteenth Century* (Berkeley: University of California Press, 1975), 131.

111. McDow, *Buying Time*, 53.

112. Guillain, *Documents Sur l'histoire*, 2:76–77.

113. Guillain, *Documents Sur l'histoire*, 2:76; Burton, *Zanzibar*, 1:21; and McDow, *Buying Time*, 53. McDow also discusses the notion of tribal/ethnic hierarchy among Omanis themselves; see pages 107–15.

114. Some family groups, like the Bani Bu Ali, would revolt against this economic disparity, only to be crushed. For more on this see chapter 3. For more on tribal discrimination in Oman in more contemporary times, see Sachedina, *Cultivating the Past*.

115. Wilkinson, *Imamate Tradition*, 222.

116. Ibn Ruzayq, *Al-Fatḥ al-Mubīn*, 1:332; and Ibn Ruzayq, *Imāms and Seyyids*, 213.

117. Nicholls, *Swahili Coast*, 83.

118. For how other groups of Indian merchants monopolized commercial networks elsewhere in the world, see Markovits, *Global World of Indian Merchants*.

119. BL, IOR/L/PS/20/C227, Selections from State Papers, regarding the East India Company's Connection with the Persian Gulf, with a Summary of Events, 1600–1800, "Report on the Commerce of Arabia and Persia by Samuel Manesty and Harford Jones," 1790, ff. 404.

120. For more background on Sultan's reign, especially his commercial policies, see Risso, *Oman and Muscat*, 191–209.

121. By 1800 Basra had obtained a critically important position in the Gulf, as a waystation for interlinked land and maritime commerce between the eastern Mediterranean and Levant, Persia, and Central Asia, and the Western Indian Ocean. See Thabit Abdullah, *Merchants, Mamluks, and Murder: The Political Economy of Trade in Eighteenth-Century Basra* (Albany: SUNY Press, 2000).

122. Ibn Ruzayq, *Al-Fatḥ al-Mubīn*, 2:362–64; and Ibn Ruzayq, *Imāms and Seyyids*, 238–41. The earliest recording of Sultan's death is MSA, Secret and Political Department Diary No. 162, November 16–December 29. 1804, ff. 4902–4908, 5090–5092. There is also a description in BL, IOR/R/15/6/16, "Political" (Aug 1, 1882–December 1, 1884), "Biographical Sketch of the late Seyyid Saeed bin Sultan Imaum of Muscat," ff. 77. See also Burton, *Zanzibar*, 1:289–90. Hamerton claims this took place in 1802, but it is likely that his dates are too early. ZNA AA3/6, Hamerton to Bombay, ff. 136. See also BL, IOR/F/4/186/3885, "Political situation at Muscat following the death of the Imam [Sayyid Sultan]" for a contemporaneous account of his death.

123. PL, PEM, MSS 230, Richard P. Waters Papers, "Thermometrical observations made at Zanzibar from 1st February to 31st March 1841," box 1, folder 5.

124. PL, PEM, MSS1624, Ahmed bin Na'man Account Book; PL MH14, box 1, folder 6, Hamed to Waters.

125. This discussion of the *Sultanah* overlaps with some works of Jeremy Prestholdt. See Prestholdt, *Domesticating the World*, 91–92; Jeremy Prestholdt, "The *Sultana* in New York: A Zanzibari Vessel between Two Worlds," in *World on the Horizon: Swahili Arts Across the Indian Ocean*, ed. Prita Meier and Allyson Purpura (Champaign: Krannert Art Museum and Kinkhead Pavilion, University of Illinois at Urbana-Champaign, 2018), 114–29; and Jeremy Prestholdt, "*Sultana*: The Biography of an Indian Ocean Vessel," in *Indian Ocean Imaginings: People, Time, and Space*, ed. Joshua Esler and Mark Fielding (Lanham, MD: Lexington Books, 2023), 59–76.

126. "From the N. Y. American: The Arabian Corvette Sultanee," *New Hampshire Sentinel*, May 27, 1840, 12, no. 22, America's Historical Newsroom, NewsBank/Readex.

127. "Captain Ahmed Bin Naman, the Commander of the Arabian Corvette 'Sultanee,' Is a Great Man," *Morning Herald*, May 15, 1840, 305 ed., 19th Century U.S. Newspapers.

128. "An Arabian Ship," *New Hampshire Sentinel*, May 20, 1940, 42, no. 21, America's Historical Newsroom, NewsBank/Readex.

129. Al-Maḥdhūrī, *Zanjabār*, 64.

130. Al-Mughairī, *Juhaynat Al-Akhbār*, 250; and Al-Maḥdhūrī, *Zanjabār*, 65.

131. Burton, *Zanzibar*, 1:268; and Prestholdt, "*Sultana*," 119.

132. I draw the word *juggernaut* here from Anthony Giddens, who refers to modernity in general as a juggernaut, "a runaway engine of enormous power which, collectively as human beings, we can drive to some extent but which also threatens to rush out of our control and which could rend itself asunder." See Anthony Giddens, *The Consequences of Modernity* (Stanford, CA: Stanford University Press, 1990), 139.

133. Robert Brenner, *Merchants and Revolution: Commercial Change, Political Conflict, and London's Overseas Traders, 1550–1653* (Princeton, NJ: Princeton University Press, 2003), 584.

134. Janet J. Ewald, "Crossers of the Sea: Slaves, Freedmen, and Other Migrants in the Northwestern Indian Ocean, c. 1750–1914," *American Historical Review* 105, no. 1 (2000): 69–91.

135. Prestholdt, "*Sultana*," 118.

136. See Eric Gilbert, *Dhows and the Colonial Economy of Zanzibar, 1860–1970* (Oxford: James Currey, 2004).

CHAPTER 3. CONTESTING THE GULF

1. Ibn Ruzayq, *Al-Fatḥ al-Mubīn*, 2:437; Ibn Ruzayq, *Imāms and Seyyids*, 293.

2. A. M. Abū Hākima provides the best account of Rahmah's life in Aḥmad Muṣṭafā Abū Ḥākima, *Tārīkh Al-Kuwait*, vol. 2 (Kuwait: Kuwait Government Press, 1973), 46–70.

3. Ḥusayn Khalaf al-Shaykh Khazʿal, *Tārīkh Al-Kuwayt al-Siāyāsī*, vol. 1 (Beirut: Dar al-Kutub, 1962), 41.

4. For more on this see Nicholas P. Roberts, "Oceanic Wahhabism," *Journal of World History* 36, no. 1 (March 2025), 21-49.

5. This chapter overlaps with and heavily borrows from Nicholas P. Roberts, "A Tolerated Terror: Rahmah bin Jabir and the Age of Revolutions in the Gulf, 1760–1830," *Itinerario: Journal of Imperial and Global Interactions* (FirstView 2025): 1–15.

6. James Silk Buckingham, *Travels in Assyria, Media, and Persia*, 2nd ed., vol. 2 (London: Colburn, 1830), 122; and Sir Charles Belgrave, *The Pirate Coast* (London: G. Bell & Sons, 1966), 126.

7. See Charles E. Davies, *The Blood-Red Arab Flag: An Investigation into Qasimi Piracy, 1797–1820* (Exeter: University of Exeter Press, 1997), esp. 63–70. Similarly, Marcus Rediker demonstrated a "political arithmetic" of piracy as discerning acts of maritime violence. See Marcus Rediker, *Villains of All Nations: Atlantic Pirates in the Golden Age* (Boston: Beacon Press, 2004), 27. His synthesis of maritime and landed affairs in exploring the concept of piracy is similar to conclusions drawn by Marc Hanna in an Atlantic context. See Mark G. Hanna, *Pirate Nests and the Rise*

of the British Empire, 1570–1740, Omohundro Institute of Early American History and Culture (Durham, NC: University of North Carolina Press, 2015). On different manifestations of piracy reflecting local, often idiosyncratic, issues, see John Coakley, Nathan C. Kwan, and David Wilson, eds., *The Problem of Piracy in the Early Modern World: Maritime Predation, Empire, and the Construction of Authority at Sea*, Maritime Humanities, 1400–1800 (Amsterdam: Amsterdam University Press, 2024). On the creation in the English legal vocabulary in this time and space of the idea of pirates and piracy, see Lakshmi Subramanian, *The Sovereign and the Pirate: Ordering Maritime Subjects in India's Western Littoral* (New Delhi: Oxford University Press, 2016).

8. Rahmah embodies the patterns of "accommodation and selective law breaking" that Benton has investigated. See Lauren Benton, "Legal Spaces of Empire: Piracy and the Origins of Ocean Regionalism," *Comparative Studies in Society and History* 47, no. 4 (2005): 700–724.

9. As Sheikh Muḥammad bin Khalīfah al-Nabhānī put it, Rahmah was "precious" to his followers, his prestige stemming from his defiance in all matters of the Āl Khalīfah confederacy. See Muḥammad bin Khalīfa Al-Nabhānī, *Al-Tuḥfah Al-Nabhānīyah Fī Tārīkh Al-Jazīrah Al-ʿArabīyah*, 2nd ed. (Cairo: Dār Maṭbaʿa Al-Maḥmūdīyya li-l-Nashr, 1924), 138.

10. Belgrave, *Pirate Coast*, 126.

11. Lorimer, *Gazetteer*, 1:793; R. Hughes Thomas, ed., *Selections from the Records of the Bombay Government: No. XXIV* (Bombay: Bombay Education Society's Press, 1856), 525.

12. This chapter tempers the apologetic framework of Muhammad al-Qasimi's work, which claimed, "The Gulf was always a peaceful waterway" and that Qasimi maritime violence was a "myth." See Sultan Muhammad Al-Qasimi, *The Myth of Arab Piracy in the Gulf* (London: Croom Helm, 1986).

13. Charles Lockyer, *An Account of Trade in India* (London: Samuel Crouch, 1711), 206–7; and Risso, *Oman and Muscat*, 14.

14. MSA, Political Department, vol. 52/49, Kheir to Bombay, January 6, 1820, ff. 147.

15. Burton, *Trouble with Empire*.

16. For more on the Qawasim, including their background, reasons behind resorting to maritime plunder, and more, see Davies, *Blood-Red Arab Flag*.

17. Risso, *Oman and Muscat*, 173; and Davies, *Blood-Red Arab Flag*, 242. Davies used his treatment of Qasimi violence as a platform for explaining ostensible British hegemony in the region and largely ignored the role of Saʿid bin Sultan in managing the Qawasim; however, his basic argument troubling the notion of superficial understandings of "piracy" falls in line with the present chapter.

18. For a similar argument in a different geographic context, see Hanna, *Pirate Nests*, 13. This chapter augments a trend in the historiography of piracy, capitalism, and empire to show how piracy must be understood as part of a "symbiotic relationship between maritime marauders and landed communities" (416).

19. Relatively little has been written about the First Saudi State. For a basic overview see Madawi Al-Rasheed, *A History of Saudi Arabia*, 2nd ed. (Cambridge: Cambridge University Press, 2010), 13–22. Wahhabism is a reformist political-theological ideology and movement that undergirded the First Saudi State. Non-Wahhabi persons, Muslim or otherwise, used the labels *Wahhabi* or *Wahhabism* to describe the movement begun by its founder, Muḥammad Ibn ʿAbd al-Wahhāb. They used these labels in critical ways to detract from the movement and its ideology. Ibn ʿAbd al-Wahhāb and his followers did not use this label. I use it throughout this chapter because its use is accepted as convention, and challenging that particular convention is not a goal of this chapter.

20. Lorimer, *Gazetteer*, 1:135.

21. Sir John Malcolm, *Sketches of Persia* (London: John Murray, 1845), 1:15.

22. This argument is developed in Roberts, "Oceanic Wahhabism."

23. Hala Fattah, *The Politics of Regional Trade in Iraq, Arabia, and the Gulf: 1745–1900*, SUNY Series in the Social and Economic History of the Middle East (Albany: State University of New York Press, 1997), 46.

24. See the discussion in Ahmad Mustafa Abu-Hakima, *The Modern History of Kuwait, 1750–1965* (London: Luzac, 1983), 18.

25. For more on the early political context of the Saudi-Wahhai use of *shirk*, see Tarik K. Firro, "The Political Context of Early Wahhabi Discourse of Takfir," *Middle Eastern Studies* 49, no. 5 (2013): 770–89.

26. Ibn Ruzayq, *Al-Fatḥ al-Mubīn*, 2016, 1:354; and Ibn Ruzayq, *Imāms and Seyyids*, 230.

27. Muḥammad Ibn ʿAbd al-Wahhāb, *Kashf Al-Shubuhat*, ed. ʿAbd Allah bin ʿĀyaḍ Al-Qaḥṭānī, 1st ed. (Riyadh: Dar al-Ṣumayʿī li'l-nashr wa'l-tawzīʿ, 1997), 72.

28. ʿAbd al-Raḥmān bin Muḥammad bin Qāsim Al-ʿĀṣamī al-Najdī, ed., *Al-Durar al-Saniyya Fī al-Ajwiba al-Najdiyya*, 6th ed. (n.p.: n.p., 1996), 8:412.

29. Despite these cateogorical theological dictums, many Wahhabi persons traveled to non-Wahhabi lands and did business with non-Wahhabi persons, even non-Muslims. For more on this see Roberts, "Oceanic Wahhabism."

30. Lorimer, *Gazetteer*, 1:193.

31. Lorimer, *Gazetteer*, 1:193–94.

32. Ibn Ruzayq, *Al-Fatḥ al-Mubīn*, 2016, 1:274; and Ibn Ruzayq, *Imāms and Seyyids*, 248. In Arabic: *wa mā ḥaddāhum ʿalā tilka al-hāli illa iktisāb mālin.*

33. INA, Foreign Department, Secret Committee, no. 21/25, Seton to Malcolm, February 6, 1809, ff. 9.

34. Aḥmad Muṣṭafā Abū Ḥākima, ed., *Kitāb Lamʿ Al-Shihāb Fī Sīrat Muḥammad Bin ʿAbd al-Wahhāb* (Beirut: Dar Assafaka, 1967), 183–84; ʿAbd al-Allāh al-Ṣāliḥ Al-ʿUthaymīn, ed., *Lamʿ Al-Shihāb Fī Sīrat Muḥammad Bin ʿAbd al-Wahhāb*, Silsilat Maṣādir Tārīkh Al-Jazīra Al-ʿArabīyya Al-Makhṭūṭa 4 (Riyadh: Dārat Al-Mālik ʿAbd al-ʿAzīz, 2005), 290–91.

35. INA, Foreign Department, Secret Committee, no. 21/25, Seton to Malcolm, February 6, 1809, ff. 9.

36. Vincenzo Maurizi, *History of Seyd Said, Sultan of Muscat: Together with an Account of the Countries and People on the Shores of the Persian Gulf, Particularly the Wahabees* (London: John Booth, 1819), 126, 129.

37. Buckingham, *Travels*, 2:413–14. The Parsees are a Zoroastrian ethnoreligious group. Buckingham, in Muscat, would have been among both Sunni and Ibadi Omani Muslims, and both those from Bushehr and Bahrain could very likely have been Shiʿa Muslims.

38. Al-ʿUthaymīn, ed., *Lamʿ Al-Shihāb*, 146; and Abū Ḥākima, ed., *Kitāb Lamʿ Al-Shihāb*, 81.

39. NRS, GD1/633/3, ff. 92-93.

40. ʿUthmān ibn ʿAbd Allāh bin ʿUthmān Ibn Bishr, *ʿUnwān Al-Majd Fī Tārīkh Najd*, 4th ed., vol. 1, 2 vols. (Riyadh: Maṭbūʿāt Dārat Al-Malik ʿAbd Al-Azīz, 1982).

41. For more on Omani and Saudi relations in this time, see Zāmil Muḥammad al-Rashīd, *Suʿūdī Relations with Eastern Arabia and ʿUmān, 1800–1871* (London: Luzac, 1981); and Aḥmad bin Saʿīd bin ʿUbayd Al-Bādī, *Al-Būsʿīdīyun Wa Āl Saʿūd*, 2nd ed., 3 vols. (Damascus: Dār al-Farqad, 2020).

42. Aḥmad Muṣṭafā Abū Ḥākima, *Tārīkh Al-Kuwait al-Ḥadīth* (Kuwait: Dhat al-Silāsil, 1984), 139. Abu Hakima refers to this decade as the "golden age" for Wahhabi authority on the Arabian Peninsula (140).

43. Sheriff, *Slaves, Spices, and Ivory*, 22, 23. Similarly, Wilkinson and Risso both claimed that the Qawasim were dealt with primarily by the British. See Wilkinson, *Imamate Tradition*, 228; and Patricia Risso, "Cross-Cultural Perceptions of Piracy: Maritime Violence in the Western Indian Ocean and Persian Gulf Region during a Long Eighteenth Century," *Journal of World History* 12, no. 2 (2001): 316. John Wilkinson, publishing his classic work in the same year as Sheriff, maintained a similar position, claiming that soon after 1819, the Gulf was nothing more than "an extension of the British-Indian domain and Oman was totally excluded from it politically." See Wilkinson, *Imamate Tradition*, 54.

44. McDow, *Buying Time*, 66, 35.

45. Tagliacozzo, *In Asian Waters*, 121; and Sivasundaram, *Waves*, 123, 128. See also the work of David Commins, who uses British dominance for periodizing Gulf history, with 1820 being his marker for the beginning of "British supremacy." David Commins, *The Gulf States: A Modern History* (London: I. B. Tauris, 2012). On alternatives to this periodization see Bishara, "Many Voyages," 44.

46. Charles Rathbone Low, *History of the Indian Navy, 1613–1863* (London: Richard Bentley, 1877), 1:xi.

47. Quoted in Nicholls, *Swahili Coast*, 98.

48. Davies, *Blood-Red Arab Flag*, 169.

49. Low, *History of the Indian Navy*, 1:215.

50. Low, *History of the Indian Navy*, 2:577–84.

51. Low, *History of the Indian Navy*, 1:322; and Davies, *Blood-Red Arab Flag*, 140.

52. LOC, MMC 3263, reel 3, box 4; and Edmund Roberts to Louis McLane, Washington, May 14, 1834, as quoted in Bennett and Brooks, *New England Merchants*, 156.

53. Belgrave, *Pirate Coast*, 1; Bose, *Hundred Horizons*, 44; Simon Layton, "Discourses of Piracy in an Age of Revolutions," *Itinerario* 35, no. 2 (2011): 84.

54. Wilkinson, *Imamate Tradition*, 46–47.

55. For more on this in the late nineteenth and early twentieth centuries, see Matthew S. Hopper, "Enslaved Africans and the Globalization of Arabian Gulf Pearling," in *Pearls, People, and Power: Pearling and Indian Ocean Worlds*, ed. Pedro Machado, Steve Mullins, and Joseph Christensen, Indian Ocean Studies Series (Athens: Ohio University Press, 2019), 263–80.

56. Davies, *Blood-Red Arab Flag*, 219.

57. Buckingham as cited in Davies, *Blood-Red Arab Flag*, 219–20.

58. Muḥammad Mursī ʿAbd Allāh, *Imārāt Al-Sāḥil Wa ʿUmān Wa al-Dawla Al-Saʿūdiyya Al-Ūlā, 1793–1818* (Cairo: Al-Maktaba al-Miṣrīyya al-Ḥadītha, 1978), 232. Davies notes that Sultan bin Saqr's "power-base was being undermined by the Saudi ruler Suʿud. His standing had for some time past been encroached upon by Wahhabi officials." See Davies, *Blood-Red Arab Flag*, 186.

59. Ibn Ruzayq, *Al-Fatḥ al-Mubīn*, 2:470–71; Ibn Ruzayq, 320-321; and Lorimer, *Gazetteer*, 1:641–43. See also INA, Foreign Department, Secret Committee, no. 21/25, Seton to Malcolm, February 6, 1809, ff. 14.

60. BL, IOR/R/15/1/14, Bruce to Bombay, June 4, 1813, ff. 26; and BL, IOR/R/15/1/22, Bruce to Bombay, February 14, 1820, ff 15v-19.

61. ʿAbd Allāh, *Imārāt Al-Sāḥil Wa ʿUmān*, 147, 215. Today, Ras al-Khaimah is a thriving, uber-capitalist, elite tourist destination in the United Arab Emirates. Rams today is a suburb of Ras al-Khaimah.

62. Ibn Ruzayq, *Al-Fatḥ al-Mubīn*, 2:471; Ibn Ruzayq, *Imāms and Seyyids*, 321; and J. B. Kelly, *Britain and the Persian Gulf, 1795–1880* (Oxford: Oxford University Press, 1968), 112.

63. Technically, it was their second expedition, but the previous expedition in 1805–1806 was rather small compared to the 1809 and 1819 expeditions, which appear far more prominently in the sources.

64. BL, IOR/R/F/4/366/9142, February 11, 1811, ff. 19–21; Kelly, *Britain and the Persian Gulf*, 116–18; Lorimer, *Gazetteer*, 1:645–46; and Low, *History of the Indian Navy*, 1:326.

65. Low, *History of the Indian Navy*, 1877, 1:324–30; Kelly, *Britain and the Persian Gulf*, 118–19, 123; and Lorimer, *Gazetteer*, 1:192.

66. BL, IOR/R/15/1/12, Bruce to Bombay, October 9, 1811, ff. 66v.

67. BL, IOR/R/15/1/14, Bruce to Bombay, July 15, 1813, ff. 22.

68. BL, IOR/R/15/1/15, Bombay to Bruce, December 9, 1813, ff. 34–36.

69. BL, IOR/R/15/1/14, Saʿid to Bruce, May 19, 1814, ff. 85r.

70. Lorimer, *Gazetteer*, 1:651.

71. BL, IOR/R/15/1/19, Sultan bin Saqr to Bruce, December 21, 1816, ff. 2r.

72. BL, IOR/R/15/1/18, Hasan bin Rahmah to Bruce, received November 27, 1816, ff. 80v–81r.

73. BL, IOR/R/15/1/13, Smee to Bruce, June 20, 1813, ff. 136 2.

74. Thomas, *Selections*, 522.

75. BL, IOR/R/15/1/14, Rahmah bin Jabr to Bruce and Bruce to Bombay, October 27, 1814, ff. 122v-124; Thomas, 523.

76. Lorimer, *Gazetteer*, 1:649.

77. BL, IOR/R/15/1/14, Rahmah bin Jabr to Bruce and Bruce to Bombay, August 7, 1814, ff. 99–100.

78. BL, IOR/R/15/1/14, Bruce to Bombay, December 15, 1814, ff. 127v.

79. BL, IOR/R/15/1/14, Bruce to Bombay, December 15, 1814, ff. 127v.

80. BL, IOR/R/15/1/14, Bruce to Bombay, December 16, 1814, ff. 128r.

81. BL, IOR/R/15/1/14, Bruce to Basra, December 16, 1814, ff. 128v.

82. BL, IOR/R/15/1/16, Bruce to Bombay, April 15, 1815, ff. 34v.

83. MSA, Political Department Vol. 29/91, Hennell to Bombay, May 23, 1822, ff. 277.

84. BL, IOR/R/15/1/19, Bombay to Bruce, December 30, 1816, ff. 83.

85. Davies, *Blood-Red Arab Flag*, 141n19.

86. Lorimer, *Gazetteer*, 1:658.

87. Kelly, *Britain and the Persian Gulf*, 135, 138.

88. MSA, Political Department vol. 52/49, Bombay to to Keir, October 27, 1819, ff. 5.

89. BL, IOR/R/15/1/19, Bombay to Bruce, October 9, 1819, ff. 128v, ff. 130r; BL, IOR/R/15/1/19, Jukes to Bruce, November 3, 1819, ff. 134r; Lorimer, *Gazetteer*, 1:658–59; and Thomas, *Selections*, 188.

90. Patricia R. Dubuisson, "Qāsimī Piracy and the General Treaty of Peace (1820)" (master's thesis, Montreal, McGill University, 1975), 47.

91. Lorimer, *Gazetteer*, 1:667.

92. Quoted in Davies, *Blood-Red Arab Flag*, 8.

93. BL, IOR/R/15/1/22, Bruce to Bombay, February 14, 1820, ff. 15v-19.

94. Dubuisson, "Qāsimī Piracy," 60–61.

95. Almost nothing has been written about this in English, although there is one book in Arabic, almost exclusively a summary of British sources. See Aminah Al-Khāṭrī, *Al-Hamlāt al-Briṭāniyyah Ḍhid Qabilah Banī Bū ʿAlī: 1820–1823* (Sharjah: Manshūrāt Al-Qāsimī, 2015).

96. Ibn Ruzayq, *Al-Fatḥ al-Mubīn*, 2:489; and Ibn Ruzayq, *Imāms and Seyyids*, 338. The Ash-Sharqiyyah region of Oman is a governorate on the northeastern tip of the country, just south of Muscat, facing the Indian Ocean.

97. MSA, Political Department, vol. 9/44, Thompson to Bombay, December 3, 1820, ff. 178.

98. Lorimer, *Gazetteer*, 1:464.

99. BL, IOR/R/15/1/23, Thompson to Bombay, October 13, 1820, ff. 44r.

100. BL, IOR/R/15/1/23, Thompson to Bombay, October 13, 1820, ff. 45v.

101. BL IOR/R/15/1/23, Thompson to Bombay, October 13, 1820, ff. 56r. After returning to Muscat, Thompson wrote to his superiors: "The Imam [Saʿid] displayed an admirable character; and though wounded, persisted in remaining with the detachment and causing it to be supplied with provisions and camels, shoes and every assistance which his country could afford." For more on the battle see MSA, Political Department, vol. 9/44, Thompson to Bombay, November 18,1820, ff. 79-95. Thompson, who lived from 1783 to 1869, would later become a fierce abolitionist and client of William Wilberforce, and he served as the first colonial governor of Sierra Leone.

102. Lorimer, *Gazetteer*, 1:464.

103. BL, IOR/R/15/1/23, Bombay to Thompson, December 10, 1820, ff. 64r.

104. BL, IOR/R/15/1/23, Warden to Thompson, January 10, 1821, ff. 69–71. Thompson responded with a nearly point-by-point refutation to Warden's letter. See IOR/R/15/1/23, Thompson to Bombay, February 12, 1821, ff. 83–90.

105. BL, IOR/R/15/1/23, Bombay to Thompson, December 10, 1820, ff. 64r. A decade later, as Saʿid had begun more fully focusing on East African affairs and had already visited Zanzibar, the governor general in Bombay considered his own government "to be so far bound to and connected with its ally the Imaum of Muscat as to prevent his ruin and downfall by every means in its power." See INA, Foreign Department, Political Committee, February 1, 1834, ff. 7 no. 467 of 1830.

106. Ibn Ruzayq, *Al-Fatḥ al-Mubīn*, 2:493; and Ibn Ruzayq, *Imāms and Seyyids*, 344. The official British after-action report is BL IOR/R/15/1/23, ff 91–92.

107. BL, IOR/R/15/1/23, Smith to Bombay, March 15, 1821, ff. 95r; and Thomas, *Selections*, 191.

108. BL, IOR/R/15/1/33, Stannus to Bombay, May 14, 1823, ff. 119–23.

109. BL, IOR/R/15/1/33, Stannus to Bombay, December 7, 1824, ff. 50r.

110. Thomas, *Selections*; and Ibn Ruzayq, *Imāms and Seyyids*, 345, Badger's n1.

111. Lorimer, *Gazetteer*, 1:465. The Bani Bu Ali continued to appeal to the British for financial support, noting for years how their entire means of existence had been annihilated in the previous war. In 1829 the governor general wrote to the chief of the Bani Bu Ali, essentially telling him that his best bet for rebuilding his confederacy would be to appeal to the graces of Said bin Sultan. See BL IOR/R/15/1/49, ff. 2–10. He was confirming what had already been instructed to the Bani Bu Ali in 1825, when Elphinstone encouraged the chieftain to cultivate better ties with Said. See BL IOR/R/15/1/35, ff. 14–21.

112. BL, IOR/R/15/1/25, November 27, 1822, ff. 76v, 2; Thomas, *Selections*, 525–26.

113. Thomas, *Selections*, 527.

114. Al-Nabhānī, *Al-Tuḥfah*, 150–51. See also Belgrave, *Pirate Coast*, 132; and Thomas, *Selections*, 527–28.

115. Hanna, *Pirate Nests*, 11. See also Michael Kempe, "'Even in the Remotest Corners of the World': Globalized Piracy and International Law, 1500–1900," *Journal of Global History* 5 (2010): 353–72, https://doi.org/10.1017/S1740022810000185.

116. Peter Linebaugh and Marcus Rediker, *The Many-Headed Hydra: Sailors, Slaves, Commoners, and the Hidden History of the Revolutionary Atlantic* (Boston: Beacon Press, 2000).

117. As one historian put it: "The rise of Oman had been accomplished at the expense of others." Bathurst, "Ya'rubi Dynasty," 191.

118. Burton, *Trouble with Empire*; Karen Barkey, *Empire of Difference: The Ottomans in Comparative Perspective* (Cambridge: Cambridge University Press, 2008).

119. Lauren Benton and Lisa Ford, *Rage for Order: The British Empire and the Origins of International Law* (Cambridge, MA: Harvard University Press, 2016).

120. Johan Mathew, *Margins of the Market: Trafficking and Capitalism Across the Arabian Sea*, California World History Library (Oakland: University of California Press, 2016).

121. Joseph A. Schumpeter, *Capitalism, Socialism, and Democracy* (New York: Harper Perennial Modern Thought, 2008), 84; and Jonathan Levy, *Freaks of Fortune: The Emerging World of Capitalism and Risk in America* (Cambridge, MA: Harvard University Press, 2012), 4.

122. J. H. Elliott, "Atlantic History: A Circumnavigation," in *The British Atlantic World, 1500–1800*, ed. David Armitage and Michael J. Braddick, 2nd ed. (New York: Palgrave Macmillan, 2009), 259–60, 269; Vink, "Indian Ocean Studies,'" 59.

CHAPTER 4. MOVING TO ZANZIBAR

1. Roberts was following a small but growing trend of merchants looking to East Africa as a space for escaping relatively dull New England markets. Very little has been written about Americans in the Western Indian Ocean. See Bennett and Brooks, *New England Merchants*; Morrison, "Cut from the Same Cloth"; Dane A. Morrison, *True Yankees: The South Seas & the Discovery of American Identity*, The Johns Hopkins University Studies in Historical and Political Science (Baltimore, MD: The Johns Hopkins University Press, 2014); and Jane Hooper, *Yankees in the Indian Ocean: American Commerce and Whaling, 1786–1860*, Indian Ocean Studies Series (Athens: Ohio University Press, 2022).

2. LOC, Roberts to Sa'id, January 27, 1828, ff. 64715, reel 3, box 4.

3. LOC, Roberts to Woodbury, December 19, 1828, reel 3, box 4. See also Norman Robert Bennett, "Americans in Zanzibar, 1825–1845," *Essex Institute Historical Collections* 95 (1959): 243–44.

4. Roberts, *Embassy to the Eastern Courts*, 6.

5. Al-Mughairī, *Juhaynat Al-Akhbār*, 220.

6. Al-Mughairī, *Juhaynat Al-Akhbār*, 261.

7. G. R. Tibbetts, *Arab Navigation in the Indian Ocean before the Coming of the Portuguese: Being a Translation of Kitāb al-Fawā'id Fī Uṣūl al-Baḥr Wa'l-Qawā'id of Aḥmad b. Mājid al-Najdī*, Oriental Translation Fund New Series, 42 (London: The Royal Asiatic Society of Great Britain and Ireland, 1981), 208.

8. Bresnahan, *Inland from Mombasa*, 6.

9. Guillain, *Documents Sur l'histoire*, 2:302–3.

10. Log and East India Marine Society Journal of the Brig *Ann* of Salem, Charles Millet, Master, December 11, 1827, as quoted in Bennett and Brooks, *New England Merchants*, 150.

11. Fernand Braudel, *The Wheels of Commerce*, trans. Siân Reynolds, Civilization & Capitalism, 15th–18th Century (New York: Harper and Row, 1982), 2:147.

12. The best account of the Mazruʿi in Mombasa is Bresnahan, *Inland from Mombasa*. For other sources see Reginald Coupland, *East Africa and Its Invaders: From the Earliest Times to the Death of Seyyid Said in 1856* (Oxford: Clarendon Press, 1938), 217–94; Guillain, *Documents Sur l'histoire*, 1:584–89; John Gray, Roland Oliver, and Gervase Mathew, "Zanzibar and the Coastal Belt, 1840–1884," in *History of East Africa*, 3 vols. (Oxford: Clarendon Press, 1963), 1:212–52. See also F. J. Berg, "The Swahili Community of Mombasa, 1500–1900," *Journal of African History* 9, no. 1 (1968): 35–56; and Fred James Berg, "Mombasa under the Busaidi Sultanate: The City and Its Hinterlands in the Nineteenth Century" (PhD diss., University of Wisconsin–Madison, 1971).

13. Bishara, *Sea of Debt*, 5.

14. Bresnahan, *Inland from Mombasa*, especially 68–93.

15. Bhacker, *Trade and Empire*, 96.

16. Guillain, *Documents Sur l'histoire*, 1:590–91.

17. See the discussion and sources in Nicholls, *Swahili Coast*, 126; and Bhacker, *Trade and Empire*, 84.

18. Bishara, *Sea of Debt*, 13–16; and Nicholls, *Swahili Coast*, 139–42. The definitive account of this is John Gray, *The British in Mombasa, 1824–1826, Being the History of Captain Owen's Protectorate* (London: Macmillan, 1957).

19. BL, IOR/R/15/1/33, Letter no. 2 from Stannus to Bombay, February 1, 1825, ff. 63v–70.

20. BL, IOR/R/15/1/33, Letter bo. 1 from Stannus to Bombay, January 28, 1825, ff. 61v–63.

21. For more on this see Coupland, *East Africa and Its Invaders*, 143–73. As for what happened to Captain Owen: "He fades out of East African history into the mists of the North Atlantic, keeping his flag flying on his little private island," wrote Coupland with his delightful flair. See Coupland, *East Africa and Its Invaders*, 164.

22. Bhacker, *Trade and Empire*, 71.

23. INA, Foreign Department, Secret Committee, Christian to Bombay, no. 22, May 1, 1826, ff. 51.

24. Guillain, *Documents Sur l'histoire*, 1:585.

25. INA, Foreign Department, Secret Committee, Said to Bombay, January 1827, no. 12, ff. 40.

26. INA, Foreign Department, Secret Committee, Said to Bombay, January 1827, no. 12, ff. 41. See also Nicholls, *Swahili Coast*, 305.

27. Guillain, *Documents Sur l'histoire*, 1:607–8; Burton, *Zanzibar*, 1:297–98; and Nicholls, *Swahili Coast*, 308.

28. Pouwels, *Horn and Crescent*, 106.

29. See the series of proclamations beginning with Al-Mughairī, *Juhaynat Al-Akhbār*, 224.

30. Al-Mughairī, *Juhaynat Al-Akhbār*, 224.

31. Al-Mughairī, *Juhaynat Al-Akhbār*, 225.

32. For more on this see chapter 1. This even held true for Muscat. According to McDow, between 1828 and his death in 1856, Saʿid spent more than 80 percent of his time in Zanzibar, leaving domestic Omani concerns to his deputies there. See McDow, *Buying Time*, 67. See also Al-Maḥdhūrī, *Zanjibār*, 27–28.

33. Hämäläinen, *Comanche Empire*, 5.

34. Bresnahan, *Inland from Mombasa*, 118.

35. Bresnahan, *Inland from Mombasa*, 118–19.

36. Bresnahan, *Inland from Mombasa*, 120–21.

37. P. Dallons, 1804, in G. S. P. Freeman-Grenville, ed., *The East African Coast: Select Documents from the First to the Earlier Nineteenth Centuries* (Oxford: Oxford University Press, 1962), 198–201; and Nicholls, *Swahili Coast*, 80–81.

38. Nicholls, *Swahili Coast*, 113.

39. The classic work on this remains Prestholdt, *Domesticating the World*.

40. INA, FD, May 29, 1834, Saʿid to Agha Mahomed Shusteree, 6, 11, PC, received March 5, 1833.

41. McDow, *Buying Time*, 24–43.

42. Goswami, *Call of the Sea*, 60–61.

43. Roberts, *Embassy to the Eastern Courts*, 353.

44. As one emblematic example see François Albrand, *Extrait d'un Mémoire Sur Zanzibar et Sur Quiloa* (Paris: Bulletin de la Société de Géographie, 1838), 67–68.

45. PL, PEM, MH94, B François ox 3 Folder 2, Stickney to Fabens, May 31, 1846.

46. Al-Mughairī, *Juhaynat Al-Akhbār*, 222.

47. François Albrand, *Extrait d'un Mémoire Sur Zanzibar et Sur Quiloa* (Paris: Bulletin de la Société de Géographie, 1838), 72; Joseph B. F. Osgood, *Notes of Travel or Recollections of Majunga, Zanzibar, Muscat, Aden, Mocha, and Other Eastern Ports* (Salem, MA: George Creamer, 1854), 45; Burton, *Zanzibar*, 1:368; and Sheriff, *Slaves, Spices, and Ivory*, 146.

48. MSA, vol. V no. 114, 1873, Frere to Earl Granville, Enclosure 1 in no. 51, dated May 7, 1873, cited in Goswami, *Call of the Sea*, 131.

49. Burton, *Zanzibar*, 1872, 1:320; and Bishara, *Sea of Debt*, 33.

50. Goswami, *Call of the Sea*, 192–93.

51. Little is known about Yaqut, though he was likely of Ethiopian heritage. He was also a eunuch. According to Burton, he had been appointed by Saʿid's uncle; Burton did not mention exactly who. Richard F. Burton, *Zanzibar: City, Island, and Coast* (London: Tinsley Brothers, 1872), 2:471. Nicholls echoed this but claimed Saʿid's father Sultan appointed Yaqut, and that Yaqut had been manumitted by then. See Nicholls, *Swahili Coast*, 271. See also Abdul Sheriff, "History of Zanzibar to 1890," in *Oxford Research Encyclopedia of African History* (Oxford: Oxford University Press, 2020). Yaqut was almost certainly not his birth name, but was rather a name ascribed to him by his enslavers. As Beeta Baghoolizadeh lyrically stated,

"There were many Yaquts." This Yaqut was like countless other enslaved Black men trafficked throughout the Western Indian Ocean, including deep into Iran and other parts of Central and Southwest Asia, many of whom did not have the relative autonomy of this Yaqut. See Beeta Baghoolizadeh, *The Color Black: Enslavement and Erasure in Iran* (Durham, NC: Duke University Press, 2024).

52. See the description of Yaqut and his exploitation of visiting merchants in Dallons to the Captain-General, Ile de France, 1804, in Freeman-Grenville, *East African Coast*, 197–201.

53. McDow, *Buying Time*, 47.

54. Al-Maḥdhūrī, *Zanjibār*, 162; Muḥammad Rajab Ḥarrāz, *Ifrīqiyah Al-Sharqīyah Wa al-Isti'mār Al-Ūrūbbī* (Cairo: Dār al-Nahḍah al-'Arabīyah, 1968), 101; and Jamāl Zakarayā Qāsim, *Dawlat BūSa'id Fī 'Umān Wa Sharq Ifrīqiyah* (Cairo: Maktabat al-Qahirah al-Hadīthah, 1968), 198.

55. ZNA, AA12/2, Rigby to Bombay, September 17, 1860, ff. 41,

56. USNA, Sen 23B-B2, Roberts to Livingstone; and Roberts, *Embassy to the Eastern Courts*, 362.

57. The Omani scholar Al-Maḥdhūrī highlights how, no matter how critical Jairam and other Indian financiers became, the commercial apparatus of the empire always required Sa'id's close supervision. See Al-Maḥdhūrī, *Zanjabār*, 162.

58. PL, PEM, MSS 230, box 1, folder 3, February 2, 1839.

59. ZNA, AA3/6, Hamerton to Bombay, ff. 87.

60. Charles Ward to James Buchanan, March 13, 1847, in Bennett and Brooks, *New England Merchants*, 385.

61. For more on the idea of "intelligence networks" in history, see Aslanian, *From the Indian Ocean*, 87; Fernand Braudel, *The Mediterranean and the Mediterranean World in the Age of Philip II*, trans. Siân Reynolds, vol. 1 (Berkeley: University of California Press, 1995), 1:566; and Rene Barendse, "The Long Road to Livorno: The Overland Messenger Service of the Dutch East India Company in the Seventeenth Century," *Itinirario* 12 (1988): 25–45.

62. Botsford to Webster, November 10, 1842, as cited in Bennett and Brooks, *New England Merchants*, 222.

63. Guillaine, *Documents Sur l'histoire*, 2:388, also 372.

64. Immanuel Wallerstein, "Braudel on Capitalism, or Everything Upside Down," *Journal of Modern History* 63, no. 2 (1991): 354–61.

65. As quoted in Goswami, *Call of the Sea*, 195.

66. PL, PEM, MH 14, box 1, folder 6, Sa'id to Waters, October 19, 1837.

67. ANOM, Édouard Loarer, Rapport commercial, 1 partie, ff. 61.

68. Al-Mughairī, *Juhaynat Al-Akhbār*, 226.

69. Bishara, *Sea of Debt*, 52–53.

70. This paragraph draws on Sheriff, *Slaves, Spices, and Ivory*, 49–50. A *frasela* was equivalent to about thirty-five pounds.

71. For the best discussion of these different accounts see Al-Maḥdhūrī, *Zanjabār*, 44–50; and Sheriff, *Slaves, Spices, and Ivory*, 49.

72. Al-Mughairī, *Juhaynat Al-Akhbār*, 223.

73. ZNA, AA3/11, Hamerton to Bombay, March 24, 1855, ff. 245.

74. ZNA, AA3/18, Rigby to Bombay, June 1, 1860, ff. 144.

75. Sheriff, *Slaves, Spices, and Ivory*, 69.

76. Sheriff, *Slaves, Spices, and Ivory*, 51.

77. ZNA, AA3/18, Rigby to Bombay, June 1, 1860, ff. 144.

78. Sheriff, *Slaves, Spices, and Ivory*, 50–53.

79. Bishara, *Sea of Debt*, 43; Sheriff, *Slaves, Spices, and Ivory*, 249–52; and Frederick Cooper, *Plantation Slavery on the East Coast of Africa* (New Haven, CT: Yale University Press, 1977), 52.

80. Sheriff, *Slaves, Spices, and Ivory*, 127.

81. ZNA, AA3/18, Rigby to Bombay, June 1, 1860, ff. 143.

82. ZNA, AA3/18, Rigby to Bombay, June 1, 1860, ff. 144.

83. John Milner Gray, *History of Zanzibar: From the Middle Ages to 1856* (London: Oxford University Press, 1962), 167. This paragraph borrows from Sheriff, *Slaves, Spices, and Ivory*, 55.

84. For more on the law and property rights in the Omani Empire, see Bishara, *Sea of Debt.*

85. Sheriff, *Slaves, Spices, and Ivory*, 55–59. For more on Pemba see McMahon, *Slavery and Emancipation.*

86. Burton and Hamerton are quoted in McDow, *Buying Time*, 53.

87. Sheriff, *Slaves, Spices, and Ivory*, 54–55.

88. William Cunningham Bissell, *Urban Design, Chaos, and Colonial Power in Zanzibar* (Bloomington: Indiana University Press, 2011), 25–28, 30–31. My thanks to Dodie McDow for this reference.

89. Osgood, *Notes of Travel*, 27–30.

90. One primary account we have of this is the testimony of a formerly enslaved person named Chengwimbe. For his account see Zoe Marsh, ed., *East Africa through Contemporary Records* (Cambridge: Cambridge University Press, 1961), 35–43.

91. Goswami, *Call of the Sea*, 244. The estimate of 200,000 enslaved humans could be inflated. In 1844 Atkins Hamerton estimated the number of enslaved on the island as 150,000. These numbers are all estimations. To be clear, however, the point remains that the density of enslaved persons on the island would have been at the least jarring. For the Hamerton estimate see McDow, *Buying Time*, 147.

92. J. Ross Browne, *Etchings of a Whaling Cruise, with Notes of a Sojourn on the Island of Zanzibar* (New York: Harper & Brothers, 1850), 332.

93. Bresnahan, *Inland from Mombasa*; and Gooding, *On the Frontiers.* See McDow's discussion of "coastal chauvinism" in *Buying Time*, 26.

94. Gwyn Campbell, *Africa and the Indian Ocean World from Early Times to Circa 1900*, New Approaches to African History (Cambridge: Cambridge University Press, 2019), 63.

95. Although Braudel never used the phrase, the *velocity of circulation* is a theme of his works. More specifically, see Banaji, *Brief History of Commercial Capitalism*, 113–18.

96. Al-Maḥdhūrī, *Zanjabār*, 166; Roberts, *Embassy to the Eastern Courts*, 362–63; and Guillain, *Documents Sur l'histoire*, 2:396–400.

97. ANOM, OIND 2, Édouard Loarer, Rapport commercial, 1 partie, ff. 67.

98. Reginald Coupland, *The Exploitation of East Africa, 1856–1890* (London: Faber and Faber, 1939), 4; Gray, Oliver, and Mathew, "Zanzibar and the Coastal Belt, 1840–1884," 224. Sources disagree on when Saʿid introduced the *pice*. Burton said it was 1840; al-Mahdhuri cites al-Mughairi, who said it was 1848. See Burton, *Zanzibar*, 2:405; Al-Maḥdhūrī, *Zanjabār*, 168; and Al-Mughairī, *Juhaynat Al-Akhbār*, 259.

99. Al-Maḥdhūrī, *Zanjabār*, 167.

100. Guillain, *Documents Sur l'histoire*, 2:395–96.

101. Gray, *History of Zanzibar*, 144.

102. ANOM, OIND 2, Édouard Loarer, Rapport commercial, 1 partie, ff. 67.

103. Bresnahan, *Inland from Mombasa*, 123.

104. Prestholdt, *Domesticating the World*, 98. Bishara and McDow added to Prestholdt's work, seeking to reimagine the worlds of these more everyday actors.

105. Burton, *Zanzibar*, :136.

106. Coupland, *East Africa and Its Invaders*, 202.

107. Burton, *Zanzibar*, 2:318.

108. Bresnahan, *Inland from Mombasa*, 121–23.

109. Goswami, *Call of the Sea*, 199–200.

110. PL, PEM, MSS 230, box 1, folder 1, Waters to Saʿid, April 16, 1841.

111. PL, PEM, MSS 230, box 1, folder 1, Saʿid to Waters, April 18, 1841.

112. In Arabic: *wa kullu ḥājatin tabdī laka fa al-ishāratu minka, wa as-salām.*

113. Cited in Nicholls, *Swahili Coast*, 254–55.

114. The importance of the return journey, something easily taken for granted today, is a theme throughout Braudel's works. See, as one example, Braudel, *Wheels of Commerce*, 2:140.

115. One might wonder how a diver, in the nineteenth century before scuba equipment, could reach the bottom of the harbor floor. Divers employed in the Persian Gulf were legendary for their ability to hold their breath at great depths, for astonishingly long periods of time. Many of these divers were slaves employed in the pearl diving industry. In 1833 Edmund Roberts observed: "Several divers were employed to find a sword which by an accident was lost overboard in eight fathoms, where the ship was anchored; two of them went down several times, and the greatest length of time either remained under water, was *two* minutes and *five* seconds" (emphasis in original). Note that one fathom equals six feet, so the divers, according to Roberts, were descending forty-eight feet. Roberts, *Embassy to the Eastern Courts*, 356.

116. PL MSS 230, box 1, folder 3, January 18, 1842.

117. ZNA AA3/2, J. Davies to Bombay, ff. 169.

118. Roberts, *Embassy to the Eastern Courts*, 360. The Omani-British treaty, in Article 14, stipulated that local authorities would provide any necessary aid to refit

any vessel flying under British flag in need of assistance. See ZNA AA3/2, ff. 112, Bombay Correspondence.

119. David Pingree and George West Jr. to Richard P. Waters, Salem, May 3, 1841, in Bennett and Brooks, *New England Merchants*, 231.

120. Richard P. Waters, August 18, 1837, in Bennett and Brooks, *New England Merchants*, 203–4.

121. Although he focuses on mobility, McDow hints at how important the privilege of being immobile also was. See McDow, *Buying Time*, 15–16.

122. Burton, *Zanzibar*, 1:323.

123. See ZNA, AC 2/72.

124. ZNA, AA12/12, Agreement between His Highness the Imam of Muscat and Captain J. Walker.

125. See, for example, PL, PEM, MH 23, box 1, folder 7, agreement between the Master, Seamen or Mariners of the Ship Brenda of Salem.

126. ZNA, AA3/1, Hamerton to Bombay, ff. 211.

127. John Studdy Leigh, "The Zanzibar Diary of John Studdy Leigh, Part I," ed. James S. Kirkman, *International Journal of African Historical Studies* 13, no. 2 (January 1, 1980): 298; and McDow, *Buying Time*, 48.

128. Braudel, *Wheels of Commerce*, 2:264–65; and Doumani, *Rediscovering Palestine*.

129. Al-Mughairī, *Juhaynat Al-Akhbār*, 222.

CHAPTER 5. POLITICS OF THE MARKETPLACE

1. USNA, Sen 23 B-B2, Message of May 30, 1834, re commercial treaty of March 20, 1833, between U.S. and Siam; and the commercial treaty of September 21, 1833, between US and Muscat. Roberts had been chosen for this mission because of the letter he had written to his senator after returning from his disastrous voyage to Zanzibar in 1828,—as detailed in the previous chapter. That the president appointed a New England merchant to negotiate commercial treaties, central components of US foreign policy, might contain important ramifications for future work to be done by historians of the United States in the world. It not only challenges the popular perception that southern states drove foreign policy, but it also augments how entrepreneurial and commercial the US approach to the world was. The appointment of Richard Waters,—a New England merchant,—as the first consul to the Omani Empire also brings New England to the fore of American foreign policy and interests, as Joshua Morrison has suggested. See Matthew Karp, *This Vast Southern Empire: Slaveholders at the Helm of American Foreign Policy* (Cambridge, MA: Harvard University Press, 2018).

2. Ruschenberger, *Narrative of a Voyage Round the World*, 1:108, 128. The first print depicted a battle between the USS *Constitution* and HMS *Guerriere* on August 19, 1812. The *Constitution* sank the *Guerriere* and returned victorious to Boston.

The second print depicted the USS *United States* forcing the surrender of the HMS *Macedonian* on October 25, 1812.

3. Quoted in David Fitz-Enz, *Old Ironsides: Eagle of the Sea - The Story of the USS Constitution* (Lanham, MD: Taylor Trade Publishing, 2004), 146.

4. BNA, FO 54/1, Peacock to Bombay, August 27, 1834, ff. 23.

5. BNA, FO 54/4, Hamerton to Smith, No. 23 of 1841, ff. 166–67.

6. BNA, FO 54/4, Hamerton to Willoughby, August 20, 1841, ff. 164–65. Apparently the paintings were so offensive to Hamerton that Saʿid had them taken down before his next visit. He did not, however, get rid of them; rather, he had them moved to his other residence, further inland in Zanzibar, known as Mtoni. See Osgood, *Notes of Travel*, 84.

7. This chapter provides an alternative interpretation from Bose, *Hundred Horizons*, 77. It challenges the notion that Zanzibar was a mere "conveyor belt" for an industrializing West, as suggested in Tagliacozzo, *In Asian Waters*, 121, 129.

8. Fahad Bishara and Hollian Wint, "Into the Bazaar: Indian Ocean Vernaculars in the Age of Global Capitalism," *Journal of Global History* 16, no. 1 (2020): 4, 7.

9. Here I am most influenced by the work of Alison Games, who demonstrated how the expansion of what would become the British Empire was rooted not so much in strength or dominance as in "dissimulation and accommodation," learning over time how to obtain certain privileges from more powerful polities and empires throughout the world. See Games, *Web of Empire*, 12, 52. For a more recent treatment of this, see Sharman, *Empires of the Weak*. The defining work on how European capital melded with preexisting Indian Ocean economies is Ray, "Asian Capital." Some historians have already demonstrated how the expansion of British interests on the subcontinent itself depended on the help of local actors, institutions, and commerce. See Bayly, *Rulers, Townsmen and Bazaars*; and Subramanian, *Indigenous Capital and European Expansion*.

10. BNA, FO/54/2, Memorandum regarding the Political relations existing between His Highness the Imaum of Muscat, and the British Government, ff. 4–7.

11. See, for one example, BL, IOR/F/4/746. Nicholls points out how, when Moresby visited Zanzibar in 1821, it was not for commercial matters but rather to investigate the slave trade there and gather preliminary information on crafting a treaty with Saʿid to abolish it. See Nicholls, *Swahili Coast*, 139.

12. BNA, FO 54/2, Palmerston to [unclear], September 24, 1838, ff. 135.

13. LOC, Roberts papers, reel 2, box 3, Forsyth to Roberts, March 20, 1835. Granted, when looking back at this some might counter that there were imperialist, political ambitions at the core of American foreign policy in this time. While there certainly might have been, however, that they cloaked those ostensible ambitions in commercial pursuits meshed with peoples in the Omani Empire, which is exactly what they were doing, as well.

14. Roberts, *Embassy to the Eastern Courts*, 352.

15. Rockel, *Carriers of Culture*; Stephen J. Rockel, "Wage Labor and the Culture of Porterage in Nineteenth Century Tanzania: The Central Caravan Routes,"

Comparative Studies of South Asia, Africa, and the Middle East 15, no. 2 (1995): 14–24; Stephen J. Rockel, "Enterprising Partners: Caravan Women in Nineteenth Century Tanzania," *Canadian Journal of African Studies* 34, no. 3 (2000): 748–78, https://doi.org/10.1080/00083968.2000.10751213; and Stephen J. Rockel, "Slavery and Freedom in Nineteenth Century East Africa: The Case of Waungwana Caravan Porters," *African Studies* 68, no. 1 (2009): 87–109. See also McDow, *Buying Time.*

16. Jeremy Prestholdt, "On the Global Repercussions of East African Consumerism," *American Historical Review* 109, no. 3 (2004): 759. For African history more broadly, Joseph Miller emphasized in his seminal study understanding the importance of imports in reorienting Africa and Africans as more than mere producers. See Joseph C. Miller, *Way of Death: Merchant Capitalism and the Angolan Slave Trade, 1740–1830* (Madison: University of Wisconsin Press, 1988).

17. Prestholdt, "On the Global Repercussions," 760–61.

18. LOC, Roberts papers, reel 3, box 4, Roberts to Woodbury, December 26, 1828, ff. 4.

19. Nicholls, *Swahili Coast*, 158.

20. INA, Foreign Department, Political Committee, no. 16, Gore to Bombay, May 22, 1834.

21. INA, Foreign Department, Political Committee, no. 18, Gore to Bombay, May 22, 1834.

22. BL, IOR/F/4/1475, Saʿid to Bombay, February 4, 1834, ff. 35–36.

23. BL, IOR/F/4/1475, Hart to Gore, February 10, 1834, ff. 61

24. BL, IOR/F/4/1475, Hart to Gore, February 10, 1834, ff. 69.

25. LOC, Roberts papers, reel 3, box 5, "Muscat," ff. 3. See also reel 2, box 3, Roberts to McLane, ff. 65121.

26. LOC, Roberts papers, reel 3, box 5, "Edmund Roberts," ff. 2.

27. LOC, Roberts papers, reel 2, box 3, Roberts to Forsyth, October 23, 1835, ff. 65314.

28. INA, Foreign Department, Secret Committee, Seton to Bombay, April 29, 1809, Ref. No. 20-25, ff. 8.

29. LOC, Roberts papers, reel 3, box 4, Saʿid to Jackson, October 7, 1833.

30. BL, IOR/F/4/1475, Hart to Gore, February 10, 1834, ff. 85.

31. BL, IOR/F/4/1475, Hart to Gore, February 10, 1834, ff. 87.

32. New England's commerce in the Omani Empire provides another vantage for studying the commercial orientation of early Americans in the world. See especially Morrison, "Cut from the Same Cloth"; and Joshua S. C. Morrison, "Amity, Commerce, and Compromise: Americans, Indians, and the Evolution of Trade on Zanzibar and across the Western Indian Ocean, 1825–1861," *Journal of World History* 35, no. 2 (2024): 199–227. On New England's commercial orientation see Russell R. Menard, *The Economy of British America, 1607–1789* (Chapel Hill: University of North Carolina Press, 1985); Winifred Barr Rothenberg, "The Invention of American Capitalism: The Economy of New England in the Federal Period," in *Engines of Enterprise: An Economic History of New England* (Cambridge, MA:

Harvard University Press, 2000), 69–108; and Peter Temin, ed., *Engines of Enterprise: An Economic History of New England* (Cambridge, MA: Harvard University Press, 2000).

33. BL, IOR/F/4/1475, Hart to Gore, February 10, 1834, ff. 88.

34. Ruschenberger, *Voyage Round the World*, 1:66. See also LOC, Roberts papers, reel 3, box 4, Roberts to Forsyth, October 23, 1835, ff. 7.

35. ZNA, AA2/4, Return of Foreign Shipping Engaged in the Direct and Indirect Trade at the Port of Zanzibar in the Year 1859, ff. 93.

36. ZNA, AA2/4, Return of Merchant Shipping Arrivals at the Port of Zanzibar During the Last Five Years, ff. 95. See also USNA, RG 84, Records of Foreign Service Posts, Consular Posts, Zanzibar.

37. For more on this see Morrison, "Amity, Commerce, and Compromise."

38. Jonathan Goldstein, "The Andrew Jackson Administration and the Orient, 1829–]1837," *International Journal of Maritime History* 12, no. 2 (December 2000): 30; and Roberts, *Embassy to the Eastern Courts*, 5.

39. Peter Temin, introduction to *Engines of Enterprise: An Economic History of New England*, ed. Peter Temin (Cambridge, MA: Harvard University Press, 2000), 6.

40. Some readers might quibble with my use of the word *local* here. I use it to mean persons from the Indian Ocean world—Africans, Arabs, South Asians—not Europeans or Americans. See also the discussion beginning in Prestholdt, *Domesticating the World*, 63.

41. PL, PEM, MH14, box 1, folder 1, Smith to Waters, September 7, 1840.

42. PL, PEM, MH14, box 1, folder 1, Smith to Waters, September 7, 1840.

43. PL, PEM, MH14, box 1, folder 1, Invoice of Merchandise Shipped on board Bark *Cavalier*, September 10, 1840.

44. PL, PEM, MH14, box 1, folder 1, Pingree to J. Waters, September 10, 1840.

45. Another similar letter demanding "as little delay as possible" so that the same vessel could be sent back out "a second time" is in Bennett and Brooks, *New England Merchants*, 227–28.

46. PL, PEM, MH14, box 1, folder 1, Pingree to J. Waters, September 10, 1840.

47. PL, PEM, MH 14, box 1, folder 3, Pingree and West to Waters, January 28, 1841.

48. Roberts to Forsyth, October 10, 1835 in Bennett and Brooks, *New England Merchants*, 162.

49. PL, PEM, MH94, Box 2 Folder 9, Shephard to Fabens, September 15, 1844.

50. Waters to P. Starr Parker, Zanzibar, January 1, 1840, as quoted in Bishara and Wint, "Into the Bazaar," 1; and Bennett and Brooks, *New England Merchants*, 225.

51. In analyzing certain written contracts Bishara suggests that in terms of legal understanding, Jairam's customs house was understood to embody the Omani government in the Western Indian Ocean. See Bishara, *Sea of Debt*, 71.

52. Ruschenberger, *Voyage Round the World*, 1:47.

53. Bishara, *Sea of Debt*, 14–15, quoting Heaton Bowstead Robinson, ed., *Narrative of Voyages to Explore the Shores of Africa, Arabia, and Madagascar; Perofrmed in*

H.M. Ships "Leven" and "Barracouta," under the Direction of Capt. W.F. Owen, R.N. (London: Richard Bentley, 1833), 1:413.

54. INA, Foreign Department, Secret Committee, Christian to Admiralty, May 9, 1826, ff. 19. This collection of sources has never been used.

55. INA, Foreign Department, Secret Committee, Bombay to Christian, September 8, 1826, ff. 26. This collection of sources has never been used.

56. BNA FO/54/1, Owen to Palmerston, September 8, 1834, ff. 10.

57. BNA, FO 54/1, Owen to Palmerston, September 8, 1834, ff. 11.

58. BNA, FO 54/2, Norsworthy to Bombay, December 20, 1837, ff. 66.

59. BNA, FO 54/2, Cogan to Bombay, June 9, 1838, ff. 75.

60. BNA, FO 54/2, Cogan to Hobhouse, February 22, 1838, ff. 35.

61. Thomas, *Selections*, 250–51.

62. P. J. L. Frankl, "Hamerton, Atkins (Bap. 1804, d. 1857), Army Officer and First British Consul in Zanzibar," in *Oxford Dictionary of National Biography*, September 23, 2004, https://www-oxforddnb-com.proxy.library.nd.edu/view/10.1093/ref:odnb/9780198614128.001.0001/odnb-9780198614128-e-59618.

63. ZNA, AA3/1, Hamerton to Bombay, August 17, 1841, ff. 196. For Hamerton's orders see ZNA, AA12/29, Willoughby to Hamerton, January 16, 1841, ff. 8; and BL, IOR/R/15/1/96, Willoughby to Hamerton, ff. 2–8.

64. BL, IOR/F/4/1983, Hamerton to Bombay, August 30, 1841, ff. 1–2.

65. John G. Waters to Richard P. Waters, June 9, 1844, in Bennett and Brooks, *New England Merchants*, 250.

66. Bennett, "Americans in Zanzibar," 252. John G. Waters, Richard's brother, described this in a letter to George West Jr., dated May 30, 1838. See Bennett and Brooks, *New England Merchants*, 221.

67. Bennett, "Americans in Zanzibar," 252.

68. ZNA, AA3/1, Hamerton to Bombay, August 17, 1841, ff. 200. It was not just local peoples who apparently were ill disposed toward the British; the Americans, it seems, also were. Waters referred to Norsworthy as a "worthless fellow" and wrote that his wife was, apparently, "still worse." See Waters to William C. Waters, December 17, 1839, in Bennett and Brooks, *New England Merchants*, 223.

69. ZNA, AA3/1, Hamerton to Bombay, July 8, 1841, ff. 175–77.

70. ZNA, AA3/1, Hamerton to Bombay, September 6, 1841, ff. 218.

71. ZNA, AA3/1, Hamerton to Bombay, September 6, 1841, ff. 219–20.

72. Prestholdt, *Domesticating the World*, 75–76.

73. Waters to Sa'id, October 13, 1837, in Bennett and Brooks, *New England Merchants*, 220.

74. Bennett, "Americans in Zanzibar," 251–52.

75. Waters to Abji bin Siwji, September 20, 1839, in Bennett and Brooks, *New England Merchants*, 222.

76. PL, PEM, MH 23, Disbursements and port charges at Hodeda on Brenda, box 1, folder 7, September 12, 1840.

77. PL, PEM, MH 23, Disbursements and port charges at Hodeda on Brenda, box 1, folder 7, September 12, 1840.

78. PL, PEM, MH 23, Disbursements and port charges at Hodeda on Brenda, box 1, folder 7, September 18, 1840.

79. Historians Fahad Bishara and Thomas McDow paved the way in studying these contracts, or *waraqas*. For more, see Bishara, *Sea of Debt*; McDow, *Buying Time*; and Bishara and Wint, "Into the Bazaar." Hollian Wint wrote her dissertation using similar contracts. See Hollian Wint, "Credible Relations: Indian Finance and East African Society in the Indian Ocean, c. 1840–1930" (PhD diss., New York, New York University, 2016).

80. PL, PEM, MH 94, box 2, folder 9, Shephard to Fabens, September 15, 1844.

81. PL, PEM, MH 94, box 2, folder 9, Shephard to Fabens, September 15, 1844.

82. Richard P. Waters to William C. Waters, November 13, 1844, in Bennett and Brooks, *New England Merchants*, 251–52. Ultimately the Boston vessel's captain and crew were able to secure a footing in the market, despite "every effort" having been made to "force the *Mohawk* from the market." See Fabens to Shepard, January 4, 1845, in Bennett and Brooks, *New England Merchants*, 340.

83. Guillain, *Documents Sur l'histoire*, 2:34–35.

84. PL, PEM, MH 14, box 2, folder 6, dated Zanzibar, August 27, 1841. Suleiman bin Hamed was one of Sa'id's relatives, whom Sa'id deputized as a governor of Zanzibar. Obviously, he was also a prolific merchant.

85. Morrison, "Cut from the Same Cloth," 125.

86. As one example, see PL, MH 14, box 2, folder 6, contract dated Zanzibar, March 19, 1842, unsigned. As another example, see PL, MH 14, box 2, folder 6, contract signed Richard P. Waters, dated Zanzibar, April 1, 1841.

87. PL, PEM, MH 14, box 2, folder 6, contract signed Richard P. Waters and dated Zanzibar, January 9, 1844.

88. Braudel, *Wheels of Commerce*, 2:223.

89. Esau died in Zanzibar in January 1845, after Waters had departed Zanzibar. An American merchant there wrote to Waters of the news: "Your friend Esau bin abdue Rahman died about one month since. . . . He is something of a loss to Zanzibar." See Jelly to Waters, February 5, 1845, in Bennett and Brooks, *New England Merchants*, 341.

90. PL, PEM, MH 14, box 2, folder 3, Richard Waters to Sadick bin Barack, December 12, 1844.

91. Prestholdt, *Domesticating the World*, 5.

92. See Andrew David Edwards, Peter Hill, and Juan Neves-Sarriegui, "Capitalism in Global History," *Past & Present* 249, no. 1 (2020): 10.

93. This adds a new angle to that in Benton and Ford, *Rage for Order*, 4–5.

94. Joyce Appleby, "The Popular Sources of American Capitalism," *Studies in American Political Development* 9, no. 2 (Fall 1995): 457; and Rothenberg, "Invention of American Capitalism," 70.

95. Temin, introduction, 6.

96. ASCF, 1850s_079, Putnam's Journal, Z. 25/11/1850, citing Essex Institute M 656 E 184 E Ben.

97. Rothenberg, "Invention of American Capitalism," 78.

98. Rothenberg, "Invention of American Capitalism," 79.

99. As Pedro Machado showed for an earlier period, Mozambique and India were not incorporated into a global economy, as if that global economy existed unto itself; rather, they were constitutive of that global economy from its inception. The treatment of Zanzibar here extends Machado's framework geographically and temporally. Machado, *Ocean of Trade*, 14.

100. Hodgson, *Rethinking World History*, 26, 37, 42.

CHAPTER 6. ENSLAVEMENT AND HUMAN TRAFFICKING

1. The preceding is from ZNA AA3/2, LeGeyt to Bombay Government, August 21, 1844, ff. 253–56.

2. As Gwyn Campbell put it: "Forms of bondage and traffic in human beings affected the entire macro-region," meaning the Indian Ocean world, a unit he defines as a "sophisticated and durable system of long-distance exchange" linking "Africa to China and all points in between." Gwyn Campbell, "Servitude and the Changing Face of the Demand for Labor in the Indian Ocean World, c. 1800–1900," in *Indian Ocean Slavery in the Age of Abolition*, ed. Robert Harms, Bernard K. Freamon, and David W. Blight (New Haven, CT: Yale University Press, 2013), 24. Given the servitude of migrant workers in the Persian Gulf today, I purposefully use "has" here instead of "had."

3. Bishara, *Sea of Debt*, 46–50. See also the reprint of a 1989 special issue of *Slavery and Abolition:* William Gervase Clarence-Smith, *The Economics of the Indian Ocean Slave Trade in the Nineteenth Century* (London: Routledge, 2015).

4. The historical debates on slavery and capitalism have been extensive. Walter Johnson, subsequently cited, summarized the general conclusion of these debates when he stated that there would have been no capitalism in the nineteenth century without slavery. This chapter illustrates why this was the case in the Omani Empire. For the best treatment of the debate, see Scott Reynolds Nelson, "Who Put Their Capitalism in My Slavery?," *Journal of the Civil War Era* 5, no. 2 (June 2015): 289–310.

5. I agree with Edward Alpers that abolitionism was perhaps the central policy of British strategy in the region. See Edward A. Alpers, "On Becoming a British Lake: Piracy, Slaving, and British Imperialism in the Indian Ocean during the First Half of the Nineteenth Century," in *Indian Ocean Slavery in the Age of Abolition*, ed. Robert Harms, Bernard K. Freamon, and David W. Blight (New Haven, CT: Yale University Press, 2013), 15. The scholar of Islamic studies Jonathan A .C. Brown is incorrect in his historical claim that the British succeeded in ending the Indian Ocean slave trade after 1830. See Jonathan A. C. Brown, *Slavery & Islam* (London: Oneworld Publications, 2019), 51.

6. BNA, FO 54/5, Sub-Enclosure 10 in Second Enclosure in no. 269, December 7, 1840, ff. 118.

7. BNA, FO 54/5, Sub-Enclosure 10 in Second Enclosure in no. 269, December 7, 1840, ff. 118.

8. BNA, FO 54/5, Haines to Bombay, December 22, 1841, ff. 131.

9. Allen, *European Slave Trading.*

10. PL, PEM, log 1180, 19. There are accounts of traffickers taking enslaved East Africans to the Atlantic. As one example, in March 1837 American consul Richard Waters observed a European ship being loaded with three hundred slaves bound for Rio de Janeiro. Though Waters was a staunch abolitionist, the nonchalance with which he observed this in his journal reflects, perhaps, just how common such transoceanic slaving vessels were in East Africa. See Bennett and Brooks, *New England Merchants*, 192–93.

11. Alpers, *Ivory and Slaves*, 191–93.

12. Alpers, *Ivory and Slaves*, 191–93.

13. For the most recent treatment of this see Gooding, *On the Frontiers*, 64–93.

14. BL, IOR/F/4/746/20306, Extract Political Letter from Bombay, August 29, 1821, ff. 2–3.

15. Janet J. Ewald, "Africa: East Africa," in *A Historical Guide to World Slavery*, ed. Seymour Drescher and Stanley L. Engerman (New York: Oxford University Press, 1998), 41; see also Hopper, *Slaves of One Master*, 35; Campbell, "Servitude and the Changing Face of Demand for Labor," 30–31; and Jonathon Glassman, *Feasts and Riot: Revelry, Rebellion, and Popular Consciousness on the Swahili Coast, 1856–1888* (Portsmouth, NH: Heinemann, 1995), 81.

16. Prestholdt, *Domesticating the World*, 118.

17. McMahon, *Slavery and Emancipation*, 4.

18. Walter Johnson, *River of Dark Dreams: Slavery and Empire in the Cotton Kingdom* (Cambridge, MA: Belknap Press, 2013), 252.

19. Robert Harms, Bernard K. Freamon, and David W. Blight, eds., *Indian Ocean Slavery in the Age of Abolition* (New Haven, CT: Yale University Press, 2013), 13.

20. Gooding, *On the Frontiers*, 170. On scholarly consensus see Gwyn Campbell, ed., *The Structure of Slavery in Indian Ocean Africa and Asia* (London: Frank Cass, 2004), x–xi; on spectrum see Toledano, *Slavery and Abolition*, 166; and Ehud Toledano, "The Concept of Slavery in Ottoman and Other Muslim Societies: Dichotomy or Continuum," in *Slave Elites in the Middle East and Africa*, ed. Miura Toru and John Edward Phillips (London: Keagan Paul International, 2000), 173–75. For a summary of this see Robert Harms, "Introduction: Indian Ocean Slavery in the Age of Abolition," in *Indian Ocean Slavery in the Age of Abolition*, ed. Robert Harms, Bernard K. Freamon, and David W. Blight (New Haven, CT: Yale University Press, 2013), 12–14. See also Glassman, *Feasts and Riot*, esp. 80.

21. Sheriff, *Slaves, Spices, and Ivory*, 37.

22. BL, IOR/F/4/617/15321, ff. 27.

23. Rebecca Wakefield, *Memoirs of Mrs. Rebecca Wakefield, Wife of the Rev. T. Wakefield*, ed. R. Brewin (London: Hamilton, Adams, 1879), 112–13, as cited in Prestholdt, *Domesticating the World*, 96.

24. One can acknowledge this without going as far as some have in what Ehud Toledano calls the "good treatment" thesis. As Leslie Peirce has noted in the

Ottoman context, elite slaves might have had certain degrees of privilege, but that privilege was granted to them after a violent process of social death and transfer to a new, enslaved life. See Ehud R. Toledano, *As If Silent and Absent: Bonds of Enslavement in the Islamic Middle East* (New Haven, CT: Yale University Press, 2007), 16–23; and Leslie Peirce, *Morality Tales: Law and Gender in the Ottoman Court of Aintab* (Berkeley: University of California Press, 2003).

25. Orlando Patterson, *Slavery and Social Death* (Cambridge, MA: Harvard University Press, 1982).

26. This is unpacked throughout Prestholdt, *Domesticating the World*, 134–40; Pouwels, *Horn and Crescent*; and Glassman, *Feasts and Riot*. See also Paul E. Lovejoy, *Transformations in Slavery: A History of Slavery in Africa*, 2nd ed. (Cambridge: Cambridge University Press, 2000), 13–15; and Gooding, *On the Frontiers*, 170–73.

27. McMahon, *Slavery and Emancipation*, 12.

28. ZNA, AM3/1, 14, as cited in Bishara, *Sea of Debt*, 76.

29. ZNA, AA3/3, Kemball to Robertson, July 8, 1842, ff. 209.

30. Salamah bint Said, *Memoirs of an Arabian Princess*, 9.

31. For a discussion of how slaves in East Africa understood their own enslaved statuses, see Glassman, *Feasts and Riot*, 85–96.

32. For an overview of women's experiences in slavery and as slave owners, see Joseph C. Miller, "Women as Slaves and Owners of Slaves: Experiences from Africa, the Indian Ocean World, and the Early Atlantic," in *Women and Slavery: Africa, the Indian Ocean World, and the Medieval North Atlantic*, ed. Gwyn Campbell, Suzanne Miers, and Joseph C. Miller, 2 vols. (Athens: Ohio University Press, 2007), 1:1–42. There is a distinguished literature on women and slavery in the Indian Ocean and in East Africa. For some of this literature see Marcia Wright, *Strategies of Slaves and Women in East Central Africa* (Bloomington: University of Indiana Press, 1989); Claire C. Robertson and Martin A. Klein, eds., *Women and Slavery in Africa* (Madison: University of Wisconsin Press, 1983); McMahon, *Slavery and Emancipation*; Gwyn Campbell, Suzanne Miers, and Joseph C. Miller, eds., *Women and Slavery: Africa, the Indian Ocean World, and the Medieval North Atlantic*, vol. 1, 2 vols. (Athens: Ohio University Press, 2007).

33. For a discussion of concubinage and its connections with Islamic law, see Kecia Ali, *Sexual Ethics and Islam: Feminist Reflections on Qur'an, Hadith, and Jurisprudence*, rev. ed. (London: Oneworld, 2016), 50–71. See also Abdul Sheriff, "Suria: Concubine or Secondary Slave Wife? The Case of Zanzibar in the Nineteenth Century," in *Sex, Power and Slavery*, ed. Gwyn Campbell and Elizabeth Elbourne (Athens, OH: Ohio University Press, 2014), 99–120.

34. Salamah bint Said, *Memoirs of an Arabian Princess*, 11.

35. Salamah bint Said, *Memoirs of an Arabian Princess*, 11.

36. Personal observation, Bayt as-Sahel Palace Museum, Stone Town Zanzibar, April 15, 2018.

37. Sarah K. Croucher, *Capitalism and Cloves: An Archaeology of Plantation Life on Nineteenth Century Zanzibar* (New York: Springer, 2015), 13; and Glassman, *Feasts and Riot*, 90. The song comes from Mtoro bin Mwinyi Bakari, *The Customs*

of the Swahili People, trans. J. W. T. Allen (Berkeley: University of California Press, 1981), 125–26.

38. BL, IOR/F/4/2014, extract para. 5 of a letter from the Native Agent at Muscat, February 5, 1843, ff. 29–30.

39. BNA, FO 54/5, Hamerton to Bombay, January 2, 1842, ff. 143; and ZNA, AA3/1, Hamerton to Bombay, January 2, 1842, ff. 268.

40. BNA, FO 54/5, Hamerton to Bombay, January 2, 1842, ff. 143–44.

41. PL, PEM, log 1180, 20. Other than Osgood's depiction here, I have not found a single other depiction of what the actual slave vessel was like from the first half of the nineteenth century. They are also notoriously difficult to find from the second half of the century, given that Arab slave dealers had no interest in describing their ships, and as Mandana Limbert has pointed out, British officers who seized these ships had little interest in the actual plight of the enslaved. As Limbert noted, however, in 1872, the *Times of India* published a piece on the British capture of an Arab slave vessel and included a graphic description of where the slaves were kept that aligns with Osgood's poem: "The hold, from which an intolerable stench proceeded, was several inches deep in the foulest bilge-water and refuse. Down below, there were numbers of children and wretched beings in the most loathsome stages of small-pox and scrofula of every description. A more disgusting and degrading spectacle of humanity could hardly be seen, whilst the foulness of the dhow was such that the sailors could hardly endure it." See Mandana E. Limbert, "'If You Catch Me Again at It, Put Me to Death': Slave Trading, Paper Trails, and British Bureaucracy in the Indian Ocean," in *Indian Ocean Slavery in the Age of Abolition*, ed. Roert Harms, Bernard K. Freamon, and David W. Blight (New Haven, CT: Yale University Press, 2013), 124.

42. Extract from Michael W. Shepard log, 1844, in Bennett and Brooks, *New England Merchants*, 262.

43. PL, PEM, log 1180, 20.

44. Ruschenberger, *Narrative of a Voyage Round the World*, 1:40. Burton also confirmed seeing this cage for holding slaves. See Burton, *Zanzibar*, 1:351.

45. "Lines of negroes stood like beasts," recalled Burton. See Burton, *Zanzibar*, 1:353. For more on animal metaphors and slavery see Johnson, *River of Dark Dreams*, particularly chapter 7.

46. PL, PEM, log 1180, 20; and BL, IOR/F/4/617/15321, ff. 21.

47. BL, IOR/F/4/617/15321, ff. 21. This report from the British Africa Institution, written by leading abolitionists of the time, might be construed as having exaggerated accounts, given the firebrand ideologies of its authors, like William Wilberforce. However, it also contains descriptions of how slaves sold to Arabs were relatively lucky, drawing upon a common perception of Arabs as treating their slaves well. If this report was in fact one of exaggerated ideology seeking to provide scathing evidence for why the British government needed to do more to stop the slave trade, one wonders why the authors reported on the Arabs treating their slaves so well.

48. PL, PEM, log 1180, 20.

49. BL, IOR/R/15/1/56, Wilson to Bombay, January 28, 1831, ff. 2r. For more on sex and prices of slaves see Lovejoy, *Transformations in Slavery*, 5–6.

50. BNA, FO 54/5, Haines to Willoughby, July 3, 1841, ff. 121; and ZNA, AA3/3, Hamerton to Robertson, July 8, 1842, ff. 206. For another report on the prices of slaves see Bennett and Brooks, *New England Merchants*, 253.

51. BL, IOR/F/4/1699, Memorandum by the Political Secretary, December 1, 1835.

52. INA, Foreign Department, Political Committee, September 19, 1836, Native Agent at Mocha to Bombay, May 14, 1836, ff. 10–11.

53. My focus in the preceding section was on East Africa and exports of slaves mostly toward the northwest Indian Ocean; however, as Richard Allen has pointed out, countless slaves were exported westward, from South Asia into East Africa, as well. Allen, *European Slave Trading*, 4–5.

54. BL, IOR/F/4/746, Saʿid to Farquhar, December 13, 1821, ff. 178.

55. BL, IOR/F/4/746, Bruce to Bombay, February 25, 1822, ff. 189–91.

56. BL, IOR/F/4/2014, Malcolm to Court of Directors, February 25, 1843, ff. 1–15.

57. By 1849 the British realized Saʿid had tricked them with this strategic move. See ZNA, AA3/9, Bombay to Hennell, June 27, 1849.

58. ZNA, AA12/2, Rigby to [unknown], May 14, 1861, ff. 114–18.

59. BL, IOR/F/4/2066, Aberdeen to the Secretary to the India Board, July 12, 1842, ff. 7–9.

60. BNA, FO54/5, Saeed bin Sultan to Earl of Aberdeen, February 11, 1842, ff. 142–43. At the same time, Saʿid wrote letters using almost identical language to Queen Victoria and Viscount Palmerston. See the same collection.

61. BNA, FO54/5, Hamerton to Aberdeen, May 21, 1842, ff. 166.

62. BNA, FO54/5, Aberdeen to Saeed Ali Bin Nasir, July 12, 1842, ff. 166. The British government's insistence upon a total end to the slave trade is repeated in sources throughout multiple archives.

63. BL, IOR/F/4/2066, extract from the Instructions of His Highness the Imaum of Muscat to Ali Bin Nasir, Envoy on a Special Mission to Her Majesty the Queen of Great Britain, February 1842, ff. 29–31; and BNA, FO54/5, Second Enclosure no. 85, February 1842, ff. 168.

64. BL, IOR/F/4/2066, extract from the Instructions of His Highness the Imaum of Muscat to Ali Bin Nasir, Envoy on a Special Mission to Her Majesty the Queen of Great Britain, February 1842, ff. 29–31; BNA, FO54/5, Second Enclosure no. 85, February 1842, ff. 168.

65. BNA, FO 54/5, The Imaum of Muscat to the Earl of Aberdeen, February 11, 1842.

66. Johnson, *River of Dark Dreams*, 254.

67. The popular writer Stuart Laing is incorrect when he asserts that the ivory trade was not usually connected with the slave trade in East Africa. See Stuart Laing, *Tippu Tip: Ivory, Slavery, and Discovery in the Scramble for Africa* (Surrey, UK: Medina Publishing, 2017), 4.

68. Here and subsequently in this chapter I am engaging with Rockel, *Carriers of Culture.*

69. ZNA, AA3/1, Hamerton to Bombay, July 1, 1841, ff. 169.

70. ZNA, AA3/1, Hamerton to Bombay, September 28, 1841, ff. 227.

71. BNA, FO 54/5, Cogan to Forbes, October 28, 1842, ff. 149.

72. BNA, FO 54/5, Hamerton to Bombay, January 2, 1842, ff. 144.

73. ZNA, AA3/8, Hamerton to Bombay, October 25, 1849, no number. It seems almost as if Richard Burton had met with Hamerton. He recalled in his memoir that, as a "result of our interference" "slavery had increased in horrors . . . the average quantity of the wretched merchandise had not been diminished" and pointed out how many British abolitionists at the time "opined that nothing save the special interposition of Providence could end that which had so long baffled many best efforts." Burton, *Zanzibar*, 1:455.

74. ZNA, AA3/8, Hamerton to Bombay, February 15, 1850, ff. 161.

75. Harms, "Introduction: Indian Ocean Slavery," 6. This number becomes more astonishing when one remembers that Zanzibar is only 50 miles long. The entire island is 643 square miles.

76. BNA, FO 54/6, Hamerton to Earl of Aberdeen, January 2, 1844, ff. 121.

77. I am borrowing here from Jürgen Osterhammel, *The Transformation of the World: A Global History of the Nineteenth Century*, trans. Patrick Camiller (Princeton, NJ: Princeton University Press, 2014), 670.

78. John C. Wilkinson, *Water and Tribal Settlement in South-East Arabia: A Study of the Aflaj of Oman* (Oxford: Clarendon Press, 1977).

79. PL, PEM, log 1180 Emily Wilder (Bark) Journal.

80. I agree with Cooper's conceptualization of what a plantation was: "Plantations were large-scale, specialized units that developed in order to serve the needs of a vast and widespread market for particular commodities." See Cooper, *Plantation Slavery*, 3. However, perhaps the best definition comes from the anthropologists Eric Wolf and Sidney Mintz, who conceptualized a plantation as "an agricultural estate, operated by dominate owners . . . and a dependent labor force, organized to supply a large-scale market by means of abundant capital, in which the factors of production are employed primarily to further capital accumulation without reference to the status needs of the owners." See Eric R. Wolf and Sidney W. Mintz, "Haciendas and Plantations in Middle America and the Antilles," *Social and Economic Studies* 6, no. 3 (1957): 380. For a discussion of the plantation as an object, see Croucher, *Capitalism and Cloves*, 60–64.

81. I am borrowing here from Richard White, *The Organic Machine: The Remaking of the Columbia River* (New York: Hill and Wang, 1995). Harnessing nature to transcend its natural limits was a crucial part of capitalism's emergence in modern history. Ellen Wood provides an overview of this in Ellen Meiksins Wood, *The Origin of Capitalism: A Longer View* (London: Verso, 2002). Similarly, understanding how Omanis in the nineteenth century expropriated land from indigenous peoples and commodified the countryside helps us understand this process in a more global manner, as parallel to similar processes taking shape throughout the world. See

Charles S. Maier, *Leviathan 2.0: Inventing Modern Statehood* (Cambridge, MA: Belknap Press, 2012).

82. James C. Scott, *Seeing Like a State: How Certain Schemes to Improve the Human Condition Have Failed* (New Haven, CT: Yale University Press, 1998), 21.

83. PL, PEM, log 1180 Emily Wilder (Bark) Journal.

84. Burton, *Zanzibar*, 1:29.

85. LOC, Edmund Roberts papers, reel 1, box 1, ff. 65510.

86. LOC, Edmund Roberts Papers, reel 1, box 1, ff. 65513.

87. Ruschenberger, *Narrative of a Voyage Round the World*, 1:71. Roberts recalled that the central house was overlooking "a great extent of very beautiful and very picturesque country; the clove plantation of His Highness radiating from the house in every direction." LOC, Edmund Roberts papers, reel 1, box 1, ff. 65512.

88. PL, PEM, log 1180 ff. 21. Ruschenberger also noted that some individuals owned up to 2,000 slaves. See Ruschenberger, *Narrative of a Voyage Round the World*, 1:40. See also Cooper, *Plantation Slavery*, 43.

89. As Frederick Cooper put it, slaves in East Africa simultaneously experienced a high degree of dependence and independence. See Cooper, *Plantation Slavery*, 241.

90. PL, PEM, log 1180 Emily Wilder (Bark) Journal, ff. 18.

91. Ruschenberger, *Narrative of a Voyage Round the World*, 1:71–72.

92. Ruschenberger, *Narrative of a Voyage Round the World*, 1:71. In 1837, when Waters visited Saʿid's main plantation at Mtoni, he estimated that Saʿid had 200,000 clove trees. See Bennett and Brooks, *New England Merchants*, 201.

93. The preceding paragraph is from PL, PEM, log 1180 Emily Wilder (Bark) Journal, ff. 18; and Ruschenberger, *Narrative of a Voyage Round the World*, 1:64.

94. Croucher, *Capitalism and Cloves*, 29.

95. BNA, FO/54/5, Hamerton to Bombay, January 2, 1842, ff. 143.

96. Burton, *Zanzibar*, 1:382.

97. The following discussion of Thani bin Amir borrows heavily from McDow, *Buying Time*, 86–88.

98. Richard Burton, as quoted in McDow, *Buying Time*, 88.

99. Rockel, *Carriers of Culture*, 3.

100. As quoted in Rockel, *Carriers of Culture*, 4.

101. Rockel, *Carriers of Culture*, 4.

102. W. H. Whiteley, trans., *Maisha Ya Hamed Bin Muhammed El Murjebi Yaani Tippu Tip, Kwa Maneno Yake Mwenyewe* (Arusha, Tanzania: Beauchamp Print Co., 1959).

103. I am drawing here from Robert Harms, *The Diligent: A Voyage through the Worlds of the Slave Trade* (New York: Basic Books, 2002), xix.

104. McDow cogently picks apart what he calls "the myth of return." See chapter 4 in *Buying Time*. One might counter that Jairam Shivji did, in fact, return to Gujarat and die there. This is true, and many other emigrants to East Africa ended up returning to their respective homes, but countless others remained, and in fact, the Al-Harthi family and other Indian families remain prominent fixtures in Zanzibar

today. As Sebouh David Aslanian put it, "We should be careful about privileging mobility and movement over permanence and immobility." See Aslanian, *From the Indian Ocean*, 14.

105. The will is recorded as appendix 3 in Bhacker, *Trade and Empire*, 201–2; and Cooper, *Plantation Slavery*, 203 (emphasis added).

106. Cooper, *Plantation Slavery*, 44–45.

107. PL, PEM, log 1180 Emily Wilder (Bark) Journal.

108. PL, PEM, log 1180 Emily Wilder (Bark) Journal.

109. PL, PEM, log 1180 Emily Wilder (Bark) Journal. Numerous sources corroborate this. See Ruschenberger, *Narrative of a Voyage Round the World*, 1:38; and BL, IOR/F/4/617/15321, ff. 25; BNA, FO 54/5, ff. 377.

110. PL, PEM, log 1180 Emily Wilder (Bark) Journal. Numerous sources corroborate this. See Ruschenberger, *Narrative of a Voyage Round the World*, 1:38; BL, IOR/F/4/617/15321, ff. 25; and BNA, FO 54/5, ff. 377.

111. PL, PEM, log 1180, Emily Wilder (Bark) Journal, ff. 17.

112. Eric Kimball, "'What Have We to Do with Slavery?' New Englanders and the Slave Economies of the West Indies," in *Slavery's Capitalism: A New History of American Economic Development*, ed. Sven Beckert and Seth Rockman, Early American Studies (Philadelphia: University of Pennsylvania Press, 2016), 183; and Philip D. Curtin, *The Rise and Fall of the Plantation Complex: Essays in Atlantic History*, 2nd ed. (New York: Cambridge University Press, 1998).

CHAPTER 7. THE OMANI EMPIRE IN WORLD HISTORY

1. Gray, Oliver, and Mathew, "Zanzibar and the Coastal Belt," 230.

2. James Raymond Wellsted, *Travels in Arabia* (London: John Murray, 1838), 1:5.

3. ZNA AA12/29, Hamerton to Foreign Office, November 10, 1856, ffs. 118–19.

4. His daughter concluded that Said had finally succumbed to a bullet wound in his leg, which he had suffered from for decades. Salamah bint Said, *Memoirs of an Arabian Princess*, 104. See also ZNA, AA12/29, Hamerton to Foreign Office, November 10, 1856, ffs. 118–19.

5. Said-Ruete, *Said Bin Sultan*, 90.

6. ZNA AA12/2, ffs. 87–88.

7. USNA, RG 84 Foreign Service Posts, Zanzibar, vol. 098, Waters to Percival, November 23, 1844.

8. PL, MSS 901, box 98, folder 3, Waters to Pingree.

9. PL, MH 14, box 1, folder 7, Pingree to Waters.

10. Indeed, even the "Atlantic world" was not the creation of only Europeans and Americans. It was also created by Africans, as Paul Gilroy showed, sparking a body of literature in response that cannot be summarized here. See Paul Gilroy, *The Black Atlantic: Modernity and Double-Consciousness* (Cambridge, MA: Harvard University Press, 1993).

11. Al-Mughairī, *Juhaynat Al-Akhbār*, 240.

12. James Baillie Fraser, *Narrative of a Journey into Khorasan, in the Years 1821 and 1822* (London: Longman, Hurst, Rees, and Orme, 1825), 20; and Said-Ruete, *Said Bin Sultan*, 154.

13. Fraser, *Narrative of a Journey into Khorasan*, 20; and Said-Ruete, *Said Bin Sultan*, 153.

14. On Omani architecture in East Africa and how it was an expression of social practices as well as a consequence of them, see Daniel Rhodes, Colin Breen, and Wes Forsythe, "Zanzibar: A Nineteenth-Century Landscape of the Omani Elite," *International Journal of Historical Archaelogy* 19 (2015): 334–55.

15. Salamah bint Said, *Memoirs of an Arabian Princess*, 3.

16. Salamah bint Said, *Memoirs of an Arabian Princess*, 35.

17. Prestholdt, *Domesticating the World*, 96.

18. Joseph Arthur de Gobineau, *Trois Ans En Asie: De 1855 a 1858* (Paris: Librairie De L. Hachette, 1859), 93, 95–96, 98.

19. Gobineau, *Trois Ans En Asie*, 99.

20. Heinz Gaube and Abdulrahman Al-Salimi, *The Ibadis in the Region of the Indian Ocean. Section One; East Africa*, Studies on Ibadism and Oman (Hildesheim, Germany: Georg Olms Verlag, 2013), 1:428; Al-Maḥdhūrī, *Zanjabār*, 57; and Gray, Oliver, and Mathew, "Zanzibar and the Coastal Belt," 224.

21. L'Académie Française, "Négociant," in *Le Dictionnaire De L'Académie Française* (Paris: Chez J. J. Smits et Ce., 1835). The fifth edition of the same dictionary, published in 1735, also differentiated between a *négociant* and a merchant, noting that *négociants* engaged in commerce on a "grand" scale, whereas merchants engaged in commerce on smaller, more minute scales. L'Académie Française, "Négociant," in *Le Dictionnaire De L'Académie Française* (Paris: Chez J. J. Smits et Ce., 1798). The difference was clear in Loarer's commercial report, throughout which he differentiated between *marchands* and *négociants*.

22. Braudel, *Wheels of Commerce*, 2:64. See also the discussion of this throughout Harms, *The* Diligent, starting on page 33. These words and the historical concepts behind them likely would have both been captured by the Arabic *tujjār/tājir*, though within this single word, Arabs understood different stratified definitions of "grand" traders who dealt in long-distance, interoceanic, or transcontinental trade and more local traders selling goods or services from private residences. Such distinctions were especially apparent to Arabs in the Arabian Peninsula, given its centuries-long position as a waystation for movements of capital, goods, and people between Africa, the Indian Ocean, Asia, and the Levant and eastern Mediterranean.

23. See chapter 1, note 7.

24. This is drawn from NRS, GD1/633/3, ff. 100–105; and Belgrave, *Pirate Coast*, 66–67.

25. There is by now a rich literature challenging the imperialist geographic area studies paradigm. For one criticism of that paradigm in the Indian Ocean context, see Sunil S. Amrith, *Crossing the Bay of Bengal: The Furies of Nature and the*

Fortunes of Migrants (Cambridge, MA: Harvard University Press, 2013). For a more recent example see Liu, *Tea War.*

26. For a review of other recent literature revolving around similar issues, see Hollian Wint, "Empire and Capitalism in the Western Indian Ocean," *Arab Studies Journal* 26, no. 2 (2018): 181–93.

27. The phrase "waiting room of history" comes from Dipesh Chakrabarty, *Provincializing Europe: Postcolonial Thought and Historical Difference* (Princeton, NJ: Princeton University Press, 2000), 8.

28. Hodgson, *Venture of Islam*, 2:542, 548, and esp. 544.

29. Sheila Carapico, "Arabia Incognita: An Invitation to Arabian Peninsula Studies," in *Counter-Narratives: History, Contemporary Society, and Politics in Saudi Arabia and Yemen*, ed. Madawi Al-Rasheed and Robert Vitalis (New York: Palgrave Macmillan, 2004), 21.

30. When I presented aspects of this book to the Middle East faculty at a preeminent American research university, one of them responded: "All that Indian Ocean stuff is great, but can you tell us about the Middle East?"

31. Thomas Metcalf demonstrated how critical India and Indians' agencies were to what became the British colonial entity in South Asia. See Thomas R. Metcalf, *Imperial Connections: India in the Indian Ocean Arena, 1860–1920*, California World History Library (Berkeley: University of California Press, 2008). Historians have shown in other ways how local Indian Ocean peoples co-opted the existence of the British Empire for their own ends, whether political, economic, social, or spiritual. See, as only some examples, Scott Reese, *Imperial Muslims: Islam, Community and Authority in the Indian Ocean, 1839–1937* (Edinburgh: Edinburgh University Press, 2017); Alavi, *Muslim Cosmopolitanism in the Age of Empire*; James L. Gelvin and Nile Green, eds., *Global Muslims in the Age of Steam and Print* (Berkeley: University of California Press, 2014); and Rishad Choudhury, *Hajj Across Empires: Pilgrimage and Political Culture after the Mughals, 1739–1857*, Asian Connections (Cambridge: Cambridge University Press, 2023).

32. Bayly, *Birth of the Modern World*, 3.

33. See, for example, the treatment of explaining Omani history against the backdrop of what Jones and Ridout label "the Age of British Ascendancy." Jeremy Jones and Nicholas Ridout, *A History of Modern Oman* (New York: Cambridge University Press, 2015).

34. Bayly, *Birth of the Modern World*, 3. Osterhammel's conclusion for his global history is that the nineteenth century was "Europe's century." See Osterhammel, *Transformation of the World.*

35. For developments in Omani history after Saʿid's death, see Jones and Ridout, *History of Modern Oman*; Robert Geran Landen, *Oman Since 1856: Disruptive Modernization in a Traditional Arab Society* (Princeton, NJ: Princeton University Press, 1967); and Uzi Rabi, *The Emergence of States in a Tribal Society: Oman under Sa'id Bin Taymur, 1932–1970* (Eastbourne: Sussex Academic Press, 2011).

36. Sivasundaram, *Waves across the South*, 32.

37. Prestholdt, *Domesticating the World*, 105–8.

38. For another take on this argument see Frank, *ReORIENT*; and Hobson, *Multicultural Origins*.

39. Edward W. Said and Jonathan Rée, "Peoples' Rights and Literature," in "Human Rights and Peoples' Rights in Literature and the Humanities," special issue of *Alif: Journal of Comparative Poetics* 13 (1993): 195.

40. Prestholdt, *Domesticating the World*, 3. Prestholdt is drawing upon Michel-Rolph Trouillot, "The Perspective of the World: Globalization Then and Now," in *Beyond Dichotomies: Histories, Identities, Cultures, and the Challenge of Globalization*, ed. Elisabeth Mudimbe-Boyi, Explorations in Postcolonial Studies (Albany: State University of New York Press, 2002), 6–7.

41. This eloquent phrase comes from Claudia Rankine, *Just Us: An American Conversation* (Minneapolis, MN: Graywolf Press, 2020), 81.

BIBLIOGRAPHY

ARCHIVAL SOURCES

ANOM: Archives Nationales d'Outre-Mer, Aix-en-Provence, France
OIND: Ministère des Colonies, Océan Indien
ASCF: Abdul Sheriff Card File
BL: The British Library, London, England
IOR: India Office Records
BNA: The National Archives of the United Kingdom (British National Archives), Kew, Richmond, England
FO: Foreign Office
INA: National Archives of India (India National Archives), New Delhi, India
FD: Foreign Department
LOC: The United States Library of Congress, Washington, DC, USA
MMC: Miscellaneous Manuscript Collection
MSA: The Maharashtra State Archives, Mumbai, India
NRS: The National Records of Scotland, Edinburgh, Scotland
GD: Gifts and Deposits
PL: The Phillips Library, Peabody Essex Museum, Rowley, Massachusetts, USA
PEM: Peabody Essex Museum
MH: Marine History
MSS: Manuscripts
USNA: The United States National Archives, Washington, DC, USA and College Park, Maryland, USA
RG: General Records of the Department of State
ZNA: The Zanzibar National Archives, Kilimani, Zanzibar
AA: Bombay Correspondence
AC: General Correspondence
AM: General Correspondence

PUBLISHED PRIMARY SOURCES

Arabic

Abū Ḥākima, Aḥmad Muṣṭafā, ed. *Kitāb lam' al-shihāb fī sīrat Muḥammad Bin 'Abd al-Wahhāb*. Beirut: Dar al-Assakafa, 1967.

Al-Afawī, Abū Suleimān Muḥammad bin 'Āmir bin Rāshid al-Ma'walī. *Qiṣaṣ wa akhbār jarat fī 'Umān*. 2nd ed., edited by Sa'īd bin Muḥammad bin Sa'īd Al-Hāshimī. Muscat: Wizārat al-Turāth wa-al-Thaqāfah, 2014.

Al-'Āṣamī al-Najdī, 'Abd al-Raḥmān bin Muḥammad bin Qāsim, ed. *Al-durrar al-saniyyah fī al-ajwiba al-Najdiyyah*. 6th ed. Vol. 8. 16 vols. n.p.: n.p., 1996.

Al-Hamawī, Yāqūt. *Mu'jam al-buldān*. Vol. 3. 5 vols. Beirut: Dar al-Sadr, 1977.

Al-Iṣṭakhrī, Abu Isḥaq Ibrāhīm bin Mūhammad Al-Fārisī. *Kitāb masālik al-mamālik*. Leiden: Brill, 1870.

Al-Izkawī, Sirḥān bin Sa'īd. *Kashf al-ghummah: al-jāmi'a li-akhbār al-ummah*. Edited by Hassan Muḥammad 'Abd Allāh Al-Nabudah. Vol. 2. 2 vols. Beirut: Dar al-Kotob al-Ilmiyah, 2016.

Al-Mahrī, Suleimān ibn Aḥmad ibn Suleimān. "Tuḥfat al-fuḥūl fī tamhīd al-uṣūl fī 'ilm al-biḥār." Unpublished manuscript, Sohar, Oman, September 7, 1740. The British Library.

Al-Mughairī, Sa'īd bin 'Alī. *Juhaynat al-akhbār fī tārīkh Zanjabār*. 5th ed., edited by Muḥammad bin 'Alī Al-Ṣalībī and Suleimān bin 'Amīr bin Nāṣir Al-Maḥdhūrī. Muscat: Wizārat al-Turāth wa al-Thaqāfa, 2017.

Al-Nabhānī, Muḥammad bin Khalīfa. *Al-tuḥfah al-nabhānīyyah fī tārīkh al-jazīrah al-'arabīyyah*. 2nd ed. Cairo: Dār Maṭba'a Al-Maḥmūdīyya li-l-Nashr, 1924.

Al-Sālimī, 'Abdullah bin Ḥummayyidd. *Nahḍat al-a'yān bi ḥurriyyat 'Umān*. 2 vols. Sib, Oman: Maktabat al-Imām Nūr al-Dīn al-Sālimī, 2000.

Al-Sālimī, Nūr Al-Dīn 'Abd Allāh bin Ḥumayyid. *Tuḥfat al-a'yān bi-sīrat ahl 'Umān*. Vol. 2. 2 vols. Cairo: Maktabat al-Istiqāmah, 2013.

———. *Tuḥfat al-a'yān bi-sīrat ahl 'Umān*. 2nd ed., edited by Ibrāhīm bin Aṭfayish Al-Jazā'irī. 2 vols. Cairo: n.p., 1931.

Al-'Uthaymīn, 'Abd al-Allāh al-Ṣāliḥ, ed. *Lam' al-shihāb fī sīrat Muḥammad Bin 'Abd al-Wahhāb*. Silsilat Maṣādir Tārīkh Al-Jazīra Al-'Arabīyya Al-Makhṭūṭa 4. Riyadh: Dārat Al-Mālik 'Abd al-'Azīz, 2005.

Ibn 'Abd al-Wahhāb, Muḥammad. *Kashf al-shubuhat*. 1st ed., edited by 'Abd Allah bin 'Āyaḍ Al-Qaḥṭānī. Riyadh: Dār al-Ṣumay'ī li'l-nashir wa'l-tawzī', 1997.

Ibn Bishr, 'Uthmān ibn 'Abd Allāh bin 'Uthmān. *'Unwān al-majd fī tārīkh Najd*. 4th ed. Vol. 1. 2 vols. Riyadh: Maṭbū'āt Dārat Al-Malik 'Abd Al-Azīz, 1982.

Ibn Ruzayq, Ḥamīd ibn Muḥammad. *Al-fatḥ al-mubīn fī sīrat al-sādah al-Būsa'idiyīn*. 6th ed., edited by Muḥammad Ḥamīd Ṣāleh and Muḥammad bin Mubārik Al-Salīmī. 2 vols. Muscat: Wizārat al-Turāth wa al-Thaqāfa, 2016.

———. *History of the Imāms and Seyyids of 'Omān: From A.D. 661–1856*. Translated by George Percy Badger. Cambridge Library Collection. New York: Cambridge University Press, 2010.

Ibn Ruzayq, Ḥāmīd bin Muḥammad. *Al-ṣaḥīfah al-qaḥṭānniyah*. Edited by Muḥammad bin Mubārik Al-Salīmī, Muḥammad Habīb Ṣāleḥ, and ʿAllal Al-Ṣadīq Al-Ghāzī. Vol. 5. 5 vols. Muscat: Wizārat al-Turāth wa al-Thaqāfa, 2009.

English

Browne, J. Ross. *Etchings of a Whaling Cruise, with Notes of a Sojourn on the Island of Zanzibar*. New York: Harper & Brothers, 1850.

Buckingham, James Silk. *Travels in Assyria, Media, and Persia, Including a Journey from Bagdad by Mount Zagros, to Hamadan, the Ancient Ecbatana; Researches in Ispahan and the Ruins of Persepolis, and Journey from Thence by Shiraz and Shapoor to the Seashore; Description of Bussorah, Bushire, Bahrein, Ormuz, and Muscat; Narrative of an Expedition against the Pirates of the Persian Gulf, with Illustrations of the Voyage of Nearchus, and Passage by the Arabian Sea to Bombay*. 2nd ed. Vol. 2. 2 vols. London: Colburn, 1830.

Burton, Richard F. *Zanzibar: City, Island, and Coast*. 2 vols. London: Tinsley Brothers, 1872.

———. *The Lake Regions of Central Africa: From Zanzibar to Lake Tanganyika*. Vol. 1. 2 vols. Historical Adventure and Exploration Series 33. Santa Barbara, CA: The Narrative Press, 2001.

Correa, Gaspar. *Lendas Da India*. Edited by Rodrigo Jose de Lima Felner. Vol. 1. 4 vols. First published in Lisbon, 1858. Reprinted in Liechtenstein, 1976.

Fraser, James Baillie. *Narrative of a Journey into Khorasan, in the Years 1821 and 1822*. London: Longman, Hurst, Rees, and Orme, 1825.

Greenlee, William Brooks, ed. *The Voyage of Pedro Alvares Cabral to Brazil and India: From Contemporary Documents and Narratives*. London: Hakluyt Society, 1938.

Ibn Jubayr, Muhammad Ibn Ahmad. *The Travels of Ibn Jubayr, 1183–1185*. Translated by R. J. C. Broadhurst. London: Jonathan Cape, 1952.

Leigh, John Studdy. "The Zanzibar Diary of John Studdy Leigh, Part I." Edited by James S. Kirkman. *International Journal of African Historical Studies* 13, no. 2 (January 1, 1980): 281–312.

Lockyer, Charles. *An Account of Trade in India*. London: Samuel Crouch, 1711.

Malcolm, Sir John. *Sketches of Persia*. Vol. 1. 2 vols. London: John Murray, 1845.

Marsh, Zoe, ed. *East Africa through Contemporary Records*. Cambridge: Cambridge University Press, 1961.

Maurizi, Vincenzo. *History of Seyd Said, Sultan of Muscat: Together with an Account of the Countries and People on the Shores of the Persian Gulf, Particularly the Wahabees*. London: John Booth, 1819.

Morning Herald. "Captain Ahmed Bin Naman, the Commander of the Arabian Corvette 'Sultanee,' Is a Great Man." May 15, 1840, 305 ed. 19th Century U.S. Newspapers.

New Hampshire Sentinel. "An Arabian Ship." May 20, 1940, 42, no. 21 . America's Historical Newsroom, NewsBank/Readex.

———. "From the N. Y. American: The Arabian Corvette Sultanee." May 27, 1840, 42, no. 22. America's Historical Newsroom, NewsBank/Readex.
Niebuhr, Carsten. *Travels through Arabia and Other Countries in the East*. Translated by Robert Heron. Vol. 2. 2 vols. Edinburgh: G. Mudie, 1792.
Osgood, Joseph B. F. *Notes of Travel or Recollections of Majunga, Zanzibar, Muscat, Aden, Mocha, and Other Eastern Ports*. Salem, MA: George Creamer, 1854.
Ovington, John. *A Voyage to Surat in the Year 1689*. Edited by H. G. Rawlinson. London: Oxford University Press, 1929.
Owen, W. F. W. *Narrative of Voyages to Explore the Shores of Africa, Arabia, and Madagascar*. Vol. 1. 2 vols. New York: J. & J. Harper, 1833.
Pires, Tomé, and Armando Cortesão. *The Suma Oriental of Tomé Pires: An Account of the East, from the Red Sea to Japan, Written in Malacca and India in 1512–1515*. 2 vols. London: Hakluyt Society, 1944.
Roberts, Edmund. *Embassy to the Eastern Courts of Cochin-China, Siam, and Muscat: In the U.S. Sloop-of-War* Peacock, *David Geisinger, Commander, during the Years 1832–3–4*. New York: Harper & Brothers, 1837.
Robinson, Heaton Bowstead, ed. *Narrative of Voyages to Explore the Shores of Africa, Arabia, and Madagascar; Performed in H.M. Ships* "Leven" *and* "Barracouta," *under the Direction of Capt. W.F. Owen, R.N.* Vol. 1. 2 vols. London: Richard Bentley, 1833.
Ross, E. C. "Administration Report of the Persian Gulf Political Residency and Muscat Political Agency for 1882–1883: Outlines of the History of 'Oman from A.D. 1728–1883." In *Annals of Oman to 1728 of Sirhan Ibn Sa'id Ibn Sirhan*. Cambridge, UK: The Oleander Press, 2013.
Ruschenberger, W. S. W. *Narrative of a Voyage Round the World During the Years 1835, 36, and 37; Including a Narrative of an Embassy to the Sultan of Muscat and the King of Siam*. Vol. 1. 2 vols. London: Richard Bentley, 1838.
Salamah bint Said, aka Emily Ruete. *Memoirs of an Arabian Princess from Zanzibar*. Translated by Lionel Strachey. New York: Doubleday, Page, 2016.
Saʿīd b. Sirhān, Sirhān b. *Kashf Al-Ghumma* [Annals of Oman]. Translated by E. C. Ross. Calcutta: G. H. Rouse, Baptist Mission Press, 1874.
Thomas, R. Hughes, ed. *Selections from the Records of the Bombay Government: No. XXIV*. Bombay: Bombay Education Society's Press, 1856.
Tibbetts, G. R. *Arab Navigation in the Indian Ocean before the Coming of the Portuguese: Being a Translation of Kitāb al-Fawā'id Fī Uṣūl al-Baḥr Wa'l-Qawā'id of Aḥmad b. Mājid al-Najdī*. Oriental Translation Fund New Series, 42. London: The Royal Asiatic Society of Great Britain and Ireland, 1981.
Wakefield, Rebecca. *Memoirs of Mrs. Rebecca Wakefield, Wife of the Rev. T. Wakefield*. Edited by R. Brewin. London: Hamilton, Adams, 1879.
Wellsted, James Raymond. *Travels in Arabia*. Vol. 1. 2 vols. London: John Murray, 1838.
Whiteley, W. H., trans. *Maisha Ya Hamed Bin Muhammed El Murjebi Yaani Tippu Tip, Kwa Maneno Yake Mwenyewe*. Arusha, Tanzania: Beauchamp Print Co., 1959.

French

Albrand, François. *Extrait d'un mémoire sur Zanzibar et sur Quiloa*. Paris: Bulletin de la Société de Géographie, 1838.

Gobineau, Joseph Arthur de. *Trois ans en Asie: de 1855 a 1858*. Paris: Librairie De L. Hachette, 1859.

Guillain, Charles. *Documents sur l'histoire, la géographie et le commerce de l'Afrique orientale, Publiès Par Ordre Du Government*. Edited by Arthur Bértrand. 2 vols. Paris: Societé de Géographie, 1859.L'Académie Française. "Négociant." In *Le dictionnaire de L'Académie Française*. Vol. 2. Paris: Chez J. J. Smits et Ce., 1798.

———. "Négociant." In *Le dictionnaire de L'Académie Française*. Vol. 2. Paris: Chez J. J. Smits et Ce., 1835.

Martin, François. *Mémoires de François Martin, fondateur de Pondichéry (1665–1696)*. Edited by A. Martineau. Vol. 1. 3 vols. Bibliothèque d'histoire coloniale. Paris: Société d'éditions géographiques, maritimes et coloniales, 1931.

Paris, François Edmond. *Essai sur la construction navale des peuples extra-Européens ou collection des navires et pirogues construits par les habitants de l'Asie, de La Malaisie, du grand océan et de l'Amérique dessinés et mesurés par M. Paris, Capitaine de Corvette, pendant les voyages autour du monde de L'Astrolabe, La Favorite et L'Artémis*. 2 vols. Paris: Arthus Bertrand, 1841.

SECONDARY SOURCES

Arabic

ʿAbd Allāh, Muḥammad Mursī. *Imārāt al-sāḥil wa ʿUmān wa al-dawla al-Saʿūdiyya al-ūlā, 1793–1818*. Cairo: Al-Maktaba al-Miṣrīyyah al-Ḥadītha, 1978.

Abū Ḥākima, Aḥmad Muṣṭafā. *Tārīkh al-Kuwait*. Vol. 2. 3 vols. Kuwait: Kuwait Government Press, 1973.

———. *Tārīkh al-Kuwait al-ḥadīth*. Kuwait: Dhat al-Silāsil, 1984.

Al-ʿAlawī, Ṭāriq bin Khamīs. *Al-ʿalāqah bayna al-imāmah wa al-sulṭanah fī ʿUmān*. Beirut: Dar al-Farqad, 2014.

Al-Amīn, Ismāʿīl. *Al-ʿUmāniyūn: ruwwād al-baḥār*. London: Riad al-Rayyes Books, 1990.

Al-Bādī, Aḥmad bin Saʿīd bin ʿUbayd. *Al-Būsʿīdīyyūn wa Āl Saʿūd*. 2nd ed. 3 vols. Damascus: Dār al-Farqad, 2020.

———. *Qiṣaṣ wa akhbār jarat fī ʿUmān wa Zanjabār*. Al-Sīb, Oman: Maktabat al-Ḍāmirī li'l-nashr wa al-Tawzīʿa, 2019.

Al-Būsaʿīdī, Jumʿah bin Khalīfah bin Manṣūr. *Al-dawlah al-Būsaʿīdīyah al-ḥadīthah min al-imāmah ilā al-sulṭānah*. Al-Sīb, Oman: Maktabat al-Ḍāmirī li'l-nashr wa al-Tawzīʿa, 2016.

Al-Fārisī, ʿAbd Allāh ibn Ṣāliḥ. *Al-Būsaʿīdīyūn: ḥukkām Zanjabār*. 5th ed. Translated by Muḥammad Amīn ʿAbd Allāh. Muscat, Oman: Ministry of Heritage and Culture, 2015.

Al-Ismāʿīlī, Aḥmad. "ʿAqlana al-tārikh al-ʿUmāni." *Nizwa*, January 17, 2018. http://www.nizwa.com/عقلنة-التاريخ-العماني-الاجتماع-السيا/.
Al-Khāṭrī, Aminah. *Al-hamlāt al-Briṭāniyyah ḍhid qabilah Banī Bū ʿAlī: 1820–1823*. Sharjah: Manshūrāt Al-Qāsimī, 2015.
Al-Maḥdhūrī, Suleimān bin ʿUmīr bin Nāṣir. *Zanjabār fi ʿahd al-Sayyid Saʿīd bin Sulṭān: Dirāsat fi al-Tārīkh al-Iqtiṣādī, 1804–1856*. Muscat: Al-Nādī Al-Thaqāfī, 2014.
Al-Muʿammarī, Aḥmad Ḥammūd. *ʿUmān Wa Sharqī Ifrīqīyah*. 3rd ed. Translated by Muḥammad Amīn ʿAbd Allāh. Muscat: Wizārat al-Turāth wa al-Qawmī al-Thaqāfa, 2016.
Al-Riyāmī, Nāḍir bin ʿAbd Allāh. *Zanjabār: Shakhṣīyāt Wa Aḥdāth, 1828–1972*. London: Dār al-Ḥikmah, 2009.
Ḥarrāz, Muḥammad Rajab. *Ifrīqiyah Al-Sharqīyah Wa al-Istiʿmār Al-Ūrūbbī*. Cairo: Dār al-Nahḍah al-ʿArabīyah, 1968.
Khazʿal, Ḥusayn Khalaf al-Shaykh. *Tārīkh Al-Kuwayt al-Siāyāsī*. Vol. 1. 5 vols. Beirut: Dar al-Kutub, 1962.
Qāsim, Jamāl Zakarayā. *Dawlat Būsaʿīd Fī ʿUmān Wa Sharq Ifrīqiyah*. Cairo: Maktabat al-Qahirah al-Hadīthah, 1968.

English

Abdullah, Thabit. *Merchants, Mamluks, and Murder: The Political Economy of Trade in Eighteenth-Century Basra*. Albany: State University of New York Press, 2000.
Abu-Hakima, Ahmad Mustafa. *The Modern History of Kuwait, 1750–1965*. London: Luzac & Co., 1983.
Abu-Lughod, Janet L. *Before European Hegemony: The World System A.D. 1250–1350*. London: Oxford University Press, 1991.
Agius, Dionisius A. *Classic Ships of Islam: From Mesopotamia to the Indian Ocean*. Handbook of Oriental Studies 92. Leiden: Brill, 2008.
Alavi, Seema. *Muslim Cosmopolitanism in the Age of Empire*. Cambridge, MA: Harvard University Press, 2015.
Ali, Kecia. *Sexual Ethics and Islam: Feminist Reflections on Qur'an, Hadith, and Jurisprudence*. Rev. ed. London: Oneworld, 2016.
Allen, Calvin H., Jr. "The Indian Merchant Community of Masqaṭ." *Bulletin of the School of Oriental and African Studies* 44, no. 1 (1981): 39–53.
———. "Sayyids, Shets and Sulṭāns: Politics and Trade in Masqat under the Āl Bū Saʿīd, 1785–1914." PhD diss., University of Washington, 1978.
Allen, Richard B. *European Slave Trading in the Indian Ocean, 1500–1850*. Indian Ocean Studies Series. Athens: Ohio University Press, 2014.
Al-Mazruʿi, Shaykh Al-Amin bin ʿAli. *The History of the Mazruʿi Dynasty of Mombasa*. Translated by J. McL. Ritchie. Union Académique Internationale Fontes Historiae Africanae, Arabica XI. London: Oxford University Press, 1995.

Alpers, Edward A. "Indian Ocean Studies: How Did We Get Here and Where Are We Going? A Historian's Perspective." *Journal of Indian Ocean World Studies* 5, no. 2 (2021): 314–36.

———. *Ivory and Slaves: Changing Pattern of International Trade in East Central Africa to the Later Nineteenth Century.* Berkeley: University of California Press, 1975.

———. "On Becoming a British Lake: Piracy, Slaving, and British Imperialism in the Indian Ocean during the First Half of the Nineteenth Century." In *Indian Ocean Slavery in the Age of Abolition*, edited by Robert Harms, Bernard K. Freamon, and David W. Blight, 45–60. New Haven, CT: Yale University Press, 2013.

Alpers, Edward A., and Chhaya Goswami, eds. *Transregional Trade and Traders: Situating Gujarat in the Indian Ocean from Early Times to 1900*. New Delhi: Oxford University Press, 2019.

Al-Qasimi, Sultan Muhammad. *The Myth of Arab Piracy in the Gulf.* London: Croom Helm, 1986.

Al-Rasheed, Madawi. *A History of Saudi Arabia.* 2nd ed. Cambridge: Cambridge University Press, 2010.

Amrith, Sunil S. *Crossing the Bay of Bengal: The Furies of Nature and the Fortunes of Migrants.* Cambridge, MA: Harvard University Press, 2013.

Andrade, Tonio. "A Chinese Farmer, Two African Boys, and a Warlord: Toward a Global Microhistory." *Journal of World History* 21, no. 4 (December 1, 2010): 573–91.

———. *The Gunpowder Age: China, Military Innovation, and the Rise of the West in World History.* Princeton, NJ: Princeton University Press, 2016.

———. *Lost Colony: The Untold Story of China's First Great Victory over the West.* Princeton, NJ: Princeton University Press, 2011.

Ankoud, Rajae. "Prosopography: An Approach to Studying Elites and Social Groups." *AlMuntaqa: Arab Center for Research & Policy Studies* 3, no. 1 (2020): 70–85.

Appleby, Joyce. "The Popular Sources of American Capitalism." *Studies in American Political Development* 9, no. 2 (Fall 1995): 437–57.

———. *The Relentless Revolution: A History of Capitalism.* New York: W. W. Norton, 2011.

Aslanian, Sebouh David. *From the Indian Ocean to the Mediterranean: The Global Trade Networks of Armenian Merchants from New Julfa.* Berkeley: University of California Press, 2011.

Baghoolizadeh, Beeta. *The Color Black: Enslavement and Erasure in Iran.* Durham, NC: Duke University Press, 2024.

Banaji, Jairus. *A Brief History of Commercial Capitalism.* Chicago: Haymarket Books, 2020.

———. *Theory as History: Essays on Modes of Production and Exploitation.* Chicago: Haymarket Books, 2011.

Barendse, R. J. *The Arabian Seas: The Indian Ocean World of the Seventeenth Century.* London: Routledge, 2015.

Barendse, Rene. "The Long Road to Livorno: The Overland Messenger Service of the Dutch East India Company in the Seventeenth Century." *Itinerario* 12 (1988): 25–45.

Barkey, Karen. *Empire of Difference: The Ottomans in Comparative Perspective*. Cambridge: Cambridge University Press, 2008.

Bashford, Alison. "Terraqueous Histories." *Historical Journal* 60, no. 2 (2017): 253–72.

Bathurst, R. D. "The Yaʿrubi Dynasty of Oman." PhD diss., Oxford University, 1967.

Bayly, C. A. *The Birth of the Modern World: Global Connections and Comparisons, 1780–1914*. Malden, MA: Blackwell, 2004.

———. *Rulers, Townsmen, and Bazaars: North Indian Society in the Age of British Expansion, 1770–1870*. New York: Cambridge University Press, 1988.

Beckert, Sven. *Empire of Cotton: A Global History*. New York: Knopf, 2014.

Beckert, Sven, Angus Burgin, Peter James Hudson, Louis Hyman, Naomi Lamoreaux, Scott Marler, Stephen Mihm, Julia Ott, Philip Scranton, and Elizabeth Tandy Shermer. "Interchange: The History of Capitalism." *Journal of American History* 101, no. 2 (2014): 503–36.

Beckingham, C. F. "The Reign of Aḥmad Ibn Saʿīd, Imam of Oman." *Journal of the Royal Asiatic Society of Great Britain and Ireland* 3 (n.d.): 257–60.

Belgrave, Sir Charles. *The Pirate Coast*. London: G. Bell & Sons, 1966.

Bennett, Norman Robert. "Americans in Zanzibar, 1825–1845." *Essex Institute Historical Collections* 95 (1959): 239–62.

Bennett, Norman Robert, and George E. Brooks, eds. *New England Merchants in Africa: A History through Documents, 1802–1865*. Brookline, MA: Boston University Press, 1965.

Bentley, Jerry H., Sanjay Subrahmanyam, and Merry E. Wiesner-Hanks, eds. *The Construction of a Global World, 1400–1800 CE: Patterns of Change*. Vol. 6.2. 7 vols. The Cambridge World History. Cambridge: Cambridge University Press, 2017.

Benton, Lauren. "Legal Spaces of Empire: Piracy and the Origins of Ocean Regionalism." *Comparative Studies in Society and History* 47, no. 4 (2005): 700–724.

Benton, Lauren, and Lisa Ford. *Rage for Order: The British Empire and the Origins of International Law*. Cambridge, MA: Harvard University Press, 2016.

Benton, Lauren, and Nathan Perl-Rosenthal, eds. *A World at Sea: Maritime Practices and Global History*. The Early Modern Americas. Philadelphia: University of Pennsylvania Press, 2020.

Berg, F. J. "The Swahili Community of Mombasa, 1500–1900." *Journal of African History* 9, no. 1 (1968): 35–56.

Berg, Fred James. "Mombasa Under the Busaidi Sultanate: The City and Its Hinterlands in the Nineteenth Century." PhD diss., University of Wisconsin-Madison, 1971.

Bertz, Ned. "Indian Ocean World Travellers: Moving Models in Multi-Sited Research." In *Journeys and Dwellings: Indian Ocean Themes in South Asia*, edited by Helene Basu, 21–60. Hyderabad: Orient Longman, 2008.

Betty, Gerald. "Reviewed Work: The Comanche Empire by Pekka Hämäläinen." *American Historical Review* 113, no. 5 (2008): 1470–72.

Bhacker, M. Reda. *Trade and Empire in Muscat and Zanzibar: The Roots of British Domination*. London: Routledge, 1992.
Bishara, Fahad Ahmad. "The Many Voyages of Fateh Al-Khayr: Unfurling the Gulf in the Age of Oceanic History." *International Journal of Middle East Studies* 52, no. 3 (2020): 397–412.
———. "Paper Routes: Inscribing Islamic Law across the Nineteenth-Century Western Indian Ocean." *Law and History Review* 32, no. 4 (2014): 797–820.
———. *A Sea of Debt: Law and Economic Life in the Western Indian Ocean, 1780–1950*. Asian Connections. New York: Cambridge University Press, 2017.
Bishara, Fahad, and Hollian Wint. "Into the Bazaar: Indian Ocean Vernaculars in the Age of Global Capitalism." *Journal of Global History* 16, no. 1 (2021): 44–64.
Bissell, William Cunningham. *Urban Design, Chaos, and Colonial Power in Zanzibar*. Bloomington: Indiana University Press, 2011.
Blumi, Isa. *Foundations of Modernity: Human Agency and the Imperial State*. Routledge Studies in Modern History. New York: Routledge, 2012.
Bose, Sugata. *A Hundred Horizons: The Indian Ocean in the Age of Global Empire*. Cambridge, MA: Harvard University Press, 2009.
Braudel, Fernand. *The Mediterranean and the Mediterranean World in the Age of Philip II*. Translated by Siân Reynolds. Vol. 1. 2 vols. Berkeley: University of California Press, 1995.
———. *The Structures of Everyday Life: The Limits of the Possible*. Translated by Siân Renolds. Vol. 1. 3 vols. Civilization and Capitalism, 15th–18th Century. New York: Harper and Row, 1981.
———. *The Wheels of Commerce*. Translated by Siân Reynolds. Vol. 2. 3 vols. Civilization & Capitalism, 15th–18th Century. New York: Harper and Row, 1982.
Brenner, Robert. *Merchants and Revolution: Commercial Change, Political Conflict, and London's Overseas Traders, 1550–1653*. Princeton, NJ: Princeton University Press, 2003.
Bresnahan, David P. *Inland from Mombasa: East Africa and the Making of the Indian Ocean World*. Oakland: University of California Press, 2024.
Brewer, John. *The Sinews of Power: War, Money, and the English State, 1688–1783*. Cambridge, MA: Harvard University Press, 1990.
Broderick, Kylie. "Middle East and Moral Dilemmas: The Problem of Studying Capitalism." *Epoch Magazine*, December 2020. https://www.epoch-magazine.com/brodericksmoraldilemma.
Brown, Jonathan A.C. *Slavery & Islam*. London: Oneworld Publications, 2019.
Burbank, Jane, and Frederick Cooper. *Empires in World History: Power and the Politics of Difference*. Princeton, NJ: Princeton University Press, 2010.
Burns, James Robert. "'Slaves' and 'Slave Owners' or 'Enslaved People' and 'Enslavers'?" *Transactions of the Royal Historical Society* 2 (2024): 371–88.
Burton, Antoinette. *The Trouble with Empire: Challenges to Modern British Imperialism*. New York: Oxford University Press, 2015.
Burton, Antoinette, and Tony Ballantyne. *World Histories from Below: Disruption and Dissent, 1750 to the Present*. London: Bloomsbury Academic, 2016.

Calhoun, Craig, Frederick Cooper, and Kevin W. Moore, eds. *Lessons of Empire: Imperial Histories and American Empire*. New York: New Press, 2006.

Campbell, Gwyn. *Africa and the Indian Ocean World from Early Times to Circa 1900*. New Approaches to African History. Cambridge: Cambridge University Press, 2019.

———. "Servitude and the Changing Face of the Demand for Labor in the Indian Ocean World, c. 1800–1900." In *Indian Ocean Slavery in the Age of Abolition*, edited by Robert Harms, Bernard K. Freamon, and David W. Blight, 23–44. New Haven, CT: Yale University Press, 2013.

———, ed. *The Structure of Slavery in Indian Ocean Africa and Asia*. London: Frank Cass, 2004.

Campbell, Gwyn, Suzanne Miers, and Joseph C. Miller, eds. *Women and Slavery: Africa, the Indian Ocean World, and the Medieval North Atlantic*. Vol. 1. 2 vols. Athens: Ohio University Press, 2007.

Carapico, Sheila. "Arabia Incognita: An Invitation to Arabian Peninsula Studies." In *Counter-Narratives: History, Contemporary Society, and Politics in Saudi Arabia and Yemen*, edited by Madawi Al-Rasheed and Robert Vitalis, 11–33. New York: Palgrave Macmillan, 2004.

Chakrabarty, Dipesh. *Provincializing Europe: Postcolonial Thought and Historical Difference*. Princeton, NJ: Princeton University Press, 2000.

Chaudhuri, K.N. *Trade and Civilisation in the Indian Ocean: An Economic History from the Rise of Islam to 1750*. New York: Cambridge University Press, 1985.

Cheta, Omar Youssef. "The Economy by Other Means: The Historiography of Capitalism in the Modern Middle East." *History Compass* 16 (2018): 1–14.

Choudhury, Rishad. *Hajj across Empires: Pilgrimage and Political Culture after the Mughals, 1739–1857*. Asian Connections. Cambridge: Cambridge University Press, 2023.

Clarence-Smith, W. G., and Steven Topik, eds. *The Global Coffee Economy in Africa, Asia, and Latin America, 1500–1989*. Cambridge: Cambridge University Press, 2003.

Clarence-Smith, William Gervase. *The Economics of the Indian Ocean Slave Trade in the Nineteenth Century*. London: Routledge, 2015.

Clegg, John J. "Capitalism and Slavery." *Critical Historical Studies* 2, no. 2 (2015): 281–304.

Cleveland, William L., and Martin Bunton. *A History of the Modern Middle East*. 6th ed. Boulder, CO: Westview Press, 2016.

Coakley, John, Nathan C. Kwan, and David Wilson, eds. *The Problem of Piracy in the Early Modern World: Maritime Predation, Empire, and the Construction of Authority at Sea*. Maritime Humanities, 1400–1800. Amsterdam: Amsterdam University Press, 2024.

Cohen, Paul. *China Unbound: Evolving Perspectives on the Chinese Past*. London: Routledge, 2003.

Commins, David. *The Gulf States: A Modern History*. London: I. B. Tauris, 2012.

Cooper, Frederick. *Plantation Slavery on the East Coast of Africa*. New Haven, CT: Yale University Press, 1977.

———. "What Is the Concept of Globalization Good For? An African Historian's Perspective." *African Affairs* 100, no. 399 (2001): 189–213.

Coupland, Reginald. *East Africa and Its Invaders: From the Earliest Times to the Death of Seyyid Said in 1856*. Oxford: Clarendon Press, 1938.

———. *The Exploitation of East Africa, 1856–1890*. London: Faber and Faber, 1939.

Croucher, Sarah K. *Capitalism and Cloves: An Archaeology of Plantation Life on Nineteenth Century Zanzibar*. New York: Springer, 2015.

Cuno, Kenneth. *The Pasha's Peasants: Land, Society and Economy in Lower Egypt, 1740–1858*. Cambridge and New York: Cambridge University Press, 1992.

Curtin, Philip D. *Cross-Cultural Trade in World History*. Studies in Comparative World History. Cambridge: Cambridge University Press, 1984.

———. *The Rise and Fall of the Plantation Complex: Essays in Atlantic History*. 2nd ed. New York: Cambridge University Press, 1998.

Darwin, John. *After Tamerlane: The Rise and Fall of Global Empires, 1400–2000*. New York: Bloomsbury Press, 2008.

Davies, Charles E. *The Blood-Red Arab Flag: An Investigation into Qasimi Piracy, 1797–1820*. Exeter: University of Exeter Press, 1997.

Dobbin, Christine. *Asian Entrepreneurial Minorities: Conjoint Communities in the Making of the World-Economy, 1570–1940*. Nordic Institute of Asian Studies 71. Richmond: Curzon, 1996.

Doumani, Beshara. *Rediscovering Palestine: Merchants and Peasants in Jabal Nablus, 1700–1900*. Berkeley: University of California Press, 1995.

Dubuisson, Patricia R. "Qāsimī Piracy and the General Treaty of Peace (1820)." Master's thesis, McGill University, 1975.

Edwards, Andrew David, Peter Hill, and Juan Neves Sarriegui. "Capitalism in Global History." *Past & Present* 249, no. 1 (2020): e1–32.

Elliott, J. H. "Atlantic History: A Circumnavigation." In *The British Atlantic World, 1500–1800*, 2nd ed., edited by David Armitage and Michael J. Braddick, 253–70. New York: Palgrave Macmillan, 2009.

———. "A Europe of Composite Monarchies." *Past & Present* 137 (1992): 48–71.

Ennāmī, ʿAmr Khalīfah. *Studies in Ibāḍism: Al-Ibāḍīyah*. Muscat: Ministry of Endowments and Religious Affairs, 1971.

"The Evolution of Polyphony." *Musical Times and Singing Class Circular* 36, no. 630 (1895): 509–12.

Ewald, Janet J. "Africa: East Africa." In *A Historical Guide to World Slavery*, edited by Seymour Drescher and Stanley L. Engerman, 41–46. New York: Oxford University Press, 1998.

———. "Crossers of the Sea: Slaves, Freedmen, and Other Migrants in the Northwestern Indian Ocean, c. 1750–1914." *American Historical Review* 105, no. 1 (2000): 69–91.

Fattah, Hala. *The Politics of Regional Trade in Iraq, Arabia, and the Gulf: 1745–1900*. SUNY Series in the Social and Economic History of the Middle East. Albany: State University of New York Press, 1997.

Feierman, Steven. "Africa in History: The End of Universal Narratives." In *After Colonialism: Imperial Histories and Postcolonial Displacements*, edited by Gyan Prakash, 40–65. Princeton, NJ: Princeton University Press, 1995.

Felber Seligman, Andrea. "Wealth Not by Any Other Name: Inland African Material Aesthetics in Expanding Commercial Times, ca. 16th–20th Centuries." *International Journal of African Historical Studies* 48, no. 3 (2015): 449–69.

Firro, Tarik K. "The Political Context of Early Wahhabi Discourse of Takfir." *Middle Eastern Studies* 49, no. 5 (2013): 770–89.

Fitz-Enz, David. *Old Ironsides: Eagle of the Sea—The Story of the USS Constitution*. Lanham, MD: Taylor Trade Publishing, 2004.

Flores, Jorge. *Empire of Contingency: How Portugal Entered the Indo-Persian World*. Philadelphia: University of Pennsylvania Press, 2024.

Frank, Andre Gunder. "A Plea for World System History." *Journal of World History* 2, no. 1 (1991): 1–28.

———. *ReORIENT: Global Economy in the Asian Age*. Berkeley: University of California Press, 1998.

Frankl, P. J. L. "Hamerton, Atkins (Bap. 1804, d. 1857), Army Officer and First British Consul in Zanzibar." In *Oxford Dictionary of National Biography*, September 23, 2004, https://www-oxforddnb-com.proxy.library.nd.edu/view/10.1093/ref:odnb/9780198614128.001.0001/odnb-9780198614128-e-59618.

Fraser, Nancy. "Behind Marx's Hidden Abode: For an Expanded Conception of Capitalism." *New Left Review* 86 (2014): 55–72.

Freeman-Grenville, G. S. P., ed. *The East African Coast: Select Documents from the First to the Earlier Nineteenth Centuries*. Oxford: Oxford University Press, 1962.

Freitag, Ulrike. *A History of Jeddah: The Gate to Mecca in the Nineteenth and Twentieth Centuries*. Cambridge: Cambridge University Press, 2020.

Fromherz, Allen James. *The Center of the World: A Global History of the Persian Gulf from the Stone Age to the Present*. Oakland: University of California Press, 2024.

———. "Introduction: World History in the Gulf as a Gulf in World History." In *The Gulf in World History: Arabia at the Global Crossroads*. Edinburgh: Edinburgh University Press, 2020.

Games, Alison. *The Web of Empire: English Cosmopolitans in an Age of Expansion: 1560–1660*. London: Oxford University Press, 2008.

Gaube, Heinz, and Abdulrahman Al-Salimi. *The Ibadis in the Region of the Indian Ocean. Section One; East Africa*. Vol. 1. 13 vols. Studies on Ibadism and Oman. Hildesheim, Germany: Georg Olms Verlag, 2013.

Gelvin, James L. *The Modern Middle East: A History*. 5th ed. New York: Oxford University Press, 2020.

Gelvin, James L., and Nile Green, eds. *Global Muslims in the Age of Steam and Print*. Oakland: University of California Press, 2014.

Ghazal, Amal N. "Islam and Arabism in Zanzibar: The Omani Elite, the Arab World and the Making of an Identity, 1880s–1930s." ProQuest Dissertations Publishing, 2005.

Ghosh, Durba. "AHR Forum: Another Set of Imperial Turns?" *American Historical Review* 117, no. 3 (2012): 772–93.
Giddens, Anthony. *The Consequences of Modernity*. Stanford, CA: Stanford University Press, 1990.
Gilbert, Eric. *Dhows and the Colonial Economy of Zanzibar, 1860–1970*. Oxford: James Currey, 2004.
Gilroy, Paul. *The Black Atlantic: Modernity and Double-Consciousness*. Cambridge, MA: Harvard University Press, 1993.
Ginzburg, Carlo. "Clues: Roots of a Scientific Paradigm." *Theory and Society* 7, no. 3 (May 1979): 273–88.
Glassman, Jonathon. *Feasts and Riot: Revelry, Rebellion, and Popular Consciousness on the Swahili Coast, 1856–1888*. Portsmouth, NH: Heinemann, 1995.
Goldstein, Jonathan. "The Andrew Jackson Administration and the Orient, 1829–1837." *International Journal of Maritime History* 12, no. 2 (December 2000): 27–51.
Gooding, Philip. *On the Frontiers of the Indian Ocean World: A History of Lake Tanganyika, c. 1830–1890*. Cambridge Oceanic Histories. Cambridge: Cambridge University Press, 2022.
Goswami, Chhaya. *The Call of the Sea: Kachchhi Traders in Muscat and Zanzibar, c. 1800–1880*. New Delhi: Orient Blackswan, 2011.
Gran, Peter. *Islamic Roots of Capitalism: Egypt 1760–1840*. Syracuse, NY: Syracuse University Press, 1998.
Gray, John. *The British in Mombasa, 1824–1826, Being the History of Captain Owen's Protectorate*. London: Macmillan, 1957.
Gray, John, Roland Oliver, and Gervase Mathew. "Zanzibar and the Coastal Belt, 1840–1884." In *History of East Africa*, 1:212–52. Oxford: Clarendon Press, 1963.
Gray, John Milner. *History of Zanzibar: From the Middle Ages to 1856*. London: Oxford University Press, 1962.
Green, Nile. "Rethinking the 'Middle East' after the Oceanic Turn." *Comparative Studies of South Asia, Africa, and the Middle East* 3 (2014): 556–64.
Gustafsson, Harald. "The Conglomerate State: A Perspective on State Formation in Early Modern Europe." *Scandinavian Journal of History* 23 (1998): 189–214.
Hämäläinen, Pekka. *The Comanche Empire*. The Lamar Series in Western History. New Haven, CT: Yale University Press, 2008.
Hamdun, Said, and Noël King, eds. *Ibn Battuta in Black Africa*. Expanded ed. Princeton, NJ: Markus Wiener Publishers, 2010.
Hanna, Mark G. *Pirate Nests and the Rise of the British Empire, 1570–1740*. Omohundro Institute of Early American History and Culture. Durham: University of North Carolina Press, 2015.
Harms, Robert. *The Diligent: A Voyage through the Worlds of the Slave Trade*. New York: Basic Books, 2002.
———. "Introduction: Indian Ocean Slavery in the Age of Abolition." In *Indian Ocean Slavery in the Age of Abolition*, edited by Robert Harms, Bernard K. Freamon, and David W. Blight, 1–22. New Haven, CT: Yale University Press, 2013.

Harms, Robert, Bernard K. Freamon, and David W. Blight, eds. *Indian Ocean Slavery in the Age of Abolition*. New Haven, CT: Yale University Press, 2013.
Ho, Engseng. *The Graves of Tarim: Genealogy and Mobility across the Indian Ocean*. Berkeley: University of California Press, 2006.
Hobson, John M. *Multicultural Origins of the Global Economy: Beyond the Western-Centric Frontier*. Cambridge: Cambridge University Press, 2021.
Hodgson, Marshall G. S. *Rethinking World History: Essays on Europe, Islam, and World History*. Edited by Edmund Burke III. New York: Cambridge University Press, 2002.
———. *The Venture of Islam: Conscience and History in a World Civilization: The Expansion of Islam in the Middle Periods*. Vol. 2. 3 vols. Chicago: University of Chicago Press, 1974.
———. *The Venture of Islam: Conscience and History in a World Civilization: The Gunpowder Empires and Modern Times*. Vol. 3. 3 vols. Chicago: University of Chicago Press, 1974.
Hoffman, Valerie J. *The Essentials of Ibāḍī Islam*. Syracuse: Syracuse University Press, 2012.
Hofmeyr, Isabel. "Universalizing the Indian Ocean." *PMLA* 125, no. 3 (2010): 725–29.
Hooper, Jane. *Yankees in the Indian Ocean: American Commerce and Whaling, 1786–1860*. Indian Ocean Studies Series. Athens: Ohio University Press, 2022.
Hopper, Matthew S. "Enslaved Africans and the Globalization of Arabian Gulf Pearling." In *Pearls, People, and Power: Pearling and Indian Ocean Worlds*, edited by Pedro Machado, Steve Mullins, and Joseph Christensen, 263–80. Indian Ocean Studies Series. Athens: Ohio University Press, 2019.
———. "The Globalization of Dried Fruit: Transformations in the Eastern Arabian Economy, 1860s–1920s." In *Global Muslims in the Age of Steam and Print*, edited by James L. Gelvin and Nile Green, 158–82. Oakland: University of California Press, 2014.
———. *Slaves of One Master: Globalization and Slavery in Arabia in the Age of Empire*. New Haven, CT: Yale University Press, 2015.
Horton, Mark, and John Middleton. *The Swahili: The Social Landscape of a Mercantile Society*. Malden, MA: Blackwell Publishing, 2000.
Hourani, Albert. *A History of the Arab Peoples*. Cambridge, MA: Belknap Press, 2002.
Howard, M. C. "Fernand Braudel on Capitalism: A Theoretical Analysis." *Historical Reflections/Réflexions Historiques* 12, no. 3 (1985): 469–83.
Ismael, Jacqueline S. *Kuwait: Social Change in Historical Perspective*. Contemporary Issues in the Middle East. Syracuse: Syracuse University Press, 1982.
Jacob, Wilson Chacko. *For God or Empire: Sayyid Fadl and the Indian Ocean World*. Stanford, CA: Stanford University Press, 2019.
Jacoby, Karl. "Indigenous Empires and Native Nations: Beyond History and Ethnohistory in Pekka Hämäläinen's The Comanche Empire." *History and Theory* 52 (2013): 60–66.
Johnson, Walter. *River of Dark Dreams: Slavery and Empire in the Cotton Kingdom*. Cambridge, MA: Belknap Press, 2013.

Jones, Jeremy, and Nicholas Ridout. *A History of Modern Oman*. New York: Cambridge University Press, 2015.

Karp, Matthew. *This Vast Southern Empire: Slaveholders at the Helm of American Foreign Policy*. Cambridge, MA: Harvard University Press, 2018.

Kelly, J. B. *Britain and the Persian Gulf, 1795–1880*. Oxford: Oxford University Press, 1968.

Kempe, Michael. "'Even in the Remotest Corners of the World': Globalized Piracy and International Law, 1500–1900." *Journal of Global History* 5 (2010): 353–72.

Keshavarzian, Arang. *Making Space for the Gulf: Histories of Regionalism and the Middle East*. Worlding the Middle East. Stanford, CA: Stanford University Press, 2024.

Kimball, Eric. "'What Have We to Do with Slavery?' New Englanders and the Slave Economies of the West Indies." In *Slavery's Capitalism: A New History of American Economic Development*, edited by Sven Beckert and Seth Rockman, 181–94. Early American Studies. Philadelphia: University of Pennsylvania Press, 2016.

Laing, Stuart. *Tippu Tip: Ivory, Slavery, and Discovery in the Scramble for Africa*. Surrey, UK: Medina Publishing, 2017.

Landen, Robert Geran. *Oman Since 1856: Disruptive Modernization in a Traditional Arab Society*. Princeton, NJ: Princeton University Press, 1967.

Layton, Simon. "Discourses of Piracy in an Age of Revolutions." *Itinerario* 35, no. 2 (2011): 81–97.

Levy, Jonathan. "Capital as Process and the History of Capitalism." *Business History Review* 91 (2017): 483–510.

———. *Freaks of Fortune: The Emerging World of Capitalism and Risk in America*. Cambridge, MA: Harvard University Press, 2012.

Limbert, Mandana E. "Caste, Ethnicity, and the Politics of Arabness in Southern Arabia." *Comparative Studies of South Asia, Africa, and the Middle East* 34, no. 3 (2014): 590–98.

———. "'If You Catch Me Again at It, Put Me to Death': Slave Trading, Paper Trails, and British Bureaucracy in the Indian Ocean." In *Indian Ocean Slavery in the Age of Abolition*, edited by Roert Harms, Bernard K. Freamon, and David W. Blight, 120–42. New Haven, CT: Yale University Press, 2013.

Linebaugh, Peter, and Marcus Rediker. *The Many-Headed Hydra: Sailors, Slaves, Commoners, and the Hidden History of the Revolutionary Atlantic*. Boston: Beacon Press, 2000.

Lipartito, Kenneth. "Reassembling the Economic: New Departures in Historical Materialism." *American Historical Review* 121, no. 1 (February 1, 2016): 101–39.

Liu, Andrew B. *Tea War: A History of Capitalism in China and India*. Studies of the Weatherhead East Asian Institute, Columbia University. New Haven, CT: Yale University Press, 2020.

Lorimer, J. G. *Gazetteer of the Persian Gulf: 'Oman, and Central Arabia*. Vol. 1. 2 vols. Calcutta: Superintendent Government Printing, India, 1915.

Lovejoy, Paul E. *Transformations in Slavery: A History of Slavery in Africa*. 2nd ed. Cambridge: Cambridge University Press, 2000.

Low, Charles Rathbone. *History of the Indian Navy, 1613–1863*. 2 vols. London: Richard Bentley, 1877.

Low, Michael Christopher. "Introduction: The Indian Ocean and Other Middle Easts." *Comparative Studies of South Asia, Africa, and the Middle East* 34, no. 3 (2014): 549–55.

Lyne, Robert Nunez. *Zanzibar in Contemporary Times: A Short History of the Southern East in the Nineteenth Century*. London: Hurst and Blackett, 1905.

Machado, Pedro. *Ocean of Trade: South Asian Merchants, Africa, and the Indian Ocean, c. 1750–1850*. Cambridge: Cambridge University Press, 2014.

Mahajan, Nidhi. "Of Those on Shore: The Dhow Trade and Mobility in the Indian Ocean." In *Cosmopolitan Cultures and Oceanic Thought*, edited by Dilip M. Menon Menon and Nishat Zaidi, 137–51. London: Routledge, 2023.

Maier, Charles S. *Leviathan 2.0: Inventing Modern Statehood*. Cambridge, MA: Belknap Press, 2012.

Margariti, Roxani Eleni. *Aden and the Indian Ocean Trade: 150 Years in the Life of a Medieval Arabian Port*. Islamic Civilizations and Muslim Networks. Chapel Hill: University of North Carolina Press, 2007.

Markovits, Claude. *The Global World of Indian Merchants: Traders of Sind from Bukhara to Panama, 1750–1947*. Cambridge Studies in Indian History and Society. Cambridge: Cambridge University Press, 2000.

Martin, B. G. "Notes on Some Members of the Learned Classes of Zanzibar and East Africa in the Nineteenth Century." *African Historical Studies* 4, no. 3 (1971): 525–45.

Mathew, Johan. *Margins of the Market: Trafficking and Capitalism Across the Arabian Sea*. California World History Library. Oakland: University of California Press, 2016.

Mathews, Nathaniel. *Zanzibar Was a Country: Exile and Citizenship between East Africa and the Gulf*. California World History Library. Oakland: University of California Press, 2024.

Matthee, Rudi. "Was Safavid Iran an Empire?" *Journal of the Economic and Social History of the Orient* 53 (2010): 233–65.

McCabe, Ina Baghdiantz, Gelina Harlaftis, and Ionna Pepelase Minoglou, eds. *Diaspora Entrepreneurial Networks: Four Centuries of History*. Oxford: Berg Publishers, 2005.

McDow, Thomas F. *Buying Time: Debt and Mobility in the Western Indian Ocean*. New African Histories. Athens: Ohio University Press, 2018.

McMahon, Elisabeth. *Slavery and Emancipation in Islamic East Africa: From Honor to Respectability*. New York: Cambridge University Press, 2013.

McPherson, Kenneth. *The Indian Ocean: A History of People and the Sea*. Oxford: Oxford University Press, 1993.

Menard, Russell R. *The Economy of British America, 1607–1789*. Chapel Hill: University of North Carolina Press, 1985.

Menon, Dilip M., and Nishat Zaidi, eds. *Cosmopolitan Cultures and Oceanic Thought*. London: Routledge, 2023.

Metcalf, Thomas R. *Imperial Connections: India in the Indian Ocean Arena, 1860–1920*. California World History Library. Berkeley: University of California Press, 2008.

Miller, Joseph C. *Way of Death: Merchant Capitalism and the Angolan Slave Trade, 1740–1830*. Madison: University of Wisconsin Press, 1988.

———. "Women as Slaves and Owners of Slaves: Experiences from Africa, the Indian Ocean World, and the Early Atlantic." In *Women and Slavery: Africa, the Indian Ocean World, and the Medieval North Atlantic*, edited by Gwyn Campbell, Suzanne Miers, and Joseph C. Miller, 1:1–42. Athens: Ohio University Press, 2007.

Mitchell, Timothy. *Questions of Modernity*. Contradictions of Modernity. Minneapolis: University of Minnesota Press, 2000.

Morrison, Dane A. *True Yankees: The South Seas & the Discovery of American Identity*. The Johns Hopkins University Studies in Historical and Political Science. Baltimore, MD: The Johns Hopkins University Press, 2014.

Morrison, Joshua S. C. "Amity, Commerce, and Compromise: Americans, Indians, and the Evolution of Trade on Zanzibar and across the Western Indian Ocean, 1825–1861." *Journal of World History* 35, no. 2 (2024): 199–227.

Morrison, Joshua Sidney Chamberlain. "Cut from the Same Cloth: Salem, Zanzibar, and the Consolidation of the Indo-Atlantic World, 1790–1875." PhD diss., University of Virginia, 2021.

Mtoro bin Mwinyi Bakari. *The Customs of the Swahili People*. Translated by J. W. T. Allen. Berkeley: University of California Press, 1981.

Muʿammar, ʿAlī Yaḥyā. *Ibāḍism in History: The Emergence of the Ibāḍī School*. Edited by Kahlān Al-Kharūṣī. Vol. 1. Muscat: Ministry of Awqaf and Religious Affairs, 2007.

Mukherjee, Rila. "The Indian Ocean in the 'New Thalassology': Review Essay Based on Sugata Bose, *A Hundred Horizons: The Indian Ocean in the Age of Global Empire*." *Archipel* 76 (2008): 291–306.

Myuko, Okawa. "The Empire of Oman in the Formation of Oman's National History: An Analysis of School Social Studies Textbooks and Teachers' Guidelines." *Annual Report of the Middle East Society of Japan* 31, no. 1 (2015): 95–120.

Nadri, Ghulam A. *Eighteenth-Century Gujarat: The Dynamics of Its Political Economy, 1750–1800*. Leiden: Brill, 2009.

Nechtman, Tillman W. "A Jewel in the Crown? Indian Wealth in Domestic Britain in the Late Eighteenth Century." *Eighteenth-Century Studies* 41, no. 1 (Fall 2007): 71–86.

Nelson, Scott Reynolds. "Who Put Their Capitalism in My Slavery?" *Journal of the Civil War Era* 5, no. 2 (June 2015): 289–310.

Newitt, Malyn. "The Portuguese in East Africa and the Omani Reconquest of East Africa." In *Oman and Overseas*, edited by Michaela Hoffmann-Ruf and Abdulrahman Al-Sālimī, 125–40. Studies on Ibadism and Oman 2. Hildesheim, Germany: Georg Olms Verlag, 2013.

Nicholls, C. S. *The Swahili Coast: Politics, Diplomacy and Trade on the East African Littoral, 1798–1856.* St. Antony's College, Oxford, Publications, No. 2. London: George Allen & Unwin, 1971.

North, Douglass C. *Institutions, Institutional Change and Economic Performance.* New York: Cambridge University Press, 1990.

———. *Structure and Change in Economic History.* New York: W. W. Norton, 1982.

Osterhammel, Jürgen. *The Transformation of the World: A Global History of the Nineteenth Century.* Translated by Patrick Camiller. Princeton, NJ: Princeton University Press, 2014.

Pallares-Burke, Maria Lucia G., ed. *The New History: Confessions and Conversations.* Cambridge, UK: Polity Press, 2002.

Parkin, David, and Ruth Barnes, eds. *Ships and the Development of Maritime Technology in the Indian Ocean.* London: Routledge, 2002.

Patterson, Orlando. *Slavery and Social Death.* Cambridge, MA: Harvard University Press, 1982.

Pearce, F. B. *Zanzibar: The Island Metropolis of Eastern Africa.* New York: E. P. Dutton, 1920.

Pearson, Michael. *The Indian Ocean.* Seas in History. London: Routledge, 2003.

Pearson, Michael N. *Port Cities and Intruders: The Swahili Coast, India, and Portugal in the Early Modern Era.* The Johns Hopkins Symposia in Comparative History. Baltimore, MD: The Johns Hopkins University Press, 1998.

Peirce, Leslie. *Morality Tales: Law and Gender in the Ottoman Court of Aintab.* Berkeley: University of California Press, 2003.

Post, Charles. "Reviewed Work: Empire of Cotton: A Global History by Sven Beckert." *Journal of the Civil War Era* 5, no. 4 (2015): 581–83.

Pouwels, Randall L. *Horn and Crescent: Cultural Change and Traditional Islam on the East African Coast, 800–1900.* Cambridge: Cambridge University Press, 1987.

Prange, Sebastian R. *Monsoon Islam: Trade and Faith on the Medieval Malabar Coast.* Cambridge Oceanic Histories. Cambridge: Cambridge University Press, 2018.

Prestholdt, Jeremy. "As Artistry Permits and Custom May Ordain: The Social Fabric of Material Consumption in the Swahili World, Circa 1450–1600." In *Working Paper*, 3:1–49. Evanston, IL: Northwestern University Program in African Studies, 1998.

———. *Domesticating the World: African Consumerism and the Genealogies of Globalization.* California World History Library. Berkeley: University of California Press, 2008.

———. "On the Global Repercussions of East African Consumerism." *American Historical Review* 109, no. 3 (2004): 755–81.

———. "Portuguese Conceptual Categories and the 'Other' Encounter on the Swahili Coast." *Journal of Asian and African Studies* 36, no. 4 (2001): 383–406.

———. "*Sultana*: The Biography of an Indian Ocean Vessel." In *Indian Ocean Imaginings: People, Time, and Space*, edited by Joshua Esler and Mark Fielding, 59–76. Lanham, MD: Lexington Books, 2023.

———. "The *Sultana* in New York: A Zanzibari Vessel between Two Worlds." In *World on the Horizon: Swahili Arts Across the Indian Ocean*, edited by Prita Meier and Allyson Purpura, 114–29. Champaign, IL: Krannert Art Museum and Kinkhead Pavilion, University of Illinois at Urbana-Champaign, 2018.

Quataert, Donald. *Ottoman Manufacturing in the Age of the Industrial Revolution.* Cambridge Middle East Library 30. Cambridge: Cambridge University Press, 2002.

Rabi, Uzi. *The Emergence of States in a Tribal Society: Oman under Sa'id Bin Taymur, 1932–1970*. Eastbourne: Sussex Academic Press, 2011.

Rankine, Claudia. *Just Us: An American Conversation*. Minneapolis, MN: Graywolf Press, 2020.

Rashīd, Zāmil Muḥammad al-. *Su'ūdī Relations with Eastern Arabia and 'Umān, 1800–1871*. London: Luzac, 1981.

Ray, Rajat Kanta. "Asian Capital in the Age of European Domination: The Rise of the Bazaar, 1800–1914." *Modern Asian Studies* 29, no. 3 (1995): 449–554.

Rediker, Marcus. *Villains of All Nations: Atlantic Pirates in the Golden Age*. Boston: Beacon Press, 2004.

Reese, Scott. *Imperial Muslims: Islam, Community and Authority in the Indian Ocean, 1839–1937*. Edinburgh: Edinburgh University Press, 2017.

Reid, Joshua L. *The Sea Is My Country: The Maritime World of the Makahs*. New Haven, CT: Yale University Press, 2015.

Rhodes, Daniel, Colin Breen, and Wes Forsythe. "Zanzibar: A Nineteenth-Century Landscape of the Omani Elite." *International Journal of Historical Archaeology* 19 (2015): 334–55.

Risso, Patricia. "Cross-Cultural Perceptions of Piracy: Maritime Violence in the Western Indian Ocean and Persian Gulf Region during a Long Eighteenth Century." *Journal of World History* 12, no. 2 (2001): 293–319.

———. *Oman and Muscat: An Early Modern History*. New York: Croon Helm, 1986.

Roberts, Nicholas P. "Oceanic Wahhabism." *Journal of World History* 36, no. 1 (2025): 21–49.

———. "The Sultan of Muscat in Vermont: Reimagining the Middle East in World History." *Middle East Critique, Special Issue, The Gulf and the World,* ed. Isa Blumi and Jaafar Alloul, (2025): 1–16.

———. "A Tolerated Terror: Rahmah bin Jabir and the Age of Revolutions in the Gulf, 1760-1830." *Itinerario: Journal of Global and Imperial Interactions* (First-Look 2025): 1–15.

Roberts, Richard. "West Africa and the Pondicherry Textile Industry." In *Cloth and Commerce: Textiles in Colonial India*, edited by Tirthankar Roy, 142–74. Thousand Oaks, CA: Sage Publications, 1996.

Robertson, Claire C., and Martin A. Klein, eds. *Women and Slavery in Africa*. Madison: University of Wisconsin Press, 1983.

Rockel, Stephen J. *Carriers of Culture: Labor on the Road in Nineteenth-Century East Africa*. Portsmouth, NH: Heinemann, 2006.

———. "Enterprising Partners: Caravan Women in Nineteenth Century Tanzania." *Canadian Journal of African Studies* 34, no. 3 (2000): 748–78. https://doi.org/10.1080/00083968.2000.10751213.
———. "Slavery and Freedom in Nineteenth Century East Africa: The Case of Waungwana Caravan Porters." *African Studies* 68, no. 1 (2009): 87–109.
———. "Wage Labor and the Culture of Porterage in Nineteenth Century Tanzania: The Central Caravan Routes." *Comparative Studies of South Asia, Africa, and the Middle East* 15, no. 2 (1995): 14–24.
Rockman, Seth. "What Makes the History of Capitalism Newsworthy?" *Journal of the Early Republic* 34, no. 3 (2014): 439–66.
Rodinson, Maxime, and Roger Owen. *Islam and Capitalism*. Translated by Brian Pearce. London: Saqi Books, 2007.
Rogan, Eugene. *The Arabs: A History*. New York: Basic Books, 2017.
Romero, Patricia W. "Seyyid Said Bin Sultan BuSaid of Oman and Zanzibar: Women in the Life of This Arab Patriarch." *British Journal of Middle Eastern Studies* 39, no. 3 (2012): 373–92.
Rothenberg, Winifred Barr. "The Invention of American Capitalism: The Economy of New England in the Federal Period." In *Engines of Enterprise: An Economic History of New England*, 69–108. Cambridge, MA: Harvard University Press, 2000.
Sachedina, Amal. *Cultivating the Past, Living the Modern: The Politics of Time in the Sultanate of Oman*. Ithaca, NY: Cornell University Press, 2021.
Said, Edward W., and Jonathan Rée. "Peoples' Rights and Literature." In "Human Rights and Peoples' Rights in Literature and the Humanities." Special issue, *Alif: Journal of Comparative Poetics* 13 (1993): 182–95.
Said-Ruete, Rudolph. *Said Bin Sultan (1791–1856) Ruler of Zanzibar: His Place in the History of Arabia and East Africa*. London: Alexander-Ouseley, 1929.
Schumpeter, Joseph A. *Capitalism, Socialism, and Democracy*. New York: Harper Perennial Modern Thought, 2008.
Scott, James C. *Seeing Like A State: How Certain Schemes to Improve the Human Condition Have Failed*. New Haven, CT: Yale University Press, 1998.
Seligman, Andrea Felber. "Wealth Not by Any Other Name: Inland African Material Aesthetics in Expanding Commercial Times, ca. 16th–20th Centuries." *International Journal of African Historical Studies* 48, no. 3 (2015): 449–69.
Şevket, Pamuk. "Institutional Change and Economic Development in the Middle East, 700–1800." In *The Rise of Capitalism: From Ancient Origins to 1848*, edited by Larry Neal and Jeffrey G. Williamson, 1:193–224. The Cambridge History of Capitalism. Cambridge: Cambridge University Press, 2014.
Sewell, William H., Jr. *Logics of History: Social Theory and Social Transformations*. Chicago: University of Chicago Press, 2005.
Sharma, Shubham. "Capitalism and its New Historians: A Review Essay." *Studies in People's History* 7, no. 2 (2020): 221–27.
Sharman, J. C. *Empires of the Weak: The Real Story of European Expansion and the Creation of the New World Order*. Princeton, NJ: Princeton University Press, 2019.

Sheriff, Abdul. *Dhow Cultures of the Indian Ocean: Cosmopolitanism, Commerce, Islam*. New York: Columbia University Press, 2014.
———. "History of Zanzibar to 1890." In *Oxford Research Encyclopedia of African History*. Oxford: Oxford University Press, 2020.
———. *Slaves, Spices, and Ivory in Zanzibar: Integration of an East African Commercial Empire into the World Economy, 1770–1873*. Athens: Ohio University Press, 1987.
———. "Suria: Concubine or Secondary Slave Wife? The Case of Zanzibar in the Nineteenth Century." In *Sex, Power and Slavery*, edited by Gwyn Campbell and Elizabeth Elbourne, 99–120. Athens: Ohio University Press, 2014.
———. "The Swahili Coast: Africa's Window on the Indian Ocean." In *Oman and Overseas*, edited by Michaela Hoffmann-Ruf and Abdulrahman Al-Sālimī, 79–91. Studies on Ibadism and Oman 2. Hildesheim, Germany: Georg Olms Verlag, 2013.
Sheriff, Abdul, and Engseng Ho, eds. *The Indian Ocean: Oceanic Connections and the Creation of New Societies*. London: Hurst, 2014.
Sivasundaram, Sujit. *Waves across the South: A New History of Revolution and Empire*. Chicago: University of Chicago Press, 2020.
Stone, Lawrence. "Prosopography." *Daedalus* 100, no. 1 (1971): 46–79.
Subrahmanyam, Sanjay. *Improvising Empire: Portuguese Trade and Settlement in the Bay of Bengal, 1500–1700*. Delhi: Oxford University Press, 1990.
———. "Of Imarat and Tijarat: Asian Merchants and State Power in the Western Indian Ocean, 1400–1750." *Comparative Studies in Society and History* 37, no. 4 (October 1995): 750–80.
———. *The Political Economy of Commerce: Southern India, 1500–1650*. Cambridge South Asian Studies. Cambridge: Cambridge University Press, 1990.Subramanian, Lakshmi. *Indigenous Capital and European Expansion: Bombay, Surat, and the West Coast*. Oxford: Oxford University Press, 1996.
———. *The Sovereign and the Pirate: Ordering Maritime Subjects in India's Western Littoral*. New Delhi: Oxford University Press, 2016.
Tagliacozzo, Eric. *In Asian Waters: Oceanic Worlds from Yemen to Yokohama*. Princeton, NJ: Princeton University Press, 2022.
———. *The Longest Journey: Southeast Asians and the Pilgrimage to Mecca*. Oxford: Oxford University Press, 2013.
Temin, Peter, ed. *Engines of Enterprise: An Economic History of New England*. Cambridge, MA: Harvard University Press, 2000.
———. Introduction to *Engines of Enterprise: An Economic History of New England*, edited by Peter Temin, 1–9. Cambridge, MA: Harvard University Press, 2000.
Toledano, Ehud. *Slavery and Abolition in the Ottoman Middle East*. Seattle: University of Washington Press, 1998.
Toledano, Ehud. "The Concept of Slavery in Ottoman and Other Muslim Societies: Dichotomy or Continuum." In *Slave Elites in the Middle East and Africa*, edited by Miura Toru and John Edward Phillips, 159–75. London: Keagan Paul International, 2000.

Toledano, Ehud R. *As If Silent and Absent: Bonds of Enslavement in the Islamic Middle East.* New Haven, CT: Yale University Press, 2007.
Trouillot, Michel-Rolph. "The Perspective of the World: Globalization Then and Now." In *Beyond Dichotomies: Histories, Identities, Cultures, and the Challenge of Globalization*, edited by Elisabeth Mudimbe-Boyi, 3–20. Explorations in Postcolonial Studies. Albany: State University of New York Press, 2002.
Um, Nancy. *The Merchant Houses of Mocha: Trade and Architecture in an Indian Ocean Port.* Seattle: University of Washington Press, 2009.
Vink, Markus P. M. "Indian Ocean Studies and the 'New Thalassology.'" *Journal of Global History* 2, no. 1 (2007): 41–62.
Vries, Jan de. "Playing with Scales: The Global and the Micro, the Macro and the Nano." *Past & Present* 242, no. 14 (November 2019): 23–36.
Wallerstein, Immanuel. "Braudel on Capitalism, or Everything Upside Down." *Journal of Modern History* 63, no. 2 (1991): 354–61.
———. *The Modern World System.* 4 vols. Berkeley: University of California Press, 2011.
Warren, James F. *The Sulu Zone: The Dynamics of External Trade, Slavery and Ethnicity in the Transformation of a Southeast Asian Maritime State, 1768–1898.* 2nd ed. Singapore: National University of Singapore press, 2007.
White, Richard. *The Middle Ground: Indians, Empires, and Republics in the Great Lakes Region, 1650–1815.* 20th anniversary ed. Studies in North American History. Cambridge: Cambridge University Press, 2011.
———. *The Organic Machine: The Remaking of the Columbia River.* New York: Hill and Wang, 1995.
Wilkinson, John C. *The Arabs and the Scramble for Africa.* Comparative Islamic Studies. Sheffield: Equinox, 2014.
———. *The Imamate Tradition of Oman.* New York: Cambridge University Press, 1987.
———. "Oman and East Africa: New Light on Early Kilwan History from the Omani Sources." *International Journal of African Historical Studies* 14, no. 2 (1981): 272–305.
———. "The Origins of the Omani State." In *The Arabian Peninsula: Society and Politics*, 67–88. London: Allen and Unwin, 1972.
———. *Water and Tribal Settlement in South-East Arabia: A Study of the Aflaj of Oman.* Oxford: Clarendon Press, 1977.
Willis, John M. "Azad's Mecca: On the Limits of Indian Ocean Cosmopolitanism." *Comparative Studies of South Asia, Africa, and the Middle East* 34, no. 3 (2014): 574–81.
Wink, André. *Al-Hind: The Making of the Indo-Islamic World.* 3 vols. Leiden: Brill Academic, 1990.
———. *The Making of the Indo-Islamic World: C. 700–1800 CE.* Cambridge: Cambridge University Press, 2020.
Wint, Hollian. "Credible Relations: Indian Finance and East African Society in the Indian Ocean, c. 1840–1930." PhD diss., New York University, 2016.

———. "Empire and Capitalism in the Western Indian Ocean." *Arab Studies Journal* 26, no. 2 (2018): 181–93.
———. "'From Desh to Desh': The Family Firm as Trans-Local Household in the Nineteenth-Century Western Indian Ocean." *Journal of World History* 34, no. 2 (2023): 187–216.
———. "Keeping It in the Family? Her- and His-Stories among Gujarati Business Communities in the Nineteenth Century Indian Ocean." In *Perspectives of Female Researchers: Interdisciplinary Approaches to the Study of Gujarati Identities*, edited by Sharmina Mawani and Anjoom A. Mukadam, 173–88. Berlin: Logos Verlag, 2016.
Wolf, Eric R. *Europe and the People Without History*. Berkeley: University of California Press, 2010.
Wolf, Eric R., and Sidney W. Mintz. "Haciendas and Plantations in Middle America and the Antilles." *Social and Economic Studies* 6, no. 3 (1957): 380–412.
Wood, Ellen Meiksins. *The Origin of Capitalism: A Longer View*. London: Verso, 2002.
Wright, Marcia. *Strategies of Slaves and Women in East Central Africa*. Bloomington: University of Indiana Press, 1989.

INDEX

Note: Persons' names are alphabetized under first name.

Adey (interpreter), 178
Ahmad bin Na'aman, 53
Ahmad bin Sa'id Al Bu Sa'id, 45–46, 95, 203n76, 204n86
Al Bu Sa'id Dynasty: emergence of, 44–46, 203n76; family debt, 94–95; human trafficking, 142; and Shivji Topan, 49–50
Al-Izkawi, 34–35
Al-Qawasim: 1809 British expedition, 68–69; 1819 British-Omani expedition, 75–77; attacks on British shipping, 65–66; beginning of war with Sa'id, 56; inner politics, 70–71; killing of Sa'id's father, 52; and political entrepreneurship, 57–58; and slavery, 67; ties to Wahhabism and Saudi state, 60–61, 64
Al-Ya'aribah. *See* Ya'rubi Dynasty
America. *See* United States
Andrew Jackson, 10, 115, 118, 122
Arabia: migrations from and to, 3, 8, 24; part of oceanic marketplace, 11–13, 171, 177, 179. *See also* Gulf
Atkins Hamerton: arrival in Zanzibar, 130, 158; as British representative for both Crown and Company, 118; and customs master in Zanzibar, 109; description of responsibilities, 130; on killing of Sa'id's father, 206n122; offense at Sa'id's American paintings, 116, 221n6; reporting on British subordination, 116, 131; reporting on slavery, 104, 118, 149, 155, 158–59, 163, 218n91. *See also* Britain

Bahrain: and human trafficking, 151; and Omani influence, 47; Persian invasion of, 70, 74; and Rahmah bin Jabir, 57–59, 78–79; Sa'id's offering to the British, 156
Baloch, 6, 46, 104, 170, 173
Bani Bu Ali: battles with Sa'id, 77–78; embrace of Wahhabism, 77; maritime plunder, 76; Sa'id's devastation of, 78, 212n95, 213n111
Barghash bin Sa'id Al Bu Sa'id, 171, 181–82
Bayt al-Mtoni, 174–75, 232n92
Bayt al-Sahel, 171, 175
Benjamin Fabens, 8–9. *See also* United States
Bibi Moza, 6, 188n22
Britain: commercial and political weakness in East Africa, 115–18, 121–23, 129, 130; expeditions against Ras al-Khaimah, 68–69, 74–76; and human trafficking, 128, 130, 141, 143, 152–56, 158, 226n5, 229nn41,47, 231n73; and ideas of hegemony, 12, 14, 18–21, 58, 64–65, 138–39, 181–82, 221n9, 235nn31,33; naval weakness in the Gulf, 59, 65, 77; and piracy, 57–58, 65–66, 69–70; treaties, 57, 65, 76, 120–21, 127, 129–30, 219n118
Buckett (enslaved man), 147
Bushehr (Bushire), 57, 59, 62, 69, 72–74

capitalism: concept of war capitalism, 44; and definitions, 25; and formation of, 19, 23, 79, 81, 113, 117, 142, 156, 161, 169
caravan trade, 17, 20, 25, 89, 106–8, 112, 119, 136, 143, 149, 163, 165–66
cartaz, 34, 201n42
Charles Guillain, 1–4, 84, 86, 91, 98–99, 123, 134. *See also* France
Christopher Rigby, 153–54. *See also* Britain
cloves: growth of industry in Zanzibar, 102–3, 105, 129; introduction to Zanzibar, 101; production and plantations, 157, 159, 160–63; Sa'id's state policy toward, 100–1
coffee trade, 38, 45–46, 48
contracts, 20, 132–36, 223n51, 225n79
cosmopolitanism, 30, 51, 61, 196n68
currency, 106–8, 134
customs duties: 17, 34; centralization of in Zanzibar, 86, 89–93; the customs house, 25, 104, 111, 150, 167, 170; establishing a flat fee, 46–47; and the Mazru'i, 43, 44; Sa'id's policies toward, 94–100, 108, 111, 113, 119, 132; and the Shivji firm, 17–18, 49–50, 83, 87, 95–96, 108–9, 123, 126–27, 137; tax farming, 17–18, 97–98. *See also* Jairam Shivji; Shivji Topan

David Pingree, 125–26, 165, 172–73. *See also* United States
dhow: captains, 132; construction of, 29–30; in human trafficking, 150, 153, 229n41

East African consumerism, 31, 43, 53, 92, 95, 120, 126, 157, 170, 172
East India Company: representation by Hamerton, 118; sources, 59; treaties with Oman, 57
Ebji Shivji, 102, 132
Edmund Roberts: appointment by Jackson, 115–16, 118–19; characterizations of Omani Empire, 10–11, 17, 66, 177; description of Muscat, 94; first voyage to Zanzibar, 82–84, 96–97, 214n1; ratification of treaty and visit to plantation, 161–62; treaty negotiations with Sa'id, 111, 120–22. *See also* Andrew Jackson; United States
Édouard Loarer: characterization of "single state," 11, 43, 177; on "clove mania," 102; on currencies, 107; on "Mrima monopoly," 100; on Sa'id, 110–11. *See also* France
enslavement. *See* slavery
Esau bin Abdul Rahman, 135–37, 225n89
Europe: and acquiescence, 3, 7, 14–15, 24, 33, 35–36, 99, 110, 133, 183, 221n9; arrival in Western Indian Ocean, 15, 22, 27, 117; and colonialism, 182; and Eurocentrism, 13–14, 19–23, 44, 53, 138, 179, 181; trade in Western Indian Ocean, 12, 32

France: and commercial treaty, 1–2, 100, 121, 129–30; and human trafficking, 32, 49, 91–92, 94, 130, 144
Francis Erskine Loch, 177–78. *See also* Britain
frasilah, 134. *See also* currency

Gulf: British reliance on Oman in, 66; consolidation of Omani power in, 35–36, 47–48; evacuation of Portuguese from, 34–35, 40, 44; historiography, 19, 21–22; and idea of political entrepreneurs, 58–59, 79; notions of British power in, 64–54; Omani-British naval campaign, 74–78. *See also* Arabia

Hamad bin Sa'id Al Bu Sa'id, 46
Hasan bin Rahmah, 67, 70–71, 75
Henry Hart, 121–22. *See also* Britain
Henry Morton Stanley, 165. *See also* Britain
heshima, 91
Hindus, 38–39, 46, 51, 63–64
Horace Putnam, 26–28, 197n1. *See also* United States
human trafficking. *See* slavery

Ibn Ruzayq, 39–40, 56, 61–62
India. *See* South Asia

Jairam Shivji: and British commerce, 158–59; centrality to the empire, 84, 95, 98–99, 112, 137, 177, 179, 232n104;

control of commerce, 100, 108–9, 113, 120, 138; customs house as a legal institution, 223n51; and his customs system, 96–97, 134, 139, 170; and human trafficking, 150; and plantation system, 102, 166; relationship with Waters, 123–27, 130–33. *See also* customs duties; Shivji Topan
James Silk Buckingham, 57–58, 64, 67. *See also* Britain
jizya tax, 30, 38
Johan Ludwig Krapf, 91
John Waters, 125
Joseph Arthur De Gobineau, 175–77. *See also* France
Joseph Osgood, 149–50, 168–69. *See also* United States

Kachchh, 29, 93, 95. *See also* South Asia
Khamis bin Uthman, 134
Kilwa, 32, 42, 49, 88, 155–56
kinship, 15, 31, 34, 133, 138

māl. *See* wealth
marketplace, 11–12, 25
Mazru'i: depictions of, 43; meetings with William Owen, 128–29, 203n69, 215n12; power in Mombasa, 85–88; Sa'id's proclamations to, 89–90
Michael Shephard, 133. *See also* United States
minorities, legal protection of: 37–38, 51, 94–95, 104, 200n34
Mombasa: British in, 128; historical importance, 83, 103; Omani siege and influence over, 40, 42–44, 49, 82, 85–94; Portuguese in, 13, 40, 42; South Asians in, 32, 46
Mozambique: as center of human trafficking, 32; historical importance, 10, 83; Portuguese arrival, 33, 40; shifting of trade toward Zanzibar, 42, 85, 144; and South Asians, 39
Mrima monopoly, 99–100
Musa Mzuri, 164–65
Muscat: and commerce, 51; as emerging center of empire, 12, 13, 32, 43–47, 51, 79, 86–88, 92, 181, 216n32; date season, 8; depictions of, 93–94, 115–16, 119; geography and history of, 28; and maritime violence, 69, 72–73; meeting between Sa'id and Guillain, 1–3; meeting with Loch, 177–78; and Portuguese, 34–38, 40; Sa'id's final voyage to, 170–71, 175–76; slavery, 141–42, 147, 151–52; South Asian and other minorities, 36–39, 46, 63–64, 83, 95, 210n37; Wahhabi attacks, 62–63

Narutem, 37–38, 202n52. *See also* minorities
Nasir bin Murshid al-Ya'aribah, 34–37
navy: British weaknesses, 66, 69; Omani navy, 17, 35, 40–41, 44–45, 47, 62, 66, 68–69, 201n45; Qasimi-Saudi naval alliance, 64
négociant, 176, 234n21. *See also* Joseph Arthur de Gobineau
New England. *See* United States

Oman: contemporary society, 186n9; geography, 28–29, 35, 66; historical labeling, 188n26; and historiography, 12–22, 64–65; and imperialism, 12–13, 16–17, 34, 36, 40, 42–43, 49–51, 57, 59, 158, movement of peoples to East Africa, 10, 41, 93, 159, 164–65; religion, 6–7, 189n28; and the sea, 28
Omani Empire: beginning of, 33; breakup of, 181–82; as a creole entity, 179–80; descriptions of, 10–11; framing of, 4–6, 10–11, 17–19, 21–22, 177–79, 183–84; historiographic debates, 10–17, 21–23, 180–81, 191n22, 192n33

Pemba, 42, 88, 101, 103–4, 119, 145
Persia: and De Gobineau, 175; disruptions in trade, 47–48; exploitation of Omani civil war, 34–35; flow of trade through, 27, 28; and language, 6, 18; presence in Muscat, 64; relations with Rahmah bin Jabir, 58–59, 72, 78–79; relations with Sa'id, 76–77; threats to Bahrain, 70
pice, 106–8, 111–12. *See also* currency
piracy, 57–58, 69, 79–80
polyphony, 4, 25, 113, 138, 177, 179–80, 183, 186n7

Portugal: *cartaz* system, 34; in East Africa, 13, 32–33, 40–44, 85, 90–91, 144, 152; maritime violence, 34; in Oman, 34–39
profit: Burton's description, 95; and caravan trade, 165; concept in Indian Ocean societies, 23–25, 39–40, 48; driving "clove mania," 102; and human trafficking, 148–49, 166–67; problems pursuing according to Roberts, 83; Sheriff's "altar of commercial profit," 64–65; and tax farming for Shivji firm, 96, 99; and time, 106–7, 125; Waters's pursuit of, 22, 112, 124–25, 138. *See also* wealth
prosopography, 4

Rahmah bin Jabir: and 1820 General Treaty of Peace, 76; alliance with Sa'id, 74–75, 78–79; death, 79; and discriminatory violence, 71–72; and enslavement, 67; framing as part of world history, 179; as a political entrepreneur, 57–59, 79–81, 207n5; relations with British, 72–73
Ras al-Khaimah: 1809 British attack, 68–69; 1819 Omani-British attack, 74–76; 1820 General Treaty of Peace, 76–77; as base for the Qawasim, 52, 56; historical importance, 66–67; Omani attacks, 70; and slavery, 67
Red Sea: coffee trade, 45; and First Saudi State, 60; human trafficking, 151–52; interconnected trade, 8, 28, 30; minority merchants, 39, 48
ribh. *See* profit; wealth
Richard Burton: and description of geography, 19; on making profit, 95; on Omani racial attitudes, 104; on plantation culture, 112, 160–61, 164. *See also* Britain
Richard Waters: contract with Esau, 135–37; ingratiation into Zanzibari commerce, 131–32; and pursuit of profit, 22, 112, 138; relations with Sa'id, 109–11, 172–73; role as consul, 123–26, 130–31, 133–35; subjection to imperial rules, 99–100. *See also* United States
Robert Norsworthy, 129–30. *See also* Britain
Sadick bin Barack, 22, 138–39
Sa'id bin Ahmad Al Bu Sa'id, 46
Sa'id bin Sultan Al Bu Sa'id: death, 170–71; descriptions of governance, 173–74; as a keyhole for writing history, 4, 6, 15, 20, 84–85, 143–44, 177–78; myths and legacy, 4–5, 5–6; rise to power, 188n22; self-description just before death, 175–76; titles, 6–7, 173–74
Salameh bint Sa'id Al Bu Sa'id, 18, 175
Saudi state: alliance with Qawasim, 60–61, 64, 69; attacks on Oman, 61–63, 66; crumbling of First Saudi State, 74–75; emergence of First Saudi State, 57; fractures within the Qawasim, 70–71; relations with the Bani Bu Ali, 77; relations with Rahmah bin Jabir, 58, 72; relations with Sultan bin Saqr, 67–68. *See also* Wahhabism
Sayf bin Sultan Al-Ya'aribah, 41, 43–44
Shivji Topan: 17–18, 49, 87, 95–96; family firm of, 18, 50, 83, 96. *See also* customs duties
slavery: as core of empire, 5, 11, 12, 17, 104–6, 136, 142–46, 149, 152–59, 167–68; differences with Atlantic world, 143, 146–47; and domestic servants, 167; enslaved women, 147–48, 151; failure of British abolitionism, 152–59; in Gulf societies, 67–68; and naval and merchant fleets, 54, 66–67; and Omani racial notions, 5, 104; and other trade, 42, 86, 137, 155–57, 163–64, 166; and plantations, 145, 102, 159–68; slave market, 150–51; as spectrum of bondage, 42, 50–51, 142, 145–48, 165; as system of labor, 155–58; terminology and debates, 5, 146; and trafficking, 32, 40, 41, 49, 91, 94, 148–50, 166; and Ya'rubi Dynasty, 34–42
Sohar (port city), 29, 32, 35–36, 56, 141, 151, 198n14
Sohar (ship), 29–30, 54
South Asia: financiers for the Omani Empire, 35–36, 37–39, 46, 49–50, 51, 93–95, 126; and human trafficking, 31–32, 142 145, 147; movement of peoples to East Africa, 84, 158, 180; Omani attacks against Portuguese in,

41, 44; Portuguese intrusions, 35–36, 40. *See also* customs duties; Hindus; Jairam Shivji; minorities; Shivji Topan
Sultanah (ship), 52–55
Sultan bin Ahmad Al Bu Saʿid, 46, 51–52
Sultan bin Saqr: as political entrepreneur, 57–59, 69, 79–80; as a Qasimi leader, 66–67, 69–70, 75–76; relations with Saudis, 67–68; war with Saʿid, 56
Sultan bin Sayf al-Yaʿaribah, 37–40
Sur, 29, 32, 54, 84, 151
Swahili: as a coastal area, 13; language, 6, 18, 91, 174; and non-Swahili-speaking East Africans, 85; society, 15, 30–31, 103, 163, 180; society and human trafficking, 151

tax farming. *See* customs; Jairam Shivji; Shivji Topan
Thani bin Amir al-Harthi, 164–65
Tippu Tip, 166
treaties: 1798 and 1800 Omani-British Treaties, 57, 67; 1820 General Treaty of Peace, 76, 80; 1822 Moresby Treaty, 153, 221n11; 1833 American treaty, 10, 96, 100, 111, 115–16, 119–21, 132; 1840 British treaty, 100, 120–21, 129, 130, 219n118; French treaty, 1; with Ile de France, 92, 100

United States: acquiescence and success in Zanzibar, 109–11, 124, 132–34; arrival of *Sultanah*, 52–55; British-American rivalry, 7, 116–17, 118–22, 129–31, 153; East African demand for American goods, 126–28, 138; foreign policy toward Omani Empire, 115; trade in Western Indian Ocean, 8,12, 15, 22, 25, 27, 89, 92–94, 97–100, 101, 102, 108, 110, 113, 122–23, 125–26, 139; troubles faced in East Africa, 82–84. *See also* Edmund Roberts; Richard Waters

Vincenzo Maurizi, 63

Wahhabism: allegations of *shirk*, 61–62, 64, 71; influence in Oman, 63; and maritime power, 61, 64; and Qawasim, 60. *See also* Saudi state
wealth: displays of, 112–13, 145, 163–66, 173–74, 181–83; and East African societies, 119–20, 147; in enslavement and human trafficking, 42, 94, 97, 143, 144, 148, 154–55, 157–58, 166, 169; and immobility, 93, 112; and Jairam Shivji, 98–100; as *māl*, 24–25, 61–62, 64, 89–90; as part of imperial system, 89–90, 98–99; pursuit of, 15, 20, 22–25, 27, 30–31, 61–62, 81, 117, 138–39, 160, 181; in Saʿid's will, 167–68; stratification of society, 50–51, 101, 104–5, 158, 164. *See also* profit
William Owen, 87, 128–29, 153, 215n21. *See also* Britain
William Ruschenberger, 115, 161–62

Yaqut (governor of Zanzibar), 92, 96, 146, 216n51
Yaʿrubi Dynasty, 33, 44–45
Yemen, 8, 28, 39; coffee trade, 48–49, 68; human trafficking, 151; interconnected trade, 155–56, 201n45

Zanzibar: density of enslaved persons, 145, 159, 218n91; expropriation of Zanzibari peoples, 12, 33, 84, 103–4, 156–57; prior to Omani imperialism, 83; social and economic hierarchies, 49–50, 98, 103–4; transformation of, 4, 10, 27, 83, 90, 173; visitors' descriptions of, 26, 94, 168–69

THE CALIFORNIA WORLD HISTORY LIBRARY

Edited by Edmund Burke III, Kenneth Pomeranz, and Patricia Seed

1. *The Unending Frontier: Environmental History of the Early Modern World,* by John F. Richards
2. *Maps of Time: An Introduction to Big History,* by David Christian
3. *The Graves of Tarim: Genealogy and Mobility across the Indian Ocean,* by Engseng Ho
4. *Imperial Connections: India in the Indian Ocean Arena, 1860–1920,* by Thomas R. Metcalf
5. *Many Middle Passages: Forced Migration and the Making of the Modern World,* edited by Emma Christopher, Cassandra Pybus, and Marcus Rediker
6. *Domesticating the World: African Consumerism and the Genealogies of Globalization,* by Jeremy Prestholdt
7. *Servants of the Dynasty: Palace Women in World History,* edited by Anne Walthall
8. *Island World: A History of Hawai'i and the United States,* by Gary Y. Okihiro
9. *The Environment and World History,* edited by Edmund Burke III and Kenneth Pomeranz
10. *Pineapple Culture: A History of the Tropical and Temperate Zones,* by Gary Y. Okihiro
11. *The Pilgrim Art: Cultures of Porcelain in World History,* by Robert Finlay
12. *The Quest for the Lost Nation: Writing History in Germany and Japan in the American Century,* by Sebastian Conrad; translated by Alan Nothnagle
13. *The Eastern Mediterranean and the Making of Global Radicalism, 1860–1914,* by Ilham Khuri-Makdisi
14. *The Other West: Latin America from Invasion to Globalization,* by Marcello Carmagnani
15. *Mediterraneans: North Africa and Europe in an Age of Migration, c. 1800–1900,* by Julia A. Clancy-Smith
16. *History and the Testimony of Language,* by Christopher Ehret

17. *From the Indian Ocean to the Mediterranean: The Global Trade Networks of Armenian Merchants from New Julfa,* by Sebouh David Aslanian
18. *Berenike and the Ancient Maritime Spice Route,* by Steven E. Sidebotham
19. *The Haj to Utopia: The Ghadar Movement and Its Transnational Connections, 1905–1930,* by Maia Ramnath
20. *Sky Blue Stone: The Turquoise Trade in World History,* by Arash Khazeni
21. *Pirates, Merchants, Settlers, and Slaves: Colonial America and the Indo-Atlantic World,* by Kevin P. McDonald
22. *Black London: The Imperial Metropolis and Decolonization in the Twentieth Century,* by Marc Matera
23. *The New World History: A Field Guide for Teachers and Researchers,* edited by Ross E. Dunn, Laura J. Mitchell, and Kerry Ward
24. *Margins of the Market: Trafficking and Capitalism across the Arabian Sea,* by Johan Mathew
25. *A Global History of Gold Rushes,* edited by Benjamin Mountford and Stephen Tuffnell
26. *A Global History of Sexual Science, 1880–1960,* edited by Veronika Fuechtner, Douglas E. Haynes, and Ryan M. Jones
27. *Potosí: The Silver City That Changed the World,* by Kris Lane
28. *A Global History of Runaways,* edited by Marcus Rediker, Titas Chakraborty, and Matthias van Rossum
29. *The City and the Wilderness: Indo-Persian Encounters on the Burmese Frontier,* by Arash Khazeni
30. *The Bloody Flag: Mutiny in the Age of Atlantic Revolution,* by Niklas Frykman
31. *Empire of Convicts: Indian Penal Labor in Colonial Southeast Asia,* by Anand A. Yang
32. *Zanzibar Was a Country: Exile and Citizenship between East Africa and the Gulf,* by Nathaniel Mathews
33. *A Sea of Wealth: The Omani Empire and the Making of an Oceanic Marketplace,* by Nicholas P. Roberts

www.ingramcontent.com/pod-product-compliance
Lightning Source LLC
Chambersburg PA
CBHW021340230426
43666CB00006B/352
* 9 7 8 0 5 2 0 4 1 5 7 8 2 *